D0984275

Admiral William A. Moffett

SMITHSONIAN HISTORY OF AVIATION SERIES
Von Hardesty, Series Editor

On December 17, 1903, on a windy beach in North Carolina, aviation became a reality. The development of aviation over the course of little more than three-quarters of a century stands as an awe-inspiring accomplishment in both a civilian and a military context. The airplane has brought whole continents closer together; at the same time it has been a lethal instrument of war.

This series of books contributes to the overall understanding of the history of aviation—its science and technology as well as the social, cultural, and political environment in which it developed and matured. Some publications help fill the many gaps that still exist in the literature of flight; others add new information and interpretation to current knowledge. While the series appeals to a broad audience of general readers and specialists in the field, its hallmark is strong scholarly content. The series is international in scope and includes works in three major categories:

Smithsonian Studies in Aviation History: works that provide new and original knowledge.

Classics of Aviation History: carefully selected out-of-print works that are considered essential scholarship.

Contributions to Aviation History: previously unpublished documents, reports, symposia, and other materials.

Advisory Board: Roger E. Bilstein, *University of Houston;* Horst Boog, *Militärgeschichtliches Forschungsamt;* Emmanuel Chadeau, *Université Charles de Gaulle;* Tom D. Crouch, *National Air and Space Museum;* John T. Greenwood, *historian;* Terry Gwynn-Jones, *author;* R. Cargill Hall, *Center for Air Force History;* Richard P. Hallion, *Air Force Historian;* James R. Hansen, *Auburn University;* Von Hardesty, *National Air and Space Museum;* William M. Leary, *University of Georgia;* W. David Lewis, *Auburn University;* Donald S. Lopez, *National Air and Space Museum;* Air Vice-Marshal R. A. Mason, CBE MA RAF (Ret.); Colonel Phillip S. Meilinger, *Maxwell AFB;* John H. Morrow, Jr., *University of Georgia;* Richard J. Overy, *King's College London;* Dominick A. Pisano, *National Air and Space Museum;* E. T. Wooldridge, *National Air and Space Museum*

Admiral
William A. Moffett
Architect of Naval Aviation ⤳

WILLIAM F. TRIMBLE

SMITHSONIAN INSTITUTION PRESS

WASHINGTON AND LONDON

The following sources have been quoted from and cited with permission from the Columbia Oral History Research Office: Memoirs of Admiral Felix B. Stump, 1963, in the Columbia University Oral History Collection (COHC); Reminiscences of Jerome C. Hunsaker, 1960, COHC; and Reminiscences of Eugene E. Wilson, 1962, COHC.

Copy Editor: Lorraine Atherton
Production Editor: Jenelle Walthour
Designer: Kathleen Sims

Library of Congress Cataloging-in-Publication Data
Trimble, William F., 1947–
    Admiral William A. Moffett, architect of naval aviation / William F. Trimble.
        p.   cm.
    Includes bibliographical references and index.
    ISBN 1-56098-320-5 (alk. paper)
    1. Moffett, William Adger, 1869–1933. 2. Admirals—United States—Biography.
3. United States Navy—Biography. 4. United States. Navy—Aviation—History. I. Title.
V63.M57T75 1993
359'.0092—dc20
    [B]   93-7962
British Library Cataloguing-in-Publication Data is available

Manufactured in the United States of America
01 00 99 98 97 96 95 94   5 4 3 2 1

∞ The paper used in this publication meets the minimum requirements of the American National Standard for Permanence of Paper for Printed Library Materials Z39.48-1984

For permission to reproduce illustrations appearing in this book, please correspond directly with the owners of the works, as listed in the individual captions. The Smithsonian Institution Press does not retain reproduction rights for these illustrations individually, or maintain a file of addresses for photo sources.

To W. F. Trimble III

CONTENTS

ACKNOWLEDGMENTS

ANYONE EXPERIENCED IN WRITING HISTORY IS FAMILIAR WITH THE relief and satisfaction that attend the completion of a book after years of research and writing. Finishing a book also brings with it the pleasure of acknowledging those who have helped see the project through from its inception to its final stages. Foremost, I thank Professor William M. Leary of the University of Georgia, who suggested a biography of Admiral Moffett as a major contribution to the Smithsonian History of Aviation Series. Dr. Richard K. Smith, a scholar whose knowledge of aviation history far exceeds my own, offered encouragement, advice, and unparalleled insight as the study progressed. He read and commented on two versions of the manuscript, each time offering suggestions that vastly improved its content and analysis.

The timely assistance of Auburn University and its College of Liberal Arts greatly facilitated the completion of the book. In 1989 and 1991, I received two Humanities Development grants from the university, allowing me to spend more than seven weeks doing research in Washington and Annapolis, Maryland. I specifically thank Leah Rawls Atkins, director of the Arts and Humanities Center, David R. Hiley, former acting dean of the College of Liberal Arts, and Gordon C. Bond, the college's current dean, for their support in securing the grants and an accompanying quarter-long faculty development leave in the fall of 1991.

Admiral Moffett's two surviving children, Rear Adm. William A. Moffett, Jr. (Ret.), of Williamsburg Landing, Virginia, and Beverly Moffett Mohan of Deep Gap, North Carolina, welcomed me into their homes and patiently endured my questions about their father and what they remembered about life in the Moffett household. They also supplied photographs, correspondence, and other information that helped bring a more human dimension to the admiral than would have been possible otherwise. My debt to them runs long and deep.

At the National Archives and Records Administration in Washington, Barry Zerby and Richard E. von Doenhoff devoted many hours to helping me sift through the extensive records of the Bureau of Aeronautics. Their knowledge, professionalism, and, above all, patience made what could have easily been a frustrating experience rewarding and enjoyable. Alice S. Creighton and Mary R. Catalfamo in the Special Collections Department of the Nimitz Library at the United States Naval Academy made the Moffett papers available to me during two visits to Annapolis. The staffs of the MIT Archives and Special Collections, the Franklin D. Roosevelt Presidential Library, the Navy Department Library, the Operational Archives of the Naval Historical Center, and the William W. Jeffries Memorial Archives at the Naval Academy supplied microfilm and photocopies from their collections. I owe much to Archie DiFante, George Cully, and Warren Trest at the United States Air Force Historical Research Agency, Maxwell Air Force Base, for leading me to Moffett materials in their collections.

Among the many others who contributed time, advice, ideas, and information to this project were Dean C. Allard, William J. Armstrong, J. Hartley Bowen, Jr., Tom D. Crouch, James R. Hansen, Thomas C. Hone, W. David Lewis, Stephen L. McFarland, Bobbie McWeeney, Don Olliff, Lee M. Pearson, and Clark G. Reynolds. I apologize to anyone whose name I have omitted out of inadvertence, forgetfulness, or ignorance.

To my wife, Sharon, and sons, Will and Mike, I extend my heartfelt thanks for their encouragement during another long research and writing project. And I am once more indebted to Paul J. Sirovatka, his wife, Harriet, and son Jonathan of Kensington, Maryland. Over what is now more than two decades of research trips to Washington, they have opened their home to me and made me feel a part of their family.

1

THE AIR ADMIRAL

Rear Admiral William A. Moffett turned away from his tall wooden desk and walked over to one of his office windows in the Main Navy building on Constitution Avenue in Washington. Peering out, he observed that high clouds had obscured the sun and the wind had picked up. He knew enough about the changeable spring weather in Washington to realize that what had started off as a warm and pleasant morning might well deteriorate into a cold and blustery afternoon and evening. On any other occasion, Moffett, who was in his third term as chief of the Navy's Bureau of Aeronautics, would not have paid too much attention to the unsettled weather. But later that day, 3 April 1933, he planned to be aboard the Navy's big airship *Akron,* scheduled to leave her base at Lakehurst, New Jersey, about sunset. *Akron*'s skipper, Comdr. Frank C. McCord, intended to take the airship on an overnight flight up the coast to Newport, Rhode Island, to test radio direction finder (RDF) stations early the next morning.

Moffett always looked forward to flights in the Navy's airships. They offered a chance to get away from the often dull office routine in Washington, and they gave him an opportunity to observe firsthand the accom-

1

plishments and problems of the Navy's lighter-than-air people. A vigorous man whose energy belied his sixty-three years, Moffett had always found flying pleasurable, especially in the big airships, which by their sheer bulk seemed to command the sky. This would be his twelfth flight in *Akron* since her completion in September 1931.

Before leaving his office, Moffett telephoned McCord at about 1100 to make sure everything was on schedule. McCord assured him that it was. *Akron*'s executive officer, Lt. Comdr. Herbert V. Wiley, had checked with the airship's aerological officer, Lt. Herbert M. Wescoat, to get an immediate analysis of the weather. Wescoat guessed that they could get the airship out of the hangar that evening but that the weather along the coast did not look good for the RDF tests. McCord passed this information along to Moffett, who decided to bring along Comdr. Harry B. Cecil from the bureau's Plans Division to act as his aide. The officer normally assigned to this duty, Lt. Thomas H. Robbins, Jr., was unable to make the trip because of a family emergency. Moffett informed Lt. Comdr. Fred T. Berry, the commanding officer at Lakehurst, that he and Cecil would arrive at the air station sometime before 1900.

There was no question *Akron* was going to fly that day; even if the weather precluded the RDF tests, McCord reasoned that the airship could still exercise her heavier-than-air unit. *Akron* had a hook-on device, known as a trapeze, that allowed her to launch and recover Curtiss XF9C-1 biplane fighters. Normally *Akron*'s airplanes took off from Lakehurst shortly after the airship, rendezvousing with her and being swung aboard by the trapeze into a small hangar in the airship's belly. Previous operations with the airplanes had been limited but promising. McCord was determined to realize *Akron*'s full potential as a flying aircraft carrier and to demonstrate the value of the fighters in protecting the airship and extending her "eyes" in scouting operations.[1]

Still concerned about the weather, McCord and Wiley went over to Wescoat's office to look at the most recent reports and maps. To the west lay a low-pressure system, ahead of which, running through western Ohio, was a weak front. Wiley later testified that the low-pressure area was "apparently moving to the north eastward outside our area of operations and was in no way a threat." McCord then issued orders to have the airship's crew ready by 1800. He told Wiley that he wanted the heavier-than-air unit prepared to take off and join *Akron* shortly after the airship left the mooring mast.[2]

Throughout the afternoon, the weather worsened at Lakehurst, with low-hanging clouds and limited visibility. McCord and Wiley consulted the latest weather map later on in the day, and according to Wiley, "it showed considerable change" from the morning map. What exactly he meant by that is not clear, but presumably what had previously shown on the map as a weak weather system now appeared as a major storm front, and there was nothing to indicate that it would clear out anytime soon. That information, coupled with observations of the poor local conditions, led McCord to cancel the hook-on exercises, but there was no change in *Akron*'s scheduled departure time.[3]

Meanwhile, Moffett and Cecil had left Washington at about 1300 and were on their way to Lakehurst by car. Had the weather forecasts been better, Moffett would have flown to Lakehurst from Anacostia, a trip that usually took about an hour and a half. Driving on two-lane highways and forced to thread their way through the traffic of downtown Baltimore and Philadelphia, Moffett's party finally arrived in Lakehurst after about five and a half hours on the road. At the air station, Moffett met Alfred F. Masury, who had come down from New York to fly in *Akron* as Moffett's guest. An army reserve colonel and a vice president of the Mack Truck Company, Masury had previously flown in the German airship *Graf Zeppelin* and, as an officer of the International Zeppelin Transport Company, had been exploring the investment potential of commercial airships. The day before the flight, Moffett had invited Eugene E. Wilson to go along. An engineering officer who had joined the Bureau of Aeronautics in 1924, Wilson had left the Navy in late 1929 to take an executive position with United Aircraft. Wilson declined the offer, telling Moffett he was "scared to death of those powered gasbags." At 1830, the mooring mast backed *Akron* out of the hangar into the gathering twilight. Less than an hour later, she lifted off from the mast and swiftly disappeared into the dark gray clouds and mist that had settled over the base.[4]

Akron never returned. Barely five hours into the flight, she went down in heavy rain and fog off the New Jersey coast. As waves ripped the airship's hull to pieces, her crew tried to fight their way clear of the twisted wreckage and struggled through cold, storm-lashed waves. Rescuers picked up four survivors, one of whom died shortly afterward. Admiral Moffett was not among them. In a tragic turn of events, the Navy had lost not only *Akron* and most of her crew but also the man who had devoted his entire career as a flag officer to championing the cause of aviation with the fleet.

More than any other person, Rear Adm. William A. Moffett shaped naval aviation during the critical, formative years of the twenties and early thirties. He was the consummate professional, the dedicated officer who in all his thoughts and actions demonstrated an abiding loyalty to his service and its role as the nation's first line of defense. Out of Annapolis, he served in more than twenty ships ranging from old windjammers to the most modern and powerful superdreadnoughts. He retraced the well-worn path that other officers had followed to senior rank, leaving few clues in his early service record to hint at his later commitment to aviation.

At first glance it appears odd that a battleship officer like Moffett would eventually devote his career and his life to such a new and visionary element as aviation. One would think that it clashed with his sense of traditionalism. But the apparently confusing dichotomy vanishes in the realization that Moffett saw aviation as an integral, organic part of the fleet. To Moffett the airplane and the airship had utility only in how they contributed to the overall effectiveness of the Navy, its ships, and its personnel. This was not a rationalization or an intentional accommodation to the extremists on both sides of the question. It was a deeply held conviction. Moffett comprehended the tactical, strategic, and political implications of naval aviation, and he was willing to dedicate his career as a flag officer first to bringing aviation into the fleet and then to guaranteeing its role as a powerful arm of the modern Navy.

The realization of those goals was due largely to Moffett's combination of intelligence, likability, understanding of human nature, and leadership capacity. He was not a brain like Rear Admirals Bradley Fiske or David Taylor, nor was he particularly technically oriented. But neither were machines and the engineering behind them totally bewildering to him. Eugene Wilson said that the admiral "knew nothing about engineering and wanted to know even less."[5] That was not entirely true. As a young officer, Moffett had some brief engineering experience; while serving as inspector of the Eighteenth Lighthouse District in San Francisco, he applied for and received two patents for improvements to navigation lights. While serving as chief of the Bureau of Aeronautics, he submitted an application for a patent to control the rolling and pitching motions of hammocks or sleeping berths in airships.[6] They were not startling innovations, but taken together they demonstrate that Moffett had an analytical mind and that he could reduce complexities to their elemental form, allowing nearly instant perception of the correct answer to questions that perplexed others. That ability to knife through perplexing issues was part of the secret of his remarkable administrative ability. It also allowed him to understand what made people act the way they did and gave him an unusual capacity to weigh human actions and their consequences. Those qualities, in turn, may be what lay behind his superior leadership and the rare devotion and respect he elicited among subordinates and fellow officers.

Moffett's intelligence and personality were perfectly suited to the naval and official Washington bureaucracy. Although many energetic, creative, hands-on people chafe at desk jobs and the bureaucratic bickering that often goes with them, Moffett reveled in his position. He knew all the right people and knew when to work through channels and when to bypass chains of command. He did not hesitate to court favor with his superiors, politicians, and influential businessmen. And he understood the art of compromise. At the same time, he knew when he had to take a stand, no matter how unpopular it might be, to get what he needed for himself and for naval aviation.

Moffett had a masterful, almost intuitive grasp of the subtleties of Washington politics. Sensing the antimilitary mood prevailing in the capital in the twenties, he issued standing orders that no personnel under him were to wear their uniforms except when it was absolutely necessary for official duties. Moffett himself usually turned out each morning in a crisply pressed three-button suit or sport coat, giving all the appearance of a conservative, prosperous businessman. To maneuver through the rough political waters of Washington, Moffett combined thorough preparation, efficient organization, and precise timing. He never appeared before Congress without all the necessary statistics and data or without an entourage of young aides to provide details on specific subjects. If he thought he had not made his points clear during his testimony, he buttonholed lawmakers afterward in the corridor and forcefully but politely explained what he had meant.[7]

Moffett played a key role in the formation and initial operation of the Bureau of Aeronautics in 1921. Those who supported the creation of the bureau did so largely based on assurances that Moffett would become its first chief. As director of Naval Aviation in 1921, he actively lobbied for the new bureau, and as its chief he personally created its organizational structure, selected its personnel, and assigned them to their duties. He was an unusually effective administrator who delegated authority to subordinates and encouraged independence, initiative, and innovation.[8] Loyal to those under him in the bureau and expecting loyalty in return, Moffett knew he could always count on the bureau's junior officers. But in demanding absolute loyalty and tolerating little or no dissent, Moffett ran the risk of surrounding himself with amiable cronies and yes-men, thereby losing perspective on vital questions where there could be legitimate contrary opinion. Some particularly strong and opinionated officers, notably Capt. Ernest J. King, found they could not work with Moffett under such circumstances. In stressing loyalty, commitment, and consensus within the Bureau of Aeronautics, Moffett conveyed an impression of confidence and assurance that what he advocated was right both for the Navy and for the country. On the occasions when his tactics of persuasion failed, he knew exactly when to call on friends for help and, most important, how to make them feel that in assisting him they were also contributing in a material way to the benefit of the service.

Moffett was not always forthright about what he had to give up when he decided to take the job as chief of the Bureau of Aeronautics. He did not hesitate to let people know that he had foregone a promising career as a line officer and possibly higher rank and pay to devote himself to aviation. In 1930, he told his former Annapolis roommate, Claude Bailey, that he "could have gone to sea and worked up to at least Commander-in-Chief of the Battle Fleet and possibly Commander-in-Chief of the United States Fleet." Committed to the cause of naval aviation, he was willing to pay the personal cost, and as a patriot he believed that the nation needed a strong naval air arm to ensure its defense and security. How much sympathy this generated in Congress or among the general public is impossible to ascertain, but the approach was an effective addition to his already formidable arsenal of political weapons. Moffett might well have achieved higher rank outside aviation, but his desk job as bureau chief was hardly a sacrifice. His entitlement to flight pay significantly boosted his salary, and his creation of a political power base in the bureau gave him more prestige and influence than if he had gone to sea with a third star.[9]

Moffett had an impeccable sense of timing. When it came to using special investigatory committees and boards, he knew that too often personalities became enmeshed in highly controversial issues, obscuring the fundamentals and preventing their solution. But panels of experts, seemingly removed from the baggage of personality and emotions, could often accomplish what he wanted and do so in a constructive, noncontroversial manner. Moreover, boards fit well into the institutional structure and seemed less threatening than strident cries for change or a long series of clashes between highly placed individuals. The success of Moffett's tactics can be measured in the incremental growth of naval aviation during a decade generally characterized by fiscal economy and reduced military appropriations. Moffett knew how to manipulate the system.

Moffett's mastery of politics enabled him to fight and win a three-front war in Washington.[10] He had first to confront the aviators within his own service. John Rodgers, Richard E. Byrd, Henry C. Mustin, John H. Towers, Bruce Leighton, and Kenneth Whiting were among some of the lower-ranking officers who had become true believers, ardent converts to aviation and unswerving in their certainty that the airplane would revolutionize naval warfare. Some of them demanded the establishment of a separate aviation corps within the Navy, which Moffett adamantly opposed because he was convinced it would pull officers out of the mainstream of general line service and prevent the full integration of aviation into the fleet. At least part of his problem with those aviators stemmed from Moffett's own place within the Navy's administrative structure. Nominally head of a material bureau, he could only make recommendations regarding operations or the development of tactics to those responsible for aviation with the fleet. Normal procedure dictated that his channels to the operational side pass through the offices of the secretary of the Navy or the chief of Naval Operations. Thus circumscribed, Moffett faced the constant difficulty of maintaining two-way communication with the aviators and ran the risk of insulating himself from their special requirements, demands, and ideas. Moffett overcame the obstacle by establishing and maintaining close, informal contacts with operating personnel and creating a rotation system whereby aviators interspersed tours at the bureau with their flying duties.

At the opposite end of the spectrum from the aviators were the entrenched conservatives, mostly high-ranking officers desperately clinging to their turf and defending it against all usurpations, real or imagined. Led by Admirals Charles F. Hughes and Samuel S. Robison, both commanders in chief of the U.S. Fleet, and including such other senior officers as Rear Admirals William R. Shoemaker and Richard H. Leigh of the Bureau of Navigation, the group appeared intolerant of change and incapable of accommodating something as revolutionary as what the aviators advocated. The airmen derisively labeled the conservatives "battleship admirals" or scorned them as members of the Navy's "gun club." Captain Joseph Mason Reeves (later a rear admiral), a convert to aviation in the twenties, referred to them as "those old coots who command battleships."[11] Aviation advocates and historians have sometimes dismissed these officers as hopelessly narrow-minded and irrationally Luddite in their opposition to the airplane. Yet following the Washington Conference, which suspended capital ship construction for a decade, American officers for the most part were less concerned with the battleship than they were with the airplane and the aircraft carrier.[12] Generally they wanted, along with Moffett, to incorporate aviation into the fleet and to determine how to maximize the potential of the new technology. Moffett's struggle with the conservatives was not so much with a crusty group of battleship admirals or members of the exclusive gun club as it was a conflict with senior bureau chiefs in Washington. These men deeply resented Moffett's authority and influence and perceived the new Bureau of Aeronautics as a threat to their long-established prerogatives and a drain on the Navy's limited manpower and resources. When it was created, the bureau drew a large number of people away from the Bureau of Construction and Repair and the Bureau of Steam Engineering and took lesser numbers from some of the other established bureaus. Few raised objections, but when Moffett reached out to exercise control over aviation personnel, he came into conflict with the all-powerful Bureau of Navigation, which had a virtual stranglehold on personnel selection, assignment, and promotion. Moffett deftly wielded his multiple weapons of leadership, political know-how, and force of personality in the confrontation with the conservative bureaucrats within the service.

Finally, there was the third front, the believers in air power, exemplified by colorful, controversial, and flamboyant General William ("Billy") Mitchell. Mitchell saw aviation in altogether different terms from Moffett's. To him, the airplane and, to a lesser extent, the airship brought an entirely new dimension to warfare. Aviation alone could fight and win wars between nations and peoples. The long-range bomber had such enormous destructive capacity that neither navies nor armies could resist it. To realize the full potential of air power, the United States, Mitchell believed, had to establish an independent air force supplied with the most up-to-date equipment, flown by trained air personnel, and led by officers who were unencumbered by ties to either the Army or the Navy. Mitchell's views were antipathetic to Moffett, who saw aviation as a dependent force within the Navy, but in many ways Mitchell was easier to deal with than the young Turks or the old shellbacks within Moffett's service. Mitchell thrived on controversy and attracted charges like a lightning rod. Moffett knew that all he had to do was wait until Mitchell's intemperance led to his own undoing. Moffett often referred to disloyalty during the height of the Mitchell controversy during the twenties, but he rarely mentioned Mitchell's name in public. He did not have to. Moffett won the war with Mitchell using an astute combination of carefully worded jabs in the news media and the support of fiscally conservative Republican administrations that did not want to add another military service to the already existing layers of Washington bureaucracy.

Mitchellite propaganda tried to give the impression that aviation was neglected during the twenties. Nothing could be farther from the truth. Official Washington and both military services devoted an enormous amount of time and effort to the aviation question. During the decade, there were at least fifteen major investigations and numerous Navy General Board hearings dealing with aviation. The probes grappled with the problems presented in defining the federal regulatory role, keeping the aviation industry reasonably competitive and profitable, developing aviation as an offensive striking force, and determining the quantity and quality of military airplanes within coordinated, long-range procurement programs. Aviation was a major budgetary item for the Navy throughout the twenties and thirties, on an annual basis consuming ever larger portions of naval appropriations. Equally important, a number of senior naval officers had become aviation advocates by the early thirties, foremost in the flag rank being (besides Moffett) Joseph Mason Reeves, William V. Pratt, Ernest J. King, and Frank Brooks Upham. There may have been indecision, misdirection, opposition, and controversy, but aviation was not neglected.

The Mitchell-Moffett drama played itself out on all levels, but the most decisive battles took place in the field of public relations. The twenties saw the emergence of the modern mass media. The high-speed rotary press and access to international wire services gave the metropolitan newspaper unprecedented power to inform and mold opinion. Where the newspaper left off, the radio picked up, bringing an immediacy to news reporting unmatched by the press. For visual effect, nothing at the time compared with the motion picture, which after 1927 acquired the added attraction of sound. Traditionally, the Navy was the silent service and shied away from publicity, but Moffett saw great opportunities in adroitly handled public relations to promote naval aviation. In his hands the modern mass media became powerful instruments for change. Mitchell, too, recognized and exploited the power of publicity, but he failed to see beyond its immediate dramatic effect and, unlike Moffett, never understood its subtleties.

Aviation issues were central to Moffett's life and career after the creation of the Bureau of Aeronautics. The early bureau bore his personal imprint. Its people were a mix taken from the older, established bureaus; many of them were civilians. Moffett was a no-nonsense officer who ran what everyone considered a tight ship, and he molded a diverse group into a cohesive, efficient, and creative unit. Part of the success of the Bureau of Aeronautics was due to its relatively small size and informality, but it was due also to a dynamic interaction of people and their implicit belief and trust in the bureau's purpose. Jerome C. Hunsaker, head of the bureau's Plans Section in the early twenties, recalled that his relationship with Moffett was "one of great confidence."[13] There was a pervasive feeling on the third floor of Main Navy in the twenties and early thirties that everyone was cooperating toward a common goal.

Like no other single figure in the Navy at the time, Moffett carved out a personal empire. Determined not to be in charge of just another material agency, he put his personal imprint on the institutional identity of the Bureau of Aeronautics and molded it into a superbureau.[14] Under Moffett, the bureau assumed control over the design, procurement, and testing of aircraft and engines, took responsibility for all budgetary and fiscal matters concerning aviation, and established considerable authority over personnel assigned to aviation duties. Moffett resolutely defended the bureau against all challenges both from within and without the naval bureaucracy. In his most serious confrontation—with the Bureau of Navigation—he established control over the training and assignment of naval aviation personnel.

Procurement was one of the thorniest issues Moffett had to confront as bureau chief. When he took office, the nation's aviation manufacturing industry was in disarray, reeling from the cancellation of wartime contracts and a glut of surplus material flooding the market. Compounding the problem was the existence of the Naval Aircraft Factory in Philadelphia, a Navy-owned and -operated plant that had supplied a significant proportion of the Navy's flying boats during the war and retained a major productive capacity into the postwar era. Starved for orders, private aircraft manufacturers agitated for shutting down the factory altogether, blaming it for unwarranted government competition. Moffett forged a compromise whereby the factory remained as a research and development and testing center, manufacturing small numbers of experimental models only, while the bulk of production orders went to the private sector of the industry.[15]

Equally important were Moffett's tireless efforts to establish long-term, rational aircraft and engine procurement. For years, the industry had complained about government procurement policies. Aircraft manufacturers fretted about design competitions that one company might win on the basis of a superior design only to have the production order go to another firm. They were naturally unwilling to turn proprietary design rights over to the Navy, which might pass them along to competitors. Above all, the manufacturers wanted the government to put in place a multiyear program for aircraft acquisition to ensure consistency of orders and a degree of prosperity they had not enjoyed since World War I.[16]

Moffett understood the problems faced by the industry and worked to resolve them as much as political constraints allowed. He did his best to secure changes in procurement legislation to limit restrictions on competitive bidding, and he was largely responsible for legislation enacted in 1926 providing for the procurement of 1,000 aircraft over five years. The five-year program, coupled with similar legislation affecting the Army, marked the end of the postwar doldrums and the beginning of a major expansion of the aircraft manufacturing industry that carried over into the early thirties. Charles M. Melhorn, in his history of the development of early carrier aviation, called the 1926 legislation Moffett's "finest hour."[17]

The politics of procurement provided an arena where Moffett displayed his remarkably sophisticated understanding of what a later generation would call the military-industrial complex. An interactive web of public and private institutions involved in weapons development and acquisition, the military-industrial complex encompassed corporate executives and military officers working together in an informal alliance.[18] It was not at all unusual to pass aircraft executives in the corridors of the bureau when bidding was to be opened on a new airplane contract. Moffett knew most of the important aircraft manufacturers on a first-name basis and found a particular friend in Clement M. Keys of Curtiss Aeroplane, one of the industry's most influential spokesmen. He understood that he needed these people and that they needed him.

In Congress, Moffett quickly identified and befriended key representatives and senators and learned how to manipulate the legislative process, especially when it came to securing the money needed for aircraft procurement. At the same time, he recognized his responsibilities as a public official to secure the best products at the most reasonable cost. Under most circumstances he and his staff made dispassionate judgments about the material requirements of aviation and got the most out of the companies under contract to provide aircraft and aviation equipment. That procurement policy remained muddled at the time of Moffett's death could be attributed more to congressional shortsightedness and inaction than to any administrative or political failures on his part.

Moffett actively promoted qualitative as well as quantitative changes in naval aviation. Possibly most important was the introduction of the aircraft carrier. Moffett saw the carrier as the principal means of taking the airplane to sea, although initially he was circumspect about the carrier's limited offensive role in support of the battleship's striking power. Largely through Moffett's efforts, the Navy completed the conversion of *Langley* in 1922 and received appropriations for the conversion of the large carriers *Saratoga* and *Lexington,* which joined the fleet in 1927. With those vessels the United States gained valuable experience in carrier design, construction, and operations. By Moffett's second term there was a not-so-subtle change in his thinking about the offensive capabilities of the carrier. More confident of his position in the Navy bureaucracy and with a steady stream of new aircraft coming into service as a result of the 1926 five-year program, Moffett was more outspoken about the potential of the aircraft carrier as a powerful strike weapon in its own right. In the late twenties he advocated the introduction of bombing and torpedo aircraft into fleet air squadrons and closely followed the transformation of carrier tactics wrought by Rear Admiral Reeves.[19]

During Moffett's tenure, aviation in general and naval aviation in particular underwent significant technological change. Lieutenant Commanders Bruce G. Leighton and Eugene Wilson in the bureau's Engine Section spent years working with engineers and manufacturers to perfect the radial, air-cooled power plant, which greatly augmented the performance and reliability of naval aircraft, particularly those operating in the unforgiving environment of the sea. Following Moffett's concept that the airplane was most effective when it operated with the fleet, the bureau sponsored the development of catapults, permitting battleships and cruisers to operate float planes in observation, scouting, and gunnery spotting missions. Much money and time went into the perfection of metal aircraft construction during the twenties, and major advances were made with the introduction of torpedo planes and dive bombers. Moffett firmly advocated the Navy's participation in racing. Although he believed that racing "improved the breed," the reality was that the design and construction of operational aircraft rarely benefited from success in racing. For Moffett, competition was principally another means of generating favorable publicity for the Navy's air arm.

Moffett was a staunch believer in the basic research needed to bring technological change to aviation in the twenties and thirties. As chief of the Bureau of Aeronautics he filled position 3 on the main committee of the National Advisory Committee for Aeronautics (NACA). He did not assume that the position was merely honorary, and he actively participated in many of the committee's policy decisions, particularly stressing cooperation between the Navy and the NACA and trying to prevent duplication in research. Moreover, after 1922, position 4 on the main committee was held by officers close to Moffett in the bureau—first by Jerome Hunsaker and later by the bureau's assistant chiefs, in succession, Captains Emory S. Land, John H. Towers, and Arthur B. Cook. Moffett trusted all of them for their administrative abilities and technical expertise.[20]

But few technical developments generated as much interest and controversy during the twenties and thirties as the rigid airship. Throughout his tour as bureau chief Moffett touted the airship as part of the solution to the daunting strategic problem faced by the Navy in the vast reaches of the Pacific. The Navy was uncertain that in the event of war with Japan it could safely move its battle fleet across the ocean without employing large numbers of scouting cruisers. Those ships were expensive, and it was unlikely Congress would appropriate the money needed for the construction and maintenance of the numbers required. Moreover, because of treaty restrictions, base and support facilities in the western Pacific were woefully inadequate. The large rigid airship seemed the obvious solution to the dilemma. It had the speed, range, and payload capacity to augment the scout cruiser in the long-range reconnaissance role, and with a complement of airplanes it could cover thousands of square miles of ocean in advance of the fleet.[21]

It was a beguiling vision—huge silvery airships sweeping before the battle fleet as it steamed across the Pacific to engage and defeat the Japanese—but it remained little more than a dream. The Navy's costly experiment with the rigid airship foundered in a morass of technical and operational problems, some of which were of Moffett's own making. In his quest for publicity, and hampered by restrictions on funds, Moffett insisted that the Navy's airships be as visible as possible. As a result, they and their crews often embarked on hazardous overland flights and sometimes encountered unnecessary risk. As some historians have pointed out, it would have been far more practical to take those expensive assets to sea and use them in as many fleet maneuvers as possible.[22]

Given Moffett's political acumen, his seemingly quixotic advocacy of the rigid airship in the face of congressional opposition and skepticism from many within his own service is difficult to explain. It is plausible that as an old battleship sailor, Moffett enjoyed the idea of airships because they were commanded like surface vessels. In fact, the operation of a large rigid airship and the direction of its crew mimicked the time-worn procedures and equipment familiar to those experienced in surface ships.[23] Eugene Wilson may also have been right when he concluded that in the rigid airship Moffett knew he had something Mitchell and the air-power advocates did not have, and he was determined for that reason to continue its development and employ it to the maximum as a propaganda vehicle.[24] Moreover, Moffett, once committed to the multimillion-dollar airship, found it hard to compromise or back away from it. He had a strong-willed personality, clear views of right and wrong, and once he set his course, he pursued it unerringly. Despite indications by the early thirties that the rigid airship might not be the solution to the Navy's long-range reconnaissance problems and that patrol-plane technology was rapidly narrowing the gap in performance and payload capacity, Moffett may simply have found it impossible to admit that he was wrong. He would not have been the first person to be caught in such a trap.

Nearly as well known in naval circles as Moffett's advocacy of the rigid airship was his adherence to the flying-deck cruiser. Going into the 1930 London Naval Conference, which he attended as a technical adviser to the American delegation, Moffett conceived of the flying-deck cruiser as a ship to allow the United States to offset the British advantage in numbers of aircraft carriers. Limited to 135,000 tons of aircraft carriers, more than half of which was taken up by *Saratoga* and *Lexington,* the United States was in a poor position to add significantly to the number of aircraft platforms it could employ or to achieve numerical parity in carriers with Great Britain. But following the imposition of total tonnage limitations on cruisers at the 1930 conference, it became possible to charge the flying-deck cruiser against the nation's cruiser tonnage and not against its carrier limits. He saw no reason why the Navy should not use a percentage or even all of its cruiser tonnage quota for 10,000-ton ships fitted with flight decks. The logic was inescapable. As Moffett saw it, the Navy could use all of its carrier tonnage for larger ships while building smaller carriers from a portion of its cruiser allotment. Furthermore, the flying-deck cruiser was consistent with Moffett's advocacy of getting as many airplanes as possible to sea with the fleet. The insurmountable difficulty, however, was that experience showed that hybrid warships, no matter how well conceived, engineered, and constructed, were never as capable as those designed for one mission. The flying-deck cruiser, had it been built, would have made a poor aircraft carrier and a poor cruiser. But Moffett realized the limitations of the proposed ship and pressed for it only as a necessary expedient under the prevailing diplomatic and naval circumstances.[25]

The same complex interplay of technology and international limits on carrier tonnage that drew Moffett to the flying-deck cruiser led him to support the small aircraft carrier. *Saratoga* and *Lexington* were big and costly ships. Moffett believed they consumed too much of the Navy's precious carrier tonnage and its restricted budget. Although each could operate more than seventy aircraft, a similar tonnage, divided among smaller vessels, permitted the launch and recovery of a far greater number of airplanes. Moffett convinced the General Board that new, higher-performance aircraft made a smaller carrier feasible. The result was *Ranger*, a 13,800-ton ship, designed from the keel up as a carrier. Yet even before *Ranger* was completed, studies showed that Moffett had been wrong and that small carriers lacked the protection, speed, range, and seakeeping qualities of bigger ships. To his credit, Moffett recognized the shortcomings of the small carrier and initiated new analyses demonstrating the clear superiority of bigger ships. Following *Ranger*, the United States built a series of carriers of about 20,000 tons each, with higher speeds, more aircraft, and enhanced protection against air and surface attack. Moffett insisted *Ranger* was not a mistake, but he had to admit, however reluctantly, that the small aircraft carrier was more attractive in theory than in practice.[26]

In retrospect, it is easy to see that the rigid airship, the flying-deck cruiser, and the small aircraft carrier diverted Moffett and the Navy from what proved to be more fruitful areas of naval aviation. But with technology in a state of flux and with carrier tactics still evolving in the early thirties, it is understandable that Moffett and others should be sidetracked into less promising fields. More remarkable, perhaps, is that there were so few instances in which Moffett lost sight of the principal goals he had set for naval aviation and how successful he was in achieving those objectives. For Moffett, naval aviation was not just the aircraft carrier, the flying boat, the airship, or the flying-deck cruiser; it was also a complex matrix of technologies and people and organizations, all of which had to be molded into a coordinated whole. Moffett had a far more sophisticated, pluralistic vision of naval aviation than most of his contemporaries.

Throughout his life, Moffett drew a sharp line of demarcation between his professional career and his personal life, making it difficult to piece together a complete picture of what went on outside the Bureau of Aeronautics. Like many naval officers then and now, he was an intensely private man, and he kept family matters well in the background. Compounding the problem of understanding Moffett the man is that few letters to and from his mother, wife, or other family members have survived. Nevertheless, it is possible to piece together an outline of his private life. We know, for example, that he was rarely demonstrative with his family, a part of his personality reinforced by almost total commitment to his work. Mutual respect more than all-consuming, passionate love characterized his marriage to his wife, Jeannette. The union was a traditional one. Jeannette's job was to nurture the family, to take care of all the annoying and distracting details of running the household, and to bear parental responsibilities during her husband's frequent and long absences. His role, other than as provider and head of the household, was to exercise authority and ensure stability within the family.[27]

The dynamics of Moffett's relationship with his wife carried over to other members of the family. His youngest daughter remembered much later in life that he had been "a great naval officer but not a very good father." By that she meant he was neither close nor overtly affectionate with any of his children. He had little time to spare with them during their growing-up years, and he rarely did things with them that they found fun or amusing. Family outings—picnics, vacations, trips to the beach—were almost unheard of in the Moffett family. Possibly his aloofness from his children stemmed from the absence of a paternal figure during his own formative years—his father had died when he was only five. Or it may have grown from an aristocratic sense that there should remain a dignified distance between parents and their offspring. Often the boys were away at school or the girls were spending summers with relatives. It was far from an atmosphere conducive to intimacy and affection. Nevertheless, George, the eldest of the Moffett siblings and the one on whom the burdens of family tradition and responsibility fell most heavily, recalled walks with his father up Massachusetts Avenue toward Rock Creek Park. He sometimes rode on his father's shoulders, but he could remember nothing of their conversations beyond talk about the service, aviation, and the nearly incessant battles Moffett had with Congress and conservative naval officers.[28]

There was little passion or commitment in Moffett's attitudes about religion. As a young cadet at the Naval Academy, his faith in God was as unswerving as it was uncritical. That belief provided an emotional crutch through a particularly difficult stage of his life, when he was separated from his family in Charleston and had to endure the hardships of military life. Even then, he mixed devotion with an emerging sense of duty. In one of the entries in the diary he kept throughout most of his time at the academy, he confided, "I must take *duty* as my watchword for the coming year. . . . I must think of my *duty* and do it with my heavenly Father's aid." His Annapolis roommate Claude Bailey wrote that at the academy Moffett prayed every night before going to bed and kept up the practice as a young midshipman. But if religion played a continuing role in his later life, it did not manifest itself in any overt way. The family certainly did not pray together, there was no imposition of organized religion on the children, and the family did not attend services on a regular basis, if at all. While he was chief of the Bureau of Aeronautics he was not a member of any church in the Washington area. One should not be led to think that Moffett was an atheist or agnostic, but it seems clear that whatever faith he had was internalized in much the same manner as his love for his wife and family.[29]

Not surprisingly for someone who usually kept his emotions under control, Moffett rarely expressed anger at home or at work. On one occasion, however, his temper, coupled with his Southern heritage and upbringing, clashed with his loyalties to the service and the flag. Claude Bailey recalled an incident that, although it may be apocryphal, illustrates the sensitivities of Southerners in the years after the Civil War. It happened either in Moffett's second year at the Naval Academy (1887–88) or in 1889. (Bailey wrote his account long after, in 1947.) One evening, two or three hundred cadets, starved for any diversion they could find, gathered in the lyceum on the academy grounds to hear a lecture on the Civil War. The speaker, a Northerner, related the events leading up to secession, culminating in the attack on Fort Sumter, where, he said, "those dastardly South Carolina traitors started the war." Unable to contain his anger, Moffett shouted "Rats" at the speaker. A general commotion ensued, and half the audience joined in a chorus of "Rats," punctuated by handclapping and foot-stomping. The superintendent took appropriate disciplinary action against Moffett and other cadets, but some of the officers at the academy later acknowledged admiration for Moffett's spirit and willingness to stand up for what he thought was right. Nevertheless, the outburst and breach of decorum could well have led to Moffett's dismissal from the academy.[30]

For someone who emphasized loyalty and professionalism and who usually held his feelings in check, Moffett had a strong sense of humor. His son George said that he had a certain charm and that even late in life there was what may have been a mischievous twinkle in his eyes. Eugene Wilson remembered that Moffett "always had a little smile about the corners of his mouth." He displayed his humor during conversations at the bureau with some of the younger officers who wanted to establish a separate aviation corps within the Navy. A separate corps ran counter to his philosophy that aviation must be a part of the Navy and not in any way segregated from line duties. In part to assuage his juniors, Moffett said, "Hell, we won't secede from the Navy. If we are half as good as we think we are, we'll take it over." Moffett hated pomposity and often countered it with humor. In 1931, Col. W. D. Newbill, a retired army colonel and assistant adjutant general of Virginia, had been placed in charge of making preparations for an air tour of his state that would include Moffett's personal Ford Trimotor. One day Newbill pushed his way into Moffett's office, saluted, and loudly introduced himself as "Colonel Newbill from Virginia, suh!" Moffett quietly got up from his desk, walked around to face Newbill, and announced with ironic scorn, "This is Admiral Moffett from South Carolina, suh!"[31]

Any real or perceived shortcomings in his personality and the possible negative effects they had on his immediate family only reveal that Moffett was, like all of us, a human being subject to all the imperfections that befall mortals. His strengths of courage, loyalty, commitment, and determination overshadowed his frailties and proved to be fundamental ingredients for the success of naval aviation. Without Moffett's firm hand at the helm, it is unlikely that the Navy's air arm would have weathered the storms of the twenties and thirties. He was the essential man.

2

THE FORMATIVE YEARS

CHARLESTON HAD ALWAYS BEEN A CITY OF CONTRASTS. ALONG the cobblestoned, tree-lined streets of this South Carolina port city gracious Georgian-style homes and dignified Greek Revival churches stood within a few blocks of seedy tenements, saloons, and bordellos. Few American cities displayed as much prosperity and poverty, and few had more black African slaves. A submissive yet always vaguely threatening underclass, the slaves were mercilessly exploited by the dominant white Europeans, who lived in constant fear that one day they would rise up and slay their masters. The exquisite tension between black slave and free white pervaded the city through the antebellum years.

Since its founding in 1670, Charleston had endured British occupation, epidemic disease, fierce hurricanes, and ravaging fires. But nothing in the city's experience matched the searing caldron of the Civil War and its aftermath. The secession of South Carolina sparked the conflict, and the first bloodshed was at Fort Sumter in Charleston harbor. Federal forces unsuccessfully assaulted the city in 1862 and then laid siege in 1863. Charleston endured. Not until the end of the war did the city finally succumb. There then followed the unsettling years of Reconstruction as black freedmen exercised political power for the first time and white redemptioners searched for new ways to restore the old social and economic order.[1]

But redemption was many years off in the fall of 1869. A small contingent of federal troops remained in Charleston, and following a particularly tense campaign and election, the city's first Republican mayor and council were installed in office. William Adger Moffett was born into that uncertain world on 31 October 1869, the son of George H. and Elizabeth Simonton Moffett. Forty-year-old George Hall Moffett, the son of Andrew Moffett, a Scotsman who had immigrated to Charleston about 1805, was a prosperous merchant in the city. George had attended Oglethorpe University in Georgia and graduated from South Carolina College in 1849. He married Elizabeth H. Simonton, the youngest daughter of the late Charles S. Simonton, in Charleston on 13 April 1854. The Simontons were of Scotch-Irish descent and had arrived in Charleston late in the eighteenth century. Three children followed in fairly quick succession—Elizabeth Simonton on 6 December 1855, Andrew on 9 December 1857, and Anna Morris on 9 May 1860. In the years before the Civil War, George was a partner in the mercantile firm of J. E. Adger and Company.[2]

When South Carolina seceded from the Union in December 1860, George enlisted as a private and served at the epochal siege of Fort Sumter in April 1861. After spending six months in Europe buying arms for the Confederacy, he returned to Charleston in November 1861 to serve as adjutant of the 25th South Carolina Infantry, commanded by his brother-in-law Charles H. Simonton. After the unit became part of Gen. Johnson Hagood's brigade in September 1863, Moffett moved up to regimental adjutant. In the meantime, on 20 August 1862, his wife had given birth to a second son, Charles Simonton, in Spartanburg, South Carolina, a retreat safe from the imminent threat of Union attack that hung over Charleston that fall.[3]

Hagood's brigade left Charleston in the spring of 1864 to join the Army of Northern Virginia. Hagood singled out Moffett for gallantry during the Battle of Port Walthall Junction, fought on 15 and 16 May on the Appomattox River outside Petersburg. Promoted to captain, Moffett served as brigade adjutant and inspector general, participating in every major battle resisting the Union drive on Richmond. During the siege of Petersburg, Hagood's brigade suffered 1,500 casualties. Hagood said he "knew no better or braver soldier" than Moffett. "An accomplished gentleman, a Christian man, and governed in every action by an unyielding sense of the obligations of duty, he had my highest respect and I greatly valued his friendship."[4]

At the end of the war, Captain Moffett returned to Charleston and resumed his position with J. E. Adger and Company. These were not prosperous times for the Moffetts, for they had to share a large house at 65 St. Philip Street with two other families. Nevertheless, Moffett was active in civic affairs and the city's chamber of commerce, and he devoted a great deal of time to charity, including the Howard Association, which helped care for the sick during Charleston's periodic outbreaks of epidemic disease. The Moffetts had five more children. Margaret, their fifth child, was born on 5 October 1865, and George Hall followed on 27 October 1867. After William Adger came Esther Barron on 29 August 1872 and Josephine Ellison on 21 June 1875.[5]

While Elizabeth Moffett was pregnant with the couple's ninth child, George was fatally injured in a freak accident. Moffett spent the night of 11–12 June 1875 at the bedside of one of his sons, who had fallen ill. At about three o'clock in the morning, he got up to stretch his legs and went out on the second-floor piazza. Hearing the family dog barking and thinking that there might be an intruder, he leaned over the low railing to investigate, lost his balance, and fell thirty feet onto the brick pavement in the courtyard. His wife heard the fall and rushed out to find him still conscious but with a broken back. Moffett lingered in agony for two more weeks. He died on 27 June and was buried the next day in the family plot at the Second Presbyterian Church on Meeting Street. The Charleston newspaper praised Moffett for his "great physical bravery" and decried his death as a "public calamity."[6]

Suddenly widowed and facing economic hardship, Elizabeth Moffett remained in the house on St. Philip Street for another five years before moving a short distance away to a multistory frame house at 119 Coming Street. After a number of years, the family relocated a block north to a large house at 131 Coming, across from the big Episcopal Church of St. Luke and St. Paul. During this trying period, Elizabeth found strength in her children and in members of the close-knit Simonton family. Hardly knowing his father, Billy became devoted to his mother; throughout his early life he sought to please her and make her proud of him. He risked derision from his peers as a mama's boy, but he never seemed ashamed of the exceptional affection he felt for his mother. At the same time, Elizabeth Moffett instilled in all her children a strong sense of self-discipline and loyalty that carried over into their later lives and careers.[7]

Billy's childhood was otherwise unextraordinary. He attended the High School of Charleston, located in an old mansion on the northeast corner of George and Meeting streets. Nominally a public school, it functioned more like a private academy, charging tuition and drawing its students from the city's elite. There were elaborate and demeaning initiation ceremonies and a demerit system charged against students for various infractions. Billy found time from his studies to do the things that most normal boys do. He enjoyed playing baseball and marbles, walking in the country, and hunting and fishing. One of his favorite fishing holes was at West Point Mill, at the end of Boundary Street (now Calhoun Street) on the Ashley River. Apparently he was not above juvenile pranks, for he and one of his childhood friends once threw stones at the windows of St. Luke's and St. Paul's Church.[8]

Billy was especially close to his sister Josephine ("Jo"), the youngest of the Moffett clan. He recalled games of tag they played after school: "She never [played] very well but sometimes I would not play my best and would let her beat me. Then she used to be so pleased." Jo liked to help Billy fly kites. She held the kite until he was ready to run with it to get it airborne. "I had just finished one," he wrote in his cadet diary, and "ran without giving her the word to let it go at the right time and it got broken." He regretted losing his temper with her. On another occasion Billy admitted, "I once got very angry with her for going into my pigeon house and she was always after that afraid to go in." After Jo died in November 1882 at the age of seven, Billy sorrowfully wished he "had given her the pigeons, house and all."[9]

In the summer of 1886, Billy's uncle, George H. Simonton, urged him to seek an appointment to the Naval Academy. At the time, there were two avenues to Annapolis. The more usual way was direct appointment by a senator or congressman; the other was to pass a rigorous competitive examination. Evidently the direct appointment was out of the question, because Billy opted for the examination. He sought and received help from two of his teachers at the high school who were on the examination board. Although his mother thought the Naval Academy was too far from home for her son, she too encouraged Billy as he put in long hours cramming geography, history, English grammar, and mathematics. On 29 July, Billy and ten others went down to the high school to take the test, which lasted most of the day. The next morning, he remembered, "I went down to the Letter box with my heart in my mouth. . . . Prepared for the worst. . . . What was my joy and surprise to see that 'William A. Moffett' had passed [with] the best exam and therefore had received the appointment. My joy knew no bounds." Officially the nomination came from Samuel Dibble, congressman from the first district of South Carolina and a friend of Billy's father's.[10]

Nomination did not automatically mean admittance to the academy, because potential midshipmen still had to pass a special entrance examination. Billy said his good-byes and left Charleston on 3 August, headed for Fort Defiance, a small town in Virginia, where he planned to receive supplementary tutoring in the home of Milton Parkins. He stopped briefly to visit relatives and friends in Richmond before continuing on to Fort Defiance, where he arrived on 5 August. At first, sixteen-year-old Billy found the Parkins home full of distractions. He found it impossible to resist horseback rides through the beautiful Shenandoah Valley, duck hunting, and sight-seeing trips to Staunton with female friends of the Parkinses'. It took a stern remonstrance from his mother before Billy buckled down to a grinding regimen that included seven hours of study a day over the next ten days.[11]

Billy left the Parkinses on 20 August, staying in Washington overnight before leaving for Annapolis early on the morning of the twenty-first. Only then, he admitted, did he begin "to feel homesick for the first time." At the academy he met Claude Bailey, from Bellefonte, Arkansas, who was to be his roommate and closest friend for the next four years. The extra study at Fort Defiance paid off, for young Moffett passed his academic tests and entered the academy as a cadet on 6 September. The class of 1890 numbered eighty-five, of which only thirty-four graduated. Besides Moffett, eleven others achieved flag rank, notably Frank H. Schofield and Jehu V. Chase (both commanders in chief, U.S. Fleet), Charles B. McVay, Jr. (chief of the Bureau of Ordnance), and Julius L. Latimer (judge advocate general). Three Marine generals also came out of Moffett's class.[12]

There were more attractive places than the United States Naval Academy in the 1880s. Forty-one years old in 1886, the academy was a forbidding array of ramshackle wood and brick buildings along the Severn River. The battalion of cadets resided in the upper three floors of the New Quarters, a four-story, red-brick edifice derided by some as an "ugly factory." On the ground floor of the building were the mess hall, offices, reception area, and some classrooms. Completed in 1869, the New Quarters was much the worse for wear. Plaster walls were a maze of cracks, and fumes seeped up from the first-floor kitchen and laundry through holes in the floors. Other buildings were not much better; major new construction did not take place until six years after Moffett graduated.[13]

When Moffett entered Annapolis in 1886, Comdr. William T. Sampson had just begun his tour as superintendent. Sampson vowed to crack down on hazing ("running," as it was then called), grappled with discipline problems that had plagued the academy earlier in the decade, and instituted a tough new curriculum more consonant with the requirements of the emerging steam navy. Moffett and his classmates tackled courses in applied science and technical fields; in 1886, electricity and metallurgy became required subjects for the first time. Recognizing the popularity of American-style football as an intercollegiate sport, Sampson put more emphasis on athletics than had his predecessors.[14]

Despite Sampson's changes, the academy remained little more than a boys' preparatory school, and not a particularly good one. But what it lacked in academic rigor it made up for in the shared experience of young men in the atmosphere of the ship. Some bilged, or were washed out, finding the close quarters, enforced hardship, and strict behavioral codes stifling. But others thrived in the surroundings. They formed lifelong bonds and constituted a band of brothers who understood that their individual actions had to be in the communal interest—for the good of the ship. The rigid hierarchy from first classmen down to lowly plebes instilled order and discipline, absolutely necessary for the smooth functioning of the human and mechanical components of a warship. A man always knew where he was within the social and military order and understood instinctively how his personal loyalties ran up and down the ladder of command.

Moffett's first year at the academy was difficult. Only sixteen, he was neither the oldest nor the youngest in his class, the ages of incoming midshipmen ranging from fourteen to eighteen. As a September plebe, he was subject to running by the May plebes, who had just returned from the annual summer cruise and had a month to humiliate their messmates before the upperclassmen returned from leave. Homesickness added to Cadet Moffett's profound discomfiture during his first year. On the other hand, classes went fairly well, and he received acceptable marks in his English and history courses as well as in French and Spanish. He finished his first year with a 2.7 average and stood twenty-first in the class.[15]

The 1887 summer cruise aboard the old frigate *Constellation* came as a welcome change for Billy and his classmates. Billy kept a diary during the cruise and for two years thereafter; it provides an insight not only into his personality but also into life at the academy. At the end of classes in June, *Constellation* sailed from Annapolis under the command of Comdr. Charles L. Huntington. The ship visited Newport, Rhode Island, where Billy was much impressed by the beautiful houses, expansive lawns, and elaborate conservatories. The remainder of the cruise, lasting until 26 August, was unremarkable, consisting of seemingly endless gun, sail, and signal drills, punctuated by an occasional fight and hazing of the May plebes. In New London, Connecticut, on 10 August there was a hop, or dance. By then young Moffett, who had always been drawn to the charms of the opposite sex, was starting to earn a reputation as a ladies' man. *Constellation*'s decks, Moffett wrote, "were crowded with people. Some of the femmes were very pretty. I decided from the first to go & had a very very good time. Danced all the dances except the 'galop.' . . . I met a good many femmes but not the exact ones I wanted to in some instances."[16]

During his second year at Annapolis, Billy paid closer attention to his studies, but there was no commensurate improvement in his grades. He generally did well in English and history and foreign languages, but he also made a creditable showing in mechanical drawing. His worst subject was chemistry, where he barely made passing marks. In his diary there is a constant recitation of long hours of studying, or boning. Within a week of the start of classes in October, he wrote that he had made "a rule to jump up at reveille and dress etc immediately so that I can bone a half hour before breakfast." Despite the distance separating them, Moffett felt his mother's constant presence and was anxious about what she would think: "I feel oh! so dreadfully when I think of Mama's disappointment when she gets my report." Still, his second year at Annapolis was not all a grind. Billy rarely missed a dance or other social event, did his share of hazing, and actively followed sports events at the academy. His 26 November 1887 diary entry includes a detailed description of the football game with Princeton, which he said was the "event of the season."[17]

Poor health contributed to Moffett's difficulties at the academy. Through his first and second years at Annapolis he suffered from severe headaches, which he vainly tried to mitigate with adjustments to his diet. He also experienced hearing loss in his left ear and worried in the spring of 1888 that it might be bad enough to cause him to fail the annual physical examination.[18]

But those ailments paled before what befell him next. A little more than a week after he left Annapolis on 18 August to return on leave to Charleston, Billy was stricken with typhoid fever. We tend to forget how prevalent and deadly such contagious diseases were; there was no vaccine against typhoid universally available until 1911. Desperately ill, Billy was bedridden until the middle of October, and thereafter he convalesced slowly. At the end of the month, his doctor reported that he was well along toward recovery but that he had lost twenty-seven pounds and would "not be fit for duty for at least a month." To make matters worse, his older brother Andrew died on 10 October, only two months before his thirty-first birthday.[19]

On 3 November, Billy took the extraordinary step of writing to Commander Sampson to request a year's sick leave. He explained that he would not be able to return to the academy until the first of December and that even then he doubted he would be able to keep up with the rigors of Annapolis. Having already missed two months of studies, he feared that he would fall hopelessly behind his classmates, who were "more gifted than I," and would wind up in all likelihood bilging. Even if he somehow completed the academic work, he thought his class standing would be so low as to "preclude all possibility of getting into the service." Sampson denied his request, and Billy had to return to the academy before the end of 1888. Not surprisingly, his marks reflected the difficulty he had catching up; at the conclusion of the academic year, he had dropped to near the bottom of his class.[20]

By the end of classes in June 1889, Billy was fully recovered from his bout with typhoid and eagerly looked forward to the summer cruise, his second and last. Unfortunately, *Constellation,* standing down Chesapeake Bay under the command of Comdr. Purnell F. Harrington, ran aground about fifteen miles off Cape Henry amid fog and a stiff wind. The crew attempted to kedge the ship off, but they could not overcome the strong current and wind. In the meantime, the old frigate started to take on water. With the help of a tug, *Constellation* was freed the next day and towed to Norfolk, where a survey showed that the ship was in need of extensive repairs. By the middle of July, the ship's officers and complement of cadets had been detached to return to Annapolis.[21]

There was little young Moffett could do during his last year at the academy to improve his low class standing. His grades improved, including the best mark in the course on international law, but he did poorly in such subjects as ordnance and gunnery, physics and chemistry, and mathematics. He graduated on 10 June 1890 thirty-first out of thirty-four members of his class, narrowly avoiding the dubious distinction of class anchor. As a passed midshipman, a sort of apprentice ensign, Moffett still faced two years at sea before receiving his commission. Numbers were all-important at the academy, and class rank initially determined seagoing assignments. Moffett received orders to report to the steam sloop *Pensacola,* based at New York. It was far from his first choice, but it was not unexpected, and whatever disappointment Moffett felt was eased when his roommate, Claude Bailey, joined him aboard the ship.[22]

Skippered by Capt. Albert Kautz, *Pensacola* was a Civil War–vintage, 3,000-ton, 1,100-horsepower wooden steamer mounting two 60-pounder muzzle-loading rifled guns and eighteen 9-inch smoothbores. She left New York in July bound for Montevideo, Uruguay, stopping in Rio de Janeiro along the way. In November, the ship and her crew received orders to steam to Chile, where civil war had broken out. The ship labored through heavy weather in the Strait of Magellan during the first week of February 1891, then made her way up the west coast of South America, arriving at Valparaiso in early March. Tension between the United States and the revolutionaries in Chile ran high as a result of the illegal American detention of the rebel arms ship *Itata.* In June 1891, Moffett transferred from *Pensacola* to the 9,700-ton armored cruiser *Charleston,* which had been sent to Valparaiso to bolster the American presence in Chile.[23]

Five months later, on 7 November 1891, Moffett and Bailey transferred to the cruiser *Baltimore.* Captained by Winfield Scott Schley, the 4,400-ton vessel was one of the Navy's newest steel ships, boasting a formidable battery of twelve 6-inch guns. Only weeks before Moffett and Bailey joined the ship, two *Baltimore* sailors had been killed in a brawl in a Valparaiso saloon. Although the Americans were far from innocent, the United States demanded an apology from the Chilean revolutionary leadership. When it was not immediately forthcoming, an armed confrontation between the two countries appeared likely. A tense couple of months followed while both sides prepared for war, but the Chileans ended the crisis in January 1892 with a full apology and offer of reparations. On 11

December 1891, *Baltimore* sailed from Valparaiso for San Francisco, passing through the Golden Gate and docking on 5 January 1892.[24]

During the 1870s and 1880s not all passed midshipmen gained admittance into the officer corps; many completed their two-year postgraduation sea duty and then were mustered out without receiving commissions. In some cases, fewer than half the graduates in a class were retained. But the Chilean crisis brought the Navy to its highest state of readiness since the Civil War and demonstrated the need to keep most of the recent Annapolis graduates. On 18 April 1892, Moffett received instructions detaching him from *Baltimore* and ordering him to return to the academy, where he completed final examinations before finally receiving his commission as an ensign on 14 July 1892, to date from 1 July.[25]

After a welcome two-month leave in Charleston, Moffett reported to Newport on 30 June for his next assignment, the old wooden frigate *Portsmouth*. Commanded by Capt. Charles D. Sigsbee, *Portsmouth* served as a sail training ship for enlisted seamen. On her first voyage that summer, the ship crossed the Atlantic, calling at Plymouth, Lisbon, and Funchal in the Madeiras before heading back home. The westward crossing was a pleasant one, with a steady breeze carrying the ship back to Newport by early October. Later that month, *Portsmouth* sailed from Newport to New York, where she spent a month in dry dock. On 3 January 1893, the ship left for the West Indies, enduring force-12 winds and heavy squalls as she worked her way south. She arrived in Bridgetown, Barbados, on 27 January. Later the ship called at Martinique, Trinidad, St. Kitts, St. Thomas, and Santa Cruz, before returning to Newport on 2 June. *Portsmouth* was far from the best the Navy could offer, but time in the frigate riding the Atlantic swells and scudding before the trade winds allowed Moffett to hone his ship-handling skills in a way that he could not in some of the newer ships.[26]

Portsmouth provided valuable experience, but Moffett received what he thought was a much better assignment when he was detached from the ship on 2 June 1893 and ordered to report to the New York (Brooklyn) Navy Yard for service in *Chicago*. One of the Navy's newest and most powerful vessels and flagship of the North Atlantic Squadron, *Chicago* was a 4,500-ton protected steel cruiser, mounting four 8-inch, eight 6-inch, and two 5-inch rifled guns. Along with the cruisers *Atlanta* and *Boston* and the dispatch vessel *Dolphin,* she was one of the famous ABCD ships making up the Squadron of Evolution, where senior officers learned the intricacies of steam and steel in the modern Navy. *Chicago*'s commander was Capt. Alfred Thayer Mahan, whose seminal work, *The Influence of Sea Power upon History,* had been published only three years before.

Unfortunately, *Chicago* was in poor condition in the summer of 1893. Her engines badly needed repair, and her complement was ill-trained and surly. To make matters worse, Mahan thought he was being sent to sea as punishment for advocating the annexation of Hawaii in a controversial article published earlier that year. *Chicago* departed from New York on 18 June, arriving in Queenstown, Ireland, later in the month. The ship then continued on to Southampton and the start of what amounted to a triumphal tour for Mahan. In London, British military and civilian officials feted him, believing his published work had given a stamp of approval to the policies long adhered to by the Royal Navy and sensing that the United States itself was a rising naval power and potential ally in any future European conflict. After Mahan's adulatory reception in London, *Chicago* went on to Le Havre, Lisbon, and Gibraltar, then spent the next eight months circumnavigating the Mediterranean. Moffett and his shipmates prowled the bazaars of Tangier, Smyrna (now Izmir, Turkey), Beirut, and Alexandria and took time for side trips to Paris and Rome. In May 1894 *Chicago* returned to England and another social go-round for Mahan, remaining in northern European waters until October before steaming back to the Mediterranean.[27]

On 2 January 1895, while *Chicago* was in Algiers, Ensign Moffett was made one of the ship's watch and division officers. A further expansion of his responsibilities came when he and his shipmate Claude Bailey each served as Mahan's clerk, a secretarial job bringing both young officers close to the man whose ideas most affected modern naval thinking. What Moffett learned directly from Mahan is not known, but we do know that Mahan was many things Moffett was not: a cold-blooded, egotistical intellectual who inspired little respect among subordinates and had a well-deserved reputation as a complainer among his peers. Whatever lessons Moffett learned from Mahan were negative ones.[28]

Back in New York, Moffett was far from dismayed when he left *Chicago* in late March 1895 with orders to join the newly commissioned monitor *Amphitrite.* She and her sisters were surprisingly durable and capable vessels, despite their denigration by Mahanite advocates of a seagoing navy. Heavily armored and bearing four 10-inch breech-loading guns in twin turrets, the 3,990-ton *Amphitrite* was ideal for inshore operations but also capable of long ocean crossings. Joining the ship on 23 April, Moffett enjoyed his responsibilities as a watch and division officer, duties made all the more agreeable because her home port was Beaufort, South Carolina, only about seventy miles from Charleston. He sometimes invited his shipboard companions to join him on leave in Charleston as he visited family and friends and made the social rounds in the city. Moffett served aboard *Amphitrite* until April 1896.[29]

Moffett's next assignment—to the Naval War College at Newport—was a counterpoint to his education at sea. He arrived at the college in June 1896 after two months' leave and immediately threw himself into classwork. The college had been founded by Capt. Stephen B. Luce in 1885 as a postgraduate school providing instruction in naval history, strategy, planning, and the technical subjects needed by officers in the modern Navy. Mahan taught at Newport from 1885 to 1888, returning in 1892 for a brief, one-year tour as the college's president before going to sea in *Chicago*. Moffett had only four months at the college, but in that time he engaged a challenging curriculum stressing the details of staff work and the techniques of planning that junior officers needed to know as they assumed more responsibilities for the organization and operation of naval vessels and their increasingly complex equipment.[30]

For the next two years, Moffett bounced from one ship to another, accumulating by the spring of 1898 almost eight years of continuous sea duty. But there was nothing particularly extraordinary in his service record that seemed to guarantee rapid career advancement until the outbreak of the Spanish-American War. When the United States declared war on Spain on 25 April, Moffett was in Honolulu serving in *Mohican*, a 1,900-ton, Civil War–vintage, bark-rigged steamer. Four days later, the ship cleared the harbor bound for San Francisco, where she put in on 12 May. The next day, Moffett learned that he had been detached from *Mohican* and ordered to *Charleston*, which was at Mare Island hastily assembling a crew and completing preparations to sail to Hawaii. Under the command of Capt. Henry Glass, *Charleston* steamed out through the Golden Gate on 22 May, arriving a week later off Honolulu and rendezvousing with *Australia, City of Sydney,* and *City of Peking,* three chartered transports loaded with troops bound for Manila. From Hawaii, the expedition set out on 4 June on the long voyage across the Pacific with orders to invade and occupy the Spanish island of Guam in the Marianas, considered valuable as a potential coaling station for ships operating in the western Pacific.[31]

Charleston and her convoy arrived off Agana, Guam's capital, early on the morning of 20 June, but upon discovering no ships in the harbor, the small fleet made its way a short distance down the west coast of the island to the port of San Luis d'Apra. Glass took *Charleston* into the harbor and fired into Fort Santa Cruz. There were no return shots. When Spanish port officers came on board *Charleston* they were astonished to learn that the two countries were at war; they had mistakenly thought the fire from the American ship was a salute and were apologetic that they could not return it. Glass demanded the surrender of the island. When that was not forthcoming by the next day, a small landing party from *Charleston* went ashore with an ultimatum that brought nearly immediate results. The Spanish governor, his staff, and the island's sixty-man garrison surrendered, and the United States took possession of its first territory in the western Pacific. Remarkably, *Charleston* and her consorts sailed from Guam on the twenty-second without leaving behind an occupying force.[32]

The immediate need to reinforce Adm. George Dewey's blockading fleet at Manila and to support the invasion and occupation of the Philippines occasioned the Americans' hasty departure. *Charleston* and the transports pulled into Manila Bay on 30 June and took up positions off the Cavite Navy yard. Shortly thereafter, Moffett and other junior officers had an audience with Dewey and congratulated him on his spectacular victory over the Spanish fleet. When one of the officers compared the Battle of Manila Bay to Nelson's triumph at the Nile almost exactly a hundred years earlier, Moffett quickly pointed out that in contrast to Nelson, Dewey had not allowed a single enemy ship to escape destruction. It was sincere if shameless flattery on Moffett's part, but it left a positive impression on Dewey.[33]

The American assault on the city of Manila began on 13 August. *Charleston* and two other ships bombarded the Luneta Battery from positions off the Pasig River, and *Olympia* shelled Fort San Antonio de Abad. Within hours, the Spanish surrendered and American troops quickly marched in to occupy the city. Although the operation went smoothly and there had been a minimum of bloodshed, the occupying forces found Manila a shambles. Weeks of blockade had led to a nearly complete breakdown in the administration of the city and the services needed by its residents. Before any semblance of normality could return, the Americans had to clear the harbor and restore essential port facilities.[34]

Dewey assigned Glass as captain of the port of Manila, with Moffett as one of his aides. One of Moffett's tasks was removing obstructions from the harbor. Temporarily assigned on 1 December to *Culgoa,* a British steamer requisitioned as a supply ship, Moffett went about his job with unusual fervor and within a short time had most of the sunken ships and other obstacles removed. *Cebu,* a transport, presented a more difficult challenge, however. Rather than surrender the ship during the assault on the city, the Spanish had set her afire, and she sank in the Pasig River near Fort Santiago. Ignoring Army recommendations to dynamite the hulk, Moffett convinced his superiors that the remains of the ship could be salvaged and requested a full set of drawings of the ship from the Spanish. When they refused, Moffett obtained a warrant, assembled a group of armed sailors, marched into the offices of the Spanish navy department, and demanded they turn over the plans. With the drawings in hand, Moffett put together a largely Filipino salvage team and raised the wreck after a week of round-the-clock effort. The experience with *Cebu* convinced Moffett that his group could also refloat three warships scuttled by the Spanish shortly after the Battle of Manila Bay, but to his dismay he learned that Dewey had already signed an expensive contract with a Hong Kong firm to salvage the wrecks. Ensign Moffett's work in clearing the harbor at Manila earned him a nickname aptly reflecting his commitment to getting the job done—"En Seguida," Spanish for "Do it now."[35]

Moffett's assiduous execution of his duties in Manila provided an ideal opportunity for him to demonstrate his initiative and organizational capacity, but the additional responsibilities took their toll. Shortly after arriving back in *Charleston* on 13 February 1899, Moffett landed in sick bay with malaria and was confined to the naval hospital at Cavite. When it became apparent that he was not recovering from the disease as quickly as expected, Moffett was detached from *Charleston* and ordered back to the United States. He boarded the cruiser *Boston* in Manila on 17 May and the next day left for Yokohama in Japan, remaining there a month before leaving for the West Coast. When the ship finally arrived in San Francisco on 26 August (after a brief stop in Honolulu), Moffett immediately reported to the Mare Island Naval Hospital for additional medical attention. The good news was that he had received his commission as lieutenant (junior grade) on 10 June 1899, to date from 3 March, followed quickly thereafter with notification of his elevation to full lieutenant. Moffett's advancement in 1899 resulted from his superior performance at Manila as well as the Navy's urgent need for experienced officers. In contrast to those who had graduated from Annapolis only a few years before him and who had faced the prospect of tedious decades in grade, Moffett could look forward to much more rapid and gratifying promotion.[36]

Health problems dogged Moffett for the next year. After nearly three months at Mare Island, the new lieutenant was well enough to get out of the hospital and make the long rail trip across the country for a well-earned leave at the family home on Coming Street in Charleston. On 19 December 1899, he reported to New York for service in *Monongahela*, a 2,000-ton, Civil War–era, 530-horsepower screw steamer. He was with the ship less than six weeks before an attack of appendicitis in February put him in the naval hospital in New York. It is unclear whether the case was severe enough to require surgery, but it was not until May that he was well enough to resume his duties.[37]

Moffett's next assignment, to the battleship *Kentucky*, marked the beginning of sixteen months at sea. Freshly commissioned at Newport News, *Kentucky* displaced 11,540 tons and mounted four 13-inch guns in two turrets, superposed on which were two smaller turrets, each with two 8-inch guns. Her commander was Capt. Colby M. Chester. The day Moffett reported to the ship, 15 May, she was still being fitted out, and a month passed before she was ready for her shakedown cruise to Newport. After spending the rest of the summer and part of the fall in the vicinity of New York, *Kentucky* left her mooring off Staten Island on 25 October bound for Turkey and a delicate diplomatic mission to recover from the Turkish government $90,000 in damages to American property incurred during a massacre in Armenia.

Kentucky stopped in Gibraltar, Algiers, and Naples on the way to Smyrna. Dropping anchor off the Turkish port on 27 November, *Kentucky* received various military and civilian dignitaries and on 9 December fired a twenty-one-gun salute in honor of the sultan's birthday. Later, Captain Chester selected Moffett to accompany him and two other junior officers to Constantinople to assist in working out the terms of the indemnity. Following a series of dinners and dances at the foreign legations in the city, the Americans attended a special feast hosted by the sultan. There the two parties concluded a monetary settlement satisfactory to both sides. During the negotiations, the sultan offered Moffett a commission in the

Turkish navy, which had recently acquired an American-built cruiser. Moffett did not accept, but the offer was a flattering one that acknowledged his considerable technical background and skills.[38]

Kentucky weighed anchor on 18 December and set course for Port Said and the Suez Canal. After transiting the waterway, the battleship made her way to Aden, crossed the Arabian Sea to Colombo in Ceylon, and continued on to Singapore, Manila, and Hong Kong, where she arrived on 12 February 1901. The ship went into dry dock at Hong Kong, spending the better part of the month undergoing repairs and maintenance. On 7 April, she sailed for Manila, anchoring off Cavite two days later.[39]

At Manila on 24 May Lieutenant Moffett transferred to *Marietta*, a 1,000-ton steamer with six 4-inch guns. *Marietta* remained in the Philippines until 3 June, when she stood down Manila Bay bound for Singapore. From Singapore Moffett sailed with the ship across the Indian Ocean to Colombo, up the west coast of India to Bombay, then back to Aden, up the Red Sea, and through the Suez Canal on the night of 3–4 August. *Marietta* put in at Naples for a week before continuing on to Gibraltar, where she halted briefly before setting out into the Atlantic. On the two-week crossing to Bermuda, the ship encountered a vicious late-summer storm. Buffeted by the tempest, *Marietta* suffered damage to her rigging and injuries to her crew; at one point, Moffett ordered sixty men aloft to make fast a sail nearly carried away by the howling winds. After a brief stop in Bermuda, *Marietta* continued on to New York, where she anchored off Staten Island on the afternoon of 17 September.[40]

Returning from a leave in Charleston on 23 October 1901, Moffett reported as executive officer of *St. Mary's,* a 958-ton wooden sloop commissioned in 1844 and used as a sail training ship by the Public Marine School in New York. Over the next year, *St. Mary's* made numerous cruises, one of them taking Moffett around Cape Horn to Amoy in China. Back in New York in April 1902, Moffett called on his older sister Margaret, who ran an art studio in the city. There he met a young woman studying to become a nurse, Jeannette Beverly Whitton, from Kingston, Ontario. Born in London, England, on 13 November 1885, Miss Whitton was only sixteen years old. She immediately attracted Moffett, who was twice her age and seemed at last ready to settle down. Not long after their first meeting, Miss Whitton left New York for London. Coincidentally, the next cruise of *St. Mary's* took Moffett to Southampton, where he made a point of going up to London to visit the young woman. Their courtship was surprisingly brief, culminating on 26 July 1902 with marriage at the village of Fawley in Hampshire, after which the newlyweds had to make their separate ways back to the United States. Unfortunately, only pieces of Moffett's correspondence with Jeannette survive. They indicate, however, that following the initial glow of nuptial bliss, the Moffetts' marriage soon settled into a comfortable, if not deeply affectionate, relationship.[41]

Moffett left *St. Mary's* in November 1902 for the old second-class cruiser *Minneapolis,* the receiving ship at the Philadelphia Navy Yard. While the Moffetts were living in Germantown, Jeannette bore her first child, Janet Whitton, on 17 May 1903. Moffett stayed in Philadelphia for the next four months, serving in the new 12,500-ton battleship *Maine,* which had only recently been completed at the yard of William Cramp and Sons in Philadelphia. One of the most powerful ships in the Navy, *Maine* mounted four 12-inch guns in two turrets, with sixteen 6-inch guns arrayed in casemates along her hull and superstructure. Moffett worked as the ship's boiler division officer while she fitted out at Cramp's and on shakedown cruises to Hampton Roads, the West Indies, Newport, Panama, and New York.[42]

Detached from *Maine* in New York on 2 January 1904, Moffett reported to Norfolk as executive officer of *Amphitrite,* commanded by Lt. Comdr. Edwin H. Tillman. This was Moffett's second tour in the monitor, now approaching twenty years of age but still considered useful for limited coastal operations. *Amphitrite* steamed out of Norfolk on 21 January bound for Guantánamo Bay in southeastern Cuba, where the United States had recently leased land for the establishment of a naval base. Along the way, the monitor stopped at Charleston long enough for Moffett to visit relatives and briefly put in at Key West before arriving in Guantánamo early on the morning of 10 February. As dawn broke, Moffett got his first glimpse of the harbor. It was an impressive sight: the crystalline waters dotted by low-lying islands, with five other American warships clustered in the anchorage. But the shore offered only snake-infested brush and cactus, hardly an attractive place for a major naval station.[43]

Amphitrite served as temporary base headquarters as work got under way at several sites around the bay. The main naval base, including office buildings, the commandant's quarters, and a large dry dock, was located on South Toro Cay. On Fisherman's Point workers constructed a coaling station, and on Hospital Cay they erected living facilities for base personnel. Six months after arriving at Guantánamo, Moffett became captain of the yard, with responsibility for all construction activities at the naval station. Over the next two years, Moffett supervised the building of additional barracks, a radio station, an extensive rifle range in the area between Deer Point and Bay Hill, and a one-million-gallon reservoir intended to alleviate the chronic water shortage at the base. Moffett's tour was made more enjoyable because Jeannette joined him for at least part of the time. Many years later, he looked back with fondness on the times he and his wife had in Guantánamo, especially the leisurely afternoon walks along the many trails around the bay.[44]

Midway through the Cuban assignment, on 21 August 1905, Moffett returned to Washington to take the examination for promotion to lieutenant commander. He passed the rigorous physical examination, withstood three grueling days of written and oral tests, and received his new commission on 25 September 1905, to date from 1 July. After three months' leave, which he spent in Washington, Moffett headed back to Guantánamo, remaining on duty there until March 1906.[45] Moffett did not know it at the time, but the Guantánamo posting marked a turning point in his naval career. He was still to spend more years at sea, but they would be in increasingly important command positions; no longer would he be subject to tiresome watch duties. At Guantánamo he had demonstrated his potential on shore as well as at sea, which contributed incrementally to his administrative experience and service reputation.

Following his return from Guantánamo, Moffett took two months' leave at home in Washington before reporting to the Compass Office in the Bureau of Equipment, where he completed brief instruction on navigation instruments. From 1 June to 29 August 1906, he took the summer officers' course at the Naval War College in Newport. After completing his instruction there, Moffett went back to Washington for more duty with the Bureau of Equipment. During that time, the Moffetts' domestic life settled into a relatively easy routine, and a new son, George Hall, was born on 18 February 1907.[46]

After nearly two years in Washington, Moffett received orders in March 1908 dispatching him to the armored cruiser *Maryland,* based at Mare Island. Moffett reported to the ship on 6 April and immediately assumed the billet of navigator. *Maryland* was big and almost new, having gone into service in 1906. She displaced 13,680 tons and mounted four 8-inch guns in two turrets; the secondary armament included fourteen

6-inch and eighteen 3-inch guns. Commanding the cruiser was Capt.
Chauncey Thomas. During Moffett's first months with *Maryland*, the ship
steamed with the Pacific Squadron from port to port on the West Coast,
but in late August she embarked on an extended cruise taking her to
Hawaii, Samoa, back to Hawaii, and then to Magdalena Bay in Mexico.
From that point the voyage extended down the coasts of Central and
South America, with Moffett functioning from 18 November as the ship's
executive officer. *Maryland* did not return to Mare Island until July
1909.[47]

Largely because of Moffett's competence and attention to detail, *Maryland* earned a reputation as a happy and efficient ship in superb material
condition. The cruiser won the Pacific Squadron's battle efficiency trophy,
which rewarded combined excellence in gunnery and engineering. Ensign
William L. Calhoun remembered *Maryland* as "the scourge of the battleships, and of her sister cruisers. No competition was EVER over until
they heard from Moffett. Usually the announcement came that the *Maryland* had again won. . . . The name *Maryland*, engraved on every service
or athletic fleet cup, might well have been spelled *Moffett!*" Moffett also
gained a reputation as a tough but fair officer who was always accessible to
those serving under him. Calhoun said: "While Billy was kind and lovable
to a degree, he demanded and received each man's all, and God forgive
the lad who gave less. At any hour of the day or night Mr. Moffett's cabin
door was open to any one seeking advice."[48]

Moffett's tour on *Maryland* was one of the most pleasing assignments
of his early career. Jeannette and the two children joined him on the West
Coast, first taking up residence at Coronado, near San Diego, and later
moving to San Francisco. The family grew with the birth of another son,
William Adger Junior, on 16 April 1910 in San Francisco. Only a bother-
some bacterial infection (leading to an abscess that required minor surgery
three days before Christmas 1908) marred what were for Moffett some of
the brightest days in his life.[49]

Moffett's next assignment, as inspector of the Eighteenth Lighthouse
District in San Francisco, appeared to be backwater duty. But he took up
his new responsibilities on 8 October 1910 with characteristic zeal. He
significantly improved navigation aids in San Francisco Bay and along the
West Coast. Blinking navigation lights replaced fixed lights, additional fog
signals were placed at strategic points, lighthouses received 4.5 million-
candlepower lamps instead of the relatively weak 900,000-candlepower

units used previously, and at Yerba Buena Island (now a part of the San Francisco–Oakland Bay Bridge) he installed a siren to warn mariners away from that dangerous obstacle in the middle of San Francisco Bay. Moffett even found time in 1912 to collaborate on two inventions, both of which received patents: a device using a selenium photocell to produce electricity for the automatic control of signaling apparatus and an occulting mechanism using the heat from a lamp to produce a flashing light.[50]

Moffett was only a few months into his tour in San Francisco when Curtiss aviator Eugene Ely arrived in the city to attempt the first airplane landing aboard a ship. Ely had already taken off from the cruiser *Birmingham* at Hampton Roads in November 1910. Now he planned to alight on a temporary wooden platform erected over the stern of the armored cruiser *Pennsylvania*. Captain Washington Irving Chambers, who had worked with Ely on the Hampton Roads experiment, was in charge of the demonstration in San Francisco, which generated an enormous amount of publicity in the local papers. Moffett, like practically everyone else in San Francisco, closely followed the preparations for the flight, at one point reportedly offering Chambers whatever assistance he thought his office could provide to ensure the success of Ely's historic achievement on 18 January 1911.[51]

While Moffett was on the West Coast, he learned that he was eligible for promotion, and he reported to Mare Island on 3 April 1911 to take the necessary examination. As was the case for his advancement to lieutenant commander, the procedure consisted of a physical examination and oral and written tests, stretching over several days. But in this instance, the Navy later determined that one of the members of the examining board had actually been junior to Moffett and that the board had been illegally constituted. As a result, Moffett had to retake the written and oral tests the next month before finally receiving his new commission on 31 May 1911 (to date from 4 March).[52]

At the end of June 1912, Commander Moffett journeyed to Philadelphia and the Camden, New Jersey, yard of the New York Shipbuilding Company for duty on the new battleship *Arkansas*. Moffett was with *Arkansas* through her fitting out and became the ship's executive officer upon her commissioning on 17 September. Commanded by Capt. Roy C. Smith, *Arkansas* displaced 26,000 tons and with her big Parsons turbines could make more than twenty-one knots. The battleship was of the dreadnought type; she mounted the maximum number of heavy guns while eliminating weapons of intermediate caliber. In this instance, the ship's main battery consisted of twelve 12-inch guns arrayed in six turrets—two forward and four aft. Twenty-one 5-inch guns made up her secondary armament. Less than a month after she went into service, *Arkansas* participated in the Presidential Naval Review on the Hudson River in New York, and in December 1912 the ship carried President William Howard Taft to Panama for an inspection tour of the still-incomplete canal.[53]

In early 1913 *Arkansas* and other elements of the Atlantic Fleet descended on Guantánamo for winter maneuvers. There Moffett once again came into contact with aviation. Lieutenant John H. ("Jack") Towers commanded a group of aviators who had set up camp on Fisherman's Point. Living and working in tents, the young flying officers demonstrated their ability to spot submerged submarines from the air and on one occasion searched for and found the battle fleet fifteen miles outside the bay. Towers met and befriended many officers in the fleet, Moffett among them. Returning with Towers from a duck-hunting expedition up the Guantánamo River, Moffett dismissed aviation as a fad and warned Towers that if he kept on flying he would "surely get himself killed." To Moffett, "any man who sticks to it is either crazy or else a plain damned fool."[54]

Moffett's lack of appreciation for the potential of aviation was to be expected, given his preoccupation with making his way up the ladder of command in the battleship navy and the airplane's then-primitive state of development. His many years of apprenticeship at sea and on shore in progressively more responsible assignments had established him as an officer with considerable ability. He had shown himself to be an excellent seaman, a highly competent leader, and, perhaps most important for the future, a skilled administrator and organizer. His service thus far had not been spectacular, but to the discerning eye he had the makings of a successful senior officer. His opportunity came with his first command late in 1913.

3

COMMAND AT SEA AND ASHORE

COMMAND OF A SHIP WAS A CRITICAL STAGE IN A NAVAL OFFICER'S career, usually preceding advancement from the junior to the senior officer ranks. Moffett's turn came when he left *Arkansas* and reported to the Philadelphia Navy Yard on 5 November 1913 as commanding officer of the cruiser *Chester*. Here was his long-awaited chance to put to the test all he had learned about leadership from more than twenty-three years of duty at sea and on shore, and he was determined to make the most of the opportunity.

Five years old when Moffett was piped aboard for the first time, *Chester* was a sleek, 3,750-ton four-stacker mounting two 5-inch and six 3-inch guns. The ship was just emerging from two years of inactivity and, when Moffett took over, was under the temporary command of Lt. (jg.) Archibald D. Turnbull, who many years later was coauthor of an excellent history of United States naval aviation. Within hours of Moffett's assumption of command, *Chester* began coaling in preparation for a voyage to Veracruz on the Gulf coast of Mexico, where the United States had assembled major elements of the Atlantic Fleet to protect American interests and intervene if necessary in the bloody revolution in that country. *Chester* left port on 7 November, cleared the Delaware capes a day later, and made all speed for her destination, anchoring outside the breakwater at Veracruz on the thirteenth.[1]

Chester was the maid of all work for the next six weeks, shuttling back and forth between Veracruz and the northern port of Tampico with supplies and equipment for the fleet and, in one instance, transporting Mexican refugees to Havana. Moffett used the time to work the ship and her crew into a high state of efficiency and readiness; in later years, he remembered *Chester* as a particularly "tight little ship." In the early evening of 30 December, the cruiser left Veracruz on a special assignment. Aboard was John Lind, the former governor of Minnesota, who was on his way to Gulfport, Mississippi, to report to President Woodrow Wilson after having failed in his diplomatic mission to effect a cease-fire between the Mexican government and the rebels and to secure an agreement to hold free elections.[2]

At the end of 1913, the United States found itself inextricably caught up in the domestic affairs of its unstable neighbor to the south. Shortly before Wilson took office, General Victoriano Huerta had overthrown the moderate government of Francisco I. Madero. Despite assurances that Madero would not be harmed, the former president was shot and killed while "attempting to escape." Huerta's seizure of power ran contrary to Wilson's liberal sensibilities, and Wilson was determined to do whatever he could to restore justice and democracy to Mexico. He withheld diplomatic recognition from the Huerta regime, slapped an embargo on all arms shipped from the United States, and dispatched Lind to pressure Huerta into acceding to American demands. *Chester* anchored at Ship Island off the Mississippi coast on 1 January 1914 and the following day stood in to Pass Christian, where in the early evening a revenue cutter arrived carrying the president. Following a reception "with appropriate ceremonies," Wilson conferred with Lind for nearly four hours, coming away from the meeting more determined than ever to force Huerta out of power.[3]

Chester left Gulfport the next day and steamed south to rejoin the American fleet operating off the Mexican coast. She spent the next three months on routine duties at Veracruz and Puerto Mexico, with one voyage to Mobile, Alabama, in February. On 5 April the cruiser moved to Tampico, where the revolutionary violence had suddenly intensified. Located ten miles inland on the Pánuco River, Tampico was an important center for the storage and transshipment of oil from Mexico's interior, and the city was home to a large number of American nationals. For the next several days the tension was as oppressive as the Mexican heat and humidity. Then, on 9 April, Huertistas detained the crew of an American whaleboat loading supplies for the dispatch vessel *Dolphin*. A few hours later, the Mexicans released the bluejackets and issued an apology, but that was not enough for Rear Adm. Henry T. Mayo, the hot-headed commander of the American squadron. He sent Moffett ashore to hand-deliver an ultimatum demanding within twenty-four hours punishment of the Mexican officer responsible for the incident and a twenty-one-gun salute to the American flag. Huerta publicly acknowledged that his officials had been mistaken in arresting the Americans but refused to accede to the salute. Wilson seized the moment to secure from Congress approval for American intervention should further grievances occur.[4]

As events unfolded at Tampico, the Americans learned that *Ypiranga*, a German freighter, was headed for Veracruz with a cargo of arms for Huerta. Determined to prevent Huerta from receiving the munitions, secretary of the Navy Josephus Daniels, acting on the president's orders, directed the elements of the Atlantic Fleet remaining off Veracruz under the command of Rear Adm. Frank F. Fletcher to intercept the German ship, land troops, and occupy the city's customs house. Because Fletcher's force had been greatly reduced during the Tampico incident, ships from Mayo's squadron were ordered to reinforce the American fleet at Veracruz. A city of about 40,000, Veracruz was a regional administrative center with the best port facilities on the east coast and a narrow-gauge railroad connection to Mexico City. The Mexican naval academy and extensive army barracks were also located in the city.[5]

Fletcher received Daniels's instructions in a series of radio messages that streamed in late on 20 April and early the next morning. He relayed the pertinent communications to Tampico, only to find Mayo reluctant to release his ships at a time when the situation there was unresolved and American lives and property still in jeopardy. Moreover, Mayo and his staff had prepared plans for a landing in the city and had assembled the sailors and marines needed for such an operation should it be authorized. Shortly after 1000 on 20 April, *Chester*, then lying in the Pánuco off Tampico, received orders to rendezvous with the larger American ships outside the mouth of the river. Through the remainder of the day and the following morning, the ship held landing and fire control drills and took on ammunition, three-inch field guns, and a company of marines from the cruiser *Des Moines*. At 0908 on 21 April the cruiser got under way from Tampico and headed downriver, passing two Mexican gunboats, but there was no exchange other than polite recognition of the ships' colors. At 1012 *Chester* dropped anchor between the battleships *Connecticut* and *Minnesota* and brought aboard two companies of marines from them. A little more than an hour later, *Chester* cleared for action once more and, at twenty-four knots, steered south through calm seas and scattered rain showers for Veracruz.[6]

Darkness had fallen by the time *Chester* reached Veracruz. Fletcher in his flagship *Prairie* was already in the harbor. When Moffett radioed for permission to enter the harbor, Fletcher warned him that all navigation lights had been extinguished and left it to Moffett's discretion to decide whether to risk passing through the breakwater that night or to wait until daybreak. Thoroughly familiar with the harbor entrance and confident of his own skills as a ship handler, Moffett without hesitation decided to bring his vessel in. At about 2300 he darkened ship and forty-five minutes later took the conn and pointed the cruiser straight toward the narrow entrance to the inner harbor, only eighty-six-feet wide between the breakwaters. *Chester* passed through unscathed, turned to starboard, and shortly after midnight anchored bow to stern between the British cruiser *Essex* and two merchantmen, *El Gobernador*, presumed to be Mexican, and *Haakon VII*, flying the Norwegian flag. The naval academy building was only about 1,850 yards off *Chester*'s port beam. The ship was in an excellent position to land her sailors and marines and to provide gunfire support for them once they were ashore. Admiral Fletcher immediately commended Moffett and his crew with a "Well done *Chester*."[7]

An hour and a half after entering the inner harbor, Moffett went over to *Prairie* for a briefing from Fletcher and his staff on the location and strength of the Mexican forces and the plans for landing American troops in the city. Before 0300 on the twenty-second, *Chester*'s boats successfully delivered her sailors and marines to the railroad terminal wharf, and by daybreak they had taken up positions near the power plant and locomotive roundhouse. At dawn, *Chester* came under small arms fire, bullets spattering against the hull and upper works of the ship. One round narrowly missed Marine Maj. Smedley D. Butler, who was standing on the bridge at the time. The ship responded with rifle fire and shells from her three-inch guns.[8]

As the morning progressed, *Chester* was the target of intensified sniper fire, emanating from the inner breakwater and small vessels off the ship's port and starboard quarters. *Chester* returned the fire, scoring direct hits on a tug and a barge with shells from her three-inch guns. Moffett also personally directed a shot from the cruiser's aft five-inch gun that broke up a group of men crouching behind a lumber pile on the breakwater. Having suppressed the fire from those points, *Chester* now directed her attention to support of the American forces in the city. She fired five-inch and three-inch shells that helped break up concentrations of Mexican troops blocking the advance of Lt. H. W. Stone's Marine company in the vicinity of the Hidalgo Monument. Three-inch shots blasted entrenched infantry and cavalry forces near the slaughterhouse and in Fort Santiago and the naval academy. Moffett also ordered one of his three-inchers to shell a private residence and a consular building where rifle fire had been seen.[9]

Moffett kept a close watch on the naval academy, which had been the source of sporadic fire since daybreak. The cadets in the academy, determined to uphold the honor and dignity of their country and service against the gringo invaders, had partially fortified the building the day before and had borrowed small artillery pieces from the army. As Moffett observed through his binoculars, the Second Seaman Regiment, under the command of Capt. Edwin A. Anderson, turned and marched in column formation down a street a block south of the academy. There, a few minutes after 0800, the Americans came under heavy small arms and artillery fire. Within moments, *Chester* opened up with her aft five-inch and port quarter three-inch guns, sending round after round through the second-story windows and roof of the academy building. Moffett was much pleased that his gunners were "cool and not excited," and he regarded their accuracy as "exceptionally good especially as it had to be done over our own forces." When the shooting stopped at 0926, the naval academy was almost totally obscured by a cloud of red dust and firing from the cadets in the building had ceased.[10]

Throughout the engagement, *Chester* remained under nearly constant small arms fire from various positions on shore. One bullet struck a loader while he was opening ammunition boxes at the aft five-inch gun, and another wounded a seaman who had come up from the fireroom for a firsthand look at the bombardment. They were *Chester*'s only casualties. When lookouts found that most of the fire seemed to be coming from the New Market, an uncompleted building next to the naval academy, *Chester* turned her guns in that direction, and the snipers quickly dispersed. The cruiser also fired into the Military Barracks, where Mexican troops were thought to have taken up defensive positions.[11]

Early in the action, *Chester*'s spotters thought they saw riflemen firing from the Norwegian steamer *Haakon VII,* anchored off *Chester*'s port bow. Moffett warned the ship, "If we see you firing at us we will sink you." Later Captain Anderson of the Second Seaman Regiment signaled Moffett that his men were apparently being fired on from *Haakon VII.* Moffett had had enough. He ordered his officer of the deck to hail the Norwegian vessel again, this time threatening to sink her unless she immediately left. Within minutes, *Haakon VII* cut her stern lines, raised anchor, and made for the harbor's outer basin. The other merchantman, *El Gobernador,* also looked suspicious, so at 0900 Moffett dispatched an armed party under Lieutenant Turnbull to inspect her. Turnbull found the vessel under the command of the first officer and told him to move the ship out of the inner harbor, but the man refused, arguing that the ship's engine was being repaired. After a search turned up only a single revolver, Turnbull and his men returned to *Chester.* At about 1130, an officer with the *Vermont* battalion of the Second Seaman Regiment alerted *Chester* that shots from *El Gobernador* had wounded two of his men. At noon the Mexican ship got under way and was steaming toward the outer harbor; an armed boat from the battleship *Florida* stopped her, removed her crew, and delivered them to *Chester.*[12]

By early afternoon, 22 April, most of the heavy fighting had come to an end, and relative quiet returned to the streets and harbor of Veracruz. Moffett went ashore the next day to survey the scene. He was particularly concerned about his ship's fire on the private residences and the consular building, for the Americans had been under strict orders to avoid civilian casualties and to minimize damage to foreign property in the city. People at the consular building assured Moffett that no one had fired any shots, but an inspection of the roof revealed that it had recently been swept clean, removing any evidence of spent cartridges. Moffett learned, too, that fire from the top of the building had been seen by an officer attending to wounded seamen from *New Hampshire*'s battalion. Moffett was pleased to find that all of *Chester*'s shells had been properly fuzed and that they had detonated as expected. Altogether, the cruiser had fired 160 rounds. In his action report, Moffett expressed his "appreciation of the readiness, spirit, zeal, promptness, alertness, willingness, and in general . . . high efficiency" of his crew.[13]

The American seizure of the city did not come without cost. Seventeen bluejackets and marines died and another sixty-three were wounded. The Mexicans, by the best guess, suffered 126 killed and 195 wounded. President Wilson and Secretary of State Bryan, who had vainly hoped that the Mexican intervention would be bloodless, were appalled at the loss of life. Throughout Mexico anti-American feelings reached a fever pitch, and jingoism ran rampant in the United States. Argentina, Brazil, and Chile offered to mediate a settlement, but they could not reach a compromise acceptable to Wilson, Huerta, or the rebels. Eventually, Huerta, the reason for all the shooting in the first place, was forced out of office by the revolutionaries in July and fled to Spain. The American military occupation of the city ended with the evacuation of all troops on 23 November.[14]

The action at Veracruz won for Moffett the Congressional Medal of Honor. Awarded to him on 4 December 1915, it cited his "distinguished conduct in battle, engagements of Vera Cruz, April 21 and 22, 1914; brought his ship into the inner harbor during the night of the 21st and 22nd without the assistance of pilot or navigational lights, and was in a position on the morning of the 22nd to use his guns at a critical time with telling effect. His skill in mooring his ship at night was especially noticeable. He placed her nearest to the enemy and did most of the firing and received most of the hits."[15]

Thirty-seven officers and eighteen enlisted men received the Medal of Honor for Veracruz, the most ever awarded for a single battle in American history. Without in any way denigrating Moffett's skill or valor during the Veracruz operation, it is worth pointing out that before 1918 the United States military issued no other decorations for bravery in battle; it was the Medal of Honor or nothing. Furthermore, the Veracruz battle was the first time officers were eligible for the medal, which previously had been restricted to enlisted men. Major Smedley Butler returned his Medal of Honor, saying that he did not feel he had earned it.[16] As time passed, the Medal of Honor took its place at the apex of a hierarchy of decorations, but few people realized that in 1914 it had been liberally distributed for significantly lesser acts of heroism. No matter, for Moffett was now a hero, and he saw no reason to disabuse the public by insisting that his medal was not the exact equivalent of those awarded to fellow servicemen for deeds far surpassing his. The Medal of Honor, in short, became one of the many tools Moffett skillfully wielded in the coming political battles that shaped naval aviation.

In the wake of the Veracruz landings, it would be hard to blame Moffett and his crew if they regarded their ship's subsequent operations as anticlimactic. *Chester* steamed to Puerto Mexico with mail for the cruiser *Tacoma* and remained on routine duty at Veracruz for the next six weeks. Of the most interest during this otherwise dull period was the arrival of an American air unit. Lieutenant Comdr. Henry C. Mustin, an academy graduate in the class of 1896 and commanding officer of the naval aeronautic station at Pensacola, Florida, brought the old battleship *Mississippi* into the harbor on 24 April. Aboard were two Curtiss biplanes—the A-3 hydroairplane (an early floatplane) and the C-3 flying boat. Accompanying Mustin were Lt. (jg.) P. N. L. ("Pat") Bellinger, Lt. (jg.) Richard C. Saufley, two ensigns, and a handful of enlisted personnel assigned to the aviation group. The next day, Bellinger made a twenty-eight-minute reconnaissance flight in the C-3, in the process distinguishing himself as the first American naval aviator to fly in combat. Joined a month later by another aviation detachment under the command of Lt. John H. Towers, the American aviators observed enemy positions and reported on hostile troop movements outside the city.[17]

The two aviation units were still in Veracruz when *Chester* received orders to return to the United States. On 7 June, the ship eased out of the inner harbor, took on coal, transferred personnel to some of the other vessels in the fleet, and twenty-four hours later left the outer anchorage bound for Boston. Accompanied by the collier *Nereus, Chester* had an uneventful voyage, briefly stopping at Sands Key near Miami for water and at Norfolk for coal before docking at the Boston Navy Yard on 19 June. Almost immediately after tying up at the pier in Boston, *Chester* began an extensive overhaul. No sailor likes having his ship out of operation for long periods, and Moffett was no exception. He had to contend with generally lower morale, far more sailors absent without leave than he liked, and the tedium of seemingly endless inspection rounds.[18]

While in Boston, Moffett assumed temporary command of the armored cruiser *North Carolina,* with orders to deliver the ship to Hampton Roads. The ship left Boston on 4 July, arriving at her destination two days later. There Moffett went ashore to meet with Henry Mustin, the ship's prospective commanding officer. What the two men discussed we cannot be certain, but it is likely Mustin explained to Moffett the Navy's plans for converting *North Carolina* into an aviation ship to replace the ancient *Mississippi*. After relinquishing command to Mustin on 8 July, Moffett returned to Boston and a much-deserved three weeks' leave. In August, he ran into Mustin again. At the outbreak of World War I, the Navy ordered *North Carolina* back to Boston, where she hastily offloaded her aviation equipment before heading for Europe to bring home stranded American tourists.[19]

On 15 September, Moffett left *Chester*, reporting for duty two days later as commandant of the Great Lakes Naval Training Station and the Ninth, Tenth, and Eleventh naval districts. After his cruiser command, Great Lakes hardly seemed choice duty for the hero of Veracruz, but it turned out to be an assignment critical to Moffett's advancement and his involvement in naval aviation. Thirty-four miles north of Chicago at Lake Bluff, Illinois, Great Lakes had been authorized in 1904 to provide a convenient recruitment and training center for the sprawling Midwest. The thinking at the time was that recruits from wholesome families in America's heartland would be superior to those exposed to the vice and corruption of the country's port cities, and it was hoped that keeping the young men closer to home would enhance morale. Several communities vied for the new installation, but a board appointed by the secretary of the Navy preferred a location close to Chicago, the thriving economic and transportation hub of the region. When the Commercial Club of North Chicago arranged a subscription to buy the 182-acre site and offered to donate it to the government, there was little question where the new naval station would be located.[20]

In spite of what appeared to be an auspicious start, many years passed before Great Lakes was fully functioning. Work began in 1905, but not until six years later and the expenditure of $3.5 million was the station completed. It featured a permanent barracks for 1,500 recruits, a drill hall, instruction building, hospital, power plant, and breakwaters enclosing a harbor on Lake Michigan. Over the next three years, Great Lakes underwent further expansion, which included the addition of another three hundred acres to the site.[21]

When Moffett reported for duty on 17 September 1914, the war in Europe was already more than a month old. Although few suspected that the United States would be drawn into the conflict, many thought the country must pay more attention to military preparedness. Great Lakes at the time was functioning mostly as a receiving center where new recruits were assigned to other naval training stations around the country. That changed with the massive Naval Act of 1916, calling for an unprecedented capital ship construction program and more than doubling annual appropriations for the Navy. To man the vastly augmented fleet, new and expanded training centers were needed. One of the first things Moffett had to do was to devise a plan to accommodate the rapid expansion of Great Lakes to meet the Navy's requirements for new personnel. Moffett's proposal was relatively simple: establish 1,726-man regiments, each a separate and independent unit, and then add regiments as needed. Using the self-contained regiments as building blocks, the station could be expanded to virtually any size demanded by the manpower requirements of the Navy without fundamentally altering the organizational structure of the base. He also concluded leases for an additional nine hundred acres north, south, and west of the station.[22]

In the midst of his expansion program at Great Lakes, Moffett came up for promotion to captain. With his superlative record and excellent service reputation, there was little reason to doubt that he would move up in rank, but there were many officers who were unable to make the grade. Moffett was told on 12 January 1917 to report to the Washington Navy Yard for the necessary examinations. He passed easily, and the examining board recommended his promotion on 19 March, dating his new commission from 29 August 1916.[23] Thus did Moffett clear the next critical hurdle to flag rank.

Moffett's promotion came as the nation slid closer to war in the winter and early spring of 1917. At the end of January, Germany declared that her submarines would sink without warning any ships—belligerent or neutral—found within a restricted area in the eastern Atlantic. As the principal neutral power, the United States protested this violation of international law and broke diplomatic relations with Germany. With the die finally cast, there was little more to do other than wait for the inevitable, which finally came in March with the sinking of four American merchant ships. President Wilson asked for and received from Congress on 6 April a joint resolution declaring war on Germany. In the rapid mobilization following the declaration of war, the Navy called nearly all available line officers to sea duty. Moffett lost half his staff at Great Lakes. Facing a critical personnel shortage, he brought in people directly from civilian life.

Lieutenant Charles S. Dewey was one of them. Coming to Great Lakes just before the country went to war, Dewey brought his business expertise to bear as Moffett's assistant and chief adviser. Another key addition to Moffett's staff was Hugh W. Fisher, who worked throughout the war years as chief clerk. Lieutenant Comdr. Chester S. Roberts, Moffett's aide before the war, took over as executive officer of the base in early 1918. An Annapolis graduate in the class of 1909, Roberts handled most of the day-to-day problems that arose as the station swelled to nearly double its pre-war size.[24]

The sudden increase in the size of Great Lakes created a crisis in June 1917. Despite Moffett's constant entreaties to Washington, he lacked equipment, clothing, and suitable sanitary facilities for the trainees arriving by the hundreds at the station. Congressman Fred A. Britten, a member of the House Naval Affairs Committee, visited Great Lakes and found what he called a "deplorable" situation. Only 800 of the 8,200 men at the base were fully equipped, some lacked uniforms, and there were only 2,600 rifles when there should have been between 8,000 and 10,000. The detention camp, where new arrivals awaited assignment to training units, housed twice as many men as it was designed to hold. With only a single railroad line linking the station with Chicago, there were serious transportation bottlenecks, too. One officer said later that he had to keep thirty-five Pullman railway coaches in reserve in Hammond, Indiana, simply to meet the demands of moving men into and out of Great Lakes. Moffett said that he was doing what he could but needed more money if the conditions at the station were to be improved. Within twenty-four hours, secretary of the Navy Josephus Daniels promised that all the needs at Great Lakes would be taken care of as soon as possible but that everyone had been caught off guard by the number of young men who wanted to get into the service.[25]

Work started on the new facilities on 3 July. Before the end of the year, five camps had been completed to accommodate the incoming personnel. The first two, Camp Dewey and Camp Perry, were located to the west of the main station. Camp Dewey featured the largest drill hall in the country, a building that measured six hundred feet long and more than one hundred feet wide. Camp Farragut and Camp Decatur were receiving units to the south, and Camp Ross, also in the south, was an assembly section where outgoing recruits awaited further duty assignments. To meet immediate requirements, another facility, Camp Paul Jones, was established north of the main station. At first only a vast tent city, Camp Paul Jones had permanent barracks built before the end of the year using the expedient of enlisted naval personnel. The 1917 expansion cost $5.5 million and allowed the station to handle 27,000 men.[26]

Phenomenal as it was, the growth of Great Lakes during 1917 did not come close to matching that of the following year. At the cost of an additional $11.4 million the station expanded to accommodate 48,000 personnel. Camp Lawrence and Camp Barry, each housing three training regiments, supplemented the existing facilities, and there were additions to Camps Ross and Paul Jones. Camp Logan, eighteen miles to the north of the main station, provided rifle ranges for small-arms training. New barracks, drill halls, armories, and a larger hospital unit were also part of the 1918 expansion. During a three-month period in the spring and summer of 1918, Great Lakes took in nearly 54,000 apprentice seamen, averaging 750 per day in July. Altogether, 125,000 men passed through the station during the eighteen months of American involvement in the war.[27]

Not only did Great Lakes expand in the aggregate but there was also a proliferation of specialized instruction units in 1917 and 1918. Before the war, there were only two special schools at the station, providing training in signals and radio and for hospital corpsmen. After the United States joined the conflict, a company commander school was established. Headed by Lt. Ralph M. Jaeger, the school was crucial for generating the petty officers needed to fill out the regiments during the first six months of wartime growth. Other units were the gunners' mate school, which prepared students in the complexities of the manufacture, repair, and maintenance of shipboard ordnance; the armed guard school, which trained gun crews for armed merchant ships; the coxswain school, for instruction in the handling of small boats; the quartermaster school, providing instruction in deck duties, log entries, and instruments; and the yeoman school, which included clerical courses.[28]

To a great extent the rapidity and magnitude of the wartime expansion of Great Lakes were due to the organization and efficiency of the station's Public Works Department, headed by Comdr. Walter H. Allen. The department had responsibility not only for construction projects but also for the operation, repair, and maintenance of the completed facilities, freeing other units to concentrate almost entirely on recruit training. By the end of 1917, Public Works had grown to nearly a thousand men, warranting its reorganization as the Twelfth Regiment (Public Works). The regiment did much of the work at the station using its own personnel, but it also supervised $17 million in construction by private contractors. As a bonus, the regiment trained public works people for duty at other bases and dispatched specialists to inspect and supervise construction work for the Navy at Washington and overseas. Hundreds of men from Great Lakes participated in the construction of aviation stations on the coast of France, and one group helped assemble and operate the Navy's fourteen-inch railroad guns on the Western Front.[29]

While he was in command at Great Lakes, Moffett gained an understanding of the power of public relations and an appreciation of the importance of a rapport between the station and the communities around it. Moffett borrowed an editor from the city desk of the *Chicago Tribune* to start a base newspaper. During the war years, John Philip Sousa came out of retirement to head the Battalion Band, a portion of the 1,000-member Great Lakes Naval Band. Apart from the entertainment it provided at the station itself, the band went on tours of the East and Midwest, literally drumming up interest in the Navy and public support for the war effort. Sousa was effusive in his praise for Moffett: "This officer, combining the qualities of an organizer and administrator, a diplomat and a lover of music in stimulating recruiting, in entertaining, in the pomp and circumstances of military life, and in bringing to the surface all that is patriotic in us, stands among the leading figures of the war."[30]

In other ways, too, Moffett raised the public consciousness of Great Lakes. Two theater companies produced musical comedies that played in Chicago, earning goodwill in the city and $165,000 for the Navy Relief Society. Thousands flocked to Pageant Days, a series of open houses held during the summer of 1918. There they typically saw a review before Moffett and his staff, with ratings in their dress whites performing precision drills and marching to Sousa's band music. After such reviews there were mock battles on the station's parade grounds, featuring tanks, motorcycles, machine guns, three-inch artillery pieces, and smoke bombs.[31]

Believing athletic competition boosted morale and developed the character of the men under him, Moffett instituted major sports programs at Great Lakes. Boxing was not only one of the few sports that interested Moffett but it attracted a large number of recruits, too. In September 1917, former president Theodore Roosevelt visited the station and refereed a series of bouts in the gymnasium. Other activities available to recruits included swimming, basketball, baseball, football, wrestling, and tennis. In the fall of 1918, Moffett followed the Great Lakes football team to Annapolis for a game with the midshipmen. Considered an underdog, the Great Lakes squad defeated the academy's team in a close and hard-fought contest. Later, Great Lakes played a team of marines from Mare Island in the Rose Bowl, winning handily and securing the collegiate national championship for that year.[32]

Jeannette Moffett grew into her role of Navy wife and did her part to draw favorable public attention to Great Lakes during the war. The June 1918 number of the *Ladies' Home Journal* carried a major illustrated article on Mrs. Moffett and her work at the station. With efficiency and grace she handled her duties as hostess, including an unprecedented reception early in 1918 that brought together both officers and enlisted men. Worried that trainees on liberty would succumb to the illicit attractions of Chicago, she arranged weekend parties and dances for them in the homes of her prominent North Shore friends and neighbors. Normally she spent several hours a day at a desk doing paperwork for the Illinois Auxiliary of the Navy Relief Society, an agency that provided financial aid to the families and dependents of officers and enlisted men. In one instance she took a personal interest in the problems of a desperately homesick recruit from Arkansas. She invited him to her home, helped him write a letter to his mother, and arranged for a ten-day leave for the boy to visit his family after he completed training. In recognition of Jeannette Moffett's work on their behalf, the Great Lakes recruits presented her with a silver tea service at Christmas in 1917.[33]

Great Lakes brought more stability to the Moffett family than there had been in many years. Moffett and his family at first lived in the commandant's quarters on the base but in 1918 settled into a commodious frame house at 524 Sheridan Road in Lake Forest, where they became active participants in community affairs. Jeannette had given birth to another daughter—Margaret Elizabeth—on 23 December 1913, before Moffett took over as *Chester*'s commanding officer. Bright and precocious, Betty, as Margaret was known, had the most outgoing personality of all the Moffett siblings. The family continued to grow while Moffett was at Great Lakes. Charles Simonton and Anna Beverly (usually called Beverly) were born there on 29 March 1915 and 16 July 1918, respectively.[34]

At the outset of the war, the Navy sorely lacked aviation training stations, Pensacola being the only place for the instruction of aviators and ground support personnel. Although Pensacola underwent considerable expansion, no one believed it alone could handle the expected influx of new aviation students. Consequently, the Navy set up temporary training centers while planning and construction got under way on permanent bases scattered around the country.[35]

The wartime expansion of Great Lakes included the establishment of units to train aviators and aviation mechanics. The genesis of aviation instruction at Great Lakes was in Chicago. Since taking command, Moffett had become friends with many wealthy residents of the North Shore and moved easily among the city's elite business and civic leaders. One of them was J. Ogden Armour, the meat-packing baron, whose interest in aviation stemmed from his company's sponsorship of the 1911 transcontinental flight by Calbraith Perry Rodgers. Another was William Wrigley, Jr., the chewing-gum magnate and one of the most influential men in the city. An advocate of the development of aviation in Chicago, Wrigley supported the Aero Club of Illinois, which in 1916 had patriotically offered its services to the government and turned its flying field over to the military for flight training. One evening in the spring of 1917, while Moffett was visiting the Wrigley home, the conversation turned to aviation. Everyone agreed that the Navy had not done enough to promote and develop its air arm, and William Wrigley saw an opportunity to do something about it. With the support of John J. Mitchell, president of the Illinois Trust and Savings Bank, he created the Great Lakes Aeronautical Society, with Moffett as its honorary president. The society established and financed a flight training unit and an aviation mechanics school at Great Lakes.[36]

Wrigley's son Philip took initial charge of the flight school at Great Lakes. The younger Wrigley had foregone a college education to go to Australia to establish an overseas branch of the family business. Fascinated with mechanical devices, he had been drawn, like so many other wealthy young men, to the excitement and promise of the airplane. Shortly after the United States entered the war, Phil and some of his prep school buddies had enlisted in the naval reserve, hoping to be of some service to the country. With his own money and funds from the Aeronautical Society, Phil bought a well-used Curtiss flying boat for the fledgling aviation school at Great Lakes. By August, the unit had two more airplanes and twenty potential aviators undergoing instruction. In December, Phil received a commission as an ensign and was placed in charge of the flight school. Knowing how hard it had been for his son to assume responsibilities, the elder Wrigley expressed astonishment that Phil had been put in charge of a school of any sort.[37]

Besides Moffett and the Wrigleys, Lee Hammond was the other key figure in the establishment of aviation at Great Lakes. Hammond was one of the country's pioneer fliers. He participated in the 1911 International Aviation Meet in Chicago, where he won more than $1,000 flying one of Thomas Scott Baldwin's Red Devil biplanes. In the spring of 1914, Hammond became chairman of the technical committee of the Aero Club of Illinois; by 1917 he was the club's secretary. Hammond received a reserve commission as lieutenant in June 1917 and was ordered to Great Lakes, where he worked with Phil Wrigley, Lt. (jg.) Duncan Forbes, and Ens. Logan A. Vilas to get the flight school operational.[38]

Following up on a favorable report on the aviation facilities at Great Lakes by Capt. Noble E. Irwin (director of Naval Aviation in the office of the chief of Naval Operations), the Navy Department allocated money for the expansion of aviation instruction at Great Lakes. In December 1917, Franklin D. Roosevelt, the assistant secretary of the Navy, wanted the immediate allocation of $75,000 "for urgent work in connection with the establishment of aviation mechanics school at Great Lakes," which was to be in one of the large drill halls at Camp Perry. When the school became fully operational in March 1918, it had 2,000 students, many of whom had come from the apprentice seaman regiments. Largely because of Moffett's efforts, the Navy Department immediately allocated $600,000 for aviation instruction, thus preparing the way for further expansion of the unit. The money allowed all aviation instruction to be consolidated in a single regiment, which came to be housed at Camp Luce, north of the main station.[39]

Before long, the aviation training units at Great Lakes grew to the point that they alone were bigger than the entire base had been a year earlier, before the outbreak of hostilities. When completed in July, Camp Luce consisted of sixteen two-story barracks, a large machine shop, a classroom building, a forge shop, powerhouses, warehouses, engine test stands, and a hangar. The aviation regiment eventually included sixty-five officers and 5,000 men. The normal course at the aviation mechanics school lasted ten weeks and included a curriculum in engine overhaul and repair and the principles of ignition, cooling, and fuel systems. More than 2,100 men completed the course by the end of the war, training on ninety

Curtiss engines, forty-eight Liberties, and a variety of other power plants.[40]

Other aviation programs at Great Lakes were a quartermaster school, where pupils learned about fabric, paints, aircraft assembly, and the repair of wings and pontoons. The aviation armorer school included an eight-week course of specialized instruction in machine guns, small arms, synchronizing gear, and shop tools. Organized in August 1918, the armorer school was placed under the command of Lt. F. B. Christmas and by the armistice had grown to include 360 men divided among six classes.[41]

Flight instruction, which had been the reason for establishing aviation at Great Lakes in the first place, did not carry over into 1918. The Navy found that Chicago's winters, which often saw Lake Michigan freeze over, were not conducive to intensive flying-boat operations and decided to move flight training to Pensacola. In the summer of 1918, however, the Navy designated the site below the bluff on Lake Michigan, where most of the flight training had formerly taken place, as a naval air station. The aviation unit there included a ground school, and those who passed through it went on to other stations for advanced classes. The naval air station had three flying boats—two Curtiss HS-1Ls and one Curtiss HS-2L—and the mechanics school had eight airplanes of various types. Hammond and other officers flew them on a regular basis in 1918, even establishing an airmail service between the station and Chicago.[42]

Officers from the Naval Aviation office found much to praise about the aviation establishment at Great Lakes, despite some inadequacies. Lieutenant C. S. Baker assured Captain Irwin in August 1918 that Hammond had built up a "fine organization," adding that he was especially impressed by how the work had been accomplished "in the most systematic and thorough manner with a minimum loss of time." Three months later, Lt. Gordon H. Balch of Irwin's staff inspected the ground school and reported that "conditions in general" were "unsatisfactory," largely because the four instructors rotated as officers in charge of the school and because a large percentage of the students did not meet acceptable standards for aviator recruits. On the other hand, Balch determined that the facilities for instruction and housing of trainees were "excellent," drill and discipline "satisfactory," and the syllabus for the most part adequate.[43]

One of the aviation trainees at Great Lakes was Joseph Pulitzer, the thirty-three-year-old son of the owner of the *New York World* and himself editor of the *St. Louis Post-Dispatch*. Pulitzer entered the service in late August. Rated as a chief petty officer, he sought admission to the aviation school at Great Lakes and completed ground instruction before the end of the war. In the early twenties Pulitzer would sponsor a series of races pitting Army and Navy aviators against one another in an intense interservice aerial rivalry that attracted considerable public attention.[44]

The enormous expansion of Great Lakes during World War I brought with it a vast increase in the operating budget. Lieutenant Comdr. Richard S. Robertson, who had graduated from the academy in the class of 1912, headed a huge financial office, which was handling more than a million dollars weekly by the fall of 1917. On 2 November 1917, Robertson found that $3,000 had been stolen during the preparation of pay envelopes. He immediately reported the theft to Moffett, who appointed a board to investigate the incident. In its report, the board determined that Robertson had sole responsibility for the missing money but that he had been severely handicapped in his work by inadequate facilities and a shortage of trained personnel. Moffett thought the matter would go no farther, but he was wrong. The Bureau of Supplies and Accounts determined that Robertson had been guilty of negligence and ordered him to pay back the $3,000, roughly equivalent to a year's pay. Worse for the hapless officer, the secretary of the Navy ordered that he be tried by a court-martial for "neglect of duty."[45]

Realizing that failures in the paymaster's office reflected negatively on his administration of Great Lakes, Moffett defended Robertson. In a letter to the judge advocate general in April 1918, he wrote that "the personnel at the station had increased enormously but without a proportionate or even adequate increase in the personnel" in Robertson's office. "I know from personal knowledge and observation," Moffett continued, "that this officer did everything that was humanly possible at the time to safeguard the Government's interests, and know that the loss in question occurred without fault or negligence on [his] part." Moffett succeeded in getting the court-martial canceled, but Robertson still had to reimburse the Navy for the embezzled funds.[46]

Great Lakes was not the only training station to experience such graft and theft during the wartime expansion, nor was the 1917 episode an isolated case there. At least one seaman working in Robertson's office in 1918 deserted rather than face charges of theft stemming from a similar incident. A scandal involving alleged graft in connection with the discharge of men from the station followed in December 1918, but by then

Moffett had left Great Lakes.[47] He was fortunate to escape from the station with his reputation untarnished, but it was a near thing, for had he been in any way implicated with the illegal use of funds or other corruption, his future career would have been jeopardized.

For Moffett, the Great Lakes experience proved important not only for his involvement in aviation but also for the lifelong friendships he forged with prominent members of the Chicago-area business community. There may have been other connections, too. In later years, Jack Towers's wife recalled Moffett joking that had he wanted to, he could call on those he knew in the city's gangster community to have someone eliminated.[48]

Nevertheless, if he were to continue up the promotion ladder, he had to make good in a battleship command. He got his wish within weeks of the end of the war, when the Navy ordered him to assume command of *Mississippi,* one of the fleet's impressive new superdreadnoughts. Not wanting to uproot his family, which only months before had settled into the house in Lake Forest, Moffett went alone to Yorktown, Virginia, where he reported on 10 December as *Mississippi's* commanding officer.[49]

Mississippi was a dream come true for Moffett and recognition by the Navy of a job well done at Great Lakes. A handsome ship with a clipper bow and clean, almost streamlined upper works, *Mississippi* had been built by the Newport News Shipbuilding Company and commissioned in December 1917. She displaced 32,000 tons and, propelled by Westinghouse steam turbines producing 40,000 horsepower, could make more than twenty-one knots. She mounted twelve 14-inch guns in four turrets, supplemented by a secondary battery consisting of fourteen 5-inch guns. Her complement, when Moffett came aboard, was approximately eleven hundred, of whom about eighty were officers.[50]

The big ship gave Moffett another taste of the tremendous potential of naval aviation and provided a glimpse of what the future held for airplanes operating from shipboard. After a brief voyage to New York, where *Mississippi* led a group of heavy ships into the harbor as part of a 21 December victory parade, Moffett took his command in February 1919 to Guantánamo to join the Atlantic Fleet in the annual winter gunnery competition. When *Mississippi* arrived in Cuba, several of the other battleships were already there, among them *Texas,* which had had flying-off platforms erected over her number-two turret forward and number-three turret aft. The installation in *Texas* was copied from several Royal Navy battleships and in fact had been erected by a British yard in Newcastle in October 1918. The platforms enabled small aircraft to be flown off the ship, but the wheeled airplanes could not be recovered; after completing their missions, they landed ashore or ditched alongside. Awkward as the arrangement was on *Texas* and other battleships, the ship planes provided much more flexibility in the observation role than kite balloons normally towed behind the vessels. Headed by Lt. Comdr. Edward O. McDonnell and including two other pilots, the *Texas* ship plane unit consisted of a pair of Sopwith Camels and a Sopwith 1½ Strutter. McDonnell flew from the platform on the forward turret for the first time on 9 March while *Texas* was at anchor in Guantánamo Bay.[51]

Not to be outdone, Moffett had his men build flying-off platforms modeled after those he saw on *Texas*. On *Mississippi* the wooden platforms extended out over the turrets, supported by steel rings that slipped over the guns of the main battery. The platforms could be removed within minutes and did not in any way interfere with the training of the turrets or with the sighting or the balance of the guns. The big guns, however, could not be fired while an airplane rested on the platform. But Moffett insisted that the battleship could be made ready to fire in less than a minute after flying off its aircraft. *Mississippi* had two Royal Aircraft Factory SE-5 aircraft at Guantánamo but apparently operated only Sopwiths.[52]

Both battleships found the airplanes vastly superior to kite balloons for spotting gunfire. Moffett became a convert after an incident involving *Mississippi*'s kite balloon at Guantánamo. During one firing exercise, the ship sent its kite balloon up to 1,800 feet, at which point the balloon valved off hydrogen and began to sink rapidly, dragging its cable in the water behind the ship at exactly the moment the ship fired off a salvo. The blast threw the basket of the balloon up against the envelope, injuring the observer just as he parachuted out. One officer said, "I don't think the MISSISSIPPI thought much of the kite balloon . . . after that." The ship developed a system whereby radio telegraph messages from the spotting airplane came directly to a gunnery officer in the foretop, who then made the necessary range corrections before giving the orders to fire. *Mississippi* used the airplanes to remarkable effect, during one exercise straddling the target on every salvo. In 1919, Lieutenant Commander McDonnell testified before the General Board, the Navy's senior advisory body, that spotting was two hundred percent better with an airplane than from a kite balloon.[53]

Following the Guantánamo exercises, *Mississippi* returned to Hampton

Roads before receiving orders to the West Coast, where she was to form an element of the newly created Pacific Fleet under Adm. Hugh Rodman. *Mississippi* departed from Hampton Roads on 19 July, transited the Panama Canal, and arrived in San Diego in early August, carrying with her two Hanriot HD-1 ship planes. Moffett was confident that the airplanes would give a good accounting of themselves during maneuvers, stating that "we knew what we could do from the turrets. There was no mystery about it." The airplanes spent a great deal of time ashore at North Island in San Diego, operating with other units in the Pacific Fleet air detachment under the command of Henry Mustin, now a captain with headquarters in the aircraft tender *Aroostook*.[54]

Moffett's and Mustin's paths had crossed before, but this time their association held much portent for Moffett's later career. On 6 February 1920, not long after arriving on the West Coast, Mustin called on Moffett aboard *Mississippi*, reestablishing an acquaintance going back to the summer of 1914. Over the next four months they became friends, often dining together and discussing at length the potential of naval aviation and its operation with the fleet.[55]

Moffett was quick to exploit Mustin's airplanes as spotters during gunnery exercises off the coast, adding to *Mississippi*'s already strong reputation as one of the most accurate ships in the fleet. Firing practice in the spring of 1920 resulted in total scores nearly as good as those turned in by all the other ships combined. After one remarkably successful shoot on 10 June 1920, when his ship achieved a straddle on the second salvo at 23,000 yards, Moffett thanked Mustin and his fellow aviators for their help: "Ship entirely dependent on aeroplane. . . . Your aeroplanes were our salvation." He was impressed not only with Mustin but also with two other aviators at North Island, Jack Towers, who had been elevated to commander in 1918, and Lt. Comdr. Marc A. Mitscher. All three officers would emerge as some of Moffett's most knowledgeable and trusted subordinates in the naval aviation establishment.[56]

True to Moffett's proven leadership attributes, *Mississippi* was a happy and efficient ship. Never did the vessel present anything other than a spotless appearance, and her crew was always in the highest state of readiness. To maintain morale, Moffett regularly entered teams from various shipboard divisions in athletic competitions, and just as regularly those teams won. *Mississippi* provided Moffett with additional opportunities to display his already prodigious seamanship and ship-handling capabilities. Commander William L. Calhoun, the ship's gunnery officer, recalled an episode in the narrow waters of Puget Sound when *Mississippi* was steaming in close formation with *Idaho* and *New Mexico,* two other ships in her division. At one point during a complex maneuver *Idaho* turned incorrectly, and for a moment it seemed to everyone on *Mississippi*'s bridge that a collision was unavoidable. Moffett took the conn and in a calm, even voice issued orders to the helm and quickly guided the ship out of harm's way.[57]

There was, however, one incident involving Moffett that had unpleasant political overtones. In September 1919, the Pacific Fleet assembled at Seattle to prepare for a review by President Wilson. Only hours before the president's scheduled arrival on the nineteenth, the city's mayor and chief of police learned that the radical Wobblies—the Industrial Workers of the World—were planning to disrupt the visit. With the nation in the throes of the Red Scare, city officials feared violence and appealed to Admiral Rodman for help. Without hesitation, Rodman ordered Moffett to assemble a shore party of eleven hundred armed marines and sailors with orders to protect the president and to intimidate the IWW. Rodman wrote in his memoirs that the sudden and overwhelming show of force "put not only the fear of God, but the fear of the navy as well, into the I.W.W. ranks."[58] The president's stay in Seattle and the fleet review came off without a hitch, but the deployment of force from the Pacific Fleet seems in retrospect to have been an overreaction that easily could have precipitated bloodshed during what otherwise would have been a peaceful demonstration.

Moffett received instructions from the chief of Naval Operations on 12 November 1920 detaching him from command of *Mississippi* and ordering him home to await further assignment. At San Pedro on 9 December ceremonies took place on *Mississippi*'s quarterdeck transferring command from Moffett to his relief, Capt. Powers ("Pete") Symington. As an expression of the admiration of the entire crew, the ship's chief petty officers presented Moffett with a parchment certificate declaring their high regard for his personal and professional leadership qualities. Some months later, in the spring of 1921, Moffett received another gift—a silver-handled sword inscribed: "From the crew of the MISSISSIPPI to our late Captain, W. A. Moffett, after a successful two years cruise." He graciously received the sword, saying that his command of *Mississippi* was successful "because every officer and man in her never worked for himself, but always 'For the Good of the Ship.'"[59]

Few officers handled their responsibilities better than Moffett. His first command, of *Chester* at Veracruz, had led to the Congressional Medal of Honor and a reputation as a national hero. The years in charge of Great Lakes gave him the opportunity to hone his already considerable organizational abilities and to develop his reputation as an officer who cared for the people serving under him. Great Lakes, moreover, put Moffett in touch with aviation and established contacts with influential businessmen on whom he depended in later years for political favors. He had some luck, too, at Great Lakes, for had he stayed on even a few more months, the scandals there might have seriously threatened his career. But a shore command, even one as important as Great Lakes, was not enough. *Mississippi* was the crucial step forward as Moffett moved into consideration for advancement to flag rank in the battleship navy. At the same time, *Mississippi* gave Moffett a wider appreciation of the value of airplanes operating at sea with the fleet and brought him closer to some of the officers he would come to depend upon as his life and career became inseparably linked to aviation.

4

CHIEF OF THE BUREAU
OF AERONAUTICS

O N 9 DECEMBER 1920, AFTER RELINQUISHING COMMAND OF
Mississippi, Moffett left the West Coast with orders to report to
the Navy Department. He stopped at Lake Forest on the long
train ride east, arriving in Washington on the fourteenth, where he
learned from the chief of Naval Operations, Adm. Robert E. Coontz, that
he had been selected to succeed Capt. Thomas T. Craven as the director of
Naval Aviation in Coontz's office.[1] Because the director carried little administrative authority, it did not seem to be a choice assignment for a fifty-
one-year-old senior captain fresh from a successful battleship command
and in line for advancement to flag rank. But if Moffett had any ambiva-
lence about the assignment, it soon evaporated. The job was, after all, a
potentially influential staff position, and it was an opportunity to work
with Coontz, an 1885 academy graduate and former *Charleston* shipmate
from Spanish-American War days. Furthermore, Moffett had had enough
firsthand experience with aviation to see some of its latent possibilities and
may have had some assurances that his job would be incorporated into a
new bureau with broad responsibilities for all naval aviation.

Late on the nineteenth Moffett left Washington, catching an overnight train out of Union Station for Chicago to spend Christmas and New Year's with his family in Lake Forest. Back at home he unwound a little and, if only briefly, reestablished bonds with his wife and six children, one of whom, Beverly, had grown from an infant into a toddler during his absence in battleship command. The return to Lake Forest also allowed Moffett to renew the Chicago-area ties from his Great Lakes years. Those links—with the Wrigleys, J. Ogden Armour, and other members of the North Shore elite—were too important to be allowed to lapse, and he made every effort to maintain them after he moved on to Washington.[2]

When Moffett returned to Washington soon after New Year's and reported for duty in Admiral Coontz's office, he found naval aviation in a state of flux. World War I had seen much progress, particularly in the remarkable expansion of manpower, the design and development of new aircraft, the procurement of material, and the establishment of bases for training and operations. American flying boats, patrolling from air stations in the British Isles and the west coast of France, had contributed to the suppression of the German U-boat menace in the North Atlantic. Closer to home, the Naval Aircraft Factory in Philadelphia had been created in 1917 to supply at least part of the Navy's requirement for flying boats as well as to function as a yardstick to check on the cost of material acquired from private companies.[3]

Despite major cutbacks associated with the general demobilization, aviation for the time being appeared to be secure in its position within the naval establishment. Through 1919 and into 1920, flying boats had continued to operate with the fleet, plans were initiated to build or convert tenders to support their activities, flying-off platforms were constructed on battleships, and the first steps were taken to introduce the aircraft carrier. The most spectacular accomplishment was the first successful flight across the Atlantic, by the Navy's big four-engine NC-4 flying boat in May 1919.[4]

Significant as those developments were, they were not matched by an equally strong commitment to aviation within the Navy Department. The organization of aviation had grown on a largely ad hoc basis through the war years, with divided lines of responsibility and little central coordination; aviation had been grafted onto the existing bureau system rather than integrated into it. For example, the Bureau of Construction and Repair had responsibility (or "cognizance," in Navy jargon) for the design and fabrication of airframes, flying boat hulls, and wings; the Bureau of

Steam Engineering handled aircraft power plants and radio installations; the Bureau of Navigation controlled personnel and training; and the Bureau of Ordnance supplied guns, bombs, torpedoes, and other airborne weapons. It was a situation tailor-made to provoke turf battles among the various powerful bureau chiefs.[5]

Going back as far as 1914, efforts had been made to bring order out of chaos, but they had all fallen far short of the fundamental administrative reform needed. In July 1914 the Office of Naval Aeronautics was established under the secretary of the Navy. Captain Mark L. Bristol headed the new organization, which within a year shifted over to the new office of the chief of Naval Operations. Bristol had little more actual authority than his predecessor, Capt. Washington I. Chambers, but he was vigorous and forceful, and he found a powerful ally in the new chief of the Bureau of Construction and Repair, Rear Adm. David W. Taylor, who had supported much of the Navy's early aerodynamic research. Almost entirely on the power of their personalities, Bristol and Taylor laid the foundation on which naval aviation was built during World War I.[6]

No one, however, was more aware than Bristol of the unwieldy nature of the administrative structure nominally under his command. In February 1916 he appeared before the House Naval Affairs Committee to plead his case for the appropriation of $10.6 million for naval aviation. Bristol used the opportunity to inform the lawmakers about the restrictions inherent in his office. There was, he said, "no head of aviation legally. I was ordered to the department and given verbal orders to take charge of the development of naval aeronautics. The regular bureaus of the department have cognizance of all the work of aviation, as well as anything else connected with the Navy."[7]

The congressmen asked Bristol what he thought of a bill pending before the House to establish aviation as a separate corps within the service. He did not think highly of the proposal. In his opinion, a naval aviator had to be a Navy officer first and a flier second; he had to know his way around ships and how to command them. "The flying is the very simplest part," he said, "of the education or requirements of a flying officer." Bristol was unequivocal in his opposition to a separate corps and could "see no object in it whatever." Instead, he asserted, "a careful estimate of the situation . . . indicates it has become certain that air craft must form a part of any properly equipped fleet of naval vessels."[8]

Bristol's testimony highlighted an underlying problem in organizing aviation within the naval establishment. To secure the steady advance of aeronautics, there had to be recognition of its special status within the Navy. Later in 1916, Henry Mustin, then a commander, drew up a proposal calling for creation of a separate corps, roughly equivalent to the Marine Corps, which would give aviators the autonomy needed to accomplish their ends. That was unacceptable to Bristol and to many others in the service.[9] Yet something more than the divided bureau responsibilities then prevailing was essential if aviation was to progress as an integral part of the Navy.

Legislation creating the Naval Flying Corps in 1916 did little to satisfy those who wanted some autonomy for naval aviation. Aviators within the corps remained line officers; they could rise no higher than captain without spending substantial time on sea duty. Bristol's office lacked independent authority over the new aeronautics organization and, as before, had no control over money, personnel, procurement, or training. Nor did the legislation receive support from Adm. William S. Benson, the chief of Naval Operations, who considered the corps an administrative excrescence that did nothing to enhance the efficiency of aviation.[10]

Under the strain of war, with great demands placed on naval aviation for personnel and material, there was little time to consider basic organizational reform. Relieving Bristol in May 1917, Capt. Noble E. Irwin had his hands full simply coping with the wartime expansion of the aviation office. In July 1917 he had under him only six officers; by the end of the war that number had grown to more than two hundred. To manage the pressing administrative load, Irwin broke the office into three departments—executive, training, and material—and to expedite everything instituted informal weekly conferences with representatives of the various bureaus charged with aviation responsibilities. On 7 March 1918, Irwin became the first director of Naval Aviation, but the important-sounding title brought no real changes to the structure or functions of his position.[11]

An obvious solution to the organizational dilemma was the formation of a new bureau. Following the war, a sophisticated proposal to create such an entity came from Lt. Graham M. Brush, a reserve officer in the Bureau of Steam Engineering. Writing to the director of Naval Aviation on 12 March 1919, Brush suggested that the unique characteristics of the airplane and aviation warranted the formation of a new organization. The bureau, Brush proposed, would include three divisions: engineering and design, production, and operations and maintenance. Its lines of authority, however, stopped with material. For construction and personnel, the new bureau was to make recommendations to the existing bureaus of Yards and Docks and Navigation, respectively. Brush justified the new bureau on the principles of economy and efficiency, maintaining that centralization of the material functions of naval aviation would reduce paperwork, personnel, and time.[12]

Responses to the Brush proposal from the two most-affected bureaus were far from encouraging. The Bureau of Steam Engineering responded that there was "no reason why another Bureau should be added to the Navy Department for the purpose of handling aviation matter[s]." The Bureau of Construction and Repair hedged on the question, stating that "while the present organization presents disadvantages and while a change along the general lines suggested might facilitate the handling of questions in connection with aircraft, the Bureau is not prepared to state whether or not such a change would be an improvement without further study."[13]

There the matter stood until Capt. Thomas T. Craven took over as director of Naval Aviation in May 1919. An intelligent and energetic former gunnery officer, Craven had to face the organizational question head on as a consequence of intensive efforts to subsume naval aviation into a unified air force. Lieutenant Comdr. Jerome Hunsaker and Brig. Gen. William Mitchell, former head of the Army Air Service in France, were returning from Europe on the liner *Aquitania* in March 1919 when Mitchell expounded at length the lessons of the war and the importance of a separate air force encompassing naval aviation. Alarm bells went off in the Navy Department when Hunsaker warned his superiors that Mitchell meant business and that he was "fully prepared, with evidence, plans, data, propaganda posters and articles, to 'break things wide open.'" Mitchell confirmed Hunsaker's fears on 3 April when he testified before the General Board. He told the board that warships could not effectively defend themselves from air attack and that land-based aircraft could handle the defense of the nation's coastlines out as far as one hundred miles. Most worrisome to naval aviators, however, were Mitchell's assertions that they and their airplanes should be incorporated into an independent air force.[14]

Craven went before the General Board on 6 May to discuss possible changes in the administration of naval aviation. In his opinion, aviation "was not well established" and his office was "really without status." He went on to complain that under the current scheme "there is a duplication of a good deal of work—information is filed in [the Naval Aviation] office as well as other places. The thing is not harmoniously arranged at all. . . . It does not look to me from what I have seen here, and the experience I have had in aviation, that there has been a sufficient coordination of the different activities." Still unwilling to commit himself to the creation of a separate bureau, Craven suggested a "tentative plan" that promised, if anything, even more confusion. He wanted an aeronautical section in each bureau and expansion of the Bureau of Navigation to include a division devoted exclusively to aviation personnel. Exercising control over all this was to be an advisory board headed by the director of Naval Aviation and composed of representatives from each of the bureaus' aviation sections. Admittedly it was far from a perfect solution, but to Craven it seemed "to be the best scheme."[15]

Three days later, Craven was back at the General Board for more testimony. He repeated his reorganization plan, refining it with the addition to his advisory board of a select group of aviators whose job it would be to present technical information on aircraft characteristics, plans, and procurement. No more enthusiastic about bureau status for naval aviation than he had been previously, Craven told the officers that "perhaps having a single bureau responsible [for aviation] would be very desirable but at the present time I do not know it is entirely necessary as far as we are concerned."[16]

Captain Hutchinson I. Cone, who had been Adm. William S. Sims' aide for operations in Europe during the war, expressed some of the same ideas to the General Board on 23 May, but he was much more positive than Craven about the prospects for a separate bureau. He agreed that the present organization could not "keep up to date in aviation" and that there was a lack of cooperation among the material bureaus. The director of Naval Aviation, according to Cone, was "neither fish, flesh nor fowl. He is not a bureau although he is held responsible for a good many things like a bureau." Cone thought that "aviation is of enough importance and enough different from the other bureaus to develop a separate bureau for it." Yet he did not consider the time ripe to form another bureau, because "every fellow who finds a new thing wants a new Navy Department for it or a new bureau." Aviation required "extraordinary methods" to be established on a firm basis. He suggested that over the near term the other bureaus should relinquish their specialists to the director to work as a de facto bureau: "That will be the beginning of building up a separate bureau."[17]

In a memo to Rear Adm. David Taylor, Hunsaker presented an organizational solution that would simultaneously strengthen the Bureau of Construction and Repair. Hunsaker believed that a separate bureau "would be workable under the existing Navy Department organization, provided the new bureau were a material or technical Bureau, such as the Bureau of Ordnance." He elaborated: "The advantages to be anticipated would be entirely with the technical and material side, that is, a more close coordination of effort in design and construction would be obtained and a great deal of correspondence now necessary between various Bureaus . . . would be eliminated." Having a chief engineer, "who would direct and coordinate the work of the various specialists in the design and construction of aircraft," was particularly attractive to Hunsaker, who added that all European nations had a single person charged with responsibility for the technical development of naval aviation. Hunsaker emphatically did not want the new bureau's authority to extend beyond material, and he stressed that above all, planning and operations should remain in the office of the chief of Naval Operations. As he viewed it, the present director of Naval Aviation "in attempting to coordinate, accelerate and stimulate the activities of material Bureaus is frequently of great assistance and help, and also has often added confusion and friction unnecessarily by duplication of Bureaus' work and by encroachment upon proper Bureau functions." The answer, according to Hunsaker, "lies in divorcing Operations-Aviation from material functions and considering it charged with responsibility for operating aircraft, planning, and the enunciation of a fixed policy as to the development of Naval Aviation; especially the development of types of aircraft desired to fulfill military requirements." Experienced technical people would have to be assigned to the Naval Aviation office to help direct planning and policy-making. If, Hunsaker reasoned, the office were strengthened and its lines of responsibility clarified and a new material bureau created simply as a "physical concentration of functions already existing," then it made no sense to establish a separate aviation organization. Instead, he argued, create a chief engineer within the Bureau of Construction and Repair with broad authority over the technical side of aviation and funnel all aviation material through his office. The Bureau of Construction and Repair then would have "full responsibility" for aircraft development and be in a position to coordinate all such activities in a "harmonious" manner.[18]

Ingeniously self-serving and totally impractical, Hunsaker's scheme for an aviation czar within the Bureau of Construction and Repair found little support. But his ideas could not be ignored, for he was a brilliant and articulate officer with an international reputation in aerodynamic research. Known as "Jerry" to his friends, Hunsaker had graduated from Annapolis at the top of his class in 1908. He received a master's degree in engineering from the Massachusetts Institute of Technology in 1912 and the following year set up a graduate aeronautical engineering program at MIT. With the aid of his wife, Alice, Hunsaker published the first English translation of Alexandre-Gustave Eiffel's classic treatise on aerodynamics, *The Resistance of the Air.* More of an empiricist than a theoretician, Hunsaker had earned his doctorate from MIT before joining the Bureau of Construction and Repair in July 1916 as head of the Aircraft Division. Largely because of Hunsaker and the encouragement of Rear Admiral Taylor, the division expanded during the war years, attracting many talented civilians and naval officers and in the process gaining respect for its high level of expertise in aeronautical engineering.[19]

Hunsaker's ideas, unrealistic as they were, helped create an atmosphere for administrative reform. When a shakeup in Naval Operations blew Craven off his middle course, a consensus could be whipped up in favor of a separate bureau. Never a friend of aviation, Admiral Benson had been overheard to say that "the Navy doesn't need airplanes. Aviation is just a lot of noise." Few should have been surprised, therefore, when on 1 August 1919 Benson initiated a reorganization plan abolishing Craven's staff and relegating the functions of the aviation office to Naval Operations' Planning and Material divisions. Exasperated, Craven saw that the best chance to restore any semblance of his office's previous authority was to advocate the formation of a separate bureau of aeronautics.[20]

With Craven no longer sitting on the fence, supporters of bureau status for naval aviation took heart and began a more active campaign to achieve their goal. Lieutenant Comdr. Richard E. Byrd, a 1912 graduate of the academy and an aviator whose family and political ties gave him instant credibility in public circles, led the way. Shortly after the armistice, he and three fellow officers had drafted a bill proposing a bureau of aeronautics only to see it buried by unsympathetic superiors. By the end of 1919, however, the climate in Washington was much changed. Not only had Craven come over to the aviators' side but Admiral Coontz, a knowledge-able and highly respected officer, had also relieved Benson as chief of Naval Operations. Far more understanding of the aviators' cause than Benson had been, Coontz believed that "aviation had grown to be too im-portant for the small amount of consideration which it was receiving in the department." Equally crucial was support on Capitol Hill. There Con-gressman Frederick C. Hicks, a Republican from Long Island, had for some time been convinced of the necessity for administrative reform and helped orchestrate the legislative fight for the bureau.[21]

Unfortunately, General Mitchell and his indefatigable efforts in 1919–20 to push through legislation creating an independent air force stood in the way of an effective reorganization plan for naval aviation. A measure introduced in the fall of 1919 by Senator H. S. New of Indiana called for a separate air department, responsible for all military and civilian aviation. Despite intense lobbying and an extensive propaganda campaign by the Mitchell faction on behalf of the bill, it did not pass, largely be-cause of concern within the Army that it would lose control over its own air arm. Undeterred by that setback, Mitchell in April 1920 secured a rid-er to an Army appropriation bill turning all naval air stations over to the Army and restricting the Navy to "aerial operations attached to a fleet." Naval officers vigorously opposed this extraordinary act of aggression by Mitchell, which constituted a high-handed seizure of Navy property by a rival service and prevented the Navy from operating any large land-based aircraft. Reacting to the threat in the nick of time, Craven worked with legislative leaders and Navy secretary Daniels to obtain passage of a substi-tute amendment preserving the Navy's control over its land-based aircraft and support facilities. Nevertheless, the service remained limited to no more than six air stations in the continental United States, forcing the cre-ation of naval aviation reserve bases to support acceptable numbers of land-based aircraft.[22] Those two rounds of the legislative bout with Mitchell marked the beginning of a long struggle during the interwar years between the air-power advocates and the Navy over the control of military aviation.

A proposal from the National Advisory Committee for Aeronautics in early 1920 offered a possible compromise. Concerned about federal regu-lation of aviation in the aftermath of the war, the NACA recommended against the creation of either an independent air force or a central aviation department. Instead, the committee urged the establishment of separate aeronautics bureaus in the Army, the Navy, the Post Office, and the Department of Commerce. The NACA's draft legislation included a central coordinating board consisting of representatives of the four aeronautics bureaus and the NACA, which would have broad powers to assign aircraft and initiate civilian and military research projects.[23]

Hunsaker used the NACA draft legislation as a starting point in developing a counterproposal, which he presented to Admiral Taylor in February 1920. Taylor incorporated Hunsaker's suggestions in a memorandum of points, which he forwarded to Secretary Daniels on 26 February. Taylor opposed the integration of civil and military aviation and called for a strict division between the two, with the Department of Commerce responsible for the civilian side and the military services coordinating their air arms through a strengthened Joint Army and Navy Board on Aeronautics. The board had been created in 1916 and restructured in 1919, but it had never enjoyed formal legislative status and its powers were advisory only. To exercise control over naval aviation, Taylor suggested creation of a naval flying corps, administered by officers temporarily assigned to the corps from the existing bureaus. Daniels and his advisers considered Taylor's ideas generally satisfactory and passed them along to Admiral Coontz, who called a conference to consider possible legislation based on Taylor's proposal. When the conference revealed considerable antagonism to a naval flying corps, Coontz brought in Taylor and Rear Adm. Robert S. Griffin, the chief of the Bureau of Steam Engineering, and with them hammered out a draft bill incorporating both a corps and an administrative bureau.[24]

Congressman Hicks prepared a bill conforming to the basic outline of the Navy's draft legislation. Before introducing the measure, Hicks wrote to assistant secretary of the Navy Franklin D. Roosevelt to see what he thought of it. Hicks said, "For sometime I have been agitating the question of a separate Bureau for Aeronautics, similar to the other Bureaus." He worried that the Army "may absorb us" as long as "we are still going along with an office running through several bureaus" and also touted the corps as "essential in order to properly take care of the flying service." Roosevelt responded favorably to the idea of a separate bureau, which, he said, "fills a want which has existed in the Navy Department for some time. Aviation can not take its place as a Naval activity until it is fostered through some centralized control." Roosevelt hoped that the Hicks bill "may be enacted in the near future, as I feel keenly that progress in the art, economy of administration, and the building up of an Aviation organiza-tion . . . are dependent upon legalized authority such as you have out-lined."[25]

Soon after introducing his measure in early April, Hicks discovered that despite the considerable enthusiasm for the bill as drafted, he did not have a consensus among naval officers to assure its passage. During a hear-ing on the bill on 29 April, Taylor and Craven argued forcefully for both a new bureau and the flying corps. On the other hand, Adm. Thomas Washington, the chief of the Bureau of Navigation, was willing to go along with the new bureau but opposed the idea of a corps. Other high-ranking and influential officers spoke against both the bureau and the corps. Without unanimity in the Navy Department, the Hicks bill died in committee.[26]

In the wake of that failure, Hicks determined that it was better to take one issue at a time and to concentrate his effort on a new bill to create a bureau only. Although he could count on more naval officers to back his new proposal than had supported his old, Hicks was not optimistic that it would receive the approval of everyone. At that moment, however, Mitchell renewed his publicity offensive, publishing an article in the Sep-tember issue of the *Review of Reviews* calling once more for a unified air service. Anticipating another threat to naval aviation, Craven immediately shot off a memo to Coontz: "The organization of a Bureau of Aviation should be represented to Congress as an urgency, and the legislation nec-essary for the creation of a Bureau enacted at the earliest possible mo-ment."[27]

Three months later, in December 1920, the *Illustrated London News* ran two photographs of a bombing experiment carried out by the Navy on the obsolete battleship *Indiana*. Planners hoped the carefully controlled tests would tell them what changes, if any, should be made in battleship design and construction to protect the vessels from air attack. Because the target was too valuable to destroy, Navy airplanes dropped only dummy bombs. Concurrently, technicians detonated carefully sited explosives aboard and around the ship, recording and analyzing the data obtained. Considering the test and the results from it confidential, many officers were justifiably shocked to see the article, and they suspected Mitchell was behind it. Mitchell's testimony before the House Military Affairs Committee in Jan-uary 1921 did nothing to allay their suspicions. Mitchell pointedly referred to the *Indiana* tests as conclusive proof that the airplane could destroy "any ship in existence today."[28]

More than any other external factor, the fallout from the *Indiana* tests and Mitchell's statements about the battleship-killing capability of the airplane convinced many that naval aviation had to solve its organizational problems or run the risk of being absorbed into a united air service. Before the House Naval Affairs Committee on 16 December 1920, Secretary Daniels said that there had been a great deal of misinformation about the potential economic benefits of a united air service. To Daniels, "no part of our Government more heartily favors restricting expenditure than does the Navy Department, but it is a false economy to hamper the development of so important an activity as aviation by failing to provide an organization under which it can accomplish the best results." Dividing the jurisdiction of aviation among the various bureaus, Daniels said, contributed to inefficiencies and hampered the technical development of aeronautics. Daniels maintained that "a legalized bureau, with definite organization that will permit coordination of the important work confronting aviation, would give to aviation the place which properly belongs to it in our naval household." He recognized that "we are confronted with the difficult problem of molding a new and important branch into an old organization not designed to care for it. The best interests of the Navy would be served by the creation of a Bureau of Aeronautics, appropriating money directly to the office of the Secretary for the purposes of aviation, and handling the appropriation as a single fund."[29]

During additional hearings before the House Naval Affairs Committee on 17 January 1921, Hicks emphasized that the solution to naval aviation's administrative shortcomings "lies in the formation of a bureau of aviation, organized along the same lines and established with authority equal to other bureaus." Captain Craven spoke out against the formation of a united air service, saying that the Navy had to remain in control of its air arm if it were to "defeat the enemy at sea." Admiral William S. Sims, who had commanded American naval forces operating in Europe during the war and in 1921 was president of the Naval War College, emphasized on 4 February that a separate bureau would enhance the continued technical progress of aviation. Retired Rear Adm. Bradley A. Fiske, one of the Navy's brightest and most outspoken officers, also stressed the urgency of creating a bureau: "If you can get that established to-morrow it will be very much better than getting it established the next day; the quicker the better."[30]

Lieutenant Commander Byrd wanted to be sure that Moffett, who relieved Craven as director of Naval Aviation on 7 March, was fully educated on the question of a bureau of aeronautics. In a memo written only five days after Moffett assumed his new duties, Byrd presented a point-by-point case for the new bureau. He asserted that the Planning Division of Naval Operations was the "least appropriate place" for Naval Aviation, especially because the chief of Naval Operations had "insufficient time to give great attention to Aviation details." The current setup was extraordinarily inefficient, with aviation "split up in the ten divisions or bureaus of the Navy Department, each of which is a law unto itself." Byrd emphasized that there was widespread support for the bureau, emanating from the NACA, the Naval War College, the chief of Naval Operations, and in the House and Senate naval affairs committees.[31]

The congressional session expired before any action was taken on Hicks's measure, and the scene shifted from Capitol Hill back to the NACA. Still seeking a resolution of the question of federal regulation of aviation, the NACA convened a meeting at the War Department on 31 March 1921, out of which emerged an agreement to have a subcommittee explore possible avenues of compromise. Headed by Charles D. Walcott, the NACA chairman, the subcommittee included Rear Admiral Taylor and Comdr. Kenneth Whiting. Within days, the body concurred on all the major issues except the question of an independent air service incorporating the Army and Navy air arms. Rather than risk a deadlock, Walcott transmitted a majority report to President Warren G. Harding, who approved it and sent it to the Republican-controlled 67th Congress on 19 April. The report stated that the Army and the Navy "each should have complete control of the character and operations of its own air service," and that the "control of naval activities in aeronautics should be centralized in a bureau of aeronautics in the Navy Department."[32]

The NACA subcommittee report and its approval by the president bolstered the position of bureau supporters in Congress. On 11 April, Congressman Hicks introduced a bill (H.R. 273) "to create a bureau of aeronautics in the Department of the Navy," followed two days later by a similar measure (S. 656) introduced in the Senate by Republican Henry W. Keyes from New Hampshire. Meanwhile, Byrd "rushed about the city" lining up people in favor of the new bureau. He said he "preyed on my friends and acquaintances until I was about as popular as a case of small-pox." But his hard work paid off when he received assurances from Congressman Thomas Butler and Senator Carroll S. Page, chairmen of the House and Senate naval affairs committees, that they would fight for the bureau.[33]

In House Naval Affairs Committee hearings on the Hicks bill testimony ran strongly in favor of a bureau of aeronautics. Hicks set the tone on 25 April when he said it was "imperative" to approve the measure "at an early date." The new secretary of the Navy, Edwin Denby, a former marine, considered the bureau "vitally necessary" for the functioning of the Navy's air arm. "It is highly important," Denby continued, "that those activities shall be centralized under one chief, of the same rank as other bureau chiefs, and that he shall have power to administer the affairs of aviation as distinct from the other branches of the service." Admiral Coontz cast his argument for the bureau to reflect the prevailing cost-cutting mood in Washington: "This is one case where the Chief of Naval Operations is willing to give up something. He is glad to have somebody take the burden off of him; he is not reaching for any other fields to conquer, but he wants to give this thing up where it will be efficiently and economically administered."[34]

Few questions pertaining to the new bureau were more troublesome than personnel. To allay the fears of other bureau chiefs, who might view the new organization as a threat to their carefully guarded prerogatives, Coontz made it clear that matters concerning aviation officers and men would remain the responsibility of the Bureau of Navigation. He continued: "I regard aviation and its future as a component part of the fighting Navy; that aviation will be . . . a regular part of the Navy; that the men who are in aviation, as time goes by, will finally get to commanding ships and commanding fleets, and, therefore, they should all be, as all others, under the Bureau of Navigation, which will give them the personnel." Coontz saw the aviator "wearing out young, like a baseball player. . . . He will move up like any regular line officer into progressively more responsible commands."[35] Coontz hoped he had laid the personnel issue to rest, but it was by no means fully resolved and would emerge in later years as the crux of a colossal struggle for supremacy between Moffett and the Bureau of Navigation.

For the present, however, Moffett wanted to make sure Coontz knew about what he considered underhanded tactics being employed by Army opponents of the bureau of aeronautics. On 21 April, he sent a memo to Coontz regarding a questionnaire titled "Air Problems over the Sea," which General Mitchell had personally handed out to members of the House Naval Affairs Committee. Moffett took exception to the document as an "unofficial means to try to embarrass the service of Naval Aviation" and "illustrative of the extent to which members of the Army Air Service have gone to . . . damage the official status of Naval Aviation." He told Coontz that the "responsible officers" were "susceptible to censure" for misleading the congressmen into believing that the list of questions had come from famed fighter ace Eddie Rickenbacker, when in fact they had not.[36]

Before Congress, however, Moffett was much more restrained, and he studiously avoided inflammatory statements likely to arouse the resistance of legislators or the united air service lobby. During hearings held by the House Naval Affairs Committee on 25 and 26 April, Moffett candidly admitted, "When I first came to Washington to relieve Capt. Craven, I had no opinion on this matter whatever." But it had not taken Moffett much time to realize "the great difficulties under which Capt. Craven had been trying to do something for which he had no executive authority. He was acting practically . . . as a chief of a bureau and was trying to perform the work of the chief of a bureau without having any executive authority whatever." Moffett's arguments for a separate bureau focused on the popular themes of economy and efficiency and the requirement to bring order out of the present "chaotic conditions."[37]

Of concern to some in Congress was that the proposed naval aviation organization would extend its authority beyond that of traditional material bureaus. When asked by Congressman Milton Kraus, a Republican from Indiana, about the extent of the bureau's responsibilities, Moffett admitted that it would take over all the aviation activities of the bureaus of Construction and Repair and Steam Engineering and would thus constitute "a complete organization" distinct from any of the older bureaus. Within the new bureau would be planning, design, engineering, personnel, and procurement sections, which were to consolidate all aviation activities previously lodged in other bureaus. Not only were some lawmakers bothered that this might bring duplication and inefficiency but also other bureau chiefs were worried that their prerogatives would be usurped by an upstart organization.[38]

Unanimous approval from the House and Senate naval affairs committees for the bureau of aeronautics bills did not stop the complex behind-the-scenes maneuvering. Moffett told his friend Bill Wrigley, Jr., that it might take months to secure passage of separate bills. Because Hicks and his allies in Congress feared a prolonged delay would give Mitchell and the backers of a united air service more time to mobilize public opinion, they melded the House and Senate measures into an amendment to H.R. 4803, the naval appropriations bill.[39]

The strategy nearly backfired on 23 May when Senator Robert M. La Follette, the Progressive from Wisconsin, introduced an amendment stipulating that the prospective chief of the new bureau be selected from the list of flying officers in the Navy or Marine Corps. Aware that La Follette represented Mitchell's home state, Byrd was certain he knew what lay behind the amendment. "On the face of it this was a fine idea. It certainly looked as if the man who would run naval aviation ought to be able to fly. But none of the admirals, such as we should have to have to head the new bureau, had taken up airplane work yet." He raced up to Capitol Hill and buttonholed La Follette, convincing him that it was more reasonable to require the new bureau chief to be trained as an aviation observer. The next day, 24 May, La Follette revised his amendment to state that the officer selected to head the bureau of aeronautics was to qualify as an aviator or an observer within one year of his appointment as bureau chief.[40]

On the floor of the Senate, Miles Poindexter, a Republican from Washington, spoke in favor of the revised La Follette amendment. Insisting that "many qualities besides that of being able to fly are required for the proper conduct of a bureau of the Navy, even though it be a bureau of aeronautics," Poindexter aimed his barbs at Mitchell. "A man might be a flyer," he said, "and still be an egregious ass. In fact, I think there have recently been some instances of that kind." Admittedly Moffett was not an aviator, but at least in Poindexter's mind, he had a better comprehension of the potential of aviation than did officers in the Army, even those who had long involvement in aviation.[41]

Moffett closely monitored developments in Congress and made a point of keeping Bill Wrigley, Jr., informed of developments. On 11 June he wrote to Wrigley that he thought the key person was Congressman Frank W. Mondell, a Republican from Wyoming, the site of some of the Navy's important oil reserves. According to Moffett, Mondell did not "know much about the Bureau provision, and says it would cause increased expense. This is not so. If you know Mondell *personally,* or know anyone who does, it would help if you would bring influence to bear upon him, but not unless it is the strongest kind of personal influence." If only Wrigley were in Washington, Moffett mused, for then he could also intervene on behalf of the proposed bureau with the president. There was a great deal at stake, for as Moffett insisted, "If this bill does not pass through, I will have to ask for duty elsewhere."[42]

Moffett need not have worried, because the appropriations bill including the new bureau emerged from the conference committee's deliberations unscathed and received overwhelming approval in both houses of the Congress on 12 July. A day later, President Harding signed the bill into law. Section 8 of the act provided that "there is hereby created and established in the Department of the Navy a Bureau of Aeronautics," headed by a chief appointed by the president and serving a four-year term. The bureau chief was to be selected from the active list of naval officers and, in accordance with the La Follette amendment, had to qualify as an aviator or observer within one year of his appointment. Rank was to be commensurate with that of other bureau chiefs, meaning that it was to be a flag billet. Within the bureau there was to be an assistant chief and a chief clerk. The secretary of the Navy was to transfer personnel, records, and equipment to the new bureau, which also had access to all money budgeted under aviation and unspent by other bureaus. Finally, the legislation stipulated that all flying units, with the exception of aircraft carriers, were to be commanded by aviators.[43]

President Harding nominated Moffett as the first chief of the Bureau of Aeronautics less than a week after signing the law establishing the new organization. On 26 July, Moffett accepted his appointment and assumed his new duties, at the same time receiving a promotion to rear admiral, effective the day before.[44] There has been considerable speculation about how and why Moffett became the first chief. The answer is simple. By the middle of 1921, it was clear to nearly everyone that the incumbent director of Naval Aviation would fill the new position. A more pertinent question is how and why did Moffett come to be the director of Naval Aviation, for by March 1921 the congressional mill had ground far enough to ensure that there almost certainly would be a new bureau and that Moffett would be selected as its chief.

In late 1920 and early 1921, several factors converged to bring Moffett to Washington and place him in the position to assume leadership of the new bureau. The most obvious of those circumstances was that after completing a highly successful battleship command, Moffett was in line for promotion to flag rank. He had also earned the respect of Taylor, Coontz, Daniels, and others as a competent and articulate officer who knew a great deal about administration from his years at Great Lakes. For many naval aviators Moffett was the obvious choice. He had helped establish aviation training at Great Lakes and as the commanding officer of *Mississippi* had effectively used airplanes in spotting and scouting operations with the battle fleet.

Admiral J. J. ("Jock") Clark recalled that one evening in 1920, while *Mississippi* was on the West Coast, Henry Mustin sat down with Moffett and presented the case for naval aviation. So persuasive was Mustin that Moffett became an overnight convert and eagerly took up the challenge of leading the Navy into the air age.[45] It seems that by the end of 1920 Moffett himself had carefully weighed his options and, deciding that aviation was a viable alternative to more-conventional desk jobs, had concluded that heading a new aviation organization with far-reaching powers offered the most opportunity for him to leave an indelible mark on his profession. He was correct.

Upon taking over as chief, Moffett quickly completed the organizational details needed to get the new bureau off the ground. Fortunately, under Coontz the office of the director of Naval Aviation had been bolstered since the nadir of August 1919 with the addition of an assistant director (who handled plans and personnel), a clerk, and several desks responsible for the technical and material sides of the operation. In April, months before passage of the appropriations bill, Moffett had begun to strengthen the office in anticipation of favorable action by Congress. He asked Coontz to add another officer to the aviation material desk, specifying that the newcomer be a naval aviator. Moffett also conferred with other officers whose bureaus were involved with aviation in an effort to secure their advice and support during the crucial organizational phase of his own bureau.[46]

Approval for Moffett's organizational plan came from the secretary of the Navy in early August, followed on the tenth by General Order 65, which formally promulgated the new bureau. The order specifically stated that the bureau "shall be charged with matters pertaining to naval aeronautics as may be prescribed by the Secretary of the Navy" and stipulated its responsibility for "all aeronautic planning, operations and administration." Within the Bureau of Aeronautics was the power to authorize other agencies and bureaus to carry out aviation work in accordance with the new bureau's recommendations and guidelines. It also took over from the older bureaus responsibility for technical development, experimentation, procurement, and the operation of the Naval Aircraft Factory. In the hazy area of personnel, the bureau's powers were for the most part restricted to recommendations to the Bureau of Navigation as to which officers and men were to be assigned to aviation duty and how they were to be trained.[47]

Moffett worked up a proposed internal organization scheme for the Bureau of Aeronautics and circulated a draft on 1 August. The plan called for establishing four divisions—Plans, Administration, Material, and Flight—and outlined the duties of each. Two days after receiving the draft, Hunsaker sent Moffett a memo critiquing the plan. He pointed out that making the assistant chief of the bureau head of the Plans Division would result in "some confusion in distinguishing requests and suggestions of the Plans Division on other Divisions from the requests of the Chief of Bureau himself." There was also a potential problem in dividing the responsibility for procurement between the Plans and Material divisions. Hunsaker preferred a strict demarcation between those officers responsible for planning (mostly aviators) and those in charge of carrying out the plans (primarily engineers). Ideally, Plans should develop the broad characteristics for the airplane it wanted, leaving to the engineers and designers in Material the task of coming up with the finished product. Equally important, Material required a free hand in research and development. Hunsaker worried about the "zeal" and morale of the division if its technical people had to go through Plans to present innovative ideas to the bureau chief.[48] Despite Hunsaker's divergent point of view, the bureau's organization remained substantially the same as that presented in Moffett's draft. As detailed in Aviation Circular 1, dated 10 August 1921, the new bureau included the four divisions originally called for.

The Plans Division was responsible for determining the characteristics of aircraft and equipment, making recommendations to the bureau chief, and working with the Material Division in the preparation of drawings and specifications. On the procurement side, Plans prepared estimates of the numbers of new aircraft required and ensured that new aircraft met specifications before being accepted into service. Financial, legal, and management technicalities passed through the offices of the Administration Division, which also had authority to deal with interservice and interbureau problems. The Flight Division handled the details of operations and training, made recommendations on personnel to be detailed to aviation duties, and oversaw the development of radio communications, aerial photography, and aerography. Six sections comprised the Material Division. Large enough to be broken into subsections responsible for lighter-than-air, heavier-than-air, and engines, the Design Section had exclusive authority to prepare detailed specifications and drawings for airplanes, airships, and aviation equipment and to oversee their procurement. The other five sections included Maintenance, which was responsible for repairs, supply, and distribution of aviation equipment; Lighter-than-Air, which included balloons, blimps, and rigid airships; Engine, with responsibility for engine and propeller development; Scientific, which advised other sections on technical matters; and Technical Information, which accumulated, filed, and disseminated technical data.[49]

When the time came to fill key positions in the new bureau, which began functioning on 1 September 1921, Moffett paid close attention to maintaining a balance among aviators, engineers, and experienced line officers. Captain Alfred W. Johnson served as assistant bureau chief until he received orders to take command of the seaplane tender *Wright*. His replacement on 7 November 1921 was Capt. Henry Mustin, one of the people responsible for bringing Moffett into naval aviation. Mustin had begun flying in 1910, although he did not formally earn his wings until 1913. A year later, he took over as officer-in-charge of the naval aeronautic station at Pensacola, and during the war he participated in the development of the Navy's first shipboard catapults. More than anyone else, Mustin epitomized the type of officer Moffett sought in the organization of the bureau—an aviator who combined an understanding of the technical requirements of aeronautics with a sophisticated grasp of aviation in fleet operations.[50]

Of the people on the early staff, 55 percent transferred from the Bureau of Construction and Repair, the vast majority of them joining the new Material Division. One of the shining stars in Admiral Taylor's constellation and longtime head of the Aircraft Division of the Bureau of Construction and Repair, Jerome Hunsaker was a natural choice to head the new bureau's Material Division. But Hunsaker himself thought better of the idea. Possibly because of his outspoken criticism of the creation of the bureau, he realized that he might be more of a liability than an asset as the division's top man. As early as December 1920, Hunsaker had written to

Comdr. Emory S. ("Jerry") Land to see if he would be interested in the new job when it became available. Hunsaker told Land that he had "the administrative skill and savoir faire to make the thing swing better" and that he could count on "a technical staff of a very excellent order of competence—I think better than you've ever had before anywhere."[51]

Commonly described as "peppery" and energetic, Jerry Land was not in Hunsaker's or Mustin's intellectual league, but he had more than enough brains to make a name for himself among the Navy's engineers. After graduating sixth in his class from the Naval Academy in 1902, Land went on to postgraduate work at the Massachusetts Institute of Technology and joined the Construction Corps, serving on the staff of Adm. Frank F. Fletcher from 1914 to 1916. During the war, he worked closely with Hunsaker in the Bureau of Construction and Repair and came to appreciate the value and potential of aviation. Land responded modestly to Hunsaker's proposition, insisting that Hunsaker reconsider stepping aside but adding the qualifier that he was "willing to do whatever is for the best interests of the Corps and the Service." In the end, pressure from Admiral Taylor convinced Land that he should accept the position, with Hunsaker serving under him in charge of the important Design Section.[52]

The selection of Comdr. Theodore G. ("Spuds") Ellyson to head the Plans Division demonstrated Moffett's awareness of political realities in the organization of the new bureau. In 1921 Ellyson had just come out of nearly a decade of self-imposed exile from aviation, had a minimum of experience in administration, and disliked desk jobs. A 1905 academy graduate, Ellyson was selected in late 1910 as the first naval officer to be given flight instruction by Glenn Curtiss. In January 1911 he learned to fly the tricky pusher biplanes at North Island, in San Diego, where Curtiss had set up temporary operations to escape the winter cold of Hammondsport, New York. Later that year, when the Curtiss school moved back to Hammondsport, Ellyson experimented with a hydroairplane and helped design a dual-control system for training airplanes. Committed to finding a way to launch airplanes from ships' decks, Ellyson in November 1912 became the first naval aviator to make a successful catapult launch, using an installation mounted on a barge at the Washington Navy Yard. He quit aviation in April 1913 after a row with Chambers and spent the next eight years on sea duty. His most important assignments were the command of subchaser units in England during the war and outfitting former German liners for the return of American servicemen after the conflict ended. When

Moffett rediscovered him, Ellyson had made his way back into the aviation fold and was serving as executive officer of the Naval Air Station at Hampton Roads.[53]

Ellyson's biographer writes that he was "somewhat miscast" in the position.[54] That may have been so, but the appointment of the near-legendary Ellyson to Plans was calculated by Moffett to ensure that the new bureau retained close ties to naval aviation's roots. Furthermore, the assignment was as clear a signal as Moffett could send to the aviators that even though he was not a flier he was really on their side and could be trusted to uphold their interests. What better way to do so than to place naval aviator number one in a top slot?

One of the lesser known but most important figures in the bureau was Lt. Francis W. Reichelderfer, who took over the aerological desk in the Flight Division in June 1922. Reichelderfer had graduated from Northwestern University and received his meteorological training at the aviation ground school at MIT during the war. Stationed in Lisbon in 1919, Reichelderfer was responsible for weather forecasts during the latter stages of the historic transatlantic flight of NC-4. An early convert to the theories of frontal and air mass analysis advanced by the Norwegian Vilhelm Bjerknes and his son Jacob, Reichelderfer helped establish the Navy's leadership in meteorology during the twenties.[55]

In many respects, the organization and functioning of the Bureau of Aeronautics reflected Moffett's own personality. An effective administrator, Moffett delegated authority and counted on the personal loyalty of his subordinates to get the job done. He could also be a stickler for detail and demanding in what he considered to be individual attention to duty. Not long after the formation of the bureau, Moffett moved from the second floor of Main Navy into a spacious cluster of offices in a corner of the second wing on the third floor of the building, looking out over the Mall to the Lincoln Memorial. Though spare, the accommodations provided ample room for his administrative staff and left space available on the floor below for Material, the largest of the bureau's divisions.[56]

Moffett called conferences every Tuesday afternoon with his division and section chiefs. Normally he presided over the meetings, but when he was out of town or otherwise indisposed, he turned the chair over to his assistant chief—in the early years, Henry Mustin or Alfred W. Johnson. Usually the meetings were brief, lasting only twenty minutes or so, but when particularly critical or contentious issues were on the table the conferences often ran far longer. The assistant chief kept minutes of the conferences, which were typed and sent to Moffett for his approval. As the bureau's business increased, Moffett found that the weekly conferences were insufficient to deal with every important issue or problem and he instituted regular meetings with individual officers.[57]

One should not construe those and other procedures as indicators of strict formality in the day-to-day functioning of the bureau. Rather, Moffett deliberately cultivated an atmosphere of informality and made a point of being as accessible as possible to all his subordinates. Surrounded by a cadre of highly competent people and given a broad mandate from Congress, Moffett was in as strong a position as anyone could expect in the fall of 1921. That does not mean there were no potential trouble spots, for despite all the planning and preparation, the new bureau did not have complete authority over naval aviation. It had to share responsibility for the procurement of aviation instruments and weapons with the Bureau of Navigation and the Bureau of Ordnance, and the wind tunnels and other research facilities at the Washington Navy Yard remained under the nominal control of the Bureau of Construction and Repair.[58] But those were minor problems compared with personnel, where the Bureau of Aeronautics could only make recommendations to the Bureau of Navigation pertaining to the selection, training, and assignment of aviation officers and men. For the time being, however, Moffett had to put the personnel fight off. His immediate priority was to establish naval aviation as a fully integrated arm of the fleet.

The air admiral at work. Rated a naval aviation observer, Moffett made a point of flying as often as time permitted. This underscored his commitment to naval aviation and to the fliers under his command as chief of the Bureau of Aeronautics. (80-G-466366, National Archives)

Elizabeth Simonton Moffett. Billy Moffett was particularly close to his mother, whose strength of character was the guiding force in the Moffett family after the death of her husband, George Hall Moffett. (Courtesy of Rear Adm. William A. Moffett, Jr.)

Commander Moffett. This formal portrait was painted about the time of Moffett's service at Veracruz in 1914. (Courtesy of Beverly Moffett Mohan)

The protected cruiser *Chicago*. Ensign Moffett served in this ship under the command of Capt. Alfred Thayer Mahan. The ship's cruise of European and Mediterranean waters in 1893-1895 amounted to a triumphal procession for Mahan, who had recently published *The Influence of Sea Power Upon History*. (19-N-13032, National Archives)

Chicago's officers, 1893. Moffett is standing at the far left; Mahan is seated left front. (Courtesy of Rear Adm. William A. Moffett, Jr.)

The armored cruiser *Charleston*. Moffett served in this ship in the Pacific during the Spanish-American War. (19-N-11278, National Archives)

The cruiser *Chester*, Moffett's first command, as she appeared in February 1909. (19-N-33-16-11, National Archives)

The Moffett siblings at attention, Great Lakes, 1918. Left to right: George, Bill Junior, Betty, and Charles. (Courtesy of Rear Adm. William A. Moffett, Jr.)

Jeannette Moffett. Moffett's wife worked for the Navy Relief Society at Great Lakes during World War I. The agency provided financial aid to the families of officers and enlisted men. (Courtesy of Rear Adm. William A. Moffett, Jr.)

Captain Moffett and his eldest daughter, Janet, at home in Lake Forest, 1917. (Courtesy of Rear Adm. William A. Moffett, Jr.)

The battleship *Mississippi*, fresh from a refit in 1928. Moffett commanded the ship from late 1918 to late 1920. (19-N-11860, National Archives)

Moffett, director of Naval Aviation, in conversation with an unidentified Marine officer at Anacostia, April 1921. The occasion was the return of Marine aviators from a survey flight to the Virgin Islands. (80-G-459202, National Archives)

Moffett at Anacostia, April 1921. On the left is Comdr. Kenneth Whiting, one of the Navy's pioneer aviators. (80-G-459203, National Archives)

Main Navy as it appeared in the early twenties. (80-G-1024872, National Archives)

Langley at the Washington Navy Yard, June 1923. (80-G-185894, National Archives)

Moffett as rear admiral and chief of the Bureau of Aeronautics, February 1922. (80-G-650715, National Archives)

Kenneth Whiting, *Langley*'s executive officer, with President Harding on the carrier's flight deck, June 1923. Moffett, in civilian clothes, is to the president's left. (80-G-433311, National Archives)

Moffett with his wife, Jeannette (right), and daughter Janet at the St. Louis air races, 6 October 1923. (80-G-459414, National Archives)

Arctic expedition planners. In late 1923, Moffett chaired a special planning board for a proposed Navy arctic expedition, which was to have included the airship *Shenandoah*. Here Moffett (right) meets with some of the board members, including Gilbert Grosvenor, president of the National Geographic Society, third from the right. (80-HAS-2C-46, National Archives)

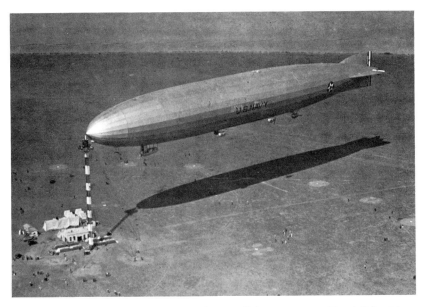

Shenandoah. The airship is moored to the expeditionary mast at North Island in San Diego at the end of her transcontinental flight in October 1924. (80-G-650737, National Archives)

Moffett in San Diego. The admiral speaks to a group of onlookers after the arrival of *Shenandoah.* Despite the hardships and dangers of the transcontinental journey, Moffett recalled it as a thoroughly enjoyable flight. (80-G-450789, National Archives)

Los Angeles moored to *Patoka*, 1926. (80-G-460456, National Archives)

Moffett disembarking from the airship *Los Angeles* at Lakehurst. (80-G-433312, National Archives)

Moffett and his sons, about 1929. George is standing behind his father, William Junior is on the left, and Charles is on the right. (Courtesy of Rear Adm. William A. Moffett, Jr.)

The admiral in dress blues and flight gear. Moffett is ready for a flight in a Douglas DT-2, at Honolulu, 18 August 1925. Note the two-star flag flying from one of the aircraft's interplane struts. (80-G-465333, National Archives)

Shenandoah crash site near Ava, Ohio, 3 September 1925. The disaster claimed the lives of fourteen men, including the airship's commanding officer, Lt. Comdr. Zachary Lansdowne. (80-MS-9, National Archives)

The carrier *Lexington* making twenty-two knots on speed trials in late 1927. (19-N-11857, National Archives)

Ranger shortly after completion in 1934. (19-N-15359, National Archives)

The flying admiral and his aviator sons, March 1932. George is on the left and William Junior on the right. (80-G-466109, National Archives)

Inspection tour of the carrier *Lexington*, late April 1930. Moffett (right) inspects the carrier with Rear Adm. Henry V. Butler and members of Congress. David Ingalls, assistant secretary of the Navy for Aeronautics, is on Moffett's right. (80-HAS-3L-22, National Archives)

Akron's maiden flight, 23 September 1931. Moffett talks to David Ingalls, assistant secretary of the Navy for Aeronautics, before the flight. To the right is secretary of the Navy Charles Francis Adams. (80-G-461226, National Archives)

Moffett and Comdr. John H. Towers, May 1929, shortly after Towers became assistant chief of the Bureau of Aeronautics. (80-G-460301, National Archives)

The top brass at the Naval Air Station, San Diego, 15 September 1932. On the left is Rear Adm. Harry Yarnell; to Moffett's right is Rear Adm. John Halligan; to his left is Capt. John Towers. (80-G-426927, National Archives)

Moffett and Lt. Comdr. Charles E. Rosendahl, *Akron*'s commanding officer, in the airship's control car during a flight in January 1932. (80-G-462258, National Archives)

Akron in flight over New York City, 1931. (80-G-458713, National Archives)

Macon's christening ceremonies in Akron, 11 March 1933. Admiral Moffett and his wife, Jeannette, are seated on the right. Jeannette Moffett was the airship's sponsor. (80-G-461819, National Archives)

A pensive Moffett gazes out the window of an airship. (Courtesy of Rear Adm. William A. Moffett, Jr.)

5

CARRIERS AND CONFERENCES

CONGRESSIONAL ACTION WAS STILL PENDING ON THE MEASURE to create the Bureau of Aeronautics on 20 June 1921 when Admiral Moffett and other naval officers embarked on the 7,750-ton transport *Henderson* at the Washington Navy Yard for an overnight run down the Potomac and Chesapeake Bay. The ship's destination lay fifty miles off the Virginia Capes, where elaborate preparations had been made for another round of bombing experiments, this time using not one old, American battleship but an aggregation of newer vessels, including German ships that were to be destroyed as part of the peace settlement. *Henderson* hove to among the fleet the next day, taking up a position with a clear view of the action as Navy aircraft bombed and sank two German U-boats. It was a reprise of the performance the day before, when Navy F-5-L flying boats had sent *U-117* plunging to the bottom of the Atlantic. Moffett was not surprised by the results of the experiment. Surfaced submarines had been shown to be vulnerable to air attack during the war, and there was little to indicate that their relatively fragile hulls would resist aerial bombs any more than they could withstand gunfire or mines.[1]

Henderson practically ran a packet schedule between Washington and the bombing test site during the summer of 1921. On 13 July, Moffett was aboard the transport again, this time to see aircraft from Billy Mitchell's First Provisional Air Brigade fly out from Langley Field to bomb and sink a German destroyer. The results were as expected that day and on the eighteenth, when Army and Navy aircraft teamed up to destroy the cruiser *Frankfurt*. Everything went like clockwork—a tribute to the thorough planning of Adm. Hilary P. Jones, the Atlantic Fleet commander, and Capt. Alfred W. Johnson, then chief of the fleet's air detachment.[2]

A spectacular climax was planned for 21 July, when Army and Navy aircraft were to attack the German dreadnought *Ostfriesland*. With hundreds of dignitaries, among them the secretaries of War and the Navy, Moffett boarded *Henderson* on the twentieth for another day-long voyage to join what had become an impressive assemblage of ships out in the Atlantic. According to the procedures worked out well in advance, Navy aircraft were to strike the target initially, followed by an inspection of the ship before Mitchell's Army bombers delivered their ordnance. Unfortunately, the Army aircraft arrived over the target earlier than scheduled and, because Mitchell said they were running low on fuel, bombed the ship first. It was a forgivable mix-up, perhaps bound to occur during such a complicated operation. But the next day, Mitchell's bombers again got off the ground early, beat the Navy airplanes to *Ostfriesland,* and sank her with 1,000-pound and 2,000-pound bombs. At no time did Navy boarding parties have a chance to inspect the damage to the ship before she capsized and went under.[3] If it was not apparent to naval officers before, they now knew that Mitchell intended to transform their carefully directed ordnance test into a publicity coup of epic proportions.

In subsequent reports on the bombing tests, Captain Johnson and others pointed out that Mitchell had failed to follow the plans he had previously agreed to, which prevented the Navy from gathering all the data it required. Sidestepping Navy complaints, Mitchell launched another propaganda campaign, focusing on the vulnerability of the battleship to air attack and questioning the Navy's traditional role as the nation's first line of defense. If Mitchell had not already drawn the line between the Navy and the air-power advocates in his unsuccessful efforts of 1919–20 to secure a united air service, he emphatically did so in the aftermath of the 1921 bombing experiments.[4]

Moffett came away from the bombing tests with mixed emotions. Dutifully he supported the Navy's contention that the experiments did not herald the impending doom of the battleship and certainly did not indicate that land-based air power was an adequate substitute for the Navy. In an interview not long after the experiments, Moffett insisted that "guns are the cheapest and most powerful weapons that we have, and, of course, the battleship and the battle cruiser are the logical ships to use them. . . . Some day aviation may develop, and probably will to a point where greater accuracy in bombing and torpedo firing will obtain. Even then, it does not seem probable that big ships will be made obsolete." Moffett echoed the conclusions of many high-ranking naval officers in his insistence that the bombing experiments were not a fair test. Not only had Mitchell's circumvention of procedures prevented the Navy from obtaining adequate information, he said, but also "all the ships attacked by aircraft were helpless. They had absolutely no means of defense, and the machinery was not manned." Had the ships been under way and armed with antiaircraft guns, Moffett was confident, "things would have been different."[5]

On the other hand, Moffett had personally witnessed the destruction of a large, well-built, and heavily armored ship by bombing aircraft. He insisted, "The bombing experiments during June and July . . . demonstrate beyond question that unhampered aircraft suitably armed can sink any type of ship." The sinking of *Ostfriesland* had a catalytic effect, convincing Moffett that the best course for the Navy was to build a well-balanced fleet, with a mix of heavy and light ships, "all of which are to be coordinated in their activities and protected by aircraft." To get sufficient aircraft to sea with the fleet as soon as possible, the Navy had to move ahead forcefully with the development and construction of aircraft carriers and equipment to permit battleships, cruisers, and other vessels to launch and recover airplanes. Noting that he had previously stated the necessity for aircraft carriers, Moffett said, "We need no less than eight big ones, because a Navy today without aircraft protection and the search-patrol, scouting-patrol, and shot-spotting facilities which aviation provides, is fatally weak when it puts to sea. . . . There is no argument against this statement. It is axiomatic." Moffett was not alone, for his conclusions meshed with those of Navy investigatory committees and high-ranking officers of the General Board who understood that in the future surface vessels would not be able to operate effectively without a protective umbrella of friendly aircraft.[6]

In the immediate aftermath of the bombing experiments, the aircraft carrier became the cornerstone of Moffett's grand plan for the development of fleet aviation. In his commitment to the carrier, Moffett followed a well-worn path. As early as June 1918, the General Board had received from the director of Naval Aviation a proposal for a large aircraft carrier fast enough to operate with the battle fleet. The board endorsed the basic concept but took no further action. Part of the reason for the board's hesitation was the dichotomy between those who wanted the flying boat and the seaplane to have priority in the postwar era and those who considered high-performance wheeled aircraft more effective in scouting and fleet-protection roles. Both sides presented convincing arguments, but in the end the carrier won out, and in April 1919, the board recommended to the secretary of the Navy that the new collier *Jupiter* be reconstructed as an aircraft carrier. Congress appropriated the necessary funds, and in March 1920 the work began. Over the next two years *Jupiter* was transformed into *Langley*, the Navy's first aircraft carrier.[7]

But *Langley* was only what in later years would be called a proof-of-concept vehicle. There were no illusions that she was fast enough or powerful enough to fill the emerging requirement for a carrier that could operate effectively with the battle fleet, and expectations in 1920 that the Navy would get its fleet carrier sooner rather than later evaporated amid the heated controversy over a unified air service. No one was surprised that Mitchell was the chief obstacle, but few would have predicted that Mitchell's support of the carrier concept was responsible. Mitchell saw the carrier, operating far out to sea, as essential to the destruction of enemy battleship forces approaching the nation's coastline. Because wheeled aircraft operated from the carrier and functioned (according to Mitchell's convoluted reasoning) in a coast-defense role, he insisted that the ship be made part of the proposed new air force.[8]

Mitchell's plans for a carrier were far more ambitious than those of the Navy. In testimony before the House Naval Affairs Committee in February 1921, Mitchell called for the conversion of the 55,000-ton liner *Leviathan*, then the world's largest ship, into a flush-deck carrier. He also thought that a purpose-built ship was a possibility, suggesting that the vessel he wanted would have a 125-foot beam and a 1,000-foot-long flush deck. When Congressman Thomas S. Butler, chairman of the committee, pointed out that a ship of that size would not be able to pass through the Panama Canal, the irrepressible Mitchell replied that the ship could be constructed with an accordionlike hull that would adjust to fit the canal's locks.[9]

Anyone who knew anything about naval architecture understood how absurd Mitchell's proposals were, but his ideas were not easily dismissed, and they placed the Navy in the awkward position of arguing against a large and powerful vessel on technical and fiscal grounds while pressing for ships that appeared, on paper at least, strikingly similar and no less expensive. Furthermore, Mitchell's skillful linkage of the carrier to a unified air force at the same time the Navy was trying to reform its administrative structure to accommodate aviation muddied the waters and made it difficult to persuade Congress to provide money for the construction of large carriers. Admiral William S. Sims, president of the Naval War College, tried to untangle the mess. Testifying before the House Naval Affairs Committee in February 1921, he dismissed the idea of a united air service on the grounds that it would hinder rather than enhance progress toward the development of an aircraft carrier and said the Navy should "go ahead immediately" with the construction or conversion of such vessels.[10]

Matters had reached an impasse by the early fall of 1921. In the wake of the bombing experiments, Mitchell had stepped up his propaganda blitz for a unified air service, which he hoped would include one or more large carriers. The General Board had developed specifications and initiated design work for the ships, but Congress had been unwilling to provide the necessary funds, particularly in light of the board's insistence that six battle cruisers left over from the massive 1916 building program had to be completed too. Amid the confusion, Moffett seized the moment to put into effect his own plans for the construction of carriers and the expansion of fleet aviation. Ironically, his opportunity came about as a direct consequence of the movement in 1921 to limit the world's major naval forces.

During the preceding two and a half years, a complicated trail of political, diplomatic, economic, and military events had led to President Harding's dramatic invitation on 11 July 1921 to the world's powers to attend a conference in Washington to address Far Eastern problems and the reduction of armaments. Although the Navy was reluctant to accede to any restrictions on its building programs, the General Board began a series of studies in preparation for the conference, eventually concluding that a ratio scheme using capital ships as a gauge was the best way to accomplish naval arms limitation. But, when asked by the State Department for recommendations for acceptable capital-ship tonnages within those ratios, the board insisted on United States parity at one million tons with Great Britain and six hundred thousand tons for Japan—figures more suitable for the expansion of naval armaments than for their restriction. Not until pressured by secretary of State Charles Evans Hughes did the board return tonnages consistent with the State Department's determination to stop current construction programs and to set a 5:5:3 capital-ship ratio among the big three naval powers.[11]

In early planning documents for the conference, the General Board suggested prohibiting military and naval aviation and restricting airplanes to commercial uses only. The rationale was that the United States was hopelessly behind the British in fleet aviation and, in the absence of approval from Congress for a large carrier, there was little expectation that the country would ever catch up. We will never know how serious the planners were, for it soon became evident that France would not give up its air force and that it would be nearly impossible to differentiate airplanes intended for peaceful commercial uses from those intended for military or naval applications.[12]

Once the board abandoned the idea of restricting aircraft, it returned to the concept of including aircraft carriers among those ships to be limited. Because the 1920 building program had incorporated 156,000 tons of carrier construction, the board suggested that figure as a starting point for negotiations and recommended extension of the 5:5:3 capital-ship ratio to aircraft carriers. In addition, the board, prophesying that the six battle cruisers being constructed under the 1916 program might be canceled in compliance with a naval disarmament treaty, initiated studies showing that one of the big ships could be economically converted into a carrier.[13]

Such was the General Board's thinking on aviation in the weeks and months before the Washington Conference. Because the conference was a State Department operation, naval officers occupied secondary advisory positions in the American delegation. The secretary of the Navy, Edwin Denby, was not even a member; instead, Theodore Roosevelt, Jr., the assistant secretary, headed the Navy group, consisting of eight officers and one civilian. Admiral Coontz, the chief of Naval Operations, was the senior officer, with Rear Adm. William V. Pratt, Moffett's former Annapolis classmate Capt. Frank H. Schofield, and Capt. Luke McNamee assigned as technical experts. Moffett's appointment as an expert assistant specializing in aviation questions came from the secretary of State on 3 November.[14]

Hughes opened the conference on 12 November 1921 with a dramatic address calling for a ten-year holiday from capital-ship construction, during which the world's maritime powers were to halt all current building programs, scrap large numbers of older vessels, and employ capital-ship tonnages as yardsticks for the restriction of lesser warships. Still reeling from Hughes's stunning speech, the delegates got down to the difficult business of hammering out the specifics of capital-ship limitation. By the middle of December, they had agreed that the United States would be limited to eighteen capital ships totaling a little over 500,000 tons, Britain to twenty-two ships and a little over 600,000 tons, and Japan left with ten ships at approximately 300,000 tons. After the ten-year moratorium, the major powers could begin replacing ships, with the United States and Britain limited to fifteen vessels and a total of 500,000 tons each, and Japan to nine ships not exceeding 300,000 tons. Of the major powers, the United States had to dismantle the greatest tonnage—nearly 850,000 tons. The British were forced to scrap more than 580,000 tons and the Japanese nearly 450,000 tons. Most of the American ships scheduled for destruction were obsolescent or had only recently begun construction.[15]

On 23 November, delegates to the conference agreed to establish a special subcommittee to consider the quantitative and qualitative limitation of aircraft. When the subcommittee met for the first time on 30 November 1921, there was a confrontation between Moffett and General Mitchell, who was attending the conference as a member of the War Department's technical staff. As Moffett recalled, "When Mitchell breezed in with a secretary, all ready to take the chair, I inquired by what authority he pretended to assume the chairmanship. He mumbled something about rank. 'Since when,' I demanded, 'does a one-star brigadier rate a two-star admiral?' That stopped him." Rather than provoke an unseemly clash in the midst of sensitive international arms negotiations, the more diplomatic Maj. Gen. Mason M. Patrick took Mitchell's place at the 8 December meeting of the subcommittee, while the Army dispatched the troublesome Mitchell to Europe on an inspection tour of military aviation facilities.[16]

With Mitchell out of the way, the aircraft subcommittee went about its business with a minimum of difficulty, holding twelve meetings. Much of the subcommittee's work was procedural, ascertaining the wishes of the conference as a whole and determining what was possible and not possible in limiting airplanes and airships. Moffett broke the subcommittee into two groups, one to study the limitation of civil and commercial aircraft and the other to put together a table representing the strengths of the air fleets of several nations. Moffett himself prepared and presented to the subcommittee for discussion on 20 December a paper examining the restriction of military aircraft. The contents of the paper closely adhered to the finding of the General Board that the limitation of military aircraft, while possible, presented insuperable difficulties, and concluded that the "international control" of military aircraft was "not practicable." A day later, Moffett delivered a letter to the subcommittee on the rules of warfare in which he dealt with the problems of visit and search of aircraft and subsurface vessels. With minor changes and additions, the documents prepared by Moffett formed the basis for the general recommendations of the subcommittee to the conference delegates.[17]

Moffett's subcommittee completed its work on 29 December and submitted its conclusions the next day. A recurrent theme in the report was the impracticality of the limitation of aircraft. Acknowledging that the restrictions imposed on German aviation by the Treaty of Versailles offered a precedent, the subcommittee warned that extending such limitations to other nations threatened to block "the natural laws of development." The subcommittee took a utopian view of the world in the air. As a potential global transportation system, aviation promised to help prevent war by accomplishing a more equitable distribution of the world's resources and, by bringing the world's peoples together, offered the possibility of peace through understanding. Because military and commercial aviation were "inseparable," imposing limits on either would be "disastrous from the point of view of world progress."[18]

In the subcommittee's view, there were technical obstacles to the limitation of aircraft. The easiest and most straightforward way to limit aviation was quantitatively, that is, by counting the numbers of airplanes and airships to conform to treaty limits. Unfortunately, political and geographical realities, combined with the capability of many nations to expand aircraft production rapidly in wartime, worked against compliance. Qualitative restrictions on the size and performance of individual airplanes were even more difficult to impose, for the subcommittee believed that no sovereign nation would permit continual inspection of its aircraft manufacturing facilities. Airships, on the other hand, lent themselves to qualitative and quantitative limitations. The subcommittee found that the inherent characteristics of large airships gave them more military capability than smaller ones, and that restrictions on their size would be comparatively simple to enforce. Moreover, because airships required mammoth protective sheds and other ground facilities, they were harder to conceal and easier to count than airplanes.[19]

The subcommittee included a peculiar paragraph in its report on the government's role in the promotion of aviation. Moffett's hand is evident in the wording: "It is possible that a far-seeing Government may stimulate the interest of its general public in aeronautics by exhibitions, general educational measures, and by the encouragement in a financial way of individuals already interested, and thus increase the adaptability of its people to aeronautics."[20] Oddly out of place in a document devoted to the possible limitation of aeronautics, the paragraph nevertheless was a succinct expression of Moffett's philosophy of the need to enhance public awareness of the accomplishments and potential of naval aviation.

In summary, the Subcommittee on Aircraft found it "not practicable to impose any effective limitations upon the numbers or characteristics of aircraft, either commercial or military, excepting in the single case of lighter-than-air craft." In the absence of any qualitative or quantitative limitations of aircraft, the subcommittee did float the idea that a later conference should consider modifications to the rules of warfare, taking into account the destructive potential of the airplane and the airship. On 7 January 1922, the conference delegates began discussing the Moffett subcommittee report, and two days later unanimously accepted its findings.[21]

Easier to limit than aircraft were aircraft carriers, which could be restricted quantitatively and qualitatively by adhering to some of the same guidelines that had been followed with other combatant vessels. Hughes had initially called for extension of the 5:5:3 capital-ship ratio to carriers, with a ceiling of 80,000 tons for the United States and Britain and 48,000 tons for Japan. No carrier could mount guns larger than eight inches. Those tonnage figures were not acceptable to the naval advisory staff, who understood that preliminary designs for large carriers envisaged ships of about 35,000 tons, thus limiting the United States to no more than two carriers. The original American proposal to retain ships already under construction did not help much, for the United States was then building only the experimental *Langley* and had no fleet carriers on the ways.[22]

At the 30 December meeting of the conference, Hughes repeated his total tonnage proposal, adding that no carrier could be constructed in excess of 27,000 tons. The various delegations could quickly calculate that under Hughes's proposal, no nation would be able to build as many ships as it wanted. Britain, for example, considered five carriers essential, which at a maximum of 27,000 tons each, meant a total of 135,000 tons. Pressed by his own naval advisers and by opposition from all the naval powers, Hughes capitulated, acceding to 135,000 tons each for the United States and Britain and, in accordance with the 5:5:3 ratio, allotting 81,000 tons to Japan. The qualitative restrictions of 27,000 tons and eight-inch guns remained.[23]

While welcoming the increased carrier tonnages, Moffett and his fellow members of the naval technical staff saw problems in the qualitative limits. Under the terms of the capital-ship agreement, the United States had to abandon construction of its six battle cruisers. Why not, then, complete two of the ships as aircraft carriers, rescuing them from the oblivion of the scrap heap and giving the United States the two big ships it needed for fleet operations? Accordingly, in January the delegates agreed to an American proposal allowing each of the major naval powers to convert two capital ships into carriers, and raised the individual tonnage restriction to 33,000 tons on those two ships only. The difficulty was that the 33,000-ton figure had been arrived at in haste and reflected a minimum rather than a maximum size. Subsequent studies indicated that the converted American ships would run about 36,000 tons—well in excess of the limit. The solution was a clause in the capital-ship agreement allowing 3,000 tons to be added to existing vessels. The additional tonnage took the form of new armor and antitorpedo bulges intended to upgrade the ships' air and underwater protection. Arbitrarily, the United States declared that the clause applied to capital ships converted to aircraft carriers and through clever semantics avoided any violations of the individual tonnage limitations.[24]

The Washington Conference closed on 6 February with the signing of three pacts. The Four-Power Treaty, including the three major naval powers and France, replaced the Anglo-Japanese alliance with a mutual guarantee to preserve the various nations' possessions in the Far East and an agreement to consult in the event of crises affecting the peace and stability of the region. The Nine-Power Treaty secured the territorial integrity of China and upheld the Open Door, considered vital to American economic interests in the Far East. In an attempt to control China's warlord armies, the treaty included a clause on arms limitation but stopped short of imposing an outright embargo. The Five-Power Naval Treaty included the complex quantitative and qualitative restrictions hammered out among the Big Three naval powers and France and Italy. Partially to mollify the Japanese, who squirmed under the inferiority explicit in the 5:5:3 ratio, the United States and Britain agreed not to expand or otherwise strengthen their base facilities or fortifications in the western Pacific. Enormously popular with the American public, the treaties fared well in the Senate, which approved them with minor reservations in March 1922. Naval officers hated to give up the immense 1916 program, which would have given the United States preeminence at sea, but many of them agreed with Rear Admiral Pratt that the five-power understanding could serve as a guideline for boosting congressional appropriations and constructing a more balanced fleet.[25]

It is not often regarded as such, but the naval treaty resulting from the Washington Conference was much more a rearmament than a disarmament agreement. The quantitative and qualitative restrictions for at least a decade effectively removed big-gun warships from the equation as far as American naval planning was concerned. Moreover, the determination by the Moffett subcommittee that the restriction of aircraft was impossible left the Navy unimpeded to pursue increases in aircraft procurement and to explore technological improvements. Finally, the agreement allowing the United States to build 135,000 tons of aircraft carriers paved the way for the construction of these ships in numbers the aviation advocates could not realistically have hoped for in the years before the Washington treaty. The conference and the treaties resulting from it heralded much promise for naval aviation, and Moffett was determined to see that promise fulfilled.

Moffett's labors at the Washington Conference, coupled with worries at the Bureau of Aeronautics, took their toll. For the most part, Moffett had assiduously segregated his personal life and professional career into two spheres, but the pressure of work in the busy winter of 1921–22 spilled over into his home. In late spring 1921, Moffett paid $14,000 for a house at 1628 Nineteenth Street, N.W., largely because, he said, he "could not stand the rent" in Washington.[26] Moves are stressful enough, but this one seemed to place an added burden on Moffett, who at work soon found himself embroiled in the controversy generated by the bombing tests at the same time he was building a working organization for the bureau and thinking about preliminary planning for the Washington Conference. The last thing he wanted or needed was discord at home.

Yet by the end of the year that was exactly what he had. He confided in his personal financial ledger on 1 January 1922 that Jeannette had made a New Year's resolution never to bring up "disagreeable topics again." The resolution, Moffett ruefully noted, lasted only until six o'clock that evening, when they had what apparently was another in a succession of quarrels. Without being specific, Moffett dismissed his often volatile wife as having "no real reason" for being suspicious of him. "If she only *knew* this," he went on, "I think everything would be as it should be & we would not have the horrible rows & scenes that are wearing me out slowly but surely & are seriously hurting my work." He emphasized how important that was: "I am enthusiastic about my work—aviation & its boundless possibilities."[27]

It is impossible to ascertain the reasons for this family dispute. Was it an isolated misunderstanding, or was it the climax of a long-standing disagreement between Moffett and his wife? How much of Jeannette's unhappiness was due to her husband's frequent and long absences and the nature of his profession? Whatever the rift was and regardless of its causes, Moffett and his wife must have reached an accommodation in their relationship. A little more than a year later, the family moved into a large, five-story brick house at 2019 Massachusetts Avenue, N.W., for which Moffett paid nearly $26,000. The surviving Moffett children remember this home best. It was roomy, tastefully decorated in the warm colors preferred by Jeannette, and was within easy walking distance of scenic Rock Creek Park. The Moffett children recall that whatever problems there were, their father and mother enjoyed a harmonious and enduring marriage.[28]

Marital tribulations aside, Moffett came away from the Washington Conference with more conviction than ever that integrating aviation with the fleet had overriding priority. He wrote to Admiral Sims on 28 February 1922 that he desired to stay "in as close touch as possible" with the Naval War College and wanted to keep Sims abreast of all aviation developments. Stating that he had "very decided opinions" about the direction naval aviation should follow, Moffett informed Sims that he was "doing the best I can to put them into effect as far as practicable." He continued: "We are feeling very much gratified that Aviation was not restricted at the [Washington] Conference, and pleased at getting two of the battle cruisers to be changed into carriers." Moffett wanted to use the opportunity presented by the conference to secure "a plan for Fleet Aviation, which will cover the next five years. . . . We are trying above all else to get Aviation afloat." There would be a "hard fight" to secure appropriations, but Moffett was confident of eventual success.[29]

Moffett had already staked out the field of battle when he appeared before the House Naval Affairs Committee on 21 February 1922. In the wake of the Washington Conference, which imposed limitations on heavy, big-gun ships, fleet aviation was more important than ever for preserving the offensive capabilities of the Navy. Moffett stressed that "the need for carriers in our fleet is greater than it was before the terms of the treaty were announced; our battleship force is cut far below the strength contemplated in the 1916 program, and we can complete no battle cruisers. Without the utilization of our full allowance of carrier tonnage . . . it will be impossible for the Navy to undertake anything but a defensive and consequently a losing naval campaign." Specifically, Moffett envisaged a multifold role for aviation units attached to the fleet. They must, he insisted, be organized, trained, and equipped to protect friendly ships from air assault by the enemy and to conduct "aggressive combat work with the control of the air as the objective." Naval aircraft were to follow through with bombing and torpedo attacks on enemy capital ships, carriers, and other vessels, while performing scouting and reconnaissance missions and spotting gunfire for friendly battleships.[30]

Aircraft carriers were central to Moffett's farsighted and comprehensive vision of air warfare at sea. Airplanes flying from catapult-equipped battleships, cruisers, and auxiliaries could begin offensive operations "on a small scale" and were essential in a support role, but in the final analysis only carriers could mass the numbers of aircraft necessary to sustain an intensive campaign. Consequently, the United States had to build to the "full allowance of carriers assigned us by the terms of the treaty." Unless the nation did so, Moffett insisted, "our Navy can never be anything but a second-best Navy, which . . . has about the same value as a second-best poker hand."

Countering arguments by some lawmakers that the United States should go slow with carrier aviation while it was still in the experimental stage, Moffett insisted that the technology was, for the most part, well in hand and was confident that with experience his people would resolve the problems of launching and recovering aircraft from ships at sea. Of critical importance was the conversion into carriers of the two large battle cruisers *Saratoga* and *Lexington,* as allowed under the Washington agreements. To

Moffett's way of thinking, "delay would not be warranted. In other words, time is a most important element."[31] Moffett knew that after 1931, when the United States began replacing battleships under the terms of the Washington treaty, there might be little money to spare for carriers.

A week after his appearance before the House Naval Affairs Committee, Moffett presented the General Board with a tentative five-year plan for the development of fleet aviation. Central to the ambitious program was getting as many airplanes as possible into operation with the fleet. According to the plan, each battleship was to be equipped with four aircraft—two fighters, one spotting airplane, and one torpedo bomber—launched from a catapult affixed to one of the aft turrets. Other warships were also to receive aircraft: each modern cruiser was to be assigned two fighters and two spotting airplanes; each destroyer division was to have six ships capable of launching airplanes, with three ships carrying scouting aircraft and three carrying fighters; as many auxiliary vessels as possible were to be modified to launch airplanes; and five aviation repair and supply ships were to be placed in operation to support flying boat squadrons.

As for carriers, the plan emphasized the urgency of building the fleet up to its full treaty limits "without unnecessary delay." *Saratoga* and *Lexington* were to be completed as quickly as possible, with the object of getting them in commission by the end of 1924. In the meantime, preliminary design work was to begin immediately on a new 23,000-ton, 29.5-knot carrier, three of which were to be completed at the rate of one per year following the completion of the two heavier ships. Finally, it was crucial "to design aircraft carriers to carry as many fighting planes and torpedo planes as possible, on at least a two to one basis, while reserving space for the necessary number of spotting planes additional to those carried by battleships."[32]

On 3 March 1922, assistant chief Henry Mustin appeared before the General Board to answer questions about the bureau's fleet aviation plan. He emphasized that the bureau's object in proposing the plan was "to direct the principal air effort on that part of the air service that is to operate from ships" and "to put fighting planes on nearly every ship in the fleet." From his experience at Pensacola in 1915 with an experimental catapult installation on *North Carolina*, Mustin was confident that equipping the much larger battleships with similar equipment would not in any way hinder their gunnery or other operations. He added that the bureau was already working on a project to demonstrate the feasibility of launching aircraft from destroyers. Turning to carriers, Mustin explained that the three 23,000-ton ships could not be built right away because of the problems of securing adequate funds from Congress and the lack of flight training facilities. After the last of the five carriers went into operation, *Langley* would be pulled out of service and have a portion of her flight deck removed so she would not count against the nation's total carrier tonnage.[33]

Of the senior officers present during Mustin's testimony, only Rear Adm. William L. Rodgers was dubious about the plan. Rodgers had no reservations about the importance of the airplane in naval operations, but he was concerned about the plan's overemphasis on aviation in the offensive. He asked Mustin point-blank, "Do you contemplate making all naval warfare in support of the air attack?" Mustin replied directly and forcefully, "No, sir. Our whole aviation program is laid out on the basis that the battleship is the dominant factor in naval warfare, provided it is properly supported by aircraft." He explained in more detail that the first objective of the program was to provide for "an adequate number of spotting planes so the battleships will get the extra advantage" in fleet engagements with other battleships. But, Mustin went on, the success of the aircraft as spotters hinged on gaining control of the air. "Consequently, we put on all the combat planes we can get aboard, after leaving enough space for carrying the necessary spotting planes and a certain number of torpedo planes for bombing and scout work."[34]

Over the next few months the bureau and the General Board played a high-stakes game of give and take with the tentative five-year aviation plan. To start with, the General Board wanted to proceed slowly with the installation of catapults and aircraft on battleships. On 27 March 1922, the director of War Plans submitted a memorandum to the chief of Naval Operations, who subsequently forwarded it to the General Board. The memorandum made it clear that the bureau was moving too quickly in its recommendations for equipping battleships with airplanes, arguing that "any planes put on the ship must be of assistance to the ship, either in the use of the battery, or in the protection of the battery; and that the battleship is in no case to be considered an airplane carrier or an airplane tender." Preliminary studies demonstrated that in one way or another airplanes, catapults, and related aviation equipment were likely to interfere considerably with a ship's primary mission and urged a "cautious and conservative" approach. Consequently, the secretary of the Navy approved the General Board's recommendation that only one spotting airplane be fitted to each battleship until experimental operations demonstrated the feasibility of the concept. The bureau also reluctantly gave way on the torpedo bomber, bowing to pressure from those who considered it too dangerous to have that type of airplane and its ordnance on the decks of battleships.[35]

The director of War Plans also objected to the bureau's proposal for putting airplanes on cruisers, finding that equipping each of the new *Omaha*-class ships with two spotting airplanes and two fighters was too expensive and would require major alterations to the design of the vessels. On 7 June 1922, the bureau agreed to delete the two fighters and cut the ships' aircraft complements to two small observation planes. But at the same time the bureau recommended that all future designs for cruisers provide for storing and launching two large, three-seat observation airplanes and two smaller fighters.[36]

The bureau also wanted smaller vessels to carry aircraft. Suggesting that submarines might be equipped to operate aircraft, the bureau proceeded with plans for a small airplane that could be disassembled, folded up, and secured in a watertight container on deck. According to this scheme, each of the Navy's large fleet submarines was to have one of the aircraft, which could be used for locating and trailing potential targets. And the bureau remained as committed as ever to the concept of operating aircraft from destroyers. By November 1922, it had developed preliminary plans for launching a floatplane using a catapult extending over the destroyer's forecastle.[37]

That the bureau remained fundamentally committed to the original concept of fleet aviation was apparent in a strongly worded letter from Moffett to the secretary of the Navy on 10 August 1922. Because of the lead time necessary to procure ships and aircraft and to train people to operate them, Moffett saw the need for long-term planning for fleet aviation. The bureau needed to "base its plans, material development, and personnel recommendations on a definite program for aeronautic activities afloat that extends several years ahead of each year's aeronautic appropriation."

To ensure that the fleet had the numbers and types of aircraft and engines it anticipated for 1925 and later, it was necessary now to provide money for experimentation. Not to do so, Moffett thought, was a false economy and jeopardized the Navy's readiness to fight another war. If requests for money from Congress were firmly based on "a definite and well considered plan for expansion of naval aviation afloat," Moffett was con-

fident, "there will be little difficulty in obtaining the required funds for annual increases." Above all, Moffett believed it was "imperative" to demonstrate a permanent commitment to aviation; otherwise, the Navy risked
disillusioning the public, who wanted more for their money than an endless round of experiments demonstrating only the "possibilities of aviation
afloat."[38]

Captain Mustin was back before the General Board on 7 November
1922 to answer questions and to clarify the changes that had been made
in the fleet aviation plan. He countered criticism that catapults and associated aircraft launching equipment would hinder ships' operations and de-
grade their offensive capabilities. "As far as battleships are concerned," he
said, "we believe we can install catapults without interfering with the fire
of the main battery." The same was true of destroyers. "We think we can
put a light plane, a type of fighting plane or a single seater observation
plane on the destroyers without interfering with their offensive power."
He repeated the purpose of the fleet aviation program, which was "to put
as many fighting planes as possible on every available bit of space on the
fleet that will not interfere with other operations."[39]

It was one thing to map out a plan for the development of fleet aviation but quite another to see that plan implemented. Ahead lay the rocks
and shoals of congressional funding restraints and the difficult technical
and operational obstacles associated with flying aircraft at sea. Of the most
immediate concern were the carriers *Saratoga* and *Lexington*. Pressed by
the urgency of beginning their conversion, the Bureau of Construction
and Repair completed preliminary designs in the early spring of 1922.
When the designs reached the Bureau of Aeronautics, they raised a flurry
among the aviators, who saw that the eight-inch gun housings aft of the
"island" on the starboard side of the ship reduced the width of the flight
deck from eighty-four to sixty feet. After an informal conference with
Mustin and Capt. Frank H. Schofield, Moffett decided to overrule the aviators and go along with the narrow flight deck. Moffett's abiding concern
was to get the carriers; he was not going to allow twenty-four feet of deck
width to stand in the way. Unfortunately, Moffett had less control over
subsequent events. Contracts to begin converting the vessels were not
signed until October and November 1922, and largely because of funding
restrictions, work on the big ships went ahead in fits and starts over the
next three years.[40]

Only slightly more satisfactory progress was made in determining the characteristics of the carriers Moffett wanted to fill out the remaining treaty tonnage. Using Aeronautics' tentative plan for a 23,000-ton, 29.5-knot vessel, the Bureau of Construction and Repair developed a series of schemes in 1922–23 for carriers ranging in size from 11,500 tons to 27,000 tons, the maximum allowable under the treaty. Speeds varied from 27 knots for a heavily armored, protected carrier with a short flight deck to 32.5 knots for a lightly armed and armored 27,000-ton ship. The studies reflected an essential compromise between the interests of the aviators, who wanted the maximum number of aircraft on each ship, and the Bureau of Construction and Repair, which had to weigh the aviators' desires against the realities of speed, size, tonnage, armor, and defensive armament.[41]

As the carrier proposals matured, it became clear that 27,000 tons was more a minimum size than a maximum, and speed became the chief variable. In response to a request from Congressman Carl Vinson, who thought it might be possible to get enough votes for a new carrier appropriation bill, the General Board convened a hearing on carrier characteristics on 24 May 1924. Echoing the aviators among his ranks, Admiral Moffett said that he wanted the carrier to have a speed of 33 knots, "if you can get it." He viewed speed as crucial to the carrier's protection in a fleet engagement, and he wanted the carrier to be able to operate the maximum number of aircraft possible. There would not be much difference in cost. A 27,000-ton, 32.5-knot carrier, Moffett estimated, would be able to carry seventy aircraft and would cost about $20 million, exclusive of aircraft, aviation equipment, armament, and armor. A ship of the same tonnage but with a speed of only 27.5 knots and ten fewer aircraft would not cost appreciably less. Unfortunately for the carrier advocates, Congress appropriated no money in 1924 or over the next five years for new carriers, and Moffett had to make do with what he had.[42]

What he had in 1922 was *Langley*. Commissioned on 20 March at the Norfolk Navy Yard, *Langley* was cumbersome and slow, but over the next several years she pointed the way to the future of fleet aviation in the United States. Tracing an incremental learning curve, *Langley*'s aviators and sailors devised relatively safe and efficient flight operations, experimented with arresting gear and catapults, worked out aircraft handling and maintenance procedures, and showed the rest of the Navy how the carrier could be tactically employed in fleet operations.

Initially, aviators had to demonstrate the basics of taking off from and landing on the ship. Takeoffs were relatively straightforward, as the ship steamed into the wind and the airplane ran the length of the deck until achieving flight speed. Lieutenant Virgil C. Griffin was the first to fly off *Langley,* doing so in a Vought VE-7 SF on the afternoon of 17 October 1922. Landings, however, were an altogether different proposition. On a vessel faster than *Langley,* the wind over the deck was usually sufficient to reduce the relative speed between the airplane and the ship, but *Langley's* top speed of fifteen knots meant that an arresting gear system was necessary to bring the airplane to a halt. In anticipation of *Langley's* requirement, experiments had begun at the Naval Air Station, Hampton Roads, in the summer of 1921 using a revolving circular platform fitted with a network of wires. Hooks on the axle of the airplane's landing gear engaged fore-and-aft wires, holding the craft down and preventing it from slewing from one side to another. At the same time, a tail hook on the airplane engaged one of the transverse wires, which, connected through sheaves to weights suspended in towers, slowed the forward momentum of the airplane. When she was commissioned, *Langley* had an arresting gear installation nearly identical to that at Hampton Roads.[43]

Off Cape Henry on 26 October 1922 Lt. Comdr. Godfrey deC. Chevalier, flying an Aeromarine 39B, accomplished the first arrested landing on *Langley.* Chevalier was the logical choice for the dangerous experiment. A 1910 Annapolis graduate, he had flown from the catapult-equipped *North Carolina,* had studied British carriers and their equipment, and had helped design and test arresting gear at Hampton Roads. Moffett flew from Anacostia to Hampton Roads on 5 November in an F-5-L flying boat and spent the next three days observing further landings and takeoffs from the carrier, some of which took place while the ship was at anchor with no wind over the deck. Ten days after Moffett returned to Washington, Comdr. Kenneth Whiting, *Langley's* executive officer, was the first to use the ship's catapult, a compressed-air model similar to those fitted to two armored cruisers before the war. Whiting flew off in a Naval Aircraft Factory twin-float PT-2 on 18 November 1922 while *Langley* was anchored in the York River.[44]

Moffett pointed to *Langley's* early success when he went before the House Appropriations Committee on 22 November 1922 to argue for more money for the development of fleet aviation. He emphasized that the experiments that fall had been "remarkable," particularly because the United States was still feeling its way with carrier aviation and as yet had suffered no major accidents or casualties. Continuing, Moffett admitted that the British were "further ahead—I would say very much further ahead—than we are on carriers." But returning to one of the principal objectives of the five-year tentative plan, Moffett added, "I think we are far ahead of them in carrying planes on board ships. . . . We are trying to get aviation in the fleet. That has been the first aim of the bureau . . . and in this way we hope to get the planes on all the battleships, destroyers, and scout cruisers, and in time we hope on the submarines."[45]

Moffett saw in *Langley* more than a means of proving the feasibility of operating aircraft at sea with the fleet. He also viewed the ship as an opportunity to promote the concept of carrier aviation to the people who made the decisions in Washington. Moffett wrote to the chief of Naval Operations in May 1923 recommending that *Langley* be sent to Washington and shown to the public during the annual Shriners' Week celebration. He believed "the exhibition of this ship at this time will do much toward putting the accomplishments of the Navy and Naval Aviation before the people throughout the country." *Langley* left Hampton Roads on 1 June and made her way up the Chesapeake Bay and the Potomac, tying up at the Washington Navy Yard the next morning. For ten days, the ship and her crew were busy with open houses and flying demonstrations on the Anacostia River and the Potomac. On 11 June, Moffett and Whiting led President Harding and several members of his cabinet on a tour of the ship. For what it was worth, Harding remarked the next day that he was "stronger than ever" in his conviction that the United States needed to go ahead with the development of fleet aviation and urged the speedy conversion of *Saratoga* and *Lexington*.[46]

Determined to maximize the public relations potential of the Navy's first carrier, Moffett arranged for *Langley* to follow her highly successful Washington visit with an extended tour of the East Coast. On 24 July, *Langley* pulled into New York Harbor and made her way up the Hudson to an anchorage off Ninety-sixth Street. For the next week, she flew off airplanes to participate in combat exercises, and in a single day she welcomed aboard more than a thousand curious New Yorkers. Moffett joined the ship on the twenty-eighth and accompanied her on visits to Newport, Boston, and Chatham, Massachusetts. Altogether, over six weeks, *Langley* called at eight New England ports, participated in a variety of community celebrations, and gave numerous flying demonstrations. Moffett was delighted with the publicity, but some officers believed that *Langley*'s tour delayed important experimental work and pointed out that the ship's valuable time would have been better spent refining air operations with the fleet.[47] For Moffett, however, the *Langley* tour was convincing evidence of the power of public relations, and thereafter he set a high priority on showing off the Navy's latest and best aviation technology.

Over the next year, *Langley* spent most of her time working with the fleet, more than meeting the expectations of Navy airmen and conclusively demonstrating the validity of the aircraft carrier. The ship operated a variety of aircraft and provided invaluable experience for her aviators and shipboard personnel. Experiments demonstrated that future carriers would have to be of the island-type, with a superstructure offset to one side of the flight deck, through which boiler stack gases would pass. With practice, *Langley*'s crew greatly reduced the time of landing and takeoff cycles, permitting the operation of many more aircraft from such ships. Other innovations pioneered by *Langley*'s personnel were the use of a landing signal officer to guide aircraft down to the arresting wires on the flight deck and indirect lighting to allow nighttime air operations.[48]

Vice Adm. Newton A. McCully, Jr., commanding the scouting forces of the U.S. Fleet in the Caribbean, was much impressed by *Langley*'s performance during maneuvers in the winter of 1923–24. He wrote to Moffett on 12 February 1924 to say he "appreciated very much having the *Langley*," adding that "she has certainly demonstrated very clearly her value to all the Fleet." During exercises off Colón, at the Atlantic entrance to the Panama Canal, *Langley*'s aircraft effectively defended the scouting fleet from attacking bombers. McCully thought such air operations had been "an eye opener for most people" and looked forward to working with *Langley* and her aircraft in the future.[49]

By the middle of 1924, *Langley* and her personnel had fulfilled a major part of Moffett's plans for fleet aviation. The other element—getting aircraft at sea on as many ships as possible—proved more difficult than Moffett had realized. Critical to the deployment of aircraft on battleships and cruisers was the turntable catapult, which could be mounted on ship superstructures or quarterdecks and trained in any direction to face the wind. Following a year of design and development work, the Naval Aircraft Factory tested the first turntable catapult on 26 October 1921. Powered by compressed air, the catapult went into production as the Mark I, three of which were fitted to the battleships *Maryland, Nevada,* and *Oklahoma* before the end of 1922. The installations, each in a separate battleship class, were successful, but they took up precious space and added considerably to unwanted topside weight. Nevertheless, Moffett emphasized the importance of such launching devices when he testified before the House Appropriations Committee on 20 March 1922: "I do not think there is any more important item in the [appropriation] bill than this one for catapults." By the middle of 1925, nine more battleships had received Mark IIs (upgraded versions of the Mark I), and each 7,000-ton *Omaha*-class scout cruiser was fitted with a pair of Mark Is.[50]

Largely because of Moffett's influence, money continued to be available for catapult development and production. Because of mechanical complexity and other limits imposed by compressed air, development concentrated after 1921 on a new launching device powered by gunpowder. Jointly designed by the bureaus of Ordnance and Aeronautics, the first of the new catapults, designated Type P Mark III, went aboard one of Moffett's old commands, the battleship *Mississippi,* in 1924. *Mississippi's* installation was typical of that on all subsequent battleships: the catapult was mounted on turret number three, supplementing the compressed-air turntable catapult remaining on the quarterdeck. By June 1925, Aeronautics had formulated plans to replace the cruisers' compressed-air catapults with a new gunpowder model, the Type P Mark V.[51]

Getting airplanes aboard destroyers, submarines, and fleet auxiliaries, as originally conceived in the tentative five-year program, proved impossible. Almost from the start, the Bureau of Ordnance was cool to the idea of aircraft on destroyers, contending in November 1922 that they would interfere with guns and torpedo tubes and would seriously detract from the ships' offensive capabilities. As for submarines, the bureau was even more negative, asserting that "just why an airplane should be carried on a submarine is not apparent" from the information and plans supplied by Aeronautics.[52]

Possibly because of that opposition, Capt. Alfred W. Johnson assured the General Board in April 1923 that the Bureau of Aeronautics was going ahead cautiously in its experiments with airplanes on destroyers and submarines. During the summer of 1923, the submarine *S1* was altered at the Portsmouth Navy Yard to accommodate a small floatplane, disassembled and stowed in a watertight cylinder aft of the conning tower. Two aircraft flew from the submarine during tests in the fall of 1923, a Martin MS and a Cox-Klemin XS, but the time required to assemble the aircraft proved excessive. Despite redesign work to improve the assembly and disassembly features and additional tests in 1926, the aircraft remained too small to be of much use. In 1927, the General Board recommended against continuing the project, but the bureau did not finally abandon it until 1931.[53]

There was little progress in the development of destroyers capable of launching aircraft. In the summer and fall of 1923, a catapult was installed on the destroyer *Charles Ausburn,* extending from just forward of the bridge to a point over the forecastle. During tests in November 1923, the ship successfully launched a Naval Aircraft Factory TS-1 floatplane, but the demonstration revealed numerous deficiencies in the installation, the most serious of which was that the catapult interfered with vision from the bridge. For a time, the bureau considered fitting a catapult over the stern of the ship, but by June 1925 it had put off the destroyer project indefinitely, determined "to get the maximum amount of information from existing service installations before taking up an entirely new type." Equipping fleet auxiliary vessels with catapults involved fewer technical problems, but plans for removing older compressed-air catapults from battleships and installing them on auxiliary ships never materialized.[54]

The failure to secure as many aviation-capable ships as he originally wanted was a setback to Moffett's ambitious plans for the rapid development of fleet aviation, but it was no less serious than the loss of Capt. Henry C. Mustin. Moffett's right-hand man and one of the most capable and innovative officers in the Bureau of Aeronautics, Mustin had helped open Moffett's eyes to the potential of naval aviation, had been instrumental in the creation of the bureau, and had done most of the hard work of putting together the five-year fleet aviation plan. But the strain proved too much for him, and his health began to decline markedly late in 1922. He entered the naval hospital in Washington in January 1923 suffering from heart disease, but there was little the doctors could do, and he was transferred on his own wishes to the naval hospital in Newport, Rhode Island. On 30 July, Mustin was relieved as the bureau's assistant chief. Moffett personally thanked him for "the exceptionally efficient, energetic and able manner in which you have performed your duties. . . . Aviation owes you a debt of gratitude." In less than a month Mustin was dead, succumbing at the age of forty-nine to an aortic aneurysm on 23 August 1923.[55]

Mustin's death was a severe blow for the Bureau of Aeronautics, but the organization he had helped forge was resilient enough to overcome the loss. To replace Mustin, Moffett appointed Capt. Alfred W. Johnson as assistant chief. Johnson had briefly served in the office before Mustin came in, he was familiar with the functioning of the bureau, and although hardly as visionary as Mustin, he was deeply committed to naval aviation. Moffett knew he could work with Johnson and was sure that despite recent disappointments, Johnson would help achieve the long-range objectives of the bureau.

In spite of the setbacks, Moffett remained confident that in the not-too-distant future aviation would become as much a part of the fleet as the battleship's big guns. In a 12 May 1924 memo to the chief of Naval Operations, he reported that "each year is seeing a steady advance both in the art and in the supply of general [aircraft] types to meet the requirements of the fleet." Fiscal constraints had "somewhat retarded the development," but there was no doubt in Moffett's mind that the airplane would become an indispensable part of any offensive operations at sea. He amplified the theme for a wider audience in the October 1925 issue of the *U.S. Naval Institute Proceedings:* "The Navy is the first line of offense and naval aviation as an advance guard of this first line must deliver the brunt of the attack. Naval aviation cannot take the offensive from shore; it must go to sea on the back of the fleet. . . . The fleet and naval aviation are one and inseparable."[56]

6

AIRPLANES, AIRSHIPS, AND AIRMEN

M OFFETT REALIZED THAT THE FULFILLMENT OF HIS ELABORATE
and farsighted plans for fleet aviation would not be easy. He and
his staff had to make decisions about aircraft procurement, establish a cooperative relationship with private industry, define a new role
for the Naval Aircraft Factory, and manage the development of the new
technologies considered essential for air warfare at sea. All would be for
nothing unless naval aviation had enough capable and experienced people.
Personnel questions centered on money, numbers of officers and enlisted
men, training, and duty status, with the further complication that the authority of Moffett's bureau extended only to making recommendations to
the influential and entrenched Bureau of Navigation, which controlled assignments of all officers and men. With characteristic vigor, Moffett took
on these formidable challenges. Some of them yielded before his considerable bureaucratic and political skills, while others proved more intractable,
frustrating his and the bureau's best efforts to achieve their objectives.

Moffett came into office in 1921 to find an American aircraft industry
in crisis. With the capacity to manufacture a little more than two thousand
aircraft annually when the nation entered the war in 1917, the industry by

the end of the conflict was able to produce more than ten times that number on a yearly basis. After the armistice, the military's postwar aircraft requirements shrank to a fraction of what they had been only a few months previously; for example, the Navy's total 1921 requirement was just 156 airplanes. Almost entirely dependent on the federal government and with no commercial or private market for its products, the American aircraft industry faced a serious overcapacity problem. What industry representatives considered government competition from the Naval Aircraft Factory made the outlook even bleaker.[1]

Created to meet the wartime needs of the Navy for large flying boats, the factory emerged in the postwar years as one of the largest aviation manufacturing plants in the country. Jerome Hunsaker estimated in 1920 that it could provide one third of the Navy's aircraft needs while also carrying out extensive repair, maintenance, and experimental activities. Needless to say, private aircraft manufacturers were less than enthusiastic about giving over such a large proportion of their already greatly reduced business to a government-owned and -operated facility. Through its principal trade association, the Aeronautical Chamber of Commerce of America, the industry protested what it considered unfair treatment and lobbied to have the factory shorn of its aircraft production responsibilities or shut down altogether.[2]

It was apparent to Moffett in the fall of 1921 that he had to resolve the question of the Naval Aircraft Factory before he could move on to a rational, long-term aircraft procurement program. Simply put, Moffett had to weigh the value of a good working relationship with the ailing private aircraft industry, which he knew the country would have to depend on in a national emergency, against the financial and institutional investment the service already had in this major aviation installation. In what turned out to be a masterful and enduring compromise, Moffett determined in January 1922 that henceforth the Naval Aircraft Factory would no longer engage in the full-scale production of aircraft but would instead concentrate on the manufacture of experimental models and continue its full range of design, research and development, and testing activities. The factory, however, would still produce a limited number of aircraft as a yardstick—that is, to provide data that could be used to gauge the costs of airplanes procured from private suppliers.[3]

Moffett's deft compromise did not entirely satisfy private manufacturers. Many believed the Navy's retention of a significant design function in both the bureau and the factory robbed their industry of its lifeblood and threatened proprietary design rights. They worried that the Navy could, if it wanted, bypass private firms and use the bureau's design and engineering staffs for all new aircraft designs, thus leaving larger and more innovative companies at a disadvantage in the competition with less competent producers. In 1925, Clement M. Keys, a Curtiss executive and self-proclaimed spokesman for the aircraft manufacturers, insisted that design and engineering "are the airplane industry" and argued that government competition in those areas was just as damaging as it was in aircraft production.[4]

On this issue, there was little Moffett could do to mollify Keys or other industry representatives short of eliminating most of the people in the Design Section of the bureau's Material Division or the staff in the factory's engineering office. In his first annual report, for fiscal year 1922, Moffett summarized the situation: "The Bureau of Aeronautics has followed the policy of encouraging design and invention outside the naval service, but has taken great care to maintain a sufficiently expert design staff so that the Navy would never be entirely dependent upon or forced to accept only such designs as might be submitted by contractors." The bureau's large design and engineering staff remained a thorn in the side of private industry throughout the interwar period.[5]

Nor was Moffett able to cut through the tangled thicket of legal contract procedures in the early and mid twenties. The Bureau of Aeronautics closely followed the law, which required it to accept the lowest bid on a contract regardless of the demonstrated competence of the lowest bidder or any doubts the bureau might have about the company's ability to fulfill the exact terms of the contract. Either inferior design or a high estimated price could disqualify a bidder. There was some flexibility in the system, however. Under certain conditions, the bureau could use negotiated contracts, a noncompetitive process whereby a contractor with a good record on previous work would receive the contract and later negotiate a price with the government for the material to be acquired. Finally, there were development contracts, which permitted a contractor to manufacture at an estimated cost an airplane designed within the bureau.

Never spelled out, but interwoven through all contract procedures, was the question of proprietary rights to aircraft and engine designs. On the one hand, manufacturers were unanimous in their insistence that they hold the rights to the design of any product developed under a Navy contract. Without those rights, the manufacturers contended, they could not recoup their research and development expenses through a production contract. The loss of their design rights also meant that aircraft manufacturers could not pursue potential commercial customers for a Navy-based aircraft design and could not produce that same design for sale abroad.[6]

On the other hand, the government, arguing for economy and competition and usually having already made a major investment in the development of the article, did not believe it could give carte blanche to any single manufacturer. Nor was it clear what a company's proprietary rights were when it took a basic Navy design and improved on it. Moffett preferred noncompetitive negotiated contracts in most instances, but he knew that they were not acceptable to Congress. As a compromise, he hoped to assuage private manufacturers by negotiating contracts for some items they considered proprietary while adhering to competitive bidding for most other articles. Publicly Moffett admitted that competitive bidding was an imperfect system, but it was not totally unworkable. The bureau, Moffett insisted, took into account the human element. When necessary, it extended the time allowed for submitting bids and made generous allowances in meeting contract deadlines. Moffett saw that it was in the Navy's interests to distribute contracts equitably, reasoning that a healthy and competitive aircraft industry was essential for naval aviation and the national defense.[7]

In line with that philosophy, Moffett made it clear that "one of the essential activities of the Bureau is keeping in touch with aircraft manufacturers. . . . and it is the desire of the Bureau to encourage those on the outside to feel at liberty at all times to present matters to the Bureau in which they are interested." The bureau was to share its technical information with all competitors on a free and equal basis and do its best to maintain an open-door policy. On a typical day, the heads of major aircraft and engine firms could be seen going from office to office in the bureau.[8] Frequently, close, informal working relationships grew up between the manufacturers, many of whom were engineers, and officers in the technical sections of the Material or Plans divisions. There was the obvious danger of conflict of interest, but Moffett tolerated the relationships because he understood the symbiosis between naval aviation and the frail American aircraft industry in the years after World War I.

All the good will in the world would amount to nothing unless Moffett had the commitment of Congress to appropriate the money to buy aircraft and related aviation equipment. He rightly believed that a long-term aircraft procurement program was needed to bring stability to the industry and furnish the types and numbers of airplanes required for fleet aviation. But circumstances largely beyond his control worked against him during his first term in office. One problem was money; budget-minded congresses were simply not willing or able to provide funds both for replacement aircraft and for the expanding needs of fleet aviation. Another problem was the enormous number of airplanes left over from the war. Not even Moffett could persuade Congress to pay for new airplanes when nearly everyone believed that the Navy could meet its immediate needs with surplus aircraft.

The best Moffett could hope for, then, was enough money over the short term for replacement aircraft and engines while the bureau proceeded with long-term plans for the development of new technologies and equipment. To the House Naval Affairs Committee in December 1922, he presented his estimates for the acquisition of 256 new airplanes worth nearly $5.8 million. He assured the lawmakers that these aircraft were replacements only, that the most efficient use was being made of surplus equipment, and that to save money, he was asking for only one spare engine for every two airplanes, rather than the usual one for each airplane. To meet future requirements, the bureau worked with engine designers on the development of a lightweight, air-cooled power plant to replace the obsolescent, though reliable, liquid-cooled engines inherited from the war years.[9]

Fleet aviation was the primary consideration the following year, when the Bureau of Aeronautics asked for $8.1 million for 234 new airplanes. More than $4.5 million of that was earmarked for airplanes to fill out the squadrons of the new carriers *Saratoga* and *Lexington*, which Moffett optimistically expected to join the fleet during fiscal year 1925. Most of the remainder of the estimates were for aircraft assigned to battleship squadrons. Appearing before the General Board on 4 April 1923 to explain the requirements, Captain Johnson, the assistant bureau chief, and Capt. Emory Land, head of the Material Division, emphasized the pressing need for new aircraft. Johnson said that he thought the Navy had been "terribly extravagant" in its use of surplus airplanes, estimating that the service would run out of its stock of F-5-L flying boats in a "very short time." Land said that he and Moffett had recently discussed the distribution of new aircraft contracts and were in agreement that the orders needed to be spread among as many manufacturers as possible. "To my mind,"

Land testified, "we ought to have a policy that would take into consideration the condition of the trade . . . irrespective of the lowest bidder."[10]

In testimony before the House Appropriations Committee on 2 December 1924, Moffett surveyed competitive bidding policies and aircraft
procurement. He said manufacturers, dissatisfied with current bidding
procedures, had suggested that the bureau develop "an approved list of
bidders," restricted to a select group of manufacturers who could count on
a steady flow of Navy contracts. Moffett was sympathetic to the idea but
worried that there might be legal obstacles; he wondered how "we could
prevent anybody else from coming in and being added to the list." The
bureau was hamstrung by competitive bidding procedures, especially on
production contracts, where it was possible, even likely, that a second
company would underbid the firm that had developed the aircraft in the
first place. Moffett saw it as the government's responsibility, in the absence of a viable commercial outlet for the products of the aviation business, to do all it could to encourage the industry, knowing that "if war
should break out there would be a tremendous urge to get what we need
in the shortest possible space of time."

Ultimately the government had to implement "a continuous building
program, so that we would have some assurance, and so that the industry
would know just what we would get not only this year and next year but
for several years." Without such a long-range plan, however, Moffett had
to accept the piecemeal approach, continuing to seek replacement aircraft
to meet immediate fleet needs. In fiscal year 1926, for example, the bureau asked for $9.3 million for new aircraft and equipment, most of which
was to be spent for the acquisition of large flying boats to replace the ag-
ing F-5-Ls attached to the scouting fleet.[11]

In spite of Moffett's and Land's arguments for new procurement policies that would give the bureau more flexibility in letting contracts and
bring a modicum of stability to the industry, change was not in the offing.
The bureau, nevertheless, remained in a strong position to influence the
direction of aircraft and engine manufacturing. By carefully distributing
development and production contracts, the bureau encouraged technological innovation and ensured that the service maintained a qualitative
lead over most of its foreign competitors.

One priority was metal aircraft construction. For naval aviation applications, metal had enormous attractions; compared with wood, steel and
aluminum alloys were more homogeneous, and they did not warp, splin-

ter, or absorb moisture. Although significantly more expensive than wood, metal promised to extend the service lives of airplanes, bringing long-term economies in operation and maintenance. Conversely, experience with light alloys (in particular, duralumin, an alloy of aluminum and copper) revealed that the metals were prone to fatigue fractures and an insidious form of intercrystalline embrittlement that greatly weakened them.[12]

Wisely, the bureau took an incremental approach to metal aircraft construction. Following through with a program that had originated in early 1920, the bureau worked with the Naval Aircraft Factory and two private firms—the Glenn L. Martin Company, a veteran aircraft manufacturer, and Charles Ward Hall, Inc., a New York City company with considerable experience with duralumin—to determine the feasibility of metal wing construction. Tests of the resulting wings in 1922 revealed significant weight savings and strength gains over wooden wings of the same size. At about the same time, Comdr. Holden C. ("Dick") Richardson, a 1901 academy graduate and holder of a master's degree in engineering from MIT, designed a series of duralumin floats for the Curtiss N-9, finding in the course of his work that thin metal sections required special protective coatings to resist corrosion in a saltwater environment.[13]

From wings and floats the Navy moved toward the complete metal airplane. By the spring of 1922, contracts had gone to Martin for the construction of observation aircraft using duralumin throughout and to the Stout Engineering Laboratories for an experimental all-metal torpedo bomber. Simultaneously, the Naval Aircraft Factory received an order for two all-metal marine expeditionary airplanes, designated NM-1, followed a year later by the inauguration of a long-term project to develop metal versions of the PN-type long-range flying boat. In 1924, Hall undertook a project to reconstruct a Curtiss TS fighter in metal, the object being to provide a direct comparison with conventional wood-and-fabric versions of the airplane. The results of these efforts in the early and mid twenties were mixed. As designers and engineers gained experience, they found that metal construction was no panacea and that much hard work remained before it would become the standard material for airplanes.[14]

The bureau's procurement policy and the key role it played in determining the course of technological change was equally evident in the development of the air-cooled radial engine. Moffett recognized that "something had to be done to reduce the weight and complication of the wartime aircraft engines," which were liquid cooled. Not only were they loaded down with heavy radiators, coolant, water pumps, and other accessories, but also the connections for their complex plumbing would loosen or come apart after several cycles of carrier landings and takeoffs.[15]

Moffett saw two courses of action open to his bureau. Either the bureau could handle the new engine design in-house, or it could establish the basic requirement and rely on the industry for design and development. He determined that the latter course was best. The Engine Section of the Material Division, rather than producing new designs, functioned as a central engineering office, setting requirements, soliciting bids from manufacturers, and testing the finished products to ensure that they met the needs of the operating forces. Proprietary rights were not as much of an issue with engines as they were with aircraft. In contrast to aircraft companies, only a handful of manufacturers supplied engines, and because of the typically long and expensive process of designing and developing a power plant and the specialized tooling needed to produce it, they had little to fear from potential competitors at the production end.[16]

The Bureau of Aeronautics inherited the air-cooled radial engine from the Bureau of Steam Engineering, which had a contract with the Lawrance Aero Engine Corporation for the design of a new power plant in the 200-horsepower category. Founded by Charles L. Lawrance in 1917, the company had worked closely with the bureau on the design and manufacture of the Model L, a three-cylinder air-cooled radial delivering 65 horsepower. In January 1920, Lawrance received a contract for the development of a nine-cylinder radial known as the Model J-1, intended for use in a new generation of airplanes designed to operate from the turret platforms of battleships. Lieutenant Comdr. Bruce G. Leighton, who had been responsible for aeronautical engine work in the Bureau of Steam Engineering, brought the Model J project with him when he came over to the new Bureau of Aeronautics to head the Engine Section. Although the first examples had trouble with the Navy's grueling fifty-hour running test, the engine showed enough promise for Jerome Hunsaker to use it as the starting point for the design of the TS-1, an exceptionally clean-looking, compact fighter intended for use aboard the carrier *Langley*. The Navy extended its commitment to the power plant by issuing a contract to Lawrance for the production of fifty J-1 engines.[17]

Oriented more to engineering than manufacturing, the Lawrance company was in a poor position to undertake even that modest production order. Realizing that and hoping to secure more competition in the field, the bureau approached the Curtiss and Wright companies in 1922 to ascertain their interest in the development and production of engines similar to the J-1. Curtiss rejected the overture, wanting to concentrate its efforts in higher-powered, liquid-cooled engines for the Army. Wright, on the other hand, had for a time considered manufacturing the J-1 for Lawrance or buying the Lawrance firm outright. After serious consideration, however, Wright rejected the bureau offer, reasoning that it was better to continue to manufacture and sell its liquid-cooled 180-horsepower Model E Hispano in an attempt to recover part of its high license fees, while simultaneously developing a more powerful air-cooled radial for the Army.[18]

Determined to get the engine it wanted, the bureau decided to force the issue with Wright. In 1922 and 1923, the bureau signed contracts with Lawrance for an additional sixty engines and advised Wright that it would not buy any more Model E Hispanos. When Army orders for its 300-horsepower Model H Hispano failed to materialize, Wright was left with few alternatives other than acceding to what the bureau wanted. Prodded by the Navy, Frederick B. Rentschler, Wright's president, worked out a deal in the spring of 1923 to buy the Lawrance company, and Charles L. Lawrance became a Wright vice president. The payoff for the bureau was immediate. Wright took over quantity production of the J-1, followed within a year by an improved version designated the J-3. The J-4, which came out in 1924, was the first to receive the famous Whirlwind name.[19]

Manipulation of production contracts and close attention to design and engineering had given the bureau the engines it wanted, but Moffett was still not entirely satisfied with the status of power-plant procurement in 1924. He recognized that the close association with Lawrance and Wright left his bureau open to political reproach for the creation of a monopoly in the air-cooled radial engine business, and he understood that the lack of competition in the industry might prevent the Navy from getting the best product at the lowest cost.[20]

Lieutenant Comdr. Eugene E. Wilson agreed with Moffett's assessment of the situation. One of Hunsaker's academy classmates in 1908, Wilson received a graduate degree in mechanical engineering from Columbia in 1915. In late December 1920, he was at Great Lakes serving as officer in charge of the Aviation Mechanics School. There he met Moffett, who stopped by the training station to see old friends while he was home in

Lake Forest on leave before assuming his new job as director of Naval Aviation. Moffett asked Wilson to join him in Washington as a technical officer in what was to become the Bureau of Aeronautics. Before doing so, however, Wilson served additional aviation duty with the seaplane tender *Wright* and for eighteen months was executive officer of the destroyer tender *Bridgeport*. Wilson finally arrived at the bureau in March 1924, succeeding Leighton as head of the Engine Section.[21]

Shortly after taking over his new responsibilities, Wilson, accompanied by Leighton, set off on a tour of engine manufacturers to measure their interest in developing a more powerful radial than the Whirlwind. Wilson reported to Moffett that Curtiss was deeply involved in liquid-cooled engines and was not proceeding quickly with an Army contract for a high-powered radial. Wright was almost wholly absorbed in production engineering for the Whirlwind but seemed willing to push the development of its large P-2 radial for the Navy and to undertake a separate project for the Simoon, a 350-horsepower engine derived from the P-2.[22]

Wilson's survey of the industry was not encouraging to Moffett, who remained determined to diversify the bureau's engine contracts. Fortunately, the opportunity to do so came when Rentschler left Wright Aeronautical in September 1924 and formed the Pratt and Whitney Aircraft Company the following year. With many of Wright's most experienced engineers and designers, Pratt and Whitney immediately went to work on a 400-horsepower radial for the Navy. Unlike its previous arrangements with Lawrance and Wright, the bureau did not pay for the company's entire development costs, but Moffett did assure Pratt and Whitney that the money would be forthcoming if the engine met the Navy's specifications. Wilson and the Engine Section staff worked closely with Rentschler's team through the summer of 1925 on the design of the new radial, guaranteeing from the start that it met the Navy's requirements. The result was the Wasp, one of the most successful radials of all time and the engine that placed Pratt and Whitney at the forefront of military and commercial aircraft engine manufacturing.[23]

Such new technologies as the metal airplane and the air-cooled radial engine were only part of Moffett's grand vision for the development of naval aviation. He also wanted the Navy actively engaged in air racing, which he justified as a means of proving high-performance airplanes and engines while nourishing cooperative relationships with aircraft and engine manufacturers. The continuing rivalry with the Army was another factor; it was easy for Moffett to rationalize Navy involvement in the sport because he knew that Mitchell had made a deep commitment to racing, and he was not about to let the Army air service go unchallenged. But his underlying motivation was his conviction that success in aerial competition would generate public excitement and interest in naval aviation.

For those reasons Moffett took a personal interest in the races sponsored by the Detroit Aviation Society in 1922. There were two major events, the Curtiss Marine Trophy Race and the more prestigious Pulitzer Trophy Race. Scheduled for 7 October 1922, the Curtiss race was an all-Navy affair, with eleven entrants flying Curtiss, Naval Aircraft Factory, Vought, and Gallaudet floatplanes. Moffett arrived for the event on the morning of the sixth, having taken a train from Washington to Chicago and then back to Toledo, where an H-16 flying boat picked him up for the short flight to Detroit. He was as disappointed as everyone else when officials delayed the race for twenty-four hours because of rain, fog, and high winds, but the results justified the wait. Navy and Marine aviators put on a spectacular performance over the twenty-mile triangular course, flying the base leg along the Detroit River downtown. The winner was Lt. A. W. ("Jake") Gorton, in a TR-1 racing variant of the Hunsaker-designed TS shipboard fighter, powered by a 220-horsepower Lawrance J-1 air-cooled radial engine.[24]

With his appetite for competition whetted by the Curtiss race, Moffett entertained great expectations for the Navy entries in the Pulitzer contest, held at Selfridge Field north of Detroit on 14 October. The Navy had originally entered eight airplanes in the competition, but three of its most advanced racers had to be withdrawn for various reasons. With nine entries, the Army enjoyed a tremendous numerical advantage. Predictably, Army Curtiss R-6s finished first and second in the race, but Navy Lieutenants Harold J. ("Hap") Brow and Alford J. Williams, Jr., came in third and fourth, both flying Curtiss CR-2s.[25]

Sorely disappointed by the Pulitzer defeat, Moffett tried to accentuate the positive by focusing on the lessons of the Curtiss Marine Trophy race. In an article in *Aviation* magazine, he wrote that the contest had been a laboratory for testing equipment and personnel under the most trying conditions and would bring long-term benefits in the form of advanced engine and airframe technology and improved operational methods. "We learned more from this contest of value in construction of material and in the training of personnel for duty under conditions approximating those of war than we could have learned in a year of ordinary operations," he wrote. "It shows the need for concentration of our effort in the Navy on the complete and thorough development of its Air Arm." On the whole, concluded Moffett, "the importance of seaplane racing in the Navy cannot be overestimated."[26]

Moffett was not being entirely candid in emphasizing the immediate technological benefits racing brought to naval aviation. Usually powered by highly tuned, liquid-cooled engines and incorporating specially designed airframes, racing airplanes were finicky thoroughbreds performing under circumstances totally alien to the normal operational requirements of naval aviation. No one would think of putting a racing engine through the rigorous fifty-hour running test required of a service engine before acceptance; racing engines were designed to produce maximum power for only brief periods, after which they usually had to be reconditioned or rebuilt. Moffett, however, felt compelled to reassure the taxpaying public that the Navy was spending its money wisely and that racing ultimately enhanced the construction and efficiency of combat aircraft; in reality, his main purpose was to show off naval aviation in a highly visible and competitive environment.

Moffett went into 1923 more determined than ever to use racing to show the country and the world the superiority of naval aviation. His resolution stemmed from both the Navy's defeat in the Pulitzer race and a feeling that he had been personally upstaged by Billy Mitchell. On 18 October 1922, Mitchell set a new world's speed record of 224.05 miles per hour over a one-kilometer course at Selfridge Field.[27] The implication was obvious: Mitchell, in contrast to the Navy's air chief, was first and foremost an aviator who had the skill and courage to do everything in the air he asked his subordinates to do.

The Navy's goal for 1923 was to win the coveted Schneider Trophy competition, an international event for seaplanes that had been renewed in 1919 after a four-year hiatus during World War I. The all-out effort included four immaculately prepared airplanes: the two Curtiss CR-2s fitted with twin floats and redesignated CR-3s, a Navy-Wright NW-2 with a huge 650-horsepower Wright T-2 engine, and the TR-3 from the 1922 Curtiss Marine Trophy Race modified with a Wright E-4 engine at the Naval Aircraft Factory and redesignated TR-3A. Arriving at Cowes, England, on 25 August, more than a month before the race was to take place, the Americans went through a carefully laid out series of trials, marred on 24 September when the engine of the NW-2 disintegrated, causing the airplane to crash. Fortunately, its pilot, Jake Gorton, was not seriously injured. Race day, 28 September, saw a resounding triumph for the Navy team, with Lieutenants David Rittenhouse and Rutledge Irvine finishing first and second in the CR-3s.[28]

The Schneider victory was only the first round in the Navy's aerial assault in the fall of 1923. Representing the service in the Pulitzer races at Lambert Field in St. Louis were four new airplanes: two Wright F2W-1s and two Curtiss R2C-1s. The Pulitzer competition was part of the National Air Races, a three-day extravaganza sponsored by the St. Louis Aeronautic Corporation and held in conjunction with the International Aeronautical Congress. Moffett arrived on time for the scheduled start of the races on 1 October, and the new rigid airship ZR-1 (later named *Shenandoah*) arrived the next day from her base at Lakehurst, New Jersey, but a soaking rain forced postponement of the events and threw everyone's plans out of kilter. Without mooring facilities, the ZR-1 could not possibly wait out the expected three-day delay in St. Louis. Reluctantly, Moffett decided to leave with the airship when she departed for Lakehurst on the second. The next two days were hectic. Determined not to miss the races, Moffett barely had time to catch up on his paperwork in Washington before boarding a Pennsylvania Railroad train with Jeannette and his daughter Janet for the trip back to St. Louis, where they arrived on the evening of the fifth.[29]

The Pulitzer races began the next afternoon. More than a hundred thousand spectators watched Al Williams flash four times around the triangular fifty-kilometer course in his R2C-1 at a blistering average speed of 243.67 miles per hour. Hap Brow finished second in the other R2C-1, followed by Marine Lt. Lawson H. Sanderson in an F2W-1 and Navy Lt. Steven W. Calloway in the other Wright racer. Exuberant with the Navy sweep, Moffett rushed over to Williams immediately after he landed and in an unusually affectionate gesture jammed his gold-braided cap on the aviator's head, saying, "You deserve it." Moffett stayed in town the next day for what he hoped would be an assault by Williams on the absolute speed record held by Army Lt. Russell Maughan, but adverse weather and the lack of trained observers caused the attempt to be postponed.[30]

With Moffett's approval Williams and Brow dueled in an exciting series of record attempts the next month at Mitchel Field, near the Curtiss factory at Garden City on Long Island. On 2 November, Brow defeated

Williams with a new record speed of 259.13 miles per hour over the three-kilometer course. Williams congratulated Brow on his achievement, vowing in the same breath that he would be back to take the honors away from him. Two days later, the pair again took to the skies. Williams went first, establishing a speed of more than 263 miles per hour, only to see Brow best it by more than 3 miles per hour. When it was Williams's turn again, he climbed to 9,000 feet and dove the R2C to within ten feet of the ground, blasting through the course at a new record speed of 274.20 miles per hour. Hearing of Williams's tactics, Moffett had second thoughts about the wisdom of continuing the dangerous contest and prohibited the aviators from diving. Unable to continue their high-speed rivalry, Williams and Brow capped off their competition on 6 November with a thrilling aerobatic display for the benefit of the Army Relief Society.[31]

With his aviators holding the Pulitzer and Schneider trophies and the world speed record, Moffett decided in January 1924 that because of fiscal constraints the Navy's only racing effort for the coming year would be the Schneider defense, planned for 24 and 25 October at Bay Shore Park outside Baltimore. On 4 August, the Navy announced that David Rittenhouse was to head the Schneider team, flying a 1923 Pulitzer R2C-1 equipped with floats and redesignated an R2C-2. Backing up Rittenhouse were Lieutenants Ralph A. Ofstie and George T. Cuddihy, in CR-3s, and Jake Gorton, whose airplane was a Wright F2W-2 modified by the Naval Aircraft Factory. Unfortunately, a combination of circumstances prevented the 1924 Schneider races. First, the Italians failed to decide on a suitable airplane in time to have it ready for the competition, then the lone British hopeful, a Gloster II, sank on its first test flight in September. Later that month, in a remarkable display of sporting magnanimity, the Baltimore Flying Club, sponsor of the Schneider race, canceled the event.[32]

Without a Schneider race and conceding the 1924 Pulitzer contest to the Army, the Navy fell back on a series of record attempts. On 27 September, Rittenhouse broke his own seaplane record in the R2C-2 with an unofficial average speed of more than 227 miles per hour over a 4.25-mile course off Port Washington, New York. No one was sure what the powerful F2W-2 might do, because Gorton lost control of the airplane and crashed during a test flight at Philadelphia on 10 October. The three remaining racers staged a series of speed trials over the Schneider course at Baltimore on 25 October. In his CR-3, Lieutenant Cuddihy established a world mark of 186.12 miles per hour over a straight 3-kilometer course, and in the other CR-3 Lieutenant Ofstie broke the old seaplane records for 100, 200, and 500 kilometers.[33]

Just as Moffett defended air racing as an opportunity to mesh technological advances with public spectacle, so too did he see the rigid airship as a means of stimulating innovation and promoting naval aviation. His initial interest in the giant lighter-than-air craft sprang from the Washington Conference. There he had developed an understanding of the strategic and tactical problems facing the Navy in the Pacific, particularly how the base fortification agreements circumscribed support of future fleet operations and how the quantitative and qualitative limits on aircraft carriers and cruisers affected the fleet's long-range scouting capabilities. The range and payload capacity of the rigid airship made it, in Moffett's mind, an ideal supplement to surface ships in the strategic reconnaissance role. To the chief of Naval Operations he wrote, shortly after taking over as bureau chief, "In the rigid airship we have a scout, capable of patrolling the Pacific in the service of information for our Fleet. . . . THE USE AND DEVELOPMENT OF RIGID AIRSHIPS IS A NAVAL NECESSITY."[34] With the airship came a bonus. The spectacular character and appearance of the airship and the nature of its operations made it perfect for showcasing naval aviation.

So inextricably has Moffett's name been linked to the rigid airship that it is easy to forget that the Navy had already made a considerable commitment to the airship well before he became bureau chief. Following the recommendations of the General Board and secretary of the Navy Daniels, Congress earmarked $7 million in 1919 for the creation of an entirely new domestic airship industry. The money was to be used for the construction of a large airship hangar at the naval air station in Lakehurst, building the airship ZR-1 in the United States, and the acquisition of the airship R-38 in Britain. Despite what appeared to be an excellent start on the airship program, it had bogged down by 1921. Progress had been agonizingly slow on the two-million-cubic-foot ZR-1, caused by delays in the airship's design and in the delivery of duralumin structural material. Girder fabrication did not start at the Naval Aircraft Factory until the middle of 1921, and actual erection of the craft at Lakehurst had to wait until the spring of 1922.[35]

Sensing that the delays threatened congressional funding and that support for the airship program was eroding in the Navy Department,

Moffett warned the chief of Naval Operations on 11 August 1921, "To fail to complete the ZR-1 will dissipate the organization of skilled technical personnel which has been built up and allow much of the material that has been assembled to deteriorate." Unless the service immediately released additional funds for the ZR-1 project, Moffett cautioned, the millions already invested by the Navy to establish the airship industry in the United States would inevitably be written off as a loss: "THE COMPLETION OF THE ZR-I IS AN ECONOMIC NECESSITY." Similar entreaties to congressmen that summer helped persuade secretary of the Navy Edwin Denby of the importance of the project and the need to channel more money in its direction.[36]

Moffett had little time to relish that victory before he had to confront additional threats to the Navy's airship program. A major blow came on 24 August 1921 when the British-built R-38 went down on a test flight in England. Built under contract to the U.S. Navy and shortly to have been commissioned in service as the ZR-2, the R-38 broke up and its hydrogen lifting gas exploded during maneuvers over the Humber River estuary. Of the forty-nine people aboard the airship, forty-four died, among them sixteen Americans. In the aftermath of the accident, Moffett said that he regretted the loss of life but hoped that development of the rigid airship would continue in the United States. He told the press, "We will carry on and build and operate as many big, rigid dirigibles as are necessary, so that these brave men shall not have given their lives in vain." Moffett also had the sad duty on 17 September of attending the funeral at the New York Navy Yard for the Americans killed in the airship disaster. Although ZR-2's loss was a severe setback to the nascent rigid airship program, it was far from terminal, and there were important lessons to be learned from the accident. Subsequent investigation revealed that the aerodynamic stresses imposed by low-altitude flight caused the airship's breakup. Studies also revealed that the airship suffered from fatal design and construction flaws, which the bureau's technicians had been worried about but were powerless to correct. Determined not to have a repetition of the ZR-2 disaster, Moffett decreed that henceforth all airships acquired from abroad must adhere strictly to bureau specifications.[37]

The loss of ZR-2 also focused attention on ZR-1, just beginning construction at Philadelphia. Determined that the American-built airship would not suffer the same fate as the British-built ZR-2 and needing to head off opposition to the Navy's airship program, Moffett in April 1922 asked the NACA to form an independent committee to review all aspects of the ZR-1's design. From June to October 1922 the committee held fifteen meetings, examined all of the Navy's aerodynamic calculations, tested material samples, and visited the Naval Aircraft Factory, where girders were being fabricated. The committee found that in general the ZR-1 design was sound, that the airship was structurally far superior to ZR-2, and that its workmanship was of the highest order. There was no danger, the committee judged, that ZR-1 would come apart as ZR-2 had during high-speed, low-altitude maneuvers.[38]

Secure in the knowledge that the airship had received a clean bill of health from the most prestigious aeronautical research organization in the country, Moffett pressed for her completion at the earliest possible date. By the middle of August 1923, the airship's hull had been finished and her gas cells inflated with nonflammable helium, but it was another few weeks before the craft was ready for her first flight. On 4 September, Moffett flew up to Lakehurst from Anacostia in a new Wright Chummy piloted by Al Williams, joining a throng of 15,000 who had gathered to see the glistening behemoth emerge from the big hangar and take to the air for the first time. During the flight, which lasted less than an hour, Moffett stayed in radio contact with the airship and her crew. Obviously pleased, he met with the press after the flight and told them he was "enthusiastic" about the results of the trial and looked forward to sending the airship on an expedition to the North Pole.[39]

As he had with the carrier *Langley*, Moffett determined that ZR-1 was to be used as much as possible to publicize the Navy's accomplishments in aeronautics. Consequently, instead of going through a rational program to prove the integrity of her design and construction, ZR-1 went out on a series of promotional flights, the longest of which was to St. Louis for the air races on 1 October. The airship's christening in Lakehurst a week later netted more commendatory publicity. The wife of Secretary Denby sponsored the airship, naming her *Shenandoah* during elaborate ceremonies in the hangar at the air station. Following the proceedings, Moffett, the Denbys, and other naval and civilian dignitaries embarked on *Shenandoah* for an hour-long flight out over the Atlantic, while motion-picture cameramen captured everything on film for newsreel audiences.[40]

In the fall of 1923, Moffett had great expectations for *Shenandoah*, and he was looking forward to the delivery of a second airship, under construction at the Luftschiffbau Zeppelin works in Friedrichshafen, Germany. The idea of obtaining a German airship had originated in 1919 with Capt. Thomas Craven, the director of Naval Aviation, but it took on new life when Billy Mitchell engineered an agreement to have the Zeppelin company provide a rigid airship with a capacity of 3.5 million cubic feet for the Army. Mitchell gave lip service to the airship's potential as a troop carrier and night bomber, but his principal objective was to use the airship as leverage in his aviation propaganda campaign. The Army airship contract added fuel to the already blazing interservice rivalry of 1919–20, particularly because it violated a 1918 understanding that rigid airship design and construction were Navy responsibilities. Furthermore, because the Senate had never approved the Treaty of Versailles, the United States and Germany were technically still at war, and the Army contract breached the Trading with the Enemy Act. As soon as he learned that the contract had been entered into despite stipulations from the Joint Army and Navy Board on Aeronautics against the purchase, secretary of War Newton D. Baker canceled the airship deal in December 1919.[41]

The plan to acquire a German airship was revived in 1921, when the Navy expressed interest in obtaining a craft from the Zeppelin company. The Versailles treaty permitted the United States to acquire two German airships as spoils of war, but their crews wrecked them before the Americans could take possession. In December 1921, following tedious diplomatic maneuvering, the Allied Conference of Ambassadors approved the construction of the airship for the United States as compensation for those destroyed, provided it was employed for civilian purposes only. Moffett dispatched Lt. Commanders Garland Fulton and Zachary Lansdowne, along with Lt. Ralph G. Pennoyer, to Germany in the winter of 1922 to iron out the details of the agreement with the Zeppelin company and to develop the general specifications of the airship. Fulton, a Construction Corps officer in the Material Division's Lighter-than-Air Section, had been transferred to Aeronautics from the Bureau of Construction and Repair with Hunsaker and possibly had more technical knowledge of airships than anyone in the bureau.[42]

As the airship project matured, the Army sent observers to Friedrichshafen to monitor progress on the craft's design and to feed technical information back to General Mitchell in Washington. When Moffett learned what Mitchell was up to, he was irate. To the American naval attaché in Berlin, Comdr. Wayman P. Beehler, Moffett sent a personal letter in May 1922 warning of interference by the Army: "There is an element in the

Army Air Service, which is sincerely and zealously advocating an independent air service, and [will] use anything they can lay their hands on as material to advance their arguments." Anticipating jealousy and friction between the services, Moffett reminded Beehler that "it is a NAVY ship and a NAVY project. The Army may and should keep in touch with it by means of such observers as they care to send, but there is no question of any joint control and in my opinion joint control will be fatal to getting results."[43]

Moffett's fears that the Army might somehow wrest control of the airship from the Navy never materialized, but Mitchell's meddling complicated the already tiresome negotiations between the Navy and the Zeppelin company and helped drag out completion of the airship's characteristics and its final design. Construction finally began in November 1922. There had been optimism that the airship would be ready by August 1923, but delays in the delivery of material and German fears that once they finished the airship the French would seize the construction facilities pushed the completion date back until August of the following year. Tests in Germany went smoothly, as did the eighty-one-hour transatlantic flight, ending on the morning of 15 October with ZR-3's arrival at Lakehurst. Moffett was not there to meet the airship or to congratulate her crew in person on their successful ocean crossing. At the moment ZR-3 touched down at the field in New Jersey, the admiral was on the other side of the country in San Diego, having recently completed a dramatic transcontinental flight in *Shenandoah*.[44]

Sensational as it was, *Shenandoah*'s flight to the West Coast was originally to have been only the first leg of a much more ambitious mission. Even before taking over as bureau chief, Moffett had had a vision of the potential of the airship for exploration. In a June 1921 press release titled "Airships and the Scientist," Moffett viewed the rigid airship as the ideal vehicle for survey flights to the Arctic. With its long range and great payload capacity, and possibly carrying airplanes as shuttles for side trips, the airship, Moffett believed, could facilitate geological, atmospheric, and astronomical research in both the Arctic and the Antarctic polar regions.[45]

In October 1923, secretary of the Navy Denby appointed Moffett to chair a seven-person board to study the feasibility of the aerial exploration of the North Pole. Moffett's committee presented an ambitious plan on 13 December. The committee proposed to dispatch *Shenandoah* across the southern tier of the country from Lakehurst to San Diego and up the Pacific Coast to Alaska. From Nome, the airship was to fly on to the pole, where it could turn around and return to its Alaskan base or, alternatively, continue on to the island of Spitsbergen in the Barents Sea north of Scandinavia. To support the airship, the expedition would require two oilers (*Patoka* and *Ramapo*), converted to seaplane tenders and fitted with mooring masts, and the erection of additional masts at Fort Worth, Texas, where the Navy had its helium production plant, and at San Diego, Camp Lewis, Washington, and Nome, Alaska. Six flying boats, operating from the tenders, were to conduct preliminary observation flights from Nome and Spitsbergen. The total cost of the expedition was to be nearly $7.5 million, but that sum was only $183,000 over the costs of normal air operations.[46]

It did not take long before the proposed expedition encountered turbulence. Moffett had become increasingly disenchanted with *Shenandoah*'s skipper, Comdr. Frank R. McCrary, who did not share his boss's enthusiasm for the rigid airship, even commenting publicly that *Shenandoah* would be lost in the Arctic wastes if she were sent on the journey. Interpreting McCrary's statement as insubordinate, Moffett saw to it that he was relieved of his command and chose Lansdowne to take over as the airship's commanding officer. In the meantime, congressional support for the project eroded. On 12 January 1924, the House Appropriations Committee, concerned about cost, weather hazards, basing arrangements, personnel, and other potential difficulties, met to consider the project. Secretary Denby explained to the congressmen that the expedition would provide an excellent test for *Shenandoah* as well as an opportunity to photograph and chart a one-million-square-mile region that was of great interest to the scientific community. If the United States did not carry out the mission within the next year, some other nation most certainly would; it was, in his opinion, a "matter of national pride." Four days later, a seventy-seven-mile-per-hour gust tore *Shenandoah* away from the mooring mast at Lakehurst, damaging her nose and top fin. Widely publicized, the accident was ample proof to many congressmen that Moffett's Arctic expedition was too risky. When the Appropriations Committee refused to allocate funds, President Coolidge canceled the project on 15 February.[47] Much to Moffett's chagrin, a little more than two years later a joint Italian-Norwegian expedition was the first to fly across the ice cap from Spitsbergen to Alaska in the Italian-built semirigid airship *Norge*.

As the year wore on, Moffett sensed that the image of naval aviation had blurred considerably. After the president canceled the Arctic expedition, the Army completed its around-the-world flight in September. The success of the flight was a particularly bitter pill to swallow, made no less distasteful by the relative lack of coverage of the Navy's crucial support role during the 175-day mission. Even worse, aviation in general and the rigid airship in particular had become targets of increasing criticism within the Navy. In an attempt to clear the air and mend political fences within the service, Moffett asked Rear Adm. Hilary P. Jones, the chairman of the General Board's executive committee, and Rear Adm. Joseph Strauss, the Navy's chief budget officer, to meet with him and other bureau officers on 23 September.

At the conference Jones wanted to know how the Navy could respond to the public relations bonus the Army had reaped from the global flight. He said, "I have yet to hear from General Patrick or General Mitchell in the public press or from the individuals or any person whatsoever on what the Navy did. What policy can you select that is going to get this thing before the public?" Lieutenant Comdr. Eugene Wilson suggested that someone in the bureau write an article praising the Army's accomplishment and the courage of its aviators while simultaneously getting in "some dirty digs about their dependency on the Navy" throughout the flight. Moffett said that the Navy had to be extremely careful: "If we gave out a criticism now on the Army around-the-world flight, the Bureau would be charged with jealousy." Captain Alfred W. Johnson directed his comments to Admiral Strauss when he insisted that the most constructive way to respond was to have everyone in the Navy come out solidly in favor of aviation.

Hoping to dispel the impression that he was opposed to aviation, Strauss explained, "I want to straighten that out because that is the reverse of true." He was opposed to the rigid airship, which he regarded as an extravagant waste of naval aviation's scarce resources. Of *Shenandoah* he said, "I have been very outspoken against it, would like to see it gotten out of the way, would like to see it stop taking 10% of your very little funds away from you which might very much better be devoted to getting airplanes." Moffett's response to Strauss was hardly forceful or convincing: "The policy of the General Board is to the effect that the SHENANDOAH is to be used to find out whether [rigid airships] are practicable for use with the fleet. We have spent nearly two million dollars on her and it is true that we are spending about 10% of the appropriation on her upkeep, but we have gone so far that the best thing to do is to go ahead."[48]

Moffett came away from the meeting convinced that a spectacular transcontinental flight by *Shenandoah* was just what naval aviation needed to bolster its sagging prestige. Because the planning had already been done for such a flight as part of the Arctic expedition, it was possible within a relatively short time to get *Shenandoah* ready for the journey, which would take her to San Diego and north up the West Coast to Seattle before turning around and retracing her course back to Lakehurst. Moffett orchestrated the publicity. He told Lansdowne that he wanted to be aboard for the flight from Lakehurst to Seattle and invited Junius B. Wood, a Chicago newspaperman, to come along as the press representative. He also wanted a cameraman on board to take movies of the flight, but he had to abandon the idea because the heavy motion-picture equipment exceeded the individual weight limits imposed by Lansdowne. Moffett himself said that he had to leave "a good many things at Lakehurst" before boarding the airship. Advance notices alerted communities along the route of the airship's estimated arrival times, assuring maximum newspaper and radio coverage. *Shenandoah* lifted off from Lakehurst on 7 October, cruising southwest over Washington, High Point, North Carolina, Atlanta, and Birmingham, Alabama, on the first leg of the flight to Fort Worth. Leaving there on the morning of 9 October, the airship climbed above the plains of West Texas and fought her way at night through the high passes of the southern Rockies, landing at North Island in San Diego early in the morning of 11 October after an all-too-exciting forty hours in the air.[49]

During the flight, Moffett spent most of his time in the control car, although he took breaks to join the crew in card games, prowl the airship's narrow catwalks, and listen to radio communications with the ground. He was impressed by the quietness and smoothness of the flight, especially compared with that of an airplane. The airship had only the simplest accommodations for the passengers and crew; Moffett slept in a tiny makeshift canvas bunk tucked away among the girders amidships and subsisted on cold sandwiches and coffee heated on a two-burner gasoline stove. Years later he wrote, "I have never before or since so thoroughly enjoyed an air voyage." The dangerous negotiation of the Rockies he regarded as a "thrilling adventure." He had nothing but praise for the cool professionalism of Lansdowne and his crew, who handled *Shenandoah* with "a great deal of nerve and skill."[50]

Shenandoah remained at San Diego for five days, while her crew repaired girders damaged when the inexperienced landing crew at North Island allowed the aft gondola to strike the ground. The airship finally slipped her moorings on 16 October, flew over units of the battle fleet exercising off San Pedro, and, bucking strong headwinds, slowly made her way up the coast. More than fifty-eight hours passed before the airship reached Camp Lewis on 18 October. There Moffett disembarked. He inspected a prospective site for an airship base at Sand Point, visited the Puget Sound Navy Yard, and toured the Boeing company's aircraft plant before boarding a train from Seattle to Minneapolis, where he delivered a speech on the twenty-seventh. In the meantime, *Shenandoah* had a comparatively uneventful return flight, arriving at Lakehurst late in the evening of 25 October.[51]

As congratulations on the flight poured in to the Bureau of Aeronautics, plans were already under way for ceremonies to christen ZR-3. Moffett insisted the event take place in Washington, despite the lack of mooring facilities at Anacostia or any other field in the area. Her gas cells inflated with scarce helium scavenged from *Shenandoah,* the airship departed Lakehurst on the morning of 25 November and appeared over the field at Anacostia that afternoon. While the ground crew struggled to hold the big ship in place, the president's wife, Grace Coolidge, braced herself against a biting wind and christened the airship *Los Angeles,* obviously in recognition of the California city but also connoting angels and peace. Moffett went aboard for the return flight to Lakehurst, where he inspected the air station the next day before flying back to Washington.[52]

Neither airship flew again for the rest of the year, but Moffett still had to be pleased with the progress that had been made since he had taken over as bureau chief. Not much had been accomplished to demonstrate how the big rigids might contribute to fleet operations, but they had generated an enormous amount of positive publicity for naval aviation. In spite of the chronic shortage of helium, the Navy had demonstrated its practicability as a lifting gas for large airships, and there had been significant improvements in ground handling and mooring mast techniques. Moffett looked forward to having both airships engage in more intensive exercises with the fleet in 1925, which he anticipated would include scouting, gunnery, refueling at sea, and possibly even hook-on experiments with airplanes.[53]

There remained, however, the problem of a shortage of airship personnel. The Bureau of Navigation had long insisted that no captain, commander, or lieutenant commander was eligible for promotion without at least two years of service at sea. Recognizing that this policy compounded the difficulty of attracting and keeping lighter-than-air officers, the Bureau of Navigation in 1923 proposed that officers could substitute two years of active service in airships for sea duty. That was unacceptable to Moffett, who argued that it discriminated against officers serving in heavier-than-air assignments and recommended that Navigation remove the lighter-than-air stipulation. In December 1923, the Bureau of Aeronautics suggested a specific alternative: "All duty performed on board cruising aircraft shall be held and considered as actual sea service on seagoing ships."

Nothing happened to the proposal until Lieutenant Commander Lansdowne complained in March 1924 that Navigation had insisted on shore-duty classification for all *Shenandoah* officers. On 8 July 1924, Moffett, Johnson, Lansdowne, and other Aeronautics representatives met with the General Board to discuss the question of sea duty for aviation personnel. Moffett explained the problem. "We found difficulty," he said, "in getting officers to go [to Lakehurst] and when they did go there they wanted to be transferred so that their promotion would not be interfered with." The ideal solution, Moffett continued, was to detach aviation officers for their obligatory two years of sea duty. But that rotation was not possible, because Aeronautics needed virtually all its officers on aviation duty and could not afford to have any of them away at sea. For the next few years, or until the number of officers undergoing aviation training increased significantly, Moffett wanted aviation duty—whether ashore or afloat in airships or airplanes—to be considered the equivalent of sea duty.[54]

The obstacles to promotion caused by aviation duty and the shortage of trained officers and enlisted men stemmed from limitations inherent in the bureau's organization and its responsibilities for personnel. General Order 65 of 10 August 1921 had specified that Aeronautics could only make recommendations to Navigation regarding the assignments and training of aviation officers and men; it could do nothing whatsoever about promotions and pay. Moffett was uncomfortable with the arrangement, but as the chief of a new bureau he did not want an immediate confrontation with the powerful Bureau of Navigation. Instead, he decided to chip away at its monolithic authority, confident that with patience and persistence Aeronautics would eventually win control of aviation personnel.

Moffett's first priority was to deal with the shortage of naval aviators.

In a letter to the chief of the Bureau of Navigation, Adm. Thomas Washington, on 19 November 1921 he said, "The lack of trained Naval aviators is now a serious consideration and one which requires immediate action if the efficiency of Naval Aviation is not to be impaired." Estimates were that the fleet air squadrons and shore units needed ninety-seven aviators by early 1922. With only sixty aviators per year graduating from Pensacola, it was impossible to make up the deficit until early 1923 or perhaps even early 1924. As fleet aviation expanded, the Navy would need about five hundred aviators in 1925, requiring Pensacola to turn out three hundred graduates over the next three years. Moffett appealed to Admiral Washington to authorize the expansion of Pensacola's biannual classes from thirty to fifty and called on him to "bring the situation squarely before the Commander-in-Chief and Commanders of all ships in the Fleet, with the request that they make every effort to obtain the required quota" of line officers for each class at Pensacola.[55]

It was not long before Moffett realized that requests for volunteers were not going to be enough to make up the shortage of naval aviators. Because "Commanding Officers and Executive Officers of the ships [in the fleet] are loath to see officers leave the ship" for aviation duty, a more direct and forceful approach was necessary. In March 1922, he called on Admiral Washington to detail two hundred recent academy graduates to aviation training at Pensacola through the middle of 1923. As another possible solution to the crisis, Moffett in June 1922 considered assigning a certain number of officers to aviation duty only, following the precedent for officers on engineering duty only. Flying officers who were "not necessarily qualified for other line duty" and some reserve officers might fit into the new classification. At the end of his first year as bureau chief, Moffett reported that "the situation regarding qualified aviation personnel is acute" and warned that "a handicap is therefore placed on the operations for the coming year."[56]

Not much happened to improve the situation in 1923. In May, Moffett informed the Bureau of Navigation that 358 aviators would be needed for fiscal year 1924, whereas on 1 July 1923, only 325 fliers would be available. The disparity between supply and demand grew alarmingly in succeeding years. Moffett said, "It can be seen that the number of Naval Aviators must be greatly increased. The rate at which officers are being assigned to aviation training at the present time is little more than sufficient to provide replacements." He suggested this time that it might be necessary to assign officers "to aviation duty regardless of the personal desires of the officers concerned." Although he was willing to educate officers in fleet and shore units of the need for aviators, Washington did not authorize any new classifications or detail recent Annapolis graduates and other officers to aviation training. He was playing a zero-sum game with Moffett. Because of a servicewide personnel shortfall in 1921–22, any additional officers and men he assigned to aviation would have to be pulled from the fleet or from shore assignments.[57]

The Naval Reserve was a potential source of naval aviators, but since the end of the war its reserve force had been allowed to run down to a condition Moffett considered "deplorable." There were two reasons for this situation. The first was that a relatively small percentage of aviation reservists passed an examination in May 1921 for transfer to the regular Navy, and those who had failed were released from service. That they did not do well was not entirely their fault, because the exam questions were biased toward the line officer who had had a great deal of sea experience. The second reason for Moffett's dismay was that no money had been set aside to allow reservists the minimum fifteen days of flight training, with the result that many aviators did not sign up again after completing their four years of service.[58]

Moffett placed a high priority on solving the reserve question over the next three years. In 1922, he succeeded in prying authorization from the Bureau of Navigation allowing the reservists to train for fifteen days with the fleet air squadrons on both coasts. He also proposed to the chief of Naval Operations a plan for thirteen new reserve units, equipped with two airplanes each, to allow the immediate enrollment of 1,000 reserve aviators and to provide preliminary flight training for 130 men annually. Later in 1922, he called on the commandants of all naval districts to organize aviation reserve units, and in 1923 he arranged the loan of Navy training aircraft to the police forces of New York, Boston, and Chicago, provided that the trainees in those cities joined the reserves. Largely as a result of a groundswell of enthusiasm among wartime aviators who wanted to keep flying, reserve units sprang up in 1923 and 1924 at Squantum, Massachusetts; Great Lakes; Hampton Roads; Pensacola; San Diego; and Lakehurst.[59]

A shortage of enlisted men in naval aviation compounded Moffett's anxieties over personnel. In April 1922, he wrote Congressman Lemuel P. Padgett, a Tennessee Democrat, that the current naval appropriation bill would result in a deficiency of nearly two thousand enlisted men, a reduction that would "cripple Naval aviation to such an extent that very little can be done for the Fleets." "I cannot bring to your attention too forcibly the above situation," Moffett concluded, "and hope that some action will be taken to provide for the number of men required for aviation duties." The cuts were not as drastic as Moffett anticipated, but for the 1923 fiscal year, enlisted personnel in aviation still declined from 4,600 to 3,700.[60]

Related to the shortage of naval aviators and enlisted men was the dearth of senior officers with aviation training. Moffett wanted his own men in important aviation commands ashore and afloat, but in 1922 few, if any, aviation officers had enough experience or seniority to fill such billets. The ingenious solution to this dilemma was the naval aviation observer. First offered by Lt. Comdr. Richard Byrd as a specific response to Mitchell's last-minute attempt to block Moffett's appointment with the requirement that the new bureau chief be an aviator, the classification became part of the 12 July 1921 bill authorizing the bureau's creation.

Captain Henry Mustin was instrumental in developing the observer's qualifications, which Moffett forwarded to the Bureau of Navigation on 27 March 1922. The observer was "a person whose duty is to relieve the pilot of a reconnaissance, or patrol airplane from the work of noting movements of enemy's vessels, aircraft, etc., in order that the pilot may concentrate solely upon his duties in connection with the manipulation of the aircraft." Following a physical examination, the officer selected for observer training went through a ground course including aerial navigation and chart reading; radio and visual communication; aerial gunnery, bombing, and fire control; naval and aerial strategy and tactics; recognition of types of surface and air craft; and aerial photography and meteorology. Before completing the course, students were taken up for "flights in aircraft in order that they may learn the practical application of the principles set forth in the ground school courses."[61]

Moffett was first to take the naval aviation observer course. After passing the physical examination, he left on 10 May 1922 for Pensacola, where he completed five weeks of training and received his observer appointment on 17 June. Everyone knew the course was little more than an expedient to ensure conformity with the letter of the law creating the Bureau of Aeronautics. But Moffett took a broader view. He saw the observer instruction at Pensacola as important indoctrination for senior nonaviation officers in the bureau. It was an opportunity for them to associate with aviators, learn some of the fundamentals of flight, do some flying themselves, and in general gain an understanding of the requirements of naval aviation. Immediately following Moffett, bureau officers Land, Hunsaker, and Lt. Commanders Sydney M. Kraus, W. W. Webster, and Robert M. Griffin received orders to report to Pensacola to take the observer course.[62]

Personnel problems extended beyond the ranks of commissioned and enlisted aviators to the bureau's technical staff. In the bureau were a considerable number of experienced engineering officers, many of whom had been inherited from the Bureau of Construction and Repair. As naval constructors these men were not line officers, and they were largely excluded from the lists of those who could advance beyond the rank of captain. There were ways to get around such restrictions, however. Some officers, like Dick Richardson, qualified as aviators, while others went through the observer course. Flight duty was important, but it was far from a guarantee of career advancement, especially with existing regulations demanding service at sea. Moffett knew that he had to do whatever was necessary to retain these bright and knowledgeable young officers.[63]

He was not entirely successful in his efforts, and there was a steady attrition of engineering officers who could see little promise in a Navy career. Hunsaker was among the first casualties. In November 1923, he received orders detaching him from the bureau and assigning him to duty as an assistant naval attaché in the American embassy in London. While overseas, Hunsaker maintained connections with the bureau. He provided useful intelligence on British and European aviation developments and assisted with the final inspection of ZR-3 before her transatlantic flight in 1924, but for all practical purposes he was lost from the bureau. In June 1926, he resigned his commission to take a job at Bell Telephone Laboratories, which he said was "an opportunity for useful employment in civil life" that he could not afford to miss. Captain George C. Westervelt, manager of the Naval Aircraft Factory and another capable engineering officer, quit the following year to go into private industry. There were similar defections from the lesser ranks; Moffett noted that fourteen other officers had either resigned or "divorced themselves from aeronautical work" by the middle of 1927.[64]

In 1924, Moffett began to wonder if he and his bureau would have to take more drastic action in the campaign to solve the personnel crisis. In a letter to Lt. Comdr. Newton H. White, Jr., an aviator serving with the

battle fleet on the West Coast, he intimated that the problem was fundamentally structural and that it was not amenable to solution through conventional organizational channels. There were more than enough graduates coming out of Annapolis to meet the staffing requirements of the
Navy as a whole and those of naval aviation, too. "It is my private opinion," he confided to White, "that the real trouble may be found to lie in
the fact that entirely too many officers of considerable experience are now
assigned to staff duties, communication duties, and similar details. There
is no doubt but that a certain number of officers must be assigned to such
work, but it seems to me that the more important assignments, such as . . .
aviation officers should be filled first."[65] Moffett's implication was that the
Bureau of Navigation had established the wrong priorities for the assignment of personnel and that ultimately the Bureau of Aeronautics would
have to assume more authority in that vital area.

After more than three years of fighting the personnel wars, Moffett
finally decided on 6 December 1924 to appoint a board headed by the bureau's assistant chief, Capt. Alfred W. Johnson, "for the purpose of inquir-
ing into and reporting upon the status of the personnel assigned to aviation duty as relating to the whole Navy." The board, which convened on
22 December, included Jerry Land, Kenneth Whiting, Lt. Comdr. Robert
R. Paunack, Lt. Comdr. Harold T. Bartlett, and Marine Lt. Col. T. C.
Turner.[66]

The Johnson board's findings, issued on 30 April 1925, amounted to a
sweeping examination of the entire aviation personnel question. Alleviation of the shortage of naval aviators demanded immediate attention. The
board recommended giving physical examinations and some flight training to midshipmen at Annapolis before sending academy graduates directly to Pensacola for flight training. The board also recommended detailing
senior officers to flight training and permanent aviation duties to bolster
the number of naval aviators eligible for command of shore units and aircraft carriers. The board saw no reason, however, to open up flight training to more enlisted men; historically, they had not done well in the
courses at Pensacola, and increasing the number of enlisted pilots meant
diverting seamen from the fleet, which already had manpower shortages.

Looking to the future, the Johnson board offered two alternative proposals. Whiting drew up the more conservative of the plans. It called for
obtaining 1,500 aviators by 1935 by increasing the classes at Pensacola
and detailing officers to tours on aviation duty. The Whiting plan ac-

knowledged that for some time senior command positions ashore and at sea would have to be filled by nonaviation officers. Lieutenant Commander Bartlett offered the second, more radical proposal, which suggested extending the bureau's control over aviation personnel through the creation of a separate air corps within the Navy. Moffett forwarded the Johnson board report to the secretary of the Navy on 3 July 1925. He concurred with the recommendations for increasing the class sizes and assigning recent academy graduates to Pensacola and for detailing other officers to aviation duty, but he did not agree with the Bartlett plan for establishing a separate corps. From the beginning he had been philosophically opposed to an air corps because of his firm belief that naval aviators should be naval officers first and fliers second.[67]

Exactly as Moffett anticipated, the report provided valuable political ammunition as the duel between the Bureau of Aeronautics and the Bureau of Navigation reached a flash point in 1925. Rear Adm. William R. Shoemaker, the chief of the Bureau of Navigation, developed a plan in June 1925 for the rotation of line officers to aviation duty. He insisted that aviators were no more specialized than other officers and that like their brethren they had to do their share of sea duty before taking on aviation assignments. To Shoemaker, the shortage of aviators could be easily made up by increasing the number of enlisted pilots, who he believed were just as good as if not better than aviators coming from the ranks of officers. The Johnson report was, in Shoemaker's opinion, "built about a predetermined opinion as to the position and specialized status of the naval aviator in the Navy, as distinct from an attempt to solve the aviation personnel problem of the Navy for the best interests of the service."[68]

As important as the personnel issue was in 1925, Moffett soon discovered that it was only one of many crises he had to face that year. He began the year with great expectations for increased aviation appropriations and for progress toward the approval of a long-term program for the procurement of aircraft. Another high priority was the continued development of fleet aviation, the construction of permanent fleet air bases in Hawaii and the Canal Zone, the early completion of the carriers *Saratoga* and *Lexington,* and the anticipation of the construction of a pair of five-million-cubic-foot airships to complement the two smaller craft already in the fleet.[69] Many of those objectives had to wait as the surge of events in 1925 swept Moffett and naval aviation along a more dangerous and unpredictable course than anyone could have expected only a few months before.

7

MOFFETT, MITCHELL, AND MORROW

IN MARCH 1923, MOFFETT RECEIVED A REPORT OF A BOARD HEADED
by Army Maj. Gen. William Lassiter. The Lassiter board found American aviation to be in a chaotic state and recommended creation of a semiautonomous air force organized to expand rapidly in time of national emergency and to undertake offensive missions independently of conventional military and naval forces. It also called for a ten-year program for the development of the peacetime Army air service, at the same time urging the Navy to come up with a similar plan to meet its own requirements.[1]

Secretary of the Navy Edwin Denby accepted the board's findings in principle before forwarding them to the Joint Army-Navy Board for further consideration. The Joint Board recommended pooling military aviation appropriations, with 60 percent going to the Army and 40 percent to the Navy. That was totally unacceptable to Denby, who on 18 February 1924 wrote that he discerned no "reason for proportioning the monies made available between the Army and the Navy." As far as Moffett was concerned, the proposal at best guaranteed permanent inferiority for the Navy in aviation appropriations and at worst sounded like the first steps in the creation of Mitchell's unified air force.[2] There was also the threat implicit in the Joint Board recommendation that if the Army reduced its spending for aviation, the Navy would have to, as well.

In response to these disturbing developments, Denby's successor, Curtis D. Wilbur, issued a directive on 23 September 1924 establishing a special board chaired by the chief of Naval Operations, Adm. Edward W. Eberle. The members included the chairman of the General Board's executive committee, Adm. Hilary P. Jones; the commandant of the Marine Corps, Maj. Gen. John A. Lejeune; the president of the Naval War College, Rear Adm. Clarence S. Williams; the Navy's chief budget officer, Rear Adm. Joseph Strauss; Rear Adm. Andrew T. Long; and Rear Adm. William W. Phelps. None of the board's members was a particular friend of aviation, but with Eberle in charge, Moffett expected at least a fair hearing. An 1885 Annapolis graduate, Eberle had succeeded Coontz as chief of Naval Operations in 1923. Like his predecessor, he had considerable understanding of and appreciation for the potential of aviation and was generally supportive of the need for expanding its role in the Navy.[3]

When the Eberle board convened on 30 September, it called Moffett as its first witness. He provided the board with a summary of technical developments and a succinct analysis of naval aviation policy as it had evolved over recent years. Aviation was, and would remain for the foreseeable future, an "auxiliary arm" of the fleet, its functions being to spot gunfire and to carry out reconnaissance, scouting, and strikes against enemy vessels with bombs and torpedoes. Moffett was careful to assure those present that the battleship was still the focal point of the fleet's offensive power. In response to Eberle's question, "Do you consider any future development of airplanes is going to minimize the value of the battleship and render it obsolete?" Moffett replied, "No, sir; I think that is foolish." But he did make a strong case for continuing the bureau's plans for fleet aviation. "I think we should complete this plan of putting planes aboard all ships," Moffett said. "We should try to get carriers or anything we could that would serve the purpose" of getting as many airplanes as possible at sea with the fleet. Carriers, he insisted, were "the most important vessels we are to get. . . . We should get all we can. . . . By not having all these airplane carriers, it is holding back our program in aviation."[4]

Continuing his testimony on 2 October, Moffett addressed the issues of a united air service and aviation personnel policy. Asked by Admiral Jones if "any greater war efficiency [would] be obtained by having a united air force, under a separate command," Moffett said that doing so "would be disastrous, especially for the Navy." Having "landsmen or soldiers telling us what we needed" was unthinkable and would mean "disaster for the country." He was "unalterably opposed to it." On the personnel question, Rear Admiral Long thought that possibly aviators did not appreciate that the Navy as a whole lacked sufficient officers and men and that they needed to be more patient while the service dealt with the problem. Moffett candidly admitted that his airmen were "enthusiasts and unanimously want to sacrifice everything about the Navy for aviation." But aviation needed extra attention if it was to "catch up as soon as possible," he continued. "We should at least decide if we're going to catch up. I, personally, think we might go a little short on surface ships to let aviation catch up. When we need [aviators] we will want them very badly. Every pilot we have will become an instructor on the outbreak of war."[5]

Next day Moffett focused on the rigid airship, providing an upbeat appraisal of *Shenandoah* and her operations over the previous year. Sensitive to criticism that the airship should have been sent to sea right away, Moffett emphasized that when she went into service the Navy had only one officer who was qualified to command an airship and only a small number of enlisted men experienced in handling them. She was still experimental, and her officers and men had much to learn about operating her under various conditions. *Shenandoah*'s "operations have been very profitable," Moffett said. "I think the people who have managed her have done very well. . . . I think her performance as a new ship compares very favorably with that of new battleships. When a new battleship is commissioned it doesn't join the fleet at once."[6]

Many other officers and civilians testified before the Eberle board over the next two months, but the one attracting the most attention was Billy Mitchell, who took the stand on 10 November. Compared with his firebreathing public countenance, Mitchell was unusually cool and thoughtful. But it was not surprising that he downplayed the Navy's role in coast defense and exaggerated the capabilities of land-based aircraft. Eberle had no trouble pinning him down. When Eberle asked whether he thought land-based aircraft would be able to "control the high seas unattended by surface or sub-surface craft," Mitchell replied, "Yes, I do. That's the end we are working toward in the air, Admiral." Nor did Eberle find it difficult to get Mitchell to repeat his statements in favor of a united air service. Yet when he fielded a question about the continued need for battleships,

Mitchell said that he "absolutely" agreed with the Navy that the battle fleet should be maintained at a high level of efficiency. After a Far Eastern tour earlier in the year, Mitchell believed that war with Japan was inevitable and that the country needed the big-gun ships to lead the sea and air charge across the Pacific.[7]

With some gratification, Moffett read the board's report when it came out on 17 January 1925. The board acknowledged that aviation had "taken its place as an element of the fleet and cannot be separated from it." The airplane, the board found, had important scouting and reconnaissance roles and as a strike weapon could inflict great damage on enemy fleet units. Above all, the Navy needed to hasten completion of its two big carriers and to lay down enough new hulls to bring its carrier force up to treaty limits. On the divisive issue of personnel the Eberle panel took a middle ground. It agreed with Moffett on the need for more aviators and that "flying officers must be above all naval officers first" but did not concur with him that they should be taken away from the fleet if necessary. Doing so, the board determined, would be "most injurious to the continued efficiency of the fleet in the performance of its mission."[8]

Aviation was for the board "a new and highly important factor in warfare both on the land and on the sea," but it remained complementary to conventional military forces. With its range and payload limitations, the airplane could not replace the battleship as the Navy's main offensive weapon. The board pointed to a recent joint war game played by the Army War College and the Naval War College that "in no way modified the conception held here that the airplane in naval warfare must be considered as an auxiliary weapon and not as occupying a primary role." It followed, then, that Mitchell's arguments for a unified air service were totally unwarranted.[9]

There was a predictability in the direction taken by the Eberle board. After all, it was a creature of the General Board, and it was unlikely Eberle would allow his group to venture too far from the naval aviation policy accepted by the General Board in 1922. On the other hand, there was no telling where the special congressional committee investigating the military air services might go with its probe or what conclusions it might come to. Chaired by Congressman Florian Lampert, a Progressive Republican from Wisconsin, the committee had been created in March 1924 to look into charges of collusion by the "aviation trust" in supplying aircraft and aviation material to the armed services.[10]

Since 1922, Moffett had worked out what he thought was a reasonable compromise with the aviation industry on aircraft and engine procurement. He had removed the major production functions from the Naval Aircraft Factory and had devised what he considered a relatively flexible procurement system combining negotiated and competitive contracts. But the industry had continued its downward spiral, and its leaders were determined to use the Lampert investigation to air their grievances. The Lampert committee had just been called together when Samuel Stewart Bradley, representing the Aeronautical Chamber of Commerce of America, the manufacturers' principal trade association, informed Moffett that the industry planned to make an all-out assault on military procurement policies. Moffett assigned Lt. Ralph Ofstie from the bureau's Plans Division to monitor developments as the Lampert committee organized its investigation and to attend the committee's hearings beginning in October 1924.[11]

Moffett was not really surprised that the first intimation of trouble from the Lampert committee was not testimony by aircraft manufacturers but by General Mitchell. On 17 December, Mitchell told the committee that the United States had fallen behind other powers in the development and employment of military aviation. Since the war, the country had spent between $400 million and $500 million on aviation, with little to show for it; the Army, for example, had only twenty modern airplanes. Mitchell insisted that the only solution to such waste and inefficiency was a united air service, which he claimed would be able to defeat any land or sea force and conceivably might make conventional armies and navies obsolete.[12]

Mitchell's allegations before the committee echoed those presented in a series of articles in the *New York World* by journalist Peter Vischer. Using an impressive array of data, Vischer wrote, "Every year instead of having more planes, we have fewer. We are spending huge sums for plans and establishments, but not for planes." During the preceding five years, $350 million had been spent on aviation, but only 1,618 airplanes were on hand, "all but a fistful of them obsolete or obsolescent." The situation, Vischer continued, had come about because of a "maze of government offices and bureaus" and the lack of a "responsible head" for aviation. In comparison, Britain, France, Italy, and Japan had rational aviation programs and had made considerably more progress than the United States had in obtaining sufficient numbers of high-quality military aircraft. Unless the president or Congress took the initiative in developing an aviation policy, and did so quickly, there was little reason to expect a solution to the problem.[13]

When Moffett saw the articles and excerpts from them in the *Literary Digest*, he dashed off a letter to the *World*'s editor on 19 December. He wrote that Vischer's articles had given the entirely erroneous impression that the Navy had been wasteful in its aviation expenditures and that there had been "gross mismanagement on the part of the administration of these activities." Estimates by Vischer that $350 million had been spent on naval aviation over the past five years were wrong. For the 1923 fiscal year, the bureau had spent $14.7 million on aircraft procurement and the maintenance and repair of shore stations. Salaries, fuel costs, transportation, and ordnance could be added, bringing the figure to $34.7 million, but aviation should not be charged for those expenses, because the bureau chief had no responsibility for their disbursement. As for alleged inefficiency in aircraft procurement, Moffett pointed out that 18.5 percent of the inflated figure of $34.7 million had been used to buy aircraft, a ratio nearly identical to what the British had spent that year. To Moffett this demonstrated "that there is just so much money that can be made available for new construction out of a total aviation appropriation" and that American taxpayers were getting their money's worth from his bureau.[14]

Moffett refuted all of Mitchell's charges before the Lampert committee on the afternoon of 22 December. The United States was not behind other nations in naval aviation: "Nobody is ahead of us; in fact we are leading." If the Army's aviation component was not as strong as it should have been, then Mitchell, as assistant chief of the air service, had only himself to blame. Moffett went on to say that Mitchell had grossly overestimated the capabilities of the airplane in combat and emphasized in contrast that "I do not claim too much for aviation. I want to keep my feet on the ground when I make statements. The air has not reached the point where it can operate across the ocean." Moreover, Moffett saw no reason for a unified air service along the lines proposed by Mitchell. The Army and the Navy had vastly different requirements in aviation, it was impossible for a unified air force to coordinate offensive operations at sea, and combined training was impossible because the requirements of a naval aviator were far more rigorous than those for an Army flier.[15]

When the Lampert panel adjourned for the year-end holidays, Moffett found time to relax and escape from some of the pressure of official business. As the years slipped by, Christmas and New Year's took on added importance for the Moffetts. Typically joyous occasions, they had become the only opportunity for the entire family to be together. By the end of 1924, the older Moffett boys, George and Bill Junior, were enrolled in boarding schools and were away from home most of the year. Janet, the eldest sibling, had turned twenty-one and within the next two years would marry and strike off on a life of her own. Bill Junior had vivid memories of Christmas and New Year's as heartwarming private occasions. There was always a beautifully decorated Christmas tree, and Bill and the other children looked forward with wonderful anticipation to the opening of presents. New Year's 1925 was typical. That year a winter storm had spread a fresh blanket of snow over the city as the family gathered in the living room of the big house on Massachusetts Avenue. At the stroke of midnight, they opened the French doors at the front of the house and listened to the whistles and horns of celebrants who had taken to the streets heedless of the inclement weather. Despite Prohibition, the admiral and his wife drank champagne toasts and wished each other and their children the best for the year to come.[16]

Following the recess, the Lampert committee went back to work, hearing testimony from individual aircraft manufacturers. To a man, they blamed the government and its contract procedures for the aircraft industry's ills. The manufacturers accused the Navy of unwillingness to recognize proprietary design rights and pointed to the large design staffs in Washington and Philadelphia as evidence that the bureau wanted to deprive manufacturers of a major portion of their livelihood. Another irritant was the Navy's penchant for using a particularly innovative company to develop a new aircraft design and then rewarding the more lucrative production contract for the airplane to one of that firm's competitors. The Curtiss Aeroplane and Motor Company felt particularly slighted when it spent a great deal of money on the design for the CS torpedo bomber in 1922–23 only to lose the production order to the Martin company.[17]

Rather than responding to the critics himself, Moffett decided that it was best to let his subordinate officers testify on specific points raised by the aircraft industry. It was an effective strategy, demonstrating to the committee that he was in full control of a knowledgeable staff, in contrast to Mitchell, whose theatrical appearances were filled with rash, unsubstantiated accusations. Moffett's approach also refuted Mitchell's charges that some officers had been muzzled by their superiors to prevent them from giving testimony critical of the services. Johnson, Land, Whiting, and many junior officers appeared before the committee from the middle of January through early February 1925. They addressed a kaleidoscope of issues and answered countless questions about appropriations, pay, procurement policy and procedures, aircraft and engine costs, and the functions of the Naval Aircraft Factory.[18]

Meanwhile, Moffett stayed discreetly in the background, interjecting only when committee members asked him a specific question or when he thought clarification or amplification was necessary. On 29 January, he decided that it was time to explain the bureau's side of the CS story. He said that the bureau respected the engineering expertise of the Curtiss company and was "very anxious to help them out" with a production contract on the CS. But Curtiss's bid of $40,000 per airplane far exceeded the bureau's estimate of $25,000. The unit price "was exorbitant, and we talked to them and told them so." Eventually Curtiss reduced its bid to $30,000 per airplane. "We did try, when they came to a lower price, to give it to them as a proprietary article," Moffett said, but on the advice of the judge advocate general the secretary of the Navy put the contract out for competitive bidding. Moffett believed that the Navy had bent over backward to help Curtiss and that whatever competitive disadvantage the firm experienced was of its own making and not because of the Navy's unfairness or wrongdoing in awarding the CS contract.[19]

In further testimony on 31 January, Moffett did his best to thwart what he sensed was a rising tide of sentiment in favor of a united air service. In his years as bureau chief, he had been responsible for creating something that "was not in existence before; that is, in the way of naval aeronautics. We have built up aviation in the Navy; we have organized a fleet of planes to go with the ships; we have adopted a doctrine; we have now a definite plan for aviation which is based on the treaty Navy." He wanted to see naval aviation continue to advance as it had in the past and worried that the advocates of a united air service, by overselling the capabilities of the airplane, were doing more harm than good. Fortunately those calling for a separate air force were in the minority. He believed others—the president, the service secretaries, the Army's general staff, and the Navy's General Board—shared his opposition to a united air force and supported his ideas about the importance of having the Navy control its own aviation.[20]

Moffett studiously avoided any references to Mitchell during his appearances before the Lampert committee in early 1925, but in private he was much more willing to express his real feelings. He wrote to Capt. Pete

Symington on 16 February that the most recent dispute with Mitchell was only the latest iteration of what had been going on for the last seven years. When he relieved Craven in 1921 as director of Naval Aviation he inherited the feud. He said he had tried to handle it differently from Craven, who would no longer even speak to Mitchell, but Mitchell "attacked me personally in the newspapers, so the war was on, and I battled as well as I knew how almost alone until recently. A part of my campaign consisted of trying to let the public know that the Navy had some Aviation. This required going to the newspapers and the public." The Navy's involvement in air racing and the proposed polar flight of *Shenandoah* were all part of Moffett's concerted effort to get the message across that naval aviation was a real and potent entity. Because publicity was anathema to many officers in the Navy, his campaign against Mitchell had cost him friends and supporters within the service. Why had he done it? "It would be much easier and more comfortable to keep out of it entirely," Moffett confessed, "but what I have done in this matter I have done for what I believed to be to the best interest of the Navy, although personally I have suffered considerably."[21]

Few of Mitchell's public allegations aroused Moffett's ire more than his statement on 31 January before the Lampert committee that the Navy was suppressing the "real truth" about the results of bombing tests on the hull of the unfinished battleship *Washington*. Scheduled to be scrapped under the terms of the 1922 Five-Power Treaty, *Washington* was a modern super-dreadnought with beefed-up armored decks to protect her against aerial attack. The experiments had taken place in November 1924 about thirty miles off the Virginia Capes. Mitchell disputed the Navy's contention that the ship had stood up under a simulated bombing attack and insisted that Army bombers could have sunk the ship in a matter of minutes. Later he told the committee that the tests were totally unrealistic in that "no bombs were used on the Washington in any shape, form or fashion." Instead, Navy aircraft dropped dummy armor-piercing projectiles and set off fixed charges in the water alongside the hull to determine their blast effects. He also said that it was untrue that conventional shells sank the battleship, because she was already going down when the surface vessels opened fire.[22]

Away from the Lampert committee Moffett felt obliged to respond to Mitchell's accusations. Mitchell had asserted "in a boastful way, that Army aviators with bombing airplanes could have sunk the WASHINGTON in from two to four minutes." The object of the test was not merely to sink the ship, he said; "One sailor could have done this by simply opening the seacocks." Rather, "the Navy's purpose in the sinking of the WASHINGTON was to gain as much technical information as possible as to the actual effectiveness of various types of explosives on a ship of that design and construction." Moffett went on to explain that the Navy had dropped dummy bombs from various altitudes to determine their ability to penetrate the battleship's thick armored skin, and the underwater explosives had been detonated at specific distances from the ship to ascertain hull damage from near misses. The *Washington* experiments had yielded data "of the greatest military value" that would have been impossible to obtain had the ship been sunk by concentrated aerial bombing.[23]

An especially disturbing report emanating from the Lampert hearings was that Moffett and Mitchell were to be disciplined for their advocacy of aviation and that neither would be reappointed to their respective positions. Congressman Randolph Perkins of New Jersey, the committee examiner, said on 4 February 1925 that he had heard earlier in the year that Moffett and Mitchell had been considered too "enthusiastic and progressive" by conservatives in the Navy and the Army and that both would be demoted.[24]

Moffett had little fear of being demoted, but he did take seriously the rumors flying about Washington that he might not be reappointed as bureau chief. He knew that his reappointment ran counter to a strong tradition in the service that a bureau chief should serve only one term, but he was generally confident that he would receive special consideration because of the need for continuity in the new bureau. Nevertheless, Moffett was not taking any chances. Just as he had before his first appointment and well before Perkins revealed that his career might be in jeopardy, Moffett asked Bill Wrigley to speak to the president on his behalf. Wrigley did so, and Moffett thanked him for his intercession: "I am mighty glad you saw the Big Chief, and it was very good of you to take advantage of the opportunity the way you did."[25]

To another of his influential Chicago friends, J. Ogden Armour, Moffett wrote on 11 February that although there was "nothing to justify" the rumors of his being disciplined, "I do think that there may be some doubt as to my being reappointed as chief of the Bureau of Aeronautics." His appointment was a presidential one and due to expire soon. "I am writing to ask you if you will help me in the matter by writing to the President in such way as you may see fit, saying that you have seen this report in the newspapers and recommend that I be reappointed. . . . I think it is important to give as the cause of your writing the fact that you have seen the newspaper reports that I was to be disciplined or would not be retained; otherwise the President might feel that I was trying to use influence in the ordinary way."[26]

As it turned out, there was little question of Moffett's reappointment. Coolidge announced it at a cabinet meeting on 10 March, and the Senate confirmed it the following day, with the official reappointment coming on 13 March. Moffett wrote to Bill Wrigley that day. "I am writing at once to tell you how grateful I am to you. I feel that what you did with the President was the deciding factor." He went on to say, "My reappointment means very much to me, not only professionally but personally, for reasons which you know, and I will always feel that I am indebted to you for it."[27]

As for Mitchell, the rumors that he would not continue as assistant chief of the air service proved to be true. A series of articles by him had appeared in the *Saturday Evening Post,* the last of which, in March 1925, accused senior Army and Navy officers of myopia when it came to seeing the power and importance of military aviation. Moffett thought that it was "outrageous" that the magazine had seen fit to publish the articles. Secretary of War John W. Weeks was even more upset. He had already decided in early February that he wanted to hold up Mitchell's reappointment while he looked into some of the statements he had made in favor of a united air service. Now he had had enough. On 6 March, he recommended to the president that Mitchell be replaced by Lt. Col. James E. Fechet, formerly commanding officer of Kelly Field in Texas. Accordingly Mitchell lost his temporary rank of brigadier general and on 30 March received orders to take command of aviation in the Eighth Corps area at Fort Sam Houston, near San Antonio, Texas. It was the first step in the making of an air-power martyr, for Mitchell had vowed that he would not remain silent on matters he considered vital to the national defense.[28]

A welcome break in the battle with Mitchell came on the afternoon of 20 February, when Moffett and forty others, including assistant secretary of the Navy Theodore Douglas Robinson, boarded the airship *Los Angeles* for a trip to Bermuda. The flight and subsequent operations through the first half of the year provided experience and training for the airship's crew and allowed them to practice mooring techniques with the mast that had been erected on the stern of the fleet oiler *Patoka*. Moffett wanted to display the Navy's latest acquisition and demonstrate some of the airship's possibilities for long-distance passenger travel. In contrast to *Shenandoah*'s spartan accommodations, *Los Angeles* featured a luxurious passenger compartment consonant with her nonmilitary role. During the outbound voyage, Moffett told a newspaper reporter (who had been invited along to give firsthand impressions of the flight) that he looked forward to the trip as a vacation; after all, that was why one went to Bermuda. But in this case, it was the airship's ability to overcome time and distance that was most impressive. Moffett said he could fly to Bermuda in about twelve hours, spend two days there, and in another twelve hours be back at his desk in Washington, having lost only one full day's work. It was, he prophesied, "a forerunner to what any one may enjoy in a few years."[29]

Far from heralding a new age of airship travel, the Bermuda flight of *Los Angeles* demonstrated that lighter-than-air operations were still a long way from becoming routine. The flight to Bermuda was unremarkable, taking just under the twelve hours estimated by Moffett, but once the airship reached the island heavy squalls and contrary winds delayed the mooring procedure so long that the airship's commanding officer, Capt. George W. Steele, doubted whether the ship had enough fuel for the return trip. Steele deferred the matter to his executive officer, Comdr. Jacob H. Klein, who decided against mooring to *Patoka* and set a course back to Lakehurst. *Los Angeles* arrived at the air station early in the morning of 22 February after spending more than thirty-three hours in the air. Interviewed shortly after stepping off the airship, Moffett made the best of the flight. He was "thoroughly satisfied with the behavior of the ship." There had never been an imperative that she land at Bermuda, because the journey was merely "an experimental trip made to demonstrate the ability of the Los Angeles and to train the crew." The flight's duration convinced Moffett that *Los Angeles* had the range expected of her, and he speculated that she might even be flown to England sometime during the summer.[30]

Moffett thought of *Los Angeles* primarily as a means of promoting the commercial and military possibilities of the airship. The transatlantic flight would have garnered tremendous publicity for the Navy's airship program, but it was a technical impossibility: inflated with hydrogen, *Los Angeles* had just enough range to fly across the ocean; with helium, she did not. Instead, *Los Angeles* returned to Bermuda in April, this time successfully mooring to *Patoka*'s mast. She also made a highly publicized flight to

Puerto Rico where, using *Patoka* as a temporary base, she took on fuel, water ballast, and helium before circumnavigating the island and returning to Lakehurst. On 15 May, Moffett, Admiral Jones, assistant secretary of War Dwight F. Davis, and a large contingent of businessmen boarded *Los Angeles* at Lakehurst for a seven-hour cruise around the Philadelphia area. Moffett carefully managed the news coverage. Among the thirty-three passengers were a reporter for a local radio station and the editor and assistant editor of the *Saturday Evening Post,* invited to woo the *Post* away from the Mitchell camp. After the flight, Moffett confidently told the press that many of the industrialists now believed in the potential profitability of the airship and that there was no reason why craft of the *Los Angeles* type could not soon go into commercial service.[31] Behind Moffett's enthusiastic press releases about the immediate commercial application of the rigid airship lay his belief and expectation that the Navy had to encourage an American airship industry to support the service's lighter-than-air program.

Moffett also wanted to use the Navy's airships in 1925 to show the American public the great exploits of naval aviation and to foil Mitchell's propaganda for a unified air service. On the evening of 27 April, he gave a lecture in Baltimore before two hundred members of the local sections of the American Society of Mechanical Engineers and the American Institute of Electrical Engineers. He put on a professional performance before a professional audience. Without making any direct references to Mitchell, Moffett explained that aviation was not a panacea, that the nation would continue to rely on its traditional armed forces for defense for many years to come, and that the Navy's special requirements meant that it had to exercise control over its own air arm. Three reels of movies highlighted the speech, showing recent naval air maneuvers, landings on the carrier *Langley,* views of *Shenandoah,* and the 7 April launching of the big carrier *Saratoga* in New York. The response to the presentation was exactly what Moffett wanted. In a letter of thanks, one of the engineers said that everyone commented on Moffett's "diplomatic manner" and the "moderation and conservatism" of his arguments against a separate air service.[32]

The moderate tone of the Baltimore speech typified Moffett's nonconfrontational strategy in his rancorous quarrel with Mitchell. At every opportunity Moffett noted that the Bureau of Aeronautics cooperated with the Army air service to eliminate duplication in experimental projects, the procurement of materials, testing, and the training of personnel. Naval officers served tours at the Army air service's engineering complex at Mc-Cook Field in Ohio, and the Army reciprocated by detailing some of its people to temporary duty at the Naval Aircraft Factory. A day before Mitchell learned of his transfer from Washington to Texas, the Navy and the Army announced an understanding to pool their resources in developing three airplanes to compete in that year's Pulitzer and Schneider races, bringing to an end three years of intense head-to-head aerial rivalry between the services.[33]

Privately Moffett still chafed at the public relations coup Mitchell and the Army air service had pulled off in 1924 with the success of the around-the-world flight, and he was determined that the Navy would do something equally spectacular in the air. The transcontinental flight by *Shenandoah* had been an enormous publicity generator, but Moffett was not entirely satisfied that it had been enough to offset the Army's accomplishment. Throughout the remainder of the year, Moffett brainstormed with his staff on a project that they hoped would upstage the Army once and for all—a nonstop flight from the West Coast to Hawaii.

The Hawaii flight had its origins in a memo from Moffett to the secretary of the Navy in November 1923. Mindful that Army plans were already under way for a globe-circling flight during the summer of 1924, Moffett wanted to preempt the rival service by staging a similar flight earlier in the year. Starting from New York in January 1924, Navy aircraft were to fly across the country to San Diego, where they were to be fitted with floats. From San Diego the airplanes were to continue up the coast to San Francisco, which was to be the jumping-off point for the Pacific leg of the flight. On or about the first of February, the aircraft were to fly to Manila via Honolulu, Midway, Wake, and Guam. Continuing westward from the Philippines, the flight would cross the Indian Ocean to Ceylon, Aden, Suez, through the Mediterranean to Gibraltar, and then leap the Atlantic to return to the United States. By far the most challenging part of the odyssey was the Pacific crossing, the key to which was the 2,100 nautical miles from San Francisco to Hawaii—the longest continuous overwater stretch on the planet.

Moffett justified the flight on several levels. "There's the publicity aspect, to be sure," he admitted. "We like to go on record as being opposed to advertising in the Navy, [but] if we consider advertising a sin, why do we observe Navy Day once a year, . . . why do we have parades, send ships to various ports for Old Home Week, and aircraft to country fairs and carnivals around the country?" The operation also had strategic and tactical value. Because the fleet in all likelihood would have to cross the Pacific in the event of war with Japan, it was time to see if aircraft could accompany the ships. "A flight clear round the world over a route which includes crossing the Pacific will tell the story in no uncertain terms," he asserted. He also saw the project as another way to blunt the arguments of the unified air force advocates, who were sure to point to the Army's flight as further proof of the efficacy of air power in a global offensive role. "Since there is always the danger of political pressure taking control of Naval Aircraft out of the Navy, can we afford to let the Army beat us to a 'round-the-world flight, and place in the hands of the separate Air Force proponents an argument that the Navy left it to the land lubber to show the possibilities in one of the strongest potential weapons in warfare?" Few people were sophisticated enough to understand that the Army airplanes did not have the range to fly across the mid-Pacific and would instead have to skirt the ocean's northern rim. All they would hear was that the Army had flown around the world.[34]

Moffett's ambitious scheme to beat the Army around the world never materialized, largely because of cost considerations and Secretary Wilbur's unwillingness to pull ships away from winter maneuvers in the Caribbean, but he did not give up on the idea of flying the Pacific. On 8 November 1924, Moffett sent another proposal to the secretary of the Navy, calling for a flight from San Diego to Australia by three Dayton-Wright SDW single-engine, long-range scouts. Two of the aircraft, fitted with floats, were to refuel at sea on the first leg of the flight to Hawaii, and the other, flying as a landplane, was to make the attempt nonstop. In Honolulu, the landplane would be equipped with floats, and all three aircraft were to continue on to Brisbane by way of Palmyra and Phoenix islands, Pago Pago, Fiji, and New Caledonia.[35]

Wilbur passed the proposal on to Admiral Coontz, commander in chief of the U.S. Fleet. One of Moffett's friends in high places and deeply sympathetic to naval aviation, Coontz rejected the Pacific flight on the grounds that it would divert too many of the battle fleet's resources. Instead, he recommended that Moffett press for a nonstop flight from either San Diego or San Francisco to Hawaii, using twin-engine, long-range flying boats then under development at the Naval Aircraft Factory and the Boeing company in Seattle. Elements of the scouting fleet could be used as station ships and in logistical support roles.[36]

Moffett had hoped for more, but he was realistic enough to know that a Hawaii flight was all he was going to get at the time. He assigned the responsibility for preliminary planning for the flight to Captain Johnson, who presented the results of his work to Admiral Eberle on 14 April 1925. According to the plan, the two flying boats from the Naval Aircraft Factory were to be ready for shipment to San Diego by 1 June, and the Boeing aircraft by the middle of July. The flight was scheduled for the first week of September. Johnson was confident that "all three planes will be capable of cruising a distance of 2,000 sea miles or more on the tank capacity, and it is probable that considerable additional mileage over the ground may be obtained by taking advantage of the trade wind conditions." Guardships would be stationed at 200-mile intervals along the route from the West Coast. Eberle approved the project on 20 April.[37]

Ultimately, the success of the flight hinged on two factors: the performance of the three flying boats, and the ability to forecast the weather accurately enough to ensure that the airplanes had favorable winds. The two aircraft from the Naval Aircraft Factory, designated PN-9s, were not ready for their first flight tests until April. Even then, they did not meet the thirty-hour endurance requirement considered essential for the Hawaii flight. At Philadelphia on 2 May one of the metal-hulled PN-9s set a new flying-boat record of more than twenty-eight and a half hours, but that still did not meet the minimum necessary to reach Hawaii. Nevertheless, the assumption was that improvements to the efficiency of the PN-9 engines, combined with fortuitous weather conditions, would give the airplanes enough range to reach the islands. Encountering even more problems, Boeing did not have its airplane, designated PB-1, ready for flight tests until early August, less than a month before the scheduled date for the attempt.[38]

As for the weather, Moffett had supreme confidence in the bureau's tiny but skilled meteorological team, led by Lt. Francis W. Reichelderfer in the Flight Division. Reichelderfer believed that the flying boats would benefit from tail winds at the latitude they planned to fly, but given the state of the art in 1925 there was no way he could be certain. He was just beginning to piece together a system of weather stations, enabling him to make reasonably accurate long-range forecasts based on the Bjerknes model of frontal analysis, and he was hampered by a lack of adequately trained officers and enlisted men. The bureau had the best weather men in the business in the mid-twenties, but they were still not good enough to provide the forecasts needed for such an inherently risky operation as the Hawaii flight.[39]

Out in San Diego, Comdr. John Rodgers, an Annapolis graduate in the class of 1903 and naval aviator number two, was in charge of the flight unit. With a great deal of effort he solved most of the lingering material deficiencies of the PN-9s, which, to meet the tight schedule, had been crated and shipped from Philadelphia without a thorough inspection. On 23 August, all three flying boats converged on San Francisco, which had been selected as the jumping-off point for the flight.[40]

Moffett, meanwhile, closely monitored developments and went ahead with his own plans for a month-long inspection tour of the West Coast and Hawaii that he hoped would give him the opportunity to see the flight off. He left Washington by train on 2 August, stopping at Chicago on the way to San Francisco, where he embarked on the Dollar Line's *President Cleveland* for Honolulu, arriving there on the fourteenth. On Oahu Moffett spent nearly a week touring Army and Navy aviation facilities and inspecting the recently completed airship mooring mast at Ewa near Pearl Harbor. He told the press that the planned flight to Hawaii presaged regular airmail and passenger service with the mainland in the "near future." The flight, Moffett added expansively, was the "most important event in naval aviation since the World War." By comparison, the around-the-world flight had done little to advance the Army air service's mission, he said, and the Hawaii flight would prove the capabilities of Navy aircraft in long-range patrol operations with the fleet.[41]

Planning to see the departure of the three flying boats, Moffett boarded the liner *President Taft* in Honolulu on 20 August for the six-day return voyage to San Francisco. Unfortunately, despite all the efforts of Commander Rodgers and his unit, only two of the airplanes were ready; PB-1's engine mounts had been seriously damaged on the flight from Seattle, and repairs were not possible before the flight scheduled for 31 August. On the evening of 30 August, Moffett met with Rodgers and Lt. Comdr. James H. Strong, PB-1's commanding officer. Strong argued for a two-day delay to allow him to complete repairs on PB-1, but Moffett reluctantly decided that the attempt would be made the next day by the two PN-9s. If and when Strong got his aircraft in shape, he and his crew might be permitted to make the flight alone.[42]

Next day the two PN-9s completed fueling and preflight checks and arrived under tow at their takeoff points in San Pablo Bay by 1400. Moffett came out to the airplanes in a launch. He shook hands with Rodgers, handed him two commemorative letters to carry with him to Honolulu, and wished the aviators well on their historic journey. The heavily laden flying boats struggled into the air and turned westward through the Golden Gate as Moffett returned to shore and awaited the first reports on the progress of the flight from the guardships stationed along the route.[43]

Less than five hours into the flight, the PN-9 commanded by Lt. Allen P. Snody suffered an engine failure and made a perilous landing at sea. Early the next morning, a destroyer located the downed flying boat and took her under tow back to San Francisco. But reports from the station ships indicated that Rodgers and his aircraft were making good progress toward their goal; there was every reason to believe they would complete the flight. Later in the day, Moffett, in a gesture of confidence in PB-1 and her crew, went up in the airplane for a one-and-a-half-hour test flight around San Francisco Bay. At the time, everyone expected to hear momentarily that Rodgers and his airplane had safely arrived in Hawaii, not knowing that Rodgers had been forced down in the Pacific, more than two hundred miles short of his destination. Because of a malfunctioning radio transmitter, he and the PN-9 crew were unable to signal rescue ships of their plight.[44]

While awaiting word of Rodgers's arrival in Hawaii, Moffett had to cope with a personal crisis. He learned from the bureau early in the evening of 1 September that his ten-year-old son, Charles, who had been under a physician's care for a minor illness, had developed an ear infection and was desperately sick. Because Jeannette needed his help at home right away, and he was understandably worried about his youngest son, he decided to cut short his stay in San Francisco. Within hours he confirmed with the bureau that he was changing his plans and making arrangements to return to Washington as soon as possible by train.[45] Just as Moffett was preparing to do so, the good news came that the medical emergency with Charles had passed, and he canceled his plans. Unfortunately, the resolution of one crisis quickly led to another, for at that moment the world learned that Rodgers's aircraft was overdue in Honolulu and presumably was down at sea somewhere east of Hawaii.

Like everyone else in San Francisco late in the evening of 1 September, Moffett had high hopes that the guardships, searching along the flight path of the PN-9, would effect a speedy rescue. No one knew that as a result of a mix-up in radio bearings Rodgers had strayed far to the north of his expected position. Twenty-four hours passed without word that the aviators had been picked up. On 3 September, Moffett sent telegrams to relatives of the missing fliers, expressing his sympathy for their anxiety during this uncertain time and assuring them that the Navy was doing "everything possible" to find their loved ones. But by then, Moffett's mind had turned from a potential disaster unfolding in the Pacific to an actual one that had occurred only hours before in the skies two thousand miles to the east. Just before 0500 on the third, *Shenandoah* had been torn apart in a fierce storm over the village of Ava, in southeastern Ohio, and the stunning news was that fourteen of her crew, including her commanding officer, Zachary Lansdowne, were dead.[46]

Shenandoah's fateful last journey had been controversial almost from the start. Admiral Eberle had originally ordered a round-trip flight from Lakehurst to Minneapolis earlier in the summer, but Lansdowne, worried about the possibility of adverse weather, opposed it. Moffett engineered a compromise that delayed the Midwest flight until the end of August or early September, when there was less probability of severe thunderstorm activity. Early on the morning of 3 September, the airship was midway through the first leg of the flight, which was to have taken her to Scott Field in Illinois. Caught completely by surprise in a violent line squall, *Shenandoah*'s crew was unable to control her in turbulence that twice carried her over her pressure height, or normal operational ceiling. On the second ascent the airship's hull broke in two, and the control car dropped away, carrying Lansdowne and five others to their death. Crewmembers in the radio car and portions of the hull where the framework opened up also died, while most of those in the extreme forward and aft parts of the airship survived by free-ballooning the wreckage to earth. For days, accounts of the naval disaster in the nation's heartland shared space on the front pages of the nation's newspapers with follow-up stories on the failure of the Hawaii flight and the loss of the PN-9.[47]

In his first public statement on the *Shenandoah* accident, issued while he was still in San Francisco on 3 September, Moffett emphasized that the Navy remained committed to the development of the rigid airship. He lamented the loss of the airship's officers and men, who were "pathfinders in this particular line of duty," and insisted that *Shenandoah* had proved herself "to be perfectly reliable and structurally safe, as was evidenced by the fact that she made a transcontinental flight over the mountains and up the entire length of the Pacific Coast and back again." The crash, he believed, had been caused by a freak storm and that the airship had been "at the mercy of the elements."[48]

At Fort Sam Houston in Texas, Billy Mitchell waited until 5 September, when hope of finding Rodgers and the PN-9 crew had been given up, to make his first public comment. Even to those familiar with Mitchell's intemperance, his words were shocking: "These accidents are the result of the incompetency, criminal negligence and almost treasonable administration of our national defense by the Navy and War Departments." He had little good to say about the Army's management of aviation, but the Navy took the brunt of his criticism. The recent maneuvers of the battle fleet had been nothing more than a "Pacific parade." The Hawaii flight failed because it had been attempted with a "good-for-nothing, big, lumbering flying boat." Mitchell was not sure what had caused the loss of *Shenandoah,* but he was certain that the airship was 50 percent overweight, was structurally unsound, and had not been properly operated or equipped. Brave officers and men from the airship had died on a propaganda mission, and the survivors had been "muzzled" pending the outcome of a "whitewash board." *Shenandoah*'s crash had been brought about by "incompetence in the Navy Department and the criminal negligence in the ordering of this trip." "What business has the Navy over the mountains, anyway?" he asked. Finally, "as a patriotic American citizen," Mitchell said, "I can stand by no longer and see these disgusting performances by the Navy and the War Department at the expense of the lives of our people and the delusion of the American public." He fully expected to be disciplined for his forthrightness and was not surprised to learn a few days later that he had been recalled to Washington to stand trial before a court-martial.[49]

Moffett was preparing to return to Washington when he read Mitchell's blast in the San Francisco papers. J. J. Clark, then a lieutenant and serving as Moffett's temporary aide, remembered the admiral's outrage: "Did you read the morning papers?" he asked Clark. "Did you see what Billy Mitchell said? That son-of-a-bitch is riding over the Navy's dead to further his own interests! I'm going back to Washington and put a stop to this." He left by train as soon as he could, arriving in Washington on the ninth and immediately reporting to an uneasy Secretary Wilbur. He assured Wilbur that plans for the *Shenandoah*'s flight had been worked out months in advance and had gone through the proper channels; no political motivation was involved. Moffett did not deny that politics and publicity underlay the Hawaii flight, but behind the attempt was a great deal of careful planning and preparation. It was definitely not a stunt, as alleged by Mitchell.[50]

To everyone's surprise and great relief, word came late on 10 September that Rodgers and the PN-9 had been located by a submarine a few miles off Kauai. He and his intrepid crew were in good shape, having used sails fashioned from the airplane's lower wing fabric to navigate the remaining distance to Hawaii. Heartened by the news, Moffett received permission from Admiral Eberle to make a public statement replying to Mitchell's charges, provided it was on his "own initiative and responsibility." "In other words," he told Lt. Comdr. Eugene Wilson, "if it breaks right for the Navy . . . it's one for them, and if it breaks wrong, it's bad for me." Wilson and other officers at the Bureau of Aeronautics immediately got to work on a press release, which they rewrote several times before Moffett was satisfied. Hand-delivered to the wire services late on 13 September, it appeared in the New York papers the next morning.[51]

In the statement, Moffett abandoned his usual calculated reserve to present an angry rebuttal. Mitchell's accusations, coming as they did during a "time of national bereavement, . . . couched in the form of questions to protect their originators, are so palpably false as to make one wonder how they could have been seriously considered." Moffett continued, "Launched in a moment of great stress and intense emotion, [Mitchell's charges] have done incalculable harm to the nation. It is only now that their absurdity is beginning to be understood." To make matters worse, Mitchell's lies had been framed "in the guise of bringing about a reform in our system of national defense and of advancing aviation. As a matter of fact, they have done more to retard aviation and hamper national defense than could have been accomplished by any other means. Destructive criticism has shaken the confidence of the country in its Government. Examples of disloyal conduct have sown the seeds of discord in aviation establishments. False charges have branded loyal servants of the people with the stigma that denial can hardly efface."[52]

To Moffett, "the ambitions of these selfish men are as unbounded as their methods are unscrupulous. Their tactics are those of the demagogue. They like to pose as eagles soaring aloft with [a] keen eye for the country's defense. They have really played the part of vultures swooping on their prey once it is down." By making a "political appeal over the heads of Congress to the people," Mitchell had made the first move toward what

Moffett feared could be a military dictatorship. It was a situation that "bodes ill for the future of this Republic." Why Mitchell had made such statements was almost beyond comprehension. "The most charitable way to regard these charges is that their author is of unsound mind and is suffering from delusions of grandeur."[53]

Moffett's statement came only one day after President Coolidge announced the appointment of a high-level committee to investigate the problems of aviation in the United States. For months, the president had tried to distance himself from the growing aviation controversy, hoping that somehow it would resolve itself. But the continued economic distress of the aviation industry and the likelihood that the Mitchell imbroglio would cause irreparable damage to the military services convinced him that he had to do something.

To chair the board, Coolidge chose Dwight W. Morrow, a close friend and former Amherst classmate who had become a partner in the J. P. Morgan investment firm and was internationally recognized in financial circles. Serving on the board with Morrow were Judge Arthur C. Denison, Howard E. Coffin (chairman of the wartime Aircraft Production Board), retired Rear Adm. Frank F. Fletcher, retired Maj. Gen. James S. Harbord (president of RCA), Republican Senator Hiram Bingham of Connecticut (a former Army aviator), Democratic Congressman Carl Vinson of Georgia, Republican Congressman James S. Parker, and William F. Durand. Moffett expected at least three of the board's members to be sympathetic: Fletcher, who in 1910 had helped secure the use of the cruiser *Birmingham* at Norfolk for Eugene Ely's historic takeoff flight and had commanded the American naval force at Veracruz in 1914; Vinson, who already had a strong reputation as a champion of the Navy; and Durand, an engineering professor at Stanford University who was an 1880 graduate of the Naval Academy and one of the original members of the NACA.

The night preceding Moffett's scheduled 22 September appearance before the Morrow board, he met in his office with Wilson, Lt. Laurance T. DuBose from the bureau's Administration Division, and Capt. George C. Westervelt, manager of the Naval Aircraft Factory. As they reviewed Moffett's answers to a questionnaire from the board, the issue of a separate aviation corps came up. Westervelt, an officer in the Construction Corps, spoke strongly in favor of semiautonomy for aviation. Moffett listened for a while, paused, and then explained that he had "lived and bled in the Navy in the old days when we had an Engineering Corps. The line and the staff; the deck force and the black gang. I never could sleep if I were to impose on my friends that particular handicap. I do not recommend a separate corps." It was the only time Wilson could remember that Moffett felt so strongly about a question that he offered an explanation for his action.[54]

The next day Moffett took the witness stand at the board hearings. Beginning with a prepared statement, he attempted to paint a positive picture of the state of naval aviation in the nation. He summarized naval aviation policies and explained the functions of aircraft operating with the fleet. The Navy had at all times strictly adhered to regulations promulgated by the Joint Army and Navy Board on Aeronautics, and he professed surprise that any knowledgeable person would question those regulations as they pertained to the use of aircraft at sea. Naval aviation was, as he had said time and again, a vital "arm of the fleet," inseparable from the Navy's basic role as the nation's first line of defense. Cooperation rather than confrontation had been the key to the Navy's success in the air. Over the years, the Navy had worked closely with private industry, the Army, and the NACA and had "progressed further in naval aviation development than any nation in the world to-day." He steadfastly opposed a unified air force and a single aviation appropriation divided between the Army and the Navy.[55]

If he expected the questioning that day to focus on interservice problems related to the feud with Mitchell, Moffett was mistaken, for board members seemed much more interested in aviation personnel. Moffett patiently explained that Navy-wide manpower shortages were at the root of naval aviation's difficulties in finding qualified people. He went over the solutions suggested by the Johnson board. Then Bingham, a freshman senator and the only aviator on the Morrow panel, put Moffett on the spot when he asked whether the bureau should have total responsibility over aviation personnel. Moffett replied, simply, "It should be that way." Congressman Vinson picked up where Bingham left off, getting Moffett to say that he believed the chief of the Bureau of Navigation should be allowed to assign aviation personnel only with the "consent or approval" of Aeronautics, a clear reversal of the traditional lines of authority.[56]

Returning to his office, Moffett was depressed about how far the proceedings had gotten off track and worried that what he had said about personnel issues would be misinterpreted.[57] He had hoped to have more of an opportunity to demonstrate how illogical Mitchell was in his advocacy of a unified air service, and he wanted to impress upon the board that, all things considered, naval aviation had done remarkably well under his stewardship. Instead, he thought he had blundered into the dangerous shoal waters of personnel. The last thing he wanted to do was raise divisive intraservice issues when the overriding priority was to close ranks in the showdown with Mitchellite air-power advocates. He firmly believed that Mitchell was unscrupulous enough to try to destroy the Navy if that was the only way to achieve his ends.

Nevertheless, Moffett took heart from Mitchell's performance before the board a week later. Exhausted from the turmoil and preoccupied with preparations for his court-martial, Mitchell spent nearly two days reading a long and uninspired statement, repeating many of the charges he had made in the press. There was nothing new in Mitchell's denigration of the Navy and its air arm, and Moffett was not surprised by Mitchell's indirect attacks on him personally as one of the many "nonflying officers" in the service who had no understanding of the meaning of aviation for the future of warfare. Nor was he startled when Mitchell condemned the Navy for mishandling the *Washington* bombing tests and when he blamed the *Shenandoah* disaster and the failure of the Hawaii flight on the "bungling amateurs" in charge of naval aviation. Even during questioning, Mitchell seemed strangely distracted and unwilling or unable to bring much drama to the hearings.[58]

Now confident that he was going to win the war against Mitchell, Moffett went on the offensive during his second appearance on 7 October. In another prepared statement, he addressed Mitchell's allegations. True, the Hawaii flight had fallen short of its objectives, but it had been a calculated risk, and he was proud to say that naval aviators had not yet "reached that point where they are willing to undertake only the sure thing." He deeply regretted the *Shenandoah* tragedy, but she was an experimental airship and the Navy still had much to learn about lighter-than-air craft and their operations. He wanted the service to continue with "a steady, farsighted, progressive development," including construction of an airship with a range of more than three thousand miles and creation of a base on the West Coast to support operations with the battle fleet. Most important, Moffett wanted Congress to commit to a five-year aircraft construction program that would permit long-range planning and bring much-needed stability to the American aircraft industry.[59]

Moffett's specific recommendations to the Morrow board show that he saw the panel as a means to resolve many of the long-standing questions affecting naval aviation. He called for legislation redefining the aviation responsibilities of the Army and the Navy and removing statutory limitations on the number of naval air stations. He also requested a new airship of six million cubic feet to replace *Shenandoah* and a West Coast airship base. He wanted more flexibility in letting contracts to address some of the grievances of the aircraft industry. But Moffett was much more circumspect about personnel, requesting an increase in officers and enlisted men in the Navy to expand the pool of aviation personnel, permission to count flight duty at shore stations as sea duty, and a settlement of the flight-pay question. On the topic of expanding his bureau's responsibilities into the territory of the Bureau of Navigation, he was completely mute.[60]

Much to Moffett's delight, the report of the Morrow board, released to the public by President Coolidge on 2 December, followed many of his recommendations. A cardinal point was the board's determination that despite Mitchell's claims, aviation had too many practical limitations to be a decisive force in any foreseeable conflict. It followed, then, that there was no reason to establish a separate air force equal in status to the Army and the Navy. The board had "nothing but praise" for the high level of expertise of naval aviation personnel and the excellence of their equipment, which were "at least the equal of and in certain directions undoubtedly superior" to those of any other nation. Accusations of extravagant expenditures in naval aviation were found to be completely unsubstantiated. The board did find, however, "unrest and dissatisfaction" among naval aviators, but it offered no specific solutions other than recommending that officers be allowed to qualify for promotion with a "minimum" of dissociation from aviation and that their flight pay be continued. Further recommendations applying to naval aviation were the appointment of an assistant secretary of the Navy with responsibilities for aviation and the assignment of aviation officers as liaisons to the offices of the chief of Naval Operations and the chief of the Bureau of Navigation.[61]

The board concurred with Moffett that many of the procurement problems the bureau had encountered over the years stemmed from the failure of Congress to provide for an adequate multiyear aircraft acquisition program. It found, too, that the lack of such continuity had wreaked havoc on the American aircraft industry. Consequently, the board urged the approval of long-range aircraft production programs for the Army and Navy, allowing the timely replacement of obsolete equipment and providing sufficient business to maintain the economic health of the industry. It also recommended changing the laws requiring competitive bidding on all contracts for aircraft and related equipment and that proprietary design rights "be fully recognized."[62]

Following the report of the Morrow board, there came in quick succession the findings of the Lampert committee on 14 December, a verdict in Mitchell's sensational trial on 17 December, and the final determination of the *Shenandoah* court of inquiry on 24 December. The Lampert committee's recommendations generally paralleled those of the Morrow board, although Moffett was disappointed that the committee called for the creation of a single department of national defense. Knowing that Mitchell had been found guilty of insubordination and would later resign from the service may have given Moffett some satisfaction, but one could only guess what Mitchell would do as a civilian in the cause of air power. The naval court of inquiry on the loss of *Shenandoah* determined that the accident had been the result of unanticipated extreme weather conditions. Although the court found no single officer culpable, it determined that an error in judgment had been made in the operation of the airship, and it took issue with the policy of sending an experimental craft around the country on publicity flights.[63]

In the welter of hearings, reports, recommendations, and verdicts at the end of 1925 was a vindication of Moffett's determination and perseverance in the cause of naval aviation. Somewhere, too, in all this confusion was a mandate for change. It remained for Moffett to ascertain what the lessons of the previous year were and to apply his formidable political and organizational skills to the resolution of the problems looming in the future.

8

A THOUSAND AIRPLANES

THE MORROW REPORT WAS A MILESTONE IN THE HISTORY OF American aviation. Not much in the document was new or had not been said in one form or another for years, but the report came from a blue-ribbon presidential panel and carried with it the weight and prestige of the chief executive. It also received the widespread support of thoughtful Americans, who by the end of 1925 had become disenchanted with Billy Mitchell and favored a more moderate and constructive approach to the country's aviation problems. No one understood this more than Admiral Moffett, who went into 1926 determined to use the Morrow report as leverage in achieving specific ends that had escaped him during his first term as bureau chief. Foremost on his agenda was congressional approval for a five-year aircraft procurement program along the lines originally drawn up by Capt. Henry Mustin in 1922.[1]

Each year, Moffett and his staff at the bureau had to go through an arduous and time-consuming ritual to secure aviation appropriations. The process began with the preparation of budget estimates, usually initiated more than a year before the fiscal year in question. For example, work on the fiscal year 1927 budget had to begin in the spring of 1925. Moffett's staff asked for estimates from each of the divisions and sections and for information from the bureau's long-serving chief clerk, Lane Lacy. The bureau solicited shore installations for information and estimates regarding public works. The Plans Division compiled the information into preliminary estimates, which were run by the Navy's budget officer, the chief of Naval Operations, the General Board, and the secretary of the Navy before going on to the Bureau of the Budget in the Treasury Department. Created in 1921, the Bureau of the Budget had responsibility for balancing expenditures and revenues and for screening the money requests of all federal departments and agencies before their submission to Congress. In Congress Moffett's budget estimates underwent further scrutiny before their incorporation into the naval appropriation bill for that fiscal year.

Each year, too, Moffett reported to the Navy's budget officer on expenses, with emphasis on the economies effected during the previous twelve months. Again, Moffett's staff assembled the information from the divisions and sections in the bureau and compiled data from shore stations, material inspection offices in the field, and operating units with the fleet. All cost figures had to be broken down to conform with standard accounting procedures before being sent on to the budget office.

The crucial item in each year's budget was "Aviation, Navy," which included all direct appropriations for aircraft and engine procurement and maintenance, operations, and the miscellaneous services under the Bureau of Aeronautics' authority. Typically, Moffett employed the tactics of most administrators, asking for as much money as he thought reasonable in the expectation that he would wind up with far less after all the responsible parties wielded their fiscal knives. Some years he was also able to get money indirectly through the carryover of unexpended funds from the previous year, special deficiency bills, general "Increase of the Navy" money, and contract authorizations. But the piecemeal approach of annual appropriations did not provide a framework for long-term planning or continuity of aircraft procurement and did nothing to promote or to protect the well-being of the nation's aircraft industry.

Under severe budget constraints during his first year in office, Moffett tried any scheme he could to get more money for aviation in the naval appropriation bill for fiscal year 1923, the first for which he had full responsibility. In late 1921 and early 1922, he wrote to individual congressmen and committee chairmen, stressing the importance of naval aviation and of maintaining sufficient personnel to keep the operating forces going. As a result of the Washington Conference, the United States had a well-defined policy to build a navy at least equal to Great Britain's and 40 percent larger than Japan's. The nation, he said, needed to do all it could to build its naval air arm to a level of parity with Britain. Despite all his efforts, Moffett found his initial estimate of $21.5 million slashed by the Navy budget officer to $17.5 million and then by Congress to $14.7 million—not enough, he argued, to pay for maintenance and to construct urgently needed new shore facilities.[2]

The purse strings loosened slightly over the next two fiscal years, but not sufficiently to maintain a steady influx of new aircraft or to meet urgent requirements ashore. In 1924, "Aviation, Navy" came in at $14,647,174, roughly equal to that of the previous year. There still was not enough money to provide the numbers of new aircraft needed for fleet operations, and Moffett worried that the "falling off of production orders for aircraft has produced a situation in the aircraft industry of the country that threatens serious consequences." The next year was marginally better, with $15,150,000 earmarked for naval aviation. Some of the money came from a deficiency bill specifically for the procurement of new aircraft, and more than $500,000 covered new construction at Pearl Harbor and Coco Solo in the Canal Zone.[3]

As preparations for the fiscal year 1926 budget proceeded in 1924, undersecretary of the Navy Theodore Roosevelt, Jr., called all the bureau chiefs to his office in late August to discuss the possibility of budget cuts. He asked them to survey their requirements and indicate to him in writing what they had done to try to make ends meet and to offer suggestions for additional economies. In a memo of 19 September, Moffett reported that his bureau was going to get $16 million, down from the $32 million originally requested for fiscal year 1926 and the same amount as the previous year. To make ends meet, the bureau would have to cut back on the aircraft squadrons it had planned to have operational with the battle and scouting fleets and put on hold additional improvements to the aviation facilities at Pearl Harbor and Coco Solo. Moffett warned that up to this point the bureau had been using up surplus war material at the rate of $10 million per year and that the stocks were due to run out soon. The Bureau of the Budget pared the request down to $14.8 million, only slightly more than the bureau had received in 1923 and 1924 and less than the previous year.[4]

At hearings before the House Appropriations Committee in early December 1924, Moffett spoke of the growing crisis in naval aviation and the aircraft industry. Not only was there insufficient money but also there was, Moffett said, the "matter of continuation" and the problem that the aircraft manufacturers "do not know whether they will have work to do from year to year." European producers survived in part because of heavy government subsidies, an alternative that was not acceptable in the United States. Moffett suggested that "the best thing that could be done for the aircraft industry would be for the Government to have a building program in aviation, or a continuous building program, so that we would have some assurance, and so that the industry would know just what we would get not only this year and next year but for several years."[5]

Before the Morrow board Moffett repeated many of the same themes. He pointed out the difficulty in pursuing a rational policy for the expansion of naval aviation "when the amount of money to be available is an unknown quantity until a few months before the beginning of each fiscal year and then is known only for one year." The consequences were dire for the aviation industry, which in the absence of a commercial market for its products needed government orders to survive. It was, Moffett said, "extremely difficult for aircraft manufacturers to carry out an orderly and economic procedure" without a "continuing construction policy."[6]

Well before the Morrow board concluded its work, Moffett discerned trends in its proceedings that he hoped to use in prying more money from Congress. In a letter to an officer in the Bureau of the Budget, Moffett wrote that he was disappointed with that office's proposed cuts in the naval aviation estimates for fiscal year 1927. He insisted, "We put in exactly what we thought should be done this year, keeping in mind the necessity for economy. As things are going, and with the amounts we have been getting, we are simply getting farther behind all the time." He believed that the Morrow board was likely to recommend increased aviation appropriations, and that if it did so, "Congress is going to go very thoroughly into the question, and will deal very liberally with aviation." The Bureau of the Budget needed to weigh that consideration carefully before arriving at a figure that was too low to be consistent with the needs of naval aviation and the wishes of Congress.[7]

Largely in response to Moffett's prodding, Congress took up the question of long-term aviation appropriations in the wake of the Morrow report. In late December, Moffett presented the bureau's plans for a five-year aircraft procurement program to the House Appropriations Committee. The committee members were generally receptive to the program; to get it started, they were willing to incorporate $9.1 million into the naval appropriation bill for fiscal year 1927. Unfortunately, Moffett himself jeopardized the aircraft program by stubbornly insisting that money be included for a large fleet airship to replace *Shenandoah*.[8]

All the makings of an acrimonious intraservice controversy were in place when the House Naval Affairs Committee, chaired by Congressman Thomas S. Butler, a Republican from Pennsylvania, began its hearings on the naval bill in January 1926. Secretary Wilbur explained to the committee that the rigid airship was still in the experimental phase and indicated that the Navy needed to explore all potential avenues of development before committing itself to a big and expensive new craft. There was, he pointed out, a proposal from Henry Ford's Aircraft Development Corporation in Detroit to build a pressure airship known as a metalclad, incorporating thin duralumin sheets for its envelope instead of the rubberized fabric used on conventional blimps. Admiral Hilary P. Jones was hostile to the new airship, believing its inclusion in the next naval appropriation bill took money away from the construction of badly needed surface warships.[9]

Butler knew that he had a growing conflict on his hands, and he wanted to avoid a public break in the Navy's ranks, especially in the aftermath of the Army's bitter internecine battle with the Mitchellites. Rather than force the issue immediately, he decided to let the naval bill go through minus any money for aircraft but with assurances that his committee would thoroughly investigate the entire question of the five-year program and the construction of a new rigid airship. The compromise measure passed the House on 25 January.[10]

Unhappy with the action by the House, Moffett told Butler's committee on 28 January that he preferred that the new airship be paid for through general appropriations. After all, he said, the craft was to be designed and built as a fleet airship; it had as legitimate a place in the fleet as battleships, cruisers, and carriers and the airplanes that operated from them. He reminded the committee that the General Board had approved the construction of a new airship, and he defended its potential as a long-range scout for the fleet. Large airships were not as vulnerable as their critics believed and had "passed the stage of [being] fair-weather vessels." Omitting such craft from general naval appropriations made no more sense to Moffett than excluding airplanes and surface ships.[11]

Moffett seemed willing at that point to sacrifice the five-year program and the fleet airship on the altar of principle; then he learned that Mitchell would be testifying before the House Military Affairs Committee in favor of proposed legislation for a unified air service. He knew that Mitchell had been discredited following his court-martial and sentence suspending him from rank and duties, but the forces favoring a unified air force still had to be reckoned with. They began in January 1926 with the introduction of H.R. 8533, a bill to abolish the Navy Department and create an independent air force within a new department of defense. Certain that Mitchell's lingering influence lay behind the measure, Moffett spoke in the strongest possible terms against the bill during hearings held by the House Military Affairs Committee on 23 February. Pointing out that the Navy and War departments and the Morrow board had specifically recommended against the establishment of a separate air force, he told the congressmen that a careful reading of the bill showed that it "fatally restricted" the Navy in the fulfillment of its role in the nation's defense and gravely impaired naval aviation.

He had said it many times before, but Moffett again patiently explained the Navy's traditional missions in defending the nation and the disadvantages of consolidating naval aviation into a unified air force. Much had been done to promote cooperation and to avoid duplication between the Army and the Navy in aviation, and there was little reason to suppose that unification would do anything to enhance the efficiency of the two services' air arms. In response to a question about the desirability of unity of command, Moffett agreed that it was a good idea in principle but that "modern military operations on land and operations at sea are so distinctly different and complicated that it is life work to master one or the other. It would require a superman to personally direct the Army and Navy in war and our military system doesn't provide for the training of such men." Anything the members of the committee had heard about the airplane's rendering surface ships obsolete was not true, Moffett added. The airplane was nothing more than "another weapon that the surface ship has to contend with," and aircraft carriers offered the fleet one of its best defenses against air attacks.[12]

Later in the day, Moffett repeated his opposition to the proposed legislation in testimony before the House Naval Affairs Committee. This time he emphasized that the bill threatened to eliminate the Navy's operations from land bases and drastically alter the Navy's coast defense role. Over time, the service secretaries had reached an understanding on sharing the coast defense mission between the Army and the Navy, yet some Army officers remained "dissatisfied" with existing policy. In contrast, the Navy had "played the game by strictly adhering to the joint decisions of the departments relative to aviation missions." In a jab at Mitchell, Moffett stated, "The Navy feels that effective coordination between naval aviation and the Army Air Service requires only loyalty to tried and approved policies and a willingness to set aside contrary personal opinions."

Those who challenged the Navy's control of shore air bases failed to understand how essential it was for the Navy to coordinate all air and sea operations in the coast defense mission. Moreover, it made no more sense for the Navy to turn over its land bases to the Army or the proposed unified air force than it did to surrender control of its navy yards. As Moffett asked, "What has the place from which aircraft start got to do with it? All ships have to start from land bases too. There is only one true method of determining whether aircraft should belong to the Army or the Navy, and that is, the primary function for which the craft are designed. If the primary function is for use over the water, they should be naval aircraft; if for primary use over the land, they should be Army aircraft." He concluded, "For reasons which I have but briefly enumerated and discussed, I strongly recommend as Chief of the Bureau of Aeronautics that this bill be not enacted into law."[13] It was not, but the attempt reminded Moffett that he could take no chances; the idea of a unified air force had enough backers in high places to remain a serious threat to the integrity of naval aviation.

With sentiment for a unified air force still running strong in early 1926, neither Moffett nor Butler wanted to provide the Mitchellite forces with any ammunition whatsoever, and both saw the five-year aircraft program as the most effective demonstration of the Navy's long-term commitment to its air arm. Moffett had a plan ready for Butler's committee on 4 February. Largely the work of Lt. Comdr. John H. Gunnell, one of the bureau's budget officers, the proposal called for the acquisition of 2,102 airplanes, costing, with engines and spares, just under $134 million, or an average of about $64,000 per unit. It nearly doubled the Navy's inventory, from 638 to 1,248 serviceable aircraft. The program did not include money for a new rigid airship; previous experience had convinced Moffett that it stood a better chance of winning separate funding. But the plan did add aircraft for a 23,000-ton carrier and for six new scout cruisers. In a statement to the press later that day, Moffett made his motives clear: "We feel that it is a moderate program. It is constructive in every way. We have been accused of being asleep at the switch in the matter of aviation. I want to say that this is not the case. We have a very definite program of aircraft development laid out. We know what we want to do for the next five years."[14]

Forty-eight hours after dropping his multimillion-dollar bombshell on Mitchell's united air force, Moffett shared the speaker's podium with secretary of War Dwight F. Davis at the National Republican Club in New York. While Davis meekly defended current military aviation policies, Moffett took the offensive. He explained that the five-year program was "carefully considered" and demonstrated the Navy's resolve to develop aviation in full accord with the spirit and the letter of the Morrow report. An independent air force was "absolutely unsound in conception." "The Air Force of this country should be a naval air force, not a separate air force based on shore." Everyone knew whom he was referring to when he said, "To my mind the single biggest handicap under which aviation has had to suffer is the repeated attacks and charges on the part of individuals who are totally ignorant of the Navy and its problems and who have been impelled, largely by unworthy motives, in their efforts to discredit us." The Navy and its people were, however, "not concerned, for the record of our achievement is a solid bulwark against the ravings and rantings of publicity seekers."[15]

Once the initial hoopla over the five-year program died down and Moffett was sure that he had put the unified air force advocates on the defensive, he and his staff worked with Butler on ways to reduce the scope of the plan. The scaled-down program emerging from their negotiations proposed a force of 1,000 airplanes by 1931, to cost $85 million over five years. Eliminated in the new draft legislation were the carrier's aircraft complement and airplanes for the six cruisers. Also cut was the number of airplanes planned for Pearl Harbor and Coco Solo and for naval air stations in the continental United States. Despite the reductions, Moffett was delighted with the finished product. On 17 February, the day Butler introduced the measure to the House as H.R. 9453, he told Capt. Jerry Land, "We won a great triumph this morning."[16]

It was, indeed, a remarkable victory, but a great deal of legislative maneuvering lay ahead. One of the questions still unresolved was that of the new rigid airship, which was not included in H.R. 9453. At the time,

H.R. 7375, a bill providing for the construction of a replacement for *Shenandoah,* was pending. Moffett and Butler decided that the best strategy was to fold H.R. 7375 into H.R. 9453, at the same time asking for not one but two new rigid airships of six million cubic feet each. The result was a new bill, H.R. 9690, introduced to the House by Butler on 23 February. Up to this point, Coolidge had been characteristically silent on the Navy aircraft program, but when the proposed cost of the measure finally sank in, he summoned Butler to the White House on 1 March to tell him that the proposal was far too rich for his blood.[17]

For some time Moffett had been worried about what he called "scarehead figures" in the newspapers, which had greatly exaggerated the size and cost of the five-year program. An Associated Press reporter had put the expansion plan at a much higher cost than what Moffett had originally proposed. With additions of $70 million in aircraft maintenance costs over five years and $46 million for a new 23,000-ton aircraft carrier, the initial $134 million jumped to what at that time was a phenomenal quarter of a billion dollars. Moffett knew that the tightfisted Coolidge would find such an expenditure completely unacceptable, and without the president's support, the program stood little chance of success. Consequently, he wrote to Capt. Adolphus Andrews, a personal friend who had the ear of the president, to explain that the press reports were misleading, that the plan had been considerably reduced since its first introduction, and that "any action by the House Naval Affairs Committee is entirely legislative and does not appropriate money unless and until it has gone through the Budget and the Appropriations Committee of the House. . . . If you do have an opportunity of explaining this to the president," Moffett said, "I would appreciate it very much if you would do so."[18]

Andrews was not the only person Moffett approached in his behind-the-scenes lobbying for the five-year program. He also sent a carefully worded letter to Dwight Morrow on 2 March. "I have been doing my best, as far as the Bureau of Aeronautics is concerned," he wrote, "to put into effect the recommendations of the President's Aircraft Board, and this five-year building program I think [is] one of the most important." He went on to explain the details of the bill and what it meant for naval aviation and the aircraft industry. But it needed Coolidge's support. "I feel that I am in a rather delicate position, because my first thought is to meet the President's wishes in every way and not to even try doing anything that he would not approve." Morrow was not obtuse. He knew that

Moffett wanted him to intervene with Coolidge on behalf of the proposed legislation. Moffett's letter-writing campaign paid off, for within two weeks the administration announced its unequivocal support for the program.[19]

Even with the authority of the chief executive behind it, the measure still had to be shepherded through the often byzantine legislative process. Moffett confided to his friend Bill Wrigley, Jr., who was sunning himself at his estate on California's Catalina Island, that he was "tired of the grind here. No one enjoys a battle, I believe, more than I do, but the one here has been going on for five years." Nevertheless, he was sure the five-year program was in capable hands. Butler and Vinson brilliantly orchestrated two days of debate on the bill in the House, during which there was only a minimum of opposition. Resistance came from expected sources: pacifists, who did not see how a military expansion program fostered world peace, and such diehard backers of a united air service as Congressman Fiorello La Guardia of New York, who saw the program as a needless duplication and questioned naval officers' understanding and administration of air matters. The bill passed on 12 April by a vote of 297 to 40, with 93 abstentions. At the same time, the House voted in favor of a second bill creating an assistant secretary of the Navy for aeronautics.[20]

Both pieces of legislation went on to the Senate, where Frederick Hale, a Republican from Maine and chairman of the Naval Affairs Committee, took charge. One of his first steps was to incorporate the second bill, providing for an assistant secretary of the Navy, into H.R. 9690 as an amendment. Meanwhile, Moffett was more than an interested observer. As the legislative mill ground on, he heard rumors that the Senate was not going to vote on the Navy measure before considering a bill to establish a semi-autonomous Army air corps. Sensing trouble, he wrote again to Dwight Morrow on 26 April, informing him that the air corps bill had not yet been taken up by the House and warning him that unless the Senate acted quickly on the Navy bill, there was a strong chance that the congressional session would end without any aviation legislation at all. Such a failure, "after all these investigations and all this excitement," he believed, "will be used with effect against the administration." Moffett urged Morrow to inform the president about the situation. "You will know best how to handle the matter and what is best to be done."[21]

Morrow may have approached the president, secretary of Commerce Herbert Hoover, or key members of Congress, but in any case events moved swiftly after Moffett's letter. The Army air corps bill passed the Senate and received quick approval in the House, removing what Moffett feared was a potential·obstacle to the Navy five-year program. Senator Hale reported the Navy bill out of committee on 18 May, and with no debate, the Senate voted to pass the measure on 3 June. All that remained was for House-Senate conferees to approve the amendment including the assistant secretary of Navy for aeronautics and agree to various other minor changes before the Senate voted to send the bill on to the president for his signature.[22]

Signed by Coolidge on 24 June, the Naval Aircraft Expansion Act authorized the procurement of 1,614 airplanes over five years, giving the Navy 1,000 operational aircraft by the end of 1931. The cost of the program was estimated at $85,078,750 (not including an additional $8 million for the construction of two fleet airships and $300,000 for an experimental metalclad), for an average of about $53,000 per unit. Broken down by years, the program called for 235 airplanes in fiscal year 1927, at $12,285,000; 313 airplanes in fiscal year 1928, at $16,223,750; 335 airplanes in fiscal year 1929, at $17,582,500; 357 airplanes in fiscal year 1930, at $18,941,250; and 374 airplanes in fiscal year 1931, at $20,046,250. The act provided for acquiring 333 more airplanes each year thereafter, to maintain the 1,000-airplane level.[23]

A significant provision of the 1926 legislation was the creation of the new position of assistant secretary of the Navy for aeronautics. Coolidge appointed Edward P. Warner, a dynamic professor of aeronautical engineering at MIT and one of Jerome Hunsaker's brightest protégés. By 1926, Warner's experience as a member of the NACA Committee on Aerodynamics, as an author of aviation legislation in Massachusetts, and as a consultant for the Morrow board had earned him a reputation as one of the nation's most knowledgeable aviation experts. Warner took office on 12 July and threw himself into his work with remarkable zest and enthusiasm, spending long hours in his office and traveling thousands of miles inspecting Navy aviation facilities around the country. He also instituted a statistical study of naval aviation accidents with a view toward improving safety. Moffett respected Warner for his vigorous opposition to Mitchell and the unified air force, but his relationship with the arrogant new assistant secretary was never more than politely formal. Warner's personal secretary remembered that her boss's personality put Moffett off; he was, she said, "not accustomed to being talked to as a student."[24]

In light of the traditional apolitical nature of American naval officers, Moffett's active intervention in the legislative process was extraordinary. He and his staff drafted the aircraft bill, collaborated with Congressman Butler and the House Naval Affairs Committee as the measure made its way through the legislative process, promoted the bill in public, and used inside political connections to help secure its passage. Hitherto, military officers had for the most part restricted their roles to recommending and implementing policy, leaving actual policy-making to civilians in the executive and legislative branches. In taking such bold action, Moffett expanded the authority of his office far beyond the traditional limits adhered to by highly placed naval officers.

It is important to keep in mind, also, that the 1926 act was an authorization only; Congress had not yet appropriated any money to implement the five-year program. Moffett's first move was to request a supplement to the appropriation for fiscal year 1927 covering the cost of the first year of the expansion program and to pay for the two new airships. But the Bureau of the Budget rejected the proposal, and Congress failed to include the extra money to start the program. In an attempt to salvage something for the first year of the program, Moffett put together a plan to acquire 137 new aircraft, costing a little more than $9 million, and added another $3.3 million from separate "Increase of the Navy" funds for 78 aircraft for the new carriers *Saratoga* and *Lexington*. Moffett got fewer airplanes than he wanted, but it was a start, and he could always make adjustments to keep the program on track through succeeding years.[25]

Crucial to the success of the five-year program was the right mix of aircraft to be procured. Moffett knew from experience that determining the numbers and types of airplanes needed would occupy nearly all his time through the remainder of the year, so he decided to get away from Washington at the first opportunity. Starting on 1 September, he took a well-deserved leave and headed with his eldest son, George, for Desbarats, Ontario, not far from Sault Ste. Marie, where James O. Heyworth, a friend from Lake Forest, owned a rustic, two-bedroom cabin. Moffett found the cool, blue lakes and the lush forests of the north woods agreeable and enjoyed some success hunting and fishing, but he missed his wife and family. Thinking about a possible vacation home, Moffett told Jeannette that land was cheap in Canada but that a place closer to Washington would be more practical. Later in the month, Moffett traveled to the West Coast with

Comdr. Bruce Leighton and assistant secretary Warner. On the tour, the trio inspected fleet aviation facilities in San Diego, Los Angeles, and San Francisco and visited the Boeing factory at Seattle.[26]

Back at his desk in early October and refreshed by his time away from the demands of official Washington, Moffett was determined that subsequent planning should reflect the immediate aircraft requirements of the fleet. In response to an inquiry from Warner in December, Moffett replied that the bureau had been studying the situation intensively and had decided to concentrate on aircraft of proven design for the next year or so. In accordance with that policy, the bureau would postpone buying sixty-one examples of the so-called three-purpose airplane, a craft that was to fill the roles of bomber, torpedo plane, and scout, until more experimentation was completed. The immediate need was for new fighters, trainers, and observation aircraft.[27]

For fiscal year 1928, "Aviation, Navy" came in at $25,135,000, of which $13,557,000 was earmarked for acquisition of new aircraft under the five-year program. Despite a special increment of $300,000 allowing additional aircraft for *Saratoga* and *Lexington,* the figure was still more than $2 million less than had been authorized. During the year, 156 more airplanes entered the inventory, bringing the total to 624, a sizable increase but fewer than called for by the 1926 legislation. As had been the case in the previous fiscal year, the emphasis was on aircraft to meet immediate service requirements. The Martin company had won the design competition for the three-purpose airplane, but a quantity purchase was again deferred until further tests had been carried out.[28]

Planning for fiscal year 1929, the third year of the five-year aircraft program, began in the spring of 1927. Moffett originally wanted $45.6 million in direct aviation appropriations, but he acceded to a reduction by the Navy budget officer to $31.5 million, plus a special $10 million contract authorization for new aircraft purchases. At a conference with the secretary of the Navy in July, Moffett said the cuts meant that only 267 new aircraft could be acquired, instead of the 335 needed to keep on track with the five-year program. Wilbur authorized the bureau to revise its budget upward to $38.5 million, keeping the extra $10 million in contract authorizations. But that estimate was not acceptable to the Navy budget officer, who eliminated the contract authorizations and slashed the "Aviation, Navy" figure to $22.1 million. Moffett complained that his bureau was being forced to absorb a disproportionate share of the overall budget cuts and pleaded that "sufficient funds be assigned this Bureau to permit of at least an approximation to the authorized program."[29]

Sympathetic to the bureau's dilemma, assistant secretary Warner urged the Navy budget officer, in a letter at the end of August, to reinstate at least the $10 million in contract authorizations. If that were not done, he saw no chance "of buying even enough new airplanes to make up for the actual current wastage of operating machines of the fleet," much less adding the new aircraft authorized under the five-year program. "It is the declared intention of the administration," Warner insisted, "that the five-year program for the procurement of naval aircraft shall be carried out at least so far as its ultimate goal is concerned." Moffett's and Warner's perseverance paid off with the restoration of the contract authorization money. The 1929 appropriation of $32,189,000 included $16.5 million for the purchase of 396 airplanes, bringing the total to 829 and keeping the 1,000-airplane goal within reach.[30]

Knowing that budget officials were unlikely to make up any deficiencies in the last year of the program, Moffett wanted to do everything possible to ensure there was ample money for new aircraft purchases in fiscal year 1930. He began early, presenting an estimate of $50.1 million to the Navy budget officer in January 1928. This time around there were only minor reductions, which cut the appropriation to $46.8 million, a figure that included $10 million in contract authorizations. Moffett said the number of airplanes would decrease from 357 to 332, and he worried that more than 400 would have to be bought in the last year of the program, resulting in "a most undesirable fluctuation in orders placed with the trade." In the end, Moffett received $31,430,000 for "Aviation, Navy" in fiscal year 1930, of which $13.4 million went to buy 359 new aircraft, bringing the total by the end of the fiscal year to 952.[31]

As work proceeded on the budget for fiscal year 1931, Moffett found his initial request for $53 million in total aviation appropriations reduced by the Navy budget officer to $35 million. Moffett complained that the $14.8 million set aside for new aircraft in the revised estimates was about half that needed to complete the five-year program on time and would leave the Navy about 150 airplanes short of the authorized objective. When subsequent revisions brought the budget down to $31.4 million, Moffett wrote to the new secretary of the Navy, Charles Francis Adams, in August 1929 to inform him that the "failure to carry out the Five Year

Aircraft Program will have the most unfortunate effect politically and in Congress. The public and Congress have been led to believe that the Five Year Program will be carried out. The public generally has great faith in Aviation and in what it can do and looks upon it as a modern, up-to-date weapon. It is believed that the appropriations for Aviation to carry out the Five Year Program and to maintain it would meet with popular and Congressional approval, and failure to do so would result in corresponding criticism." He urged Adams to add $13.8 million to the budget estimates to procure additional aircraft.[32]

"Aviation, Navy" for fiscal year 1931 finally came in at $32,032,211, including $12.3 million for 279 new aircraft. It gave the Navy just enough airplanes by 30 June 1931 to attain the hard-fought 1,000-airplane objective. Moffett was justifiably proud of reaching that goal with an expenditure more than $20 million under the original estimate. Appearing before the House Appropriations Committee on 4 March 1932, Moffett expressed his "appreciation of the action of Congress in appropriating funds sufficient to permit the timely completion of this most important naval aircraft program." He reported that the Navy had accomplished the feat by reducing the quantity of aircraft slated for Pearl Harbor and Coco Solo, cutting the number of aircraft lost through accidents, achieving significant savings on aircraft production contracts, and requiring a smaller percentage of spare engines.[33]

Linked to the law authorizing the five-year program were clauses in the 1926 Army Air Corps Act aimed at reforming some of the more ambiguous aspects of aircraft procurement policy, particularly the requirements for competitive bidding and the recognition of design rights. Because neither the services nor the industry had been entirely happy with existing laws, the Lampert committee and the Morrow board devoted a great deal of time to the procurement question. In late January 1925, for example, Moffett told the Lampert panel that the bureau had done its best to be fair to Curtiss in the CS contract, even to the point of trying to have the airplane declared a proprietary article as a means of getting around the requirement for competitive bidding. But only so much could be done within the confines of the law. Before the Morrow board in September 1925, Moffett urged that existing procurement regulations be revised to allow negotiated contracts with the approval of the secretary of the Navy, that contractors be selected from a list of responsible bidders, and that proprietary rights be redefined to allow the manufacturer who won the contract for the design of an aircraft to produce it in quantity.[34]

Moffett told the General Board in February 1926 that the bureau had been able to tolerate the existing procurement laws but that they had created "friction and a great deal of delay" in the acquisition of certain aviation materials. He explained, "When we have to make a contract, we have to make sure whether it is a proprietary article or whether we must advertise and take the lowest bid." Legislation reforming the procurement system, Moffett said, would make it "easier for us to get our planes and motors. We are willing to try it and have recommended it." There was also the issue of design rights. Moffett maintained that the bureau had always recognized the rights of manufacturers in the design of engines and aircraft accessories and no longer insisted on the purchase of the design rights to airplanes.[35]

Following recommendations from the Morrow board and the Lampert committee that existing legislation be changed to permit contracts without competitive bidding, the Army and the Navy agreed to work together on revisions to the law. The collaboration resulted in Section 10 of the Army Air Corps Act, signed by the president on 2 July 1926. The new law gave the services four different means of acquiring aviation material: design competition, whereby the Army and Navy advertised for designs and provided all prospective bidders with complete specifications for the article; noncompetitive contracts for experimental equipment; noncompetitive procurement in quantity of material designed before the passage of the 1926 act; and quantity procurement from the lowest responsible bidder.[36]

For Moffett, however, the new procurement provisions were only a marginal improvement over older regulations, because they still limited the bureau to competitive bidding in nearly all production orders. In a 10 November 1926 memorandum to the judge advocate general, Rear Adm. Edward H. Campbell, Moffett wrote, "Competition must be had before such procurement can be had." In almost every case, the 1926 law required advertising, whether the article was experimental or not. Only in the quantity procurement of essentially identical articles that had been under development for some time by several different manufacturers did Moffett believe it possible for the bureau to enter into contracts without advertisement and competitive bidding. The issue, as far as he was concerned, remained undecided.[37]

Unresolved, too, was the matter of personnel, even though lawmakers recognized the need for additional officers and enlisted men in aviation and had addressed the question in the 1926 legislation authorizing the five-year aircraft program. The act formally defined "naval aviator," "naval aviation observer," and "aviation pilot" (enlisted flier). In an attempt to provide more aviation personnel, the law set an arbitrary quota: by 1 July 1928, 30 percent of the total number of aviators must be enlisted aviation pilots. Part of the act, too, stated that lieutenant commanders and commanders who had served on aviation duty could move up to the next higher pay grade as partial compensation for their years of specialized aviation duty. As for the most fundamental personnel problems, in Moffett's eyes—the classification of aviation duty as sea duty, flight pay, the status of specialized engineering officers, and the responsibilities of the bureau in assigning officers and enlisted men to aviation—the law was silent.[38]

The personnel question transcended nearly all other issues and went to the heart of an ongoing dispute within the Navy over the autonomy of the Bureau of Aeronautics. Unless and until Moffett wrested from the Bureau of Navigation at least de facto authority over the training and assignment of officers and men, he would not be satisfied that naval aviation had been placed on a secure foundation. Whereas he had generally been able to get along with Adm. Thomas Washington as chief of the Bureau of Navigation, Moffett found Washington's successor, Rear Adm. William R. Shoemaker, far less tractable. Shoemaker set the tone in January 1925 when he responded to a request from Moffett that Navigation comply with General Order 65 and allow Aeronautics to review the appointment of supply officers to aviation duty. Shoemaker insisted that the order applied only to line officers and that he "did not consider it practicable to refer to the Bureau of Aeronautics all contemplated exchanges of officers to and from duty that might be connected with aeronautics. . . . Such assignments are not referred to other Bureaus whose financial interests are involved."[39] It was apparent to Moffett that he had a fight on his hands and that Shoemaker was not prepared to surrender any of his bureau's authority over personnel.

In a confidential letter to Secretary Wilbur on 26 June 1925, Shoemaker proposed a career track that in effect penalized those choosing aviation duty. Aviators were to start their careers with two years of sea duty, followed by five years in aviation, another two years in line service, four years in aviation, and then finish their first fifteen years with a second two-year tour in general line responsibilities. Fifty percent of those officers could go on aviation duty for five years, at which point they would all return to the line unless they were specifically designated for aviation duty only. It was a rotation system strongly biased toward traditional sea service, and to Moffett's way of thinking, it was not remotely acceptable as a solution to the shortage of aviators.

None of Shoemaker's other suggestions about managing aviation personnel matters was any more palatable. His basic philosophy was that aviation was no different from other specialties in the Navy and that naval aviators should not be accorded preferential treatment. It was beyond him why the bureau did not tap the Navy's enlisted ranks more than it did to make up for the shortage of aviators. Did the Bureau of Aeronautics have to have officers for all flying duties, he asked, when young, properly trained enlisted men were perfectly adequate for nearly all of its requirements? Flight pay was another sore point for Shoemaker. Comparing aviators to submariners, he suggested that one of the reasons officers remained in aviation duty longer than they did in submarines was the additional 50-percent compensation they received in flight pay. Would it not be fair, he asked, to reduce flight pay to 10 percent or possibly to eliminate it altogether? Doing so, he believed, would also effect badly needed economies in the service.[40]

When Moffett sought a replacement for Captain Johnson as assistant bureau chief in the summer of 1925, it became even clearer that his ideas on personnel were strongly at variance with those of Shoemaker. In June, Moffett indicated to Wilbur that his choice for the job was Capt. Emory Land, the Construction Corps officer who had served more than three years as head of the Material·Division. Admiral Shoemaker vigorously opposed the appointment on the grounds that the assistant bureau chief should be a line officer and not a member of a specialized corps. Moffett took exception to Shoemaker's position in a letter to the secretary of the Navy on 1 August, insisting that there was no legal requirement to select a line officer, only that the assistant chief be either a naval aviator or a naval aviation observer. Land, Moffett pointed out, had been qualified as an observer since 1922.

The wording of Moffett's letter was polite, but it was obvious he was indignant about Shoemaker's intercession in an internal bureau matter. "As Chief of the Bureau of Aeronautics, it is my belief that, unless for some very important basic reason involving a principle, I should have the right to choose my own assistants, subject of course to your approval, just as a flag officer at sea selects his own assistants, and I think I am in the best position to tell who is best fitted to perform these duties." He went on to explain that Land was eminently qualified for the job, based on his expert knowledge and experience in the material side of aviation. Furthermore, his appointment would boost morale by signaling other specialist officers in the bureau that there were no impediments to their moving up to important command assignments. Despite Moffett's declaration that "Captain Land is my choice for this position," Shoemaker's obstructionism prevented Land from taking over as assistant bureau chief until January 1926, at which time Johnson went to sea as commanding officer of the cruiser *Raleigh*.[41]

Shoemaker also irritated Moffett in the way he handled the findings of the Johnson board. After sitting on the report for months, Shoemaker submitted a long and critical endorsement letter to the secretary of the Navy on 29 August 1925. He described the report as "built about a predetermined opinion as to the position and specialized status of the naval aviator in the Navy, as distinct from an attempt to solve the aviation personnel problem of the Navy for the best interests of the service." The Bureau of Navigation, Shoemaker insisted, was far less narrow-minded and wanted to solve the problem in the best interests of the Navy, instead of "establishing obligations for the Navy to fulfill to a group of permanently designated operating specialists." He did not concur with either the Bartlett or the Whiting plans put forth in the Johnson report.[42]

Shoemaker's ideas on enlisted pilots and flight pay struck deep into the heart of Moffett's plans for attracting and retaining a highly skilled and motivated cadre of naval aviation personnel. Moffett explained his bureau's policy on enlisted pilots to Admiral Eberle in April 1925. Because of financial exigencies, enlisted pilots had been recruited and trained in 1921 and 1922 and had been sent to observation squadrons attached to the battle fleet. But there had been problems. In the first place, officer aviators did not trust the enlisted men's abilities to handle the full range of situations a flier might encounter in combat. Moffett believed that unless all fliers had "full confidence in the skill and judgment of the other pilots," they would not be fully effective as naval aviators. Much of his rationale stemmed from his agreement with Kenneth Whiting that naval aviators were more than "aerial chauffeurs." Moffett argued, "The primary operations of naval aviation in peace time consist of the development of material needs and methods of coordinating the offensive, defensive and auxiliary activities of the air units with those of the surface fleet. It is impossible, obviously, to limit the duties of the pilot of an airplane on a fleet mission simply to piloting of the airplane as directed by another person in the plane." To establish fixed ratios of aviation pilots to naval aviators, as Shoemaker called for, disregarded fundamental organizational and administrative realities.[43]

The resistance to flight pay, Moffett believed, also displayed the ignorance of the Bureau of Navigation. Since the establishment of the Bureau of Aeronautics, Moffett had strongly supported flight pay as an incentive and a reward to those who assumed the inevitable risks of naval flying. Admiral Shoemaker, on the other hand, saw flight pay as inherently discriminatory and prone to abuse. The "pay hop" many naval constructors and other nonflying officers took each month to qualify for the salary increment bothered him immensely. Instead, he suggested that additional insurance was a fairer and more economical way to provide extra compensation for aviators.

In a memorandum to the secretary of the Navy in April 1925, Moffett responded that "flight pay and insurance are separate and distinct and bear little or no relation to one another." It had been recognized for some time that flying was hazardous duty and that flight pay was justified; insurance was "entirely a personal matter," best left to the individual aviator according to his circumstances. "Opposition to flight pay comes from people who have not volunteered for flying themselves and have little knowledge of the psychology of flying personnel or of what carefully thought out measures are necessary to keep up their efficiency." If flight pay were reduced or eliminated altogether, Moffett averred, "flying personnel would dwindle to a handful, morale and efficiency would materially suffer, and in general it would wreck Naval Aviation."[44]

Knowing that Aeronautics and Navigation were on a collision course, Admiral Eberle recommended that another board be appointed to consider the personnel question. He suggested that the board examine and make recommendations on the percentage of enlisted aviation pilots in the service and develop a system for rotating senior officers from aviation duty to sea duty, allegedly to "broaden their careers to fit them for higher commands in aviation." Moffett, however, wanted a more comprehensive approach to the problem. On 17 September, he wrote to the secretary of the Navy asking that the board deal with the question of a naval flying corps. He was not in favor of such a corps, but he believed that Mitchell's agitation for an independent air force had had "a most adverse effect on the morale of the personnel of Naval Aviation" and that the advocates of a separate corps should have the opportunity to be heard. He also suggested that the board include at least three naval aviators, who would have the "opportunity to present their case."[45]

Although Eberle concurred with Moffett on including aviators on the new board and attempted to make the panel as representative as possible, its final composition left Moffett with doubts about its objectivity. Heading the panel was Rear Adm. Montgomery Meigs Taylor, one of Moffett's fellow cadets in the academy class of 1890 and a highly capable officer but no particular friend of aviation. In addition to Taylor the board included three nonaviators: Capt. John R. Y. Blakely, Capt. Walter R. Gherardi, and Capt. Harry E. Yarnell. Commanders John Rodgers and Ken Whiting and Lt. Commanders Robert R. Paunack and Marc A. Mitscher represented Aeronautics, and Maj. E. H. Brainerd Marine Corps aviation. The board was not exactly stacked in favor of the Bureau of Navigation, but all of its senior members were nonaviators who were more likely to favor traditional lines of authority on the personnel issue.[46]

The Taylor report, released on 20 January 1926, found "widely divergent" opinions on personnel matters and tried to strike a balance between the extreme positions on both sides. The board recommended that all Annapolis graduates have two years of sea experience before going to Pensacola for aviation training but called for only one more year of sea duty for all aviators as a prerequisite for promotion to the rank of commander. The board also determined that aviators must have the required experience at sea before assuming billets as commanding officers, executive officers, or department heads. Because there were insufficient naval aviators in the senior grades, the board recommended that captains be detailed from line duties to the command of aircraft carriers. The belief was that a strong background in the operation and administration of ships was more important than flying experience and that prospective carrier captains could, if necessary, rush through an abbreviated flight training program at Pensacola.

Two other major questions addressed by the Taylor board were the status of specialist officers and the numbers of enlisted naval aviation pilots. The board believed it was a needless expense to require flight training for engineering officers attached to the Bureau of Aeronautics. Such officers could carry out all their responsibilities from the ground and on shore; if a particular inspection job demanded that they fly, they could hitch rides as passengers in the airplanes. The Taylor board could see no reason to assign naval constructors permanently to carriers or other aviation ships, where, in any case, there were insufficient officer quarters. As for aviation pilots, the board did not recommend establishing a fixed ratio between them and officer aviators, opting instead to train personnel as needed to meet operating force requirements.

Three members of the board—Whiting, Paunack, and Brainerd—submitted a minority report. They took issue with the board's finding that senior officers in line for carrier command could take a short course at Pensacola. Older officers, no matter how skilled, were unlikely to make good aviators; better, the minority opinion ran, to send them through the observer training program already in place at Pensacola. On the other hand, the minority report stipulated that all officers below the grade of commander assigned to aviation should pass the full naval aviator course. The report also recommended restricting sea duty for aviation officers and allowing recent academy graduates to go directly to Pensacola for flight instruction if they volunteered for aviation duty. Staff and specialist officers were not to be discriminated against. If they successfully completed aviation instruction, they should be accorded naval aviator status.[47]

It is possible Moffett would have accepted the Taylor report modified along the lines suggested by the minority opinion, but Shoemaker accused the board of bias in favor of aviation and extensively revised the report before endorsing it on 26 January. Among the changes he insisted on were the imposition of a quota on enlisted pilots and additional sea duty for aviators in line for promotion to captain. He saw no reason whatsoever for engineers to have flight training, insisting that "there appears to be no need for constructors in aircraft at sea." He took an uncompromising position on Navigation's ultimate authority in all decisions affecting flying personnel.[48]

Upon receiving the report as revised by Shoemaker, Moffett dismissed it as merely the opinions of one person who was out of touch with the wider views of the service. He accused Shoemaker of presenting false information, particularly in regard to the flight status of specialized aeronautical engineers, and censured him for changing the report without letting him see the original first. Finally, Moffett criticized the Taylor board for not conferring with him or calling upon aviators for their testimony. Only Captain Land from Aeronautics had testified before the board, and from all appearances his views on the need to give special consideration to technical officers had been completely ignored.[49]

To make matters worse, conservatives used the minority opinion expressed in the Taylor report to attack Moffett and others in the Bureau of Aeronautics. On 15 March 1926, the commander in chief of the U.S. Fleet, Adm. Samuel S. Robison, vented his spleen in a long letter to the secretary of the Navy. The board had overstepped its bounds in applying the "principle of self-determination to aviators" and had extended certain "privileges" to aviation personnel that other officers and men did not enjoy. It made no sense to Robison that command of aircraft carriers, "the largest and most powerfully engined ships that our Navy has ever possessed," be given to aviators. Not only that, but these same aviators who were so adamant about command of aircraft carriers refused to accept even minimum sea duty. "No officer or body of officers in a military service who claim that they should select or determine who their commanding officer shall be is an asset to such service; on the contrary, they are a menace," Robison declared.

To Robison it was nothing short of insubordination when a group of officers felt they could not take orders from someone who did not have particular knowledge of their specialty. Furthermore, the blame for this situation rested on the top officers, especially on Whiting and Moffett, who, out of self-aggrandizement, had been the most vocal in their demands to have all aviation personnel brought under the control of the Bureau of Aeronautics. Robison wanted them "warned that it is not part of their duty to determine the qualifications of commanding officers of ships, nor to spend any portion of their time in attempting to establish and secure exclusive privileges for aviators." Moffett needed to be "informed that his duties are primarily with material, that his duties for personnel are completely secondary," and that he had "exceeded his authority and usurped the functions of the Secretary of the Navy and Chief of the Bureau of Navigation" in trying to expand the responsibilities of his office.[50]

More than two years passed before Moffett learned of Robison's letter. When it finally came to his attention in November 1928, he angrily wrote to Lt. Comdr. Dewitt C. ("Duke") Ramsey, an experienced carrier aviator, to say that he was "amazed and astonished" by its contents and that had he known of it earlier, he "would have taken immediate and very active steps in the matter." It was almost beyond comprehension that "a Commander in Chief should so impugn my motives . . . and those of Whiting and aviators in general." Moffett explained that Robison's accusations were totally false. He had not advocated that aviators command carriers, except in the case of Jack Towers, who was "in every way capable of performing the line duties" associated with carrier command. Yes, Moffett admitted, he did want bureau control over personnel, but that was an expedient necessary during the formative stages of naval aviation. Robison's attack was the "first written severe criticism" directed toward him in his forty-two-year career. As such, it was "unfair and unjust and has done a great deal of harm to the Bureau and to my efforts in performing my duty."[51]

Robison's charges displayed a deep-seated resentment against Moffett on the personnel question. Toward the end of March 1926, Moffett wrote to Capt. Joseph Mason Reeves, the battle fleet's commander of Aircraft Squadrons, to say he probably would not get out to the West Coast to see aviation operations with the fleet. Running through Moffett's letter was a tone of exasperation with the dissension in the service and the criticism he had endured as a result of his stand on personnel. "I have done everything I could while I have been here," Moffett wrote, "to play ball and play the game, and to meet the situation as best I can." He went on: "I am sorry that in some quarters,—in some cases very high ones,—I have not been understood, and that Aviation has not been understood. However, I will say this, that the [mis]understanding and lack of knowledge that exists is reflecting more on the Navy as a whole than on the Aviation part of the Navy, a situation which no one regrets more than I do."[52]

Nowhere was the growing discord more apparent than among aeronautical engineering officers. Increasingly, Moffett believed, these men were the key to the success of naval aviation, for without their technical know-how it was impossible to guarantee the best available aircraft for the Navy. In a memo for his files in January 1926, Moffett wrote that "to build up a group of suitably qualified technical officers, they must be trained, must be encouraged through recognition of their work, must be clothed with the requisite authority, and must be protected against discrimination on account of their specialization." He wanted to do everything necessary to keep them and to encourage others to join them by setting aside positions and by upgrading their postgraduate education at engineering schools in the United States and abroad. But above all, they should be offered "a reasonable ladder of promotion" and should be permitted to "devote their full career, without interruption of sea duty, to the technical phases of aeronautics."[53]

A bill before Congress in early 1926 proposed the transfer of all naval constructors to line duties, effectively removing them from their area of specialization and depriving the bureau of their technical expertise. Moffett detected what he thought was Shoemaker's nefarious hand in the measure and wrote to him on 29 April to register his opposition to the proposed legislation. The bill ran against the Morrow board's recommendation that the career paths of technical officers be made as straightforward and attractive as possible. In praise of the work of naval constructors assigned to the bureau, Moffett wrote that they were "by far the best aeronautical engineers in the Navy" and had "served the interests of the Navy zealously and loyally." Some line officers also worked in technical areas at the bureau, detailed to engineering duty only, but they were essentially part-timers, and he considered it "essential to the best efficiency that important questions of design be handled by whole-time or permanent specialists." To mandate line duties for all technical officers would, in effect, make them part-time technicians and "would be detrimental to the interests of the Navy."[54]

Moffett bypassed Shoemaker and appealed directly to Secretary Wilbur. On 13 July 1927, he wrote to Wilbur that the issue was "vital to the interests of the service and especially to the Aeronautic Organization." He criticized Shoemaker's endorsement of the recommendations of the Taylor board as they applied to specialists and pointed out that "to be thoroughly familiar with the technical side of aeronautics in its highest phase, a man must give his entire time to the work; it is a life work." It was impossible for anyone to be "everything required of a line officer and an aviator as well, and perform any duties efficiently and thoroughly, both afloat and ashore, including the duties of Constructor." Moffett recommended that the service recognize and set aside within the bureau "a group of trained specialists (Naval Constructors or line officers for engineering duty only), who will give their entire time to aircraft engineering, research, and design, and who will not be required to alternate shore and sea duty." He suggested, too, that specialist careers be made more attractive by allowing officers to qualify as full-fledged naval aviators and opening up the promotion process to give them a smooth path all the way up to flag rank.[55]

Moffett's arguments eventually carried the day. Despite the opposition of the Bureau of Navigation and its new chief, Rear Adm. Richard H. ("Reddy") Leigh, Wilbur and assistant secretary of the Navy Warner took steps to resolve the issue. They opposed legislation to shift all aviation technical officers to line duties and instituted a study of the problem aimed at developing a policy for such personnel. Moffett in July 1928 proposed the assignment of fifty-five officers to aeronautical engineering duty to fill out an estimated ninety-two billets for technical specialists. Leigh, on the other hand, wanted a much lower number. In the end, Moffett acceded to a compromise. On 1 March 1929, the secretary of the Navy determined that thirty-three naval constructors and one line officer restricted to engineering duty were to be immediately assigned to the bureau on a permanent basis. Additional specialist officers were to be detailed to the bureau as deemed necessary. The following year the category of aeronautical engineering duty officer was created, allowing technical specialists to pursue careers in aviation while bypassing the time-consuming sea duty required of their brother line officers. The new category was a signal triumph for Moffett in the personnel controversy, giving him complete authority over an entire group of officers independent of the Bureau of Navigation.[56]

During the war over personnel, one of the fiercest battles centered on Moffett's reappointment to a third term as bureau chief. In early 1928, Moffett was not altogether sure that he wanted or would actively pursue a third term when his current appointment expired in March 1929. In May, he wrote to Julius Rosenwald, another of his influential Chicago friends, that he was "very much disgusted with the way Aviation is going in the Navy" and that "things have reached the point where my position is almost untenable consistent with self-respect." He calculated that he could retire for age with nearly forty-two years of service under his belt. But the prospect of living the remainder of his life in quiet leisure was even more disturbing to Moffett, who had never known inactivity, and he wondered if Rosenwald could find "something worth while" for him in the event he had to retire. As late as January 1929, when his reappointment was still not a sure thing, Moffett wrote of the possibility of taking a position with one of the aircraft manufacturing companies, possibly one of the firms managed by Clement Keys or with Boeing in Seattle.[57]

Dejected over the nearly continuous battle with the Bureau of Navigation and doubts about his reappointment, Moffett suffered a wrenching personal blow with the death of his fourteen-year-old daughter Betty in

April 1928. A gifted student with a talent for writing, Betty attended the Eastman School in Washington, where she ranked first in her class in 1927. She was particularly close to her older brother Bill Junior, who entered the Naval Academy in the fall of 1926 at the age of sixteen. She wrote to him during his difficult first year at Annapolis to tell him that the whole family was "squeezing" for him to do well and that all anyone could expect of him was that he do his best. "I'd like to see anyone who can do more than that," she offered in cheery encouragement.[58]

Betty fell ill with influenza in the third week of March, and her condition worsened when pneumonia set in. The physicians could do little besides watch and wait as she battled for her life through early April, finally succumbing in the predawn hours on the ninth. After a quiet funeral service in their home two days later, the Moffetts laid their daughter to rest in Arlington. In a poignant note in his personal financial ledger on 22 April, Moffett wrote, "This book records nothing to date of the agony that has been ours" in the weeks leading up to and immediately following Betty's death. Bill Junior recalled many years later that he rushed home from the academy but was not able to talk to his sister before she died. He remembered her death as the "worst thing that ever happened" to the family, worse even than the loss of his father five years later. Both Bill Junior and Beverly remembered that their mother took Betty's death especially hard, suffering from depression for months afterward. Moffett at least had his work to help him through the grieving process, but the emotional scars from the tragedy remained throughout the rest of his life.[59]

By the fall of 1928, Moffett had resolved to seek a third term as chief and inaugurated another letter-writing offensive to garner support. He began with Bill Wrigley, Jr., whose intervention with President Coolidge had helped secure his second term. Acknowledging that third terms for bureau chiefs were "almost unknown," Moffett forecast that Admiral Leigh would oppose his reappointment. "There is no question," Moffett asserted, "that the whole Navy does not appreciate Aviation and its importance, and the majority still consider battleships and surface vessels of infinitely greater importance." He believed Leigh would work hard to have him reassigned to a sea command, and declared, "My knowledge of Aviation and my fitness to remain here is not based on knowledge of battleships, cruisers and Naval craft but on aircraft."[60]

For Moffett the thought of being shuffled off to a sea command was almost unbearable, and he knew he faced stiff opposition to his reappointment. Secretary Wilbur, although personally preferring to keep Moffett on, deferred to Admiral Leigh and assistant secretary Warner on the matter. Neither of them wanted Moffett; Leigh suggested Joseph Mason Reeves as the next chief, and Warner thought Capt. Henry V. Butler, a former Aircraft Squadrons commander for the battle fleet, was best for the job. Knowing where the opposition stood made Moffett more determined than ever to secure a third term. He called on W. F. Durand of Stanford University, whom he knew well from his work on the Morrow board three years earlier, to intervene on his behalf with president-elect Hoover. Wrigley received word a little later: Moffett wanted him to write to Hoover "as soon as possible," before "influences antagonistic to me" gained the president's ear and caused him to "make up his mind adversely." Wasting no time, Wrigley sent a letter to Hoover on 19 February urging Moffett's reappointment. By the first week of March, Hoover had received twenty-one letters from congressmen, senators, and businessmen supporting Moffett's reappointment.[61]

Moffett also took up his case directly with Wilbur. On 21 January, he wrote that although he was "ready to undertake any duty to which I may be assigned," his staying on for at least two more years at the bureau would be of the most benefit to the service. Aviation was still not "firmly established" in the Navy, and it required "continuity of policies and administration." Moffett thought it best "to allow me to continue these policies for a while longer; that is to say, until a more favorable time for a break in continuity of administration." More specifically, he wanted to be kept on to see the five-year aircraft program through to completion, to secure more carriers and rigid airships, and to resolve some of the outstanding personnel issues. Furthermore, his "experience in and association with aeronautics has been longer than that of any other ranking officer," and he enjoyed the support and confidence of the Navy's "aviation element." Moffett's appeal may have worked, for he later learned that Wilbur was "wavering" on the reappointment question.[62]

In contrast to some of the resistance to Moffett's reappointment within the Navy, strong backing came from the press. In February 1929, the *Aeronautic Review* (published by the National Aeronautic Association, a group of businessmen and aviation enthusiasts) appealed for Moffett's retention. The article said it was an "erroneous assumption" that third terms for bureau chiefs were unprecedented, noting seven flag officers who had served more than two tours, one of whom stayed in office for eighteen years. Beyond that, there were many good reasons for keeping Moffett as chief of the bureau; among them were his knowledge of aviation matters, his record in equipping the Navy with "modern, efficient and valuable aircraft," the admiration and respect he engendered among naval aviators, and the need to have someone with his experience to guide naval aviation through the rough weather ahead. "It would be a splendid tribute to [Moffett] if he could be permitted to complete a brilliant career in 1933 as chief of the Bureau of Aeronautics," the magazine concluded.[63]

The decision on Moffett's reappointment ultimately lay with the new president, Herbert Hoover. Both Jock Clark and Adm. Felix B. Stump remembered the same story. Shortly after taking office in March, Hoover asked for and received a list of nominees from the Bureau of Navigation. Dutifully, Admiral Leigh submitted three names, none of which was Moffett's. Hoover immediately sent the list back, with a request for more names. Leigh obliged, but still excluded Moffett. A second time, Hoover returned the list. The situation seemed headed for a ludicrous battle of wills between the new president and the Bureau of Navigation when a spate of articles appeared in the press favoring Moffett's reappointment. One more time Leigh forwarded a list to Hoover, now including everyone who might remotely qualify for the job and placing Moffett's name at the bottom. Hoover looked it over and on 12 March sent a curt reply to Leigh: "Approved for Admiral Moffett."[64]

Relieved when his reappointment came through, Moffett wrote to Claude Bailey, "You saying how neatly and perfectly I turned the trick was indeed flattering, but it was due more to the work done by my friends than to anything I did myself." From the start, "comparatively few people" had thought he had much of a chance, but they had not counted on his intensive lobbying effort. Moffett candidly admitted, "As a politician I carried on a rather active campaign, and as somebody remarked, they felt that Mr. Hoover was glad I was not running for a Cabinet job." But he was wise enough to know that the victory had not come without cost and that more battles lay ahead. "I am watching my step now, for as the Good Book says, 'Pride goeth before destruction and a haughty spirit before a fall.'"[65] The experience was sobering, for Moffett came away from that important political victory convinced that he could lose many of the gains from the past eight years if he did not remain perpetually on guard.

The acrimony between Moffett and the Bureau of Navigation in the late twenties tended to obscure the real problem of getting and keeping enough personnel to operate and maintain the aircraft acquired under the five-year program. Moffett did his best to rise above the interbureau controversy and applied his energies to putting together a personnel package consonant with the objectives of the five-year plan. On 5 March 1926, Moffett explained to the General Board that over five years more than eight hundred naval aviators would be needed, nearly double the number currently in the service. In the bureau's annual report for fiscal year 1926, Moffett noted that there had been a net gain of only forty-four naval aviators over the previous fiscal year and that the rate of increase would have to rise. To meet the personnel requirements implicit in the five-year aircraft program, Moffett approved doubling the classes at Pensacola from two to four per year and accepted a recommendation by Lieutenant Commander Paunack to increase the class size from sixty-five students to eighty.[66]

In 1927, the seriousness of the personnel crisis became apparent to everyone. The number of aviators that year increased from 426 to 472, still far short of what was needed for full implementation of the five-year program. In his annual report for fiscal year 1927, Moffett explained that the bureau had, in addition to increasing the number and size of the classes at Pensacola, provided aviation indoctrination for midshipmen at Annapolis and instituted preflight courses at Hampton Roads and San Diego for all ensigns. But it still was not enough. In a 10 August 1927 memorandum to Moffett, Warner pessimistically reported that after his own study of the problem, he had the "gravest concern . . . of ever securing and maintaining a number of regular aviators adequate to our needs." He saw the problem as "distinctly critical" and did not believe that the regular line would be able to meet the increased demand. It would be "necessary to press the training of all available members of Naval Academy classes to the very limit of possibility in order to secure by 1933 a number of naval aviators concordant with the five-year program." He suggested increasing the size of academy classes and possibly reducing the physical standards for aviation recruits. In an effort to reach a consensus, he asked the Aeronautics and Navigation bureaus to study the problem.[67]

Aeronautics completed its analysis and reported to Warner on 28 September that 664 naval aviators would be needed over the next five years. Among the bureau's recommendations for increasing the number of fliers was administering a physical examination to all Annapolis entrants and requiring those who passed to answer a questionnaire aimed at determining their interest in becoming naval aviators. The bureau projected that two years after graduation, 85 percent would still be physically qualified. If only a little more than half of them volunteered for aviation and 75 percent completed the course at Pensacola, ninety additional aviators per year would be available. Another suggestion was anathema to the Bureau of Navigation: eliminate the requirement that Annapolis graduates serve two years of sea duty before being sent to Pensacola for flight training.[68]

Predictably, Admiral Leigh disagreed with Aeronautics' statistics and with the proposal to cut sea duty. Leigh offered as an alternative increasing the percentage of enlisted aviation pilots from the 30 percent already called for in the five-year aircraft act. Aeronautics' response was just as predictable. Capt. Emory Land wrote to the chief of Naval Operations: "This Bureau has always maintained . . . that an excess of enlisted pilots above the minimum allowance now established by law would be against the best military and tactical interests of the service and would provide too great a number of pilot personnel inferior in quality to the best material available."[69]

Warner expressed dismay that the two bureaus seemed as far apart as ever and that an immediate solution to the problem did not appear possible. He agreed with Moffett that increasing the number of enlisted pilots was not the answer, but he did not concur on the wisdom of waiving the requirement for two years' sea duty for recent academy graduates. Warner proposed that all officers be solicited to see if they were interested in aviation, that physical examinations be given to all line officers to determine their qualification for aviation duties, and that the age limit for flight training be temporarily raised. Unfortunately, his suggestions did not represent fundamental changes, and he was unable to bring the two bureaus any closer together than they had been previously.[70]

Needing to provide aviators for the newly commissioned carriers *Saratoga* and *Lexington,* on top of the demands already imposed by the five-year program, Moffett became more aggressive in his campaign to secure sufficient aviators for the expanded aircraft program. In April 1928, he wrote to Admiral Leigh that there was still a "serious shortage" of naval aviators but that he did not see an increase in enlisted pilots as an effective means of making up the deficit. In fact, Moffett called for a reduction in the percentage of enlisted pilots from the 30 percent mandated by the 1926 five-year act to 21 percent. "This Bureau," Moffett continued, "has steadfastly and consistently maintained that the young line officers of the

Regular Service, graduates of the Naval Academy, make by far the best aviators." He renewed his request that all recent academy graduates who qualified for aviation be sent directly to Pensacola. Once these officers completed flight training, they could be detailed to carriers or other aviation vessels, where "they would gain sea experience in regular naval duties to an extent practically the same as they would gain with the former method employed of sending them to sea two years before allowing them to go to Pensacola." He also suggested that in the interim 100 reserve aviators be ordered to active duty for one year.[71]

Leigh was willing to call up the reserves as a "temporary expedient," but he was obdurate about reducing the percentage of enlisted pilots and refused to assign ensigns fresh out of Annapolis to flight instruction at Pensacola until after their two years of sea duty. On the latter point Leigh was as unyielding as Shoemaker had been: "If the present policy of the Bureau were changed, it would not solve the problem of an adequate yearly supply of naval aviators, but on the contrary would deprive newly made officers of a part of their training that is essential before they are fitted to take up a specialty."[72]

The impasse between the two bureaus did nothing to improve what Moffett saw at the end of the 1928 fiscal year as "an acute shortage of pilots to man the aeronautic organization." Although there had been a slight net increase in flying personnel, and 73 officers were being trained as opposed to only 28 the previous year, the number of officer aviators had declined from 472 to 466. There had been heavy attrition of enlisted pilot trainees at Pensacola, and on the whole the outlook was not bright for making up the lack of naval aviators by assigning enlisted men to aviation instruction. The situation demanded a "concerted effort on the part of the [Navy] department to meet the needs of the aeronautical organization."[73]

Signs pointed to an eventual solution of the personnel shortage in 1929. Eighty-six fliers were added that year, of which fifty-four were naval aviators and thirty-two enlisted aviation pilots. Much of the growth was due to a change in the class size at Pensacola in January 1929 from ten per week to fifty per month, a 25 percent boost in the number of students. It was an encouraging step forward, but Moffett warned in his 1929 annual report that the shortage of personnel "still remains and constitutes one of the most serious problems facing naval aviation." He urged Congress to do something about increasing pay for officers and enlisted men in naval aviation, and he wanted more administrative control over the percentage of enlisted pilots in the service.[74]

The breakthrough in aviation personnel finally came in fiscal 1930. That year, class sizes at Pensacola increased from fifty to sixty per month, and the attrition rate was markedly reduced by streamlining the syllabus. Most important, however, was the deferment of sea duty for all Annapolis graduates until after they completed flight training. The result was an increase of 164 flying personnel over the previous year, of which 90 were naval aviators. By 30 June 1930, 614 naval aviators and 244 naval aviation pilots were available, with another 184 aviators and 100 enlisted pilots undergoing instruction at Pensacola. The bureau completed a study showing that the percentage of enlisted pilots mandated by the 1926 act was too high and that 22 percent was more realistic. An outgrowth of the study was a bill empowering the secretary of the Navy to adjust the percentage of enlisted pilots to meet the needs of the service. In the depressed economy of the early thirties, Moffett urged passage of the bill as a means of saving money, arguing that training enlisted pilots was more expensive than providing instruction for officers. Signed into law in 1932, the measure reduced the percentage of enlisted pilots from 30 percent to 20 percent.[75]

In retrospect, the thousand-airplane act was one of the most notable achievements in Moffett's career as bureau chief. The law provided the numbers of aircraft needed for the expansion of fleet aviation and lent badly needed stability to the exceedingly volatile aircraft manufacturing industry. Meeting the goal of the 1926 aircraft act by the end of fiscal 1931 was remarkable under the circumstances, but it remained to be seen whether Congress would be willing to provide enough money to maintain that level or to move on to a more ambitious development program. Changes were also made in aircraft procurement policy, but it was still not clear that certain production contracts could be let without competitive bidding. Of all Moffett's accomplishments between 1926 and 1931, those relating to personnel were perhaps most significant. Not only was he able to alleviate a chronic shortage of aviators, but in a series of confrontations with the Bureau of Navigation he also made it clear that he wanted substantial control over aviation personnel. More studies, recommendations, and disputes lay ahead, but to the discerning observer it was clear that the tide of events was flowing in the direction of the Bureau of Aeronautics.

9

"This New and Powerful Weapon"

On 8 May 1930, Admiral Moffett donned his flight suit, strapped on his leather flying helmet and goggles, and climbed into a Vought O2U Corsair at the naval air station in Anacostia for a two-hour flight to the Curtiss Airport at Valley Stream, Long Island. At the controls of the airplane was Jock Clark, who had served as the admiral's temporary aide in San Francisco in 1925 and was now a lieutenant commander attached to the Bureau of Aeronautics as Moffett's personal pilot. Moffett inspected the engineering facilities of the Curtiss company at nearby Garden City later in the day and then went on to the gala New York Air Show at Madison Square Garden. Scores of aviation manufacturers displayed their products during the week-long extravaganza, traditionally one of the biggest shows of the year. The day before Moffett's arrival, more than a hundred airplanes from the battle fleet's aircraft squadrons flew in to Valley Stream from Hampton Roads and Anacostia, streaming over Manhattan in V-formation while millions watched from the ground.[1]

On the morning of the ninth, the Navy aircraft appeared over the city again, swooping in from the east to simulate a surprise bombing raid on the city before breaking off the attack and returning to their bases. The press considered it a fabulous demonstration of the nation's naval air power. Later that afternoon Moffett delivered an Army and Navy Day address over the NBC radio network. In his soft Carolina Low Country accent he explained that aircraft from the carriers *Langley, Saratoga,* and *Lexington* had not been able to participate in the flyover because they had only just returned from fleet operations in the Caribbean, and that what New Yorkers had witnessed earlier in the day was only a sampling of the Navy's mighty air force. "Seeing these planes, the fighters, the bombers, the scouts, and the torpedo planes, and this wonderful aircraft exposition makes one realize the strides that have been made in the last few years," Moffett said. In 1924, the Navy's only carrier had been *Langley.* Now, with *Saratoga* and *Lexington* the Navy had two of the most powerful ships in the world, their aircraft capable of reaching out far beyond the range of any battleship and delivering devastating blows to opposing forces. Moffett went on to emphasize that the big carriers "are not all of Naval Aviation." The Navy operated patrol aircraft from shore stations, battleships and cruisers had catapults to launch observation and spotting airplanes, and much progress had been made in the development of the rigid airship. Moffett concluded, "You have every right to be justly proud not only of Naval Aviation but aviation in all its branches."[2]

The 1926 five-year aircraft program and the alleviation of some of the most urgent personnel problems gave Moffett the foundation upon which to build an air navy. As he said in his New York radio speech, the aircraft carrier was a vital component of naval aviation, possessing tremendous offensive capability. Through the early development of fleet aviation, Moffett and others had studiously downplayed the potential of the aircraft carrier in offensive roles, particularly in comparison with the battleship. But a clear vision of a powerful naval weapon emerged with the commissioning of *Saratoga* and *Lexington* and the development of aircraft with the range and payload capacity to deliver heavy weapons against ships and land targets.

In the transformation of Moffett's ideas on the carrier there was no identifiable "eureka" moment, or point at which he instantaneously saw in vivid detail the new offensive capability of these warships. Rather, his thinking evolved in response to a range of influences, including the confrontation with Mitchell and the air-power adherents, his own more secure and influential position in the naval bureaucracy, the completion of the big new fleet carriers, and confidence that his five-year aircraft program would finally bring into the fleet adequate numbers of airplanes to carry out offensive missions.

In September 1925, as the Mitchell controversy swirled about him, Moffett appeared before the General Board to discuss his plans to equip *Saratoga* and *Lexington*. He wanted the ships to carry significant numbers of strike aircraft organized into two bomber squadrons for each carrier. Ken Whiting was also present at the hearings. When asked what he would do with the new carriers in a fleet action, he answered, "The day before the fleets engaged I would try to locate the enemy carriers to put them out of the engagement" using bombers and torpedo aircraft. With the enemy carriers sunk or disabled, Whiting said, he would then ask the commander in chief of the fleet for permission to attack other components of the enemy force, presumably including its capital ships.[3]

Experiments with *Langley* had provided direction for the future development of carrier aviation, but Moffett anxiously awaited the completion of *Saratoga* and *Lexington,* two ships with the power and speed to operate with the fleet and sufficient aircraft capacity to demonstrate the carrier's offensive capabilities. Unfortunately, there were frustrating delays in the ships' construction. Despite initial optimism that the work would go smoothly, the conversion of the vessels from the battle cruiser configuration was not as straightforward as anticipated. By the end of 1924, the ships were only a little more than 50 percent complete, and the Navy was in the embarrassing position of having to ask Congress for more money to finish them. The chief of the Bureau of Construction and Repair, Rear Adm. John D. Beuret, explained to the House Appropriations Committee on 8 December that an additional $10 million to $11 million each would be needed to complete the carriers. He went on to point out that the increases were due to a 100 percent rise in the cost of labor and material since 1916 and that extensive redesign of the ships and late changes ordered as a result of experiments with *Langley* had contributed to the delays and cost overruns. In January 1925, Congress passed a bill increasing the cost limit on the two ships from $23 million to $34 million each.[4]

Moffett followed the carriers' progress closely. He was in Camden, New Jersey, on 7 April 1925 to attend the launching ceremonies for *Saratoga* at the yards of the New York Shipbuilding Corporation, and he participated in the christening of *Lexington* at the yards of the Bethlehem Shipbuilding Corporation at Quincy, Massachusetts, on 3 October 1925. In a brief speech, he praised *Saratoga* and *Lexington* as ships "without equal anywhere else" in the world. *Lexington* embodied the principle of the offensive in naval warfare: "I am convinced that a bombing attack launched from such carriers from an unknown point, at an unknown instant, with an unknown objective, cannot be warded off" by any conventional defensive measures. Moffett was effusive: "LEXINGTON and SARATOGA! These are wonderful names in Naval history. It is particularly fitting that they should be chosen for these great vessels which are concrete evidence of the Navy's determination to utilize to its utmost this new and powerful weapon—the fleet air arm."[5]

Not until the latter part of 1927 did the new carriers join the fleet. *Saratoga* was first, in November 1927, followed by *Lexington* in December. In service the ships quickly lived up to the expectations everyone had for them. Big and powerful, they displaced 36,000 tons, had top speeds in excess of thirty-three knots, had considerable armor protection, and carried more than seventy aircraft each. But they had cost, with their aircraft complements, about $45 million apiece, and together they had consumed nearly half the American treaty allotment of 135,000 tons of aircraft carriers.

As the carriers inched toward completion, assistant secretary Edward Warner suggested in December 1926 that the time was ripe for another look at naval aviation policy, particularly because four years had passed since it had last been reviewed. Moffett took advantage of Warner's overture to present a report in which he examined the carrier forces of Britain, the United States, and Japan. He found that the Royal Navy had three big ships capable of participating in fleet operations, supplemented by three more carriers with lesser potential. Japan had a small experimental carrier and two big ships, converted from a battleship and a battle cruiser, nearing completion. Only the United States remained below her total tonnage allotment, necessitating that "definite steps be taken to obtain authorization for the construction of additional aircraft carriers." At the end of February 1927 he urged Secretary Wilbur to "review the situation in aviation, both ashore and afloat, particularly afloat, with a view to ascertaining how it can better meet the requirements of the fleet."[6]

Wilbur agreed. In April he ordered Rear Adm. Montgomery Taylor to convene a board to explore all aspects of naval aviation. Taylor was not Moffett's first choice to chair such a panel, particularly in light of the recommendations on aviation personnel made by his last board, but Moffett had little reason to complain about the new board's makeup. Moffett himself was a member, as was Capt. Joseph Mason Reeves. Other members were Capt. Harry Yarnell, who since the previous Taylor board had taken the observer's course at Pensacola and become a convert to naval aviation; Captains Henry V. Butler and James J. Raby, who had also passed through the observer's program; Comdr. Theodore Ellyson; and Lt. Comdr. Marc Mitscher. The board held daily hearings in Washington from 3 May to 6 May before adjourning and reconvening on 9 May at New York City aboard the battleship *California* for two more days of proceedings. Before the conclusion of the board's hearings, more than a dozen aviation personnel from the Bureau of Aeronautics and the fleet operating forces appeared as witnesses.[7]

The board found a wide divergence of opinion on matters relating to naval aviation, concluding that "the only way in which more satisfactory answers can be had is by trial along definite lines with the Fleet." There was general agreement with Moffett, however, on the need for additional aircraft carriers, and there were tantalizing hints that the board perceived an offensive role for the carrier beyond simply supporting the battleships in a fleet engagement. The board found carriers necessary for "service of the battle line to furnish fighting airplanes for its protection and a landing place for reservicing its airplanes; thus leaving other carriers free for scouting and offensive operations at a distance from the battle line too great to adequately serve it." More specifically, the Taylor board recommended that new naval aircraft be designed and produced to fill specific tactical and strategic roles, with priority going to new fighters, spotters, scouts, and dive bombers. In the board's hierarchy, torpedo planes and patrol aircraft had less importance than the other types.[8]

In its endorsement of the Taylor board's report in November 1927, the General Board concurred that the aircraft carrier, operating fighters and bombers well in advance of the battle fleet, was likely to play a major role in future naval actions. Accordingly, the General Board thought it imperative to authorize the construction of one new carrier immediately and complete one carrier per year thereafter until the Navy reached its treaty limits in this category of warship. The General Board also wanted the designs of new carriers to incorporate space for as many bombing aircraft as possible and emphasized that the ships had to be fully manned and maintained in the highest state of readiness.[9]

At the same time that the General Board was reviewing the Taylor report, it was deeply involved in aircraft-carrier design studies. The quantitative and qualitative ceilings imposed by the Washington treaty left the Navy with only limited options in future carrier construction. Within the 69,000 tons remaining to the United States (*Saratoga* and *Lexington* counted as 66,000 tons; *Langley* was an experimental ship and did not count against the treaty allocation), the basic alternatives were three 23,000-ton carriers, four 17,250-ton carriers, or five 13,800-ton carriers. The bureau's first recommendations, as part of Mustin's five-year plan, were for three 23,000-ton ships, but all that changed in 1926 and 1927.

Following in-depth studies by bureau staff and by the Naval War College, Moffett wrote to the General Board on 20 June 1927 with the bureau's recommendations on aircraft carrier characteristics. The analyses showed a "real and immediate need for additional carrier strength in the fleet, up to the full 135,000 tons allowed by [the] existing treaty" and that "aircraft can be handled far more expeditiously from a large number of small carriers than from a small number of large carriers." In general, the bureau found that new carrier designs should incorporate high speeds, flush decks, ample hangar space, minimum armor protection, and no guns larger than six inches. According to Moffett, the bureau had determined that combining the requirement of a flush deck with "the maximum speed, armament, and displacement that can be obtained, it appears that 14,000 tons approaches the upper limit of displacement which should be considered for carriers of the future." The bureau's studies indicated that a smaller ship, displacing no more than 10,000 tons, might also be feasible. Therefore, Moffett recommended, "We should proceed without further delay to construct one carrier of the smallest practicable size that will do the job, and with one carrier of the size which appears from present information to be the optimum size." Because of the long lead time involved in carrier design and construction, Moffett hoped to secure rapid authorization for the ships, allowing them to come into service sometime in 1931. He was confident that "this would allow ample time to take advantage of information regarding details which will be developed from SARATOGA and LEXINGTON." In conclusion, Moffett noted that it was "of vital importance that actual service experience in the use of light carriers be available as soon as possible" to help guide decisions regarding the best use of the remaining available carrier tonnage.[10]

On 18 October 1927, the General Board held hearings on carrier characteristics. Admiral Beuret presented the various design concepts examined by his bureau, with emphasis on a 13,800-ton carrier instead of the

10,000-ton ship. Moffett forcefully advocated the flush deck, stating that Aeronautics considered it "essential" based on the results of experiments with *Langley*. "We ought not to consider having the island type at all," he went on. "It affects not only the number of planes on deck but it also interferes in getting them off, to say nothing of the eddies that are set up by the stack itself which makes it difficult and more dangerous to land." He had no doubts about the advantages of building five 13,800-ton carriers as opposed to fewer larger ships. "I think . . . you don't lose much by that displacement, and it gives you another carrier under the treaty tonnage, so that your whole air force would be more mobile. You could have the air force in a greater number of places. . . . The more carriers you have the greater the number of planes you can have and the more protection you get."[11]

Moffett's views held sway as the General Board focused more intently on the 13,800-ton option during hearings on 9 March 1928. Following additional studies and discussions with Aeronautics officers and personnel from *Saratoga* and *Lexington*, which had recently entered service, the Bureau of Construction and Repair reported on the characteristics of the new ship. Speed was one of the principal considerations, important not only to provide wind over the deck for aircraft operations but also for defensive purposes. An encounter with a battleship, especially at night when the carrier could not launch strike aircraft, left little choice but to dash for safety at maximum speed. Admiral Beuret pointed out that 32.5 knots was desirable but would require a large engineering plant amidships, taking up space that could otherwise be used for aircraft, whereas a vessel with a speed of 29.5 knots needed machinery that occupied only half as much room and could be located aft if necessary. There remained the questions of numbers and types of guns the ships were to carry, with five-inch and even six-inch weapons receiving the most attention.[12]

The carrier's proposed armament bothered Moffett, who wanted to be sure that no one lost sight of the warship's principal function. He thought the General Board should "not sacrifice the aircraft feature to other activities more than is necessary." For the new carrier—the first such ship designed and built in the United States from the keel up—Moffett strongly believed that "we should not let anything interfere with the carrying of aircraft. It will be a compromise to some extent, but the sacrifice of aviation should be as little as possible. That is, on an aircraft carrier the guns should not interfere with her primary mission, which is to use aircraft. I think we must rely on the offensive use of aircraft as the principal agent for her defense against surface ships." Rather than five-inch or six-inch guns, Moffett wanted the new carrier to mount large numbers of small antiaircraft weapons.[13]

Lieutenant Comdr. Bruce Leighton, who handled most of the carrier studies in the Bureau of Aeronautics and was at Moffett's side during General Board hearings on the vessels, was in full agreement with Moffett about deleting heavy ordnance from the carrier designs and carrying as many aircraft as possible on the ships to enhance their striking power. On 7 August 1928, Leighton told the General Board that recent developments in aircraft and aircraft armament raised the "strong probability that we are only in the first stages of changes which will go a long way toward modifying our entire tactical concept of war at sea." He acknowledged that this was an "extreme view," but the General Board had to look to the long term in thinking about carrier requirements. Ten or twenty years hence, naval aircraft would have significantly enhanced performance and air operations at sea would be far more sophisticated than they were at present.[14]

While the General Board continued to weigh the specifics of carrier design, Moffett learned in August 1928 that Capt. Emory Land intended to leave his position as assistant chief and take a year of absence to serve with the Daniel Guggenheim Fund for the Promotion of Aeronautics. Moffett hated to see Land go, for he had been a capable and loyal subordinate, and Moffett knew that it would be much harder the second time around to resist pressure from the Bureau of Navigation in appointing his successor. Moffett's first choice for the job was Comdr. John Towers, who had served as *Langley*'s commanding officer since January 1927. But Towers was far too junior to be acceptable to Navigation's chief, Admiral Leigh. Almost by default, then, the position fell to Capt. Ernest J. King. King had been fourth in the academy's graduating class of 1901 and had a deserved reputation for being bright and efficient. He had completed the naval aviation observer course at Pensacola in 1926 and gone on to command the seaplane tender *Wright*. Moffett had followed King's career closely and regarded him as an officer of great potential, but he was unsure that King would be the team player he wanted as his assistant. Towers, meanwhile, came to Washington in September 1928 to head the bureau's Plans Division.[15]

The shuffling in the upper administrative echelons of the bureau in

1928 did not divert Moffett from his principal concentration on the aircraft carrier. Secretary Wilbur moved ahead to include five 13,800-ton ships in the department's proposed building program for fiscal year 1929 and beyond. Appearing before the House Naval Affairs Committee on 18 January 1928, Moffett laid out the Navy's plans for the maximum number of aircraft carriers. The carrier, he said, was a "floating flying field," essential for air operations with the fleet, particularly in far-distant waters where shore-based support facilities were nonexistent. The more aircraft carriers the United States had, the more effective such operations would be. He admitted that one small carrier was not as powerful as one large carrier, but "when there is a very real limit on total carrier tonnage—a limit imposed both by international agreement and by economical considerations—it is a basic truth that a large number of small carriers is always superior to a small number of large carriers." "Exhaustive" studies had shown that the 13,800-ton ship was best.[16]

Congress, however, rejected the department's proposal for five carriers, opting instead for fifteen large cruisers and only one carrier. Dismayed by what he considered the shortsightedness of Congress, Moffett wrote to Wilbur at the end of July 1928, repeating his contention that the United States still had "a decided inferiority" to Britain in carriers. He viewed the decision to reduce the program from five carriers to one as a "matter of very grave concern" and worried that it seriously detracted from the Navy's capabilities in future fleet actions.

Recent experiments with *Langley* had demonstrated conclusively that the carrier had considerable offensive power. Fighters and scouting airplanes flying from *Langley* could carry bombs heavy enough to inflict major damage on enemy warships. Moffett pointed out that *Langley* did not have nearly the size or speed of *Saratoga* and *Lexington*, ships able to operate significantly greater numbers of more powerful airplanes. "It is apparent therefore, that our present deficiency in aircraft carriers is retarding the Navy's readiness for war in a triple sense, involving: (a) A grave lack of an important service type of vessel, which prevents; (b) The proper determination of sound operating methods, which further precludes; (c) The development of aircraft embodying those tactical characteristics necessary in Naval operations." He urged Wilbur to do whatever he could to see that the remainder of the American carrier tonnage was finished, even if it meant sacrificing the construction of cruisers.[17]

Yet nothing either Moffett or Wilbur did changed the picture as far as the number of carriers was concerned. In February 1929, Congress passed a bill authorizing construction of the fifteen cruisers and the lone 13,800-ton carrier. Appropriations came slowly, however, and it was not until September 1931 that the new carrier, named *Ranger,* was laid down. She was an austere ship reflecting numerous compromises. Moffett's and the aviators' ideas to the contrary, the vessel did not have a flush deck, incorporating instead a small island on the starboard side amidships. Hinged stacks located aft along both sides of the hull carried boiler gases down and away from the flight deck. The ship's design included eight 5-inch guns, despite Moffett's objections, but also featured were forty light automatic antiaircraft guns lining the edges of the flight deck. *Ranger*'s hangar was significantly larger than the ones on *Saratoga* and *Lexington,* and her shops and repair facilities were laid out more efficiently. Her design provided for seventy-two aircraft, divided into two squadrons of fighters and two squadrons of dive bombers.[18]

The development of dive bombing tactics helped to shape the views of Moffett and his staff about the offensive capability of the aircraft carrier in the twenties. Apparently there were never any decisions within the upper echelons of the Navy's command structure to authorize or implement dive bombing as a doctrine. Instead, the tactic evolved during the interwar years as higher-performance aircraft became available, squadrons perfected techniques, and exercises confirmed its efficacy. In an informal, ad hoc way the Navy acquired a carrier-borne strike weapon with enormous ship-killing potential.

Marine aviators pioneered dive bombing in Haiti in 1919 and Nicaragua in 1927. Flying DH-4Bs and using fifty-pound bombs, the leathernecks found that the technique permitted remarkably accurate attacks on concentrations of native guerrilla forces. In 1926, Navy fighter units on both coasts also experimented with the technique. But for delivering effective strikes on enemy warships, Navy planners recognized the need for more robust aircraft and heavier bombs. Lieutenant Commander Leighton informed the General Board on 9 March 1928 that "the diving bomb attack . . . is not so far in the future as we are prone to believe." The fleet already had aircraft that could drop 300-pound bombs in diving attacks, and he was certain that in the near future 500-pound bombs would be employed. By the time *Ranger* joined the fleet, Leighton predicted, dive bombing would be "in full use" by the Navy.[19]

Fleet exercises confirmed Leighton's prophecy. In November 1928, simulated level bombing attacks on battleships demonstrated that intense antiaircraft fire would exact a heavy toll on the bombers. Rapid changes in altitude threw off the defenders' aim but also dramatically reduced the accuracy of the bombing. *Saratoga* and *Lexington* participated in maneuvers with the battle fleet off San Diego in May and June 1931. During exercises on 3–5 June, the carriers' torpedo bombers encountered heavy antiaircraft fire from the battleships and suffered unacceptable losses. On the other hand, dive bombers struck their targets with virtual impunity.[20]

From Moffett's presentations to the General Board it was clear that the number of aircraft platforms was the overriding consideration in all decisions as far as carriers were concerned, and he was determined to do everything possible to achieve treaty parity with Great Britain. Few objected in principle to the 13,800-ton carrier, but Moffett's desire for the maximum number of such ships ran counter to others' desire to use the Navy's limited resources to build the cruiser force up to the level of Britain's. There was seemingly no way around the dilemma: either provide sufficient carriers to match Britain or build up the Navy's strength in cruisers, but not both. This direct challenge to Moffett's considerable powers of compromise resulted in the design of a peculiar hybrid warship, the flying-deck cruiser.

Moffett was not the first to see the dual-purpose warship as a means of satisfying the Navy's requirements for both cruisers and carriers. In 1925, the General Board briefly considered a suggestion for a cruiser-carrier only to reject it because the experience of other navies with similar ships had not been positive. There was, in addition, the firm belief that a hybrid vessel would exhibit all the disadvantages of the cruiser and the carrier individually while incorporating few of those ships' advantages. Yet the idea of combination warships persisted. In 1928, Congressman James V. McClintic, a Democrat from Oklahoma and a member of the House Naval Affairs Committee, suggested fitting flight decks to all eighteen of the Navy's battleships. The following year, the Bureau of Aeronautics put forth a design study for modifying eight-inch-gun cruisers with an enclosed hangar for no fewer than eight catapult-launched floatplanes.[21] But it was not until the eve of new naval arms limitation negotiations in London, along with the pressing need to achieve parity with Britain and clear superiority over Japan, that the flying-deck cruiser emerged as a viable alternative to more conventional warships.

Moffett was looking ahead to a new naval conference when he wrote to

Wilbur in July 1928 expressing his concern about the failure of Congress to provide for additional 13,800-ton aircraft carriers. He predicted that carrier tonnage would be an important issue at the conference and that it would be imperative to determine what types of carriers were best for the United States before making any decisions about qualitative limitations. Both Britain and Japan were in position to take maximum advantage of the tonnage limitations by employing a combination of large and small carriers, and Britain's *Hermes* and Japan's *Hosho* had given them much more experience than the United States in the operation of ships in the 10,000-ton category. "This situation," Moffett continued, "is accentuated by the fact that our carrier tonnage, being embodied in larger units, cannot support in sustained operations, a number of planes equal to that capable of being supported by the same tonnage embodied in smaller units, as is the case with British and Japanese carriers."[22]

Many diplomatic, economic, and military factors led the three principal naval powers, along with France and Italy, to agree to meet in London in 1930 to consider revisions of the existing naval limitation agreements and the restriction of vessels not covered by the quantitative limits imposed by the Washington treaty. Of primary concern were the fundamental differences between the British and the Americans on numbers and types of cruisers. Put simply, the British wanted the maximum number of smaller cruisers within the total tonnage agreed on, and the United States wanted to build fewer numbers of larger, 10,000-ton, eight-inch-gun ships, the maximum size and armament permissible under the qualitative limitations of the Washington treaty. Other considerations were setting total tonnage limits on destroyers, reducing the maximum unit tonnage of capital ships, extending the Washington agreements on capital ships for another five years, and reducing the total tonnage ceilings on aircraft carriers. Caught in what appeared to be a rapidly escalating and expensive race to build more cruisers, Britain, the United States, and Japan agreed in principle to place total tonnage caps on these ships. Moreover, President Herbert Hoover had strongly pacifistic leanings and wanted to do everything possible to cut government spending as the nation faced economic uncertainties in the wake of the 1929 stock market crash.[23]

Anticipating the conference, Moffett sent a long letter on 23 November 1929 to Hoover's secretary of the Navy, Charles Francis Adams. He warned that the United States must resist attempts to reduce the total carrier tonnage below the 135,000 tons set by the Washington treaty. One or more of the powers might also attempt to restrict air strength by suggesting reductions in total aircraft. Statistics showed that the United States had a definite edge over both Britain and Japan in this category, but Moffett insisted that the numerical preponderance was deceptive. "There is a widespread and very mistaken conception on the part of many who have studied this matter only superficially, picturing aircraft as more or less self-contained agents." In truth, aircraft required an elaborate infrastructure of support facilities and personnel, and to be effective in distant offensive naval operations they had to operate from carriers. "Any comparison of effective naval air strengths," Moffett concluded, "must be predicated on a basis of available carriers."

Moffett believed that the conventional means of comparing naval strength by unit and total tonnages was "dangerously misleading" when applied to aircraft carriers. Of far more importance in gauging the capability of a carrier was the size of the ship's flight deck. It was obvious, then, that within agreed-upon total tonnage limitations, "there is a far greater flight deck area available on a large number of small ships than a small number of large ships." *Saratoga* and *Lexington* were excellent examples. The tonnage of one of those carriers could be distributed in two 16,500-ton ships, each of which could operate the same number of aircraft as the bigger vessel while enhancing mobility and operational flexibility.

Because the number of flight decks was more important than total tonnage, the United States entered the conference at a disadvantage to the British. Not only did they have six carriers to the American three but they also could replace most of those ships at will. The Washington treaty had categorized all carriers built or building before November 1921 as experimental and permitted their replacement at any time, whereas carriers completed after 1921 could not be replaced for twenty years. Under those circumstances, the British had four experimental carriers and the United States only one. Adhering to the replacement schedule and staying within the quantitative limits of the Washington pact, Britain could build seven more carriers and the United States only five, giving the British an insurmountable advantage of nine carriers to seven. "In light of the foregoing, it is of paramount importance that steps be taken in the forthcoming Armament Conference to remove this permanent handicap," Moffett concluded.

Moffett offered two recommendations. The first was to have the American representatives at the conference insist on reclassifying *Saratoga* and

Lexington as experimental. This proposal was "based on a very reasonable premise because in fact, these ships were . . . much more experimental than those of Great Britain. They were of an experimental nature even as battle cruisers; they were doubly so as converted carriers." He believed that the Japanese would support the idea, because their carriers *Kaga* and *Akagi* were converted under roughly the same circumstances as the American ships, and there were indications that Japan was leaning toward smaller carriers. Moffett's second proposal was to have the Navy indicate before attending the conference that the United States was definitely going to build two more 13,800-ton carriers. He saw this as a means of immediately making up the American disadvantage in flight decks while signaling to the British that the United States would accept nothing other than parity.[24]

His ideas received a less-than-enthusiastic reception from Rear Adm. Andrew T. Long, who coordinated the General Board's preconference planning studies. Long dismissed as totally unrealistic Moffett's recommendation that *Saratoga* and *Lexington* be reclassified as experimental carriers. On the other hand, he agreed that "any reduction of total carrier tonnage below 135,000 tons would be to the serious disadvantage of the United States." He generally agreed about the importance of counting flight decks. The question Long asked was how to translate numbers of flight decks into a quantitative ceiling on aircraft carriers without imposing unacceptable restrictions on the individual powers' ability to design and build the types of ships they needed to meet their particular requirements. What Moffett really wanted was a guideline to measure the efficiency of the nations' carrier fleets, and Long did not think there was any practical way to do so. Furthermore, he argued that Moffett had failed to take into account that the United States would have to fight a future naval war far from home in the western Pacific and would consequently rely heavily on the great size and high speed of carriers like *Saratoga* and *Lexington*. Limitation by total tonnages, he admitted, was imperfect—it "merely provides equality of opportunity, it does not guarantee equality of results"—but there were no alternatives.[25]

How, then, was the United States to catch up and maintain parity in aircraft carriers with Britain and preserve a numerical advantage over Japan? Well before the London Conference, Moffett had concluded that the only answer was to boost the number of American carriers by going outside the total carrier tonnage, in other words, counting them against either the battleship or the cruiser tonnages. Because there was little likelihood of changes in the quantitative restrictions on battleships at London, the cruiser category was all that was left in which to negotiate. But for some time it had also been apparent to Moffett that neither the Navy Department nor Congress was going to permit small carriers to take up any of the American cruiser tonnage, whatever the final figures might turn out to be. Driven by the inescapable logic of the situation and naturally drawn to compromise, Moffett saw the construction of a certain number of flying-deck cruisers as the sole possible solution.

On 4 December 1929, Moffett's orders came through to report to the secretary of the Navy for temporary duty in connection with preparations for the London Conference, followed on the last day of the year by formal notification of his appointment as a technical adviser to the American delegation. Headed by secretary of State Henry L. Stimson, the group included secretary of the Navy Adams, Ambassador Charles G. Dawes, Senators David A. Reed and Joseph T. Robinson, Hugh S. Gibson, and Dwight Morrow. Moffett was only one of many on the large advisory staff assembled by Adm. William V. Pratt, now serving as commander in chief of the U.S. Fleet. In addition to Moffett, the senior members of the technical staff were Adm. Hilary P. Jones; Rear Adm. J. R. P. Pringle, president of the Naval War College; Harry Yarnell, now a rear admiral and chief of the Bureau of Engineering; and Pratt's chief of staff, Rear Adm. Arthur J. Hepburn.[26]

Moffett was busy the entire month of December preparing for the conference. With typical thoroughness, he and his staff produced a compendium filled with detailed background information pertaining to aviation and naval arms limitation for use in developing guidelines for the conference. Meanwhile, he turned over most of his regular duties to Jack Towers, the bureau's capable assistant chief. Moffett's reservations about having Ernest King as his assistant had turned out to be justified, because the two officers mixed like oil and water. King recalled twenty years later that Land had told him it would be "easy to get along all right" with Moffett but the admiral had a propensity for playing favorites among his subordinates. Haughty and self-centered, King did not like being assistant to anyone, and he was uncomfortable with Moffett's demands for absolute loyalty and the admiral's seeming unwillingness to listen to opposing opinions on important policy matters.[27]

It is possible Moffett and King might have been able to bury their personal feelings and establish a long-term working relationship if another dispute had not arisen over aviation personnel. This time it involved an effort by Admiral Leigh to assign Lt. Al Williams to sea duty. Since 1926, Williams had been working with a private, nonprofit company to design and build a Schneider Trophy racer. Just as the airplane was nearing completion in the spring of 1929, Admiral Leigh sent through Williams's orders. Seeing Leigh's move as another attempt by the Bureau of Navigation to block Moffett's efforts to achieve authority over the assignment of aviation officers, Moffett protested. King, however, saw no reason why officers in Aeronautics or any other bureau should enjoy special privileges, and he told Moffett so. Barely able to contain his anger, Moffett replied that if King felt that strongly about the issue, then perhaps the best thing he could do was to step aside and let King take over as bureau chief. Their differences beyond reconciliation, they agreed that it was best for King to seek reassignment. King moved on to command of the Naval Air Station, Hampton Roads, and Jack Towers filled the slot at the bureau on 24 April.[28]

Towers was one of the bureau officers most trusted and admired by Moffett. The two shared a common objective in establishing aviation as an integral part of the Navy and saw the aircraft carrier as the best means of securing that end. During the nearly four months he was away from Washington in London in early 1930, Moffett corresponded with Towers on a regular basis, keeping him informed about matters and advising him on pressing bureau concerns. In Moffett's absence, Towers represented the bureau at congressional hearings dealing with appropriations for the five-year aircraft program and the construction of a second fleet airship. But he was unable to prevent the Bureau of Navigation from assigning Al Williams to sea duty with the carrier *Lexington* or to prevent Williams from resigning his Navy commission in protest on 7 March 1930.[29]

Secure in the knowledge that he could count on Towers to uphold the bureau's interests while he attended the London Conference, Moffett left Washington by train with the American delegation on 9 January 1930. The group arrived later in the day in Hoboken, New Jersey, where they boarded the United States Lines steamer *George Washington*. On the eight-day voyage Moffett talked individually to the civilian members of the delegation about aviation issues, although there was no general meeting to discuss policy. The ship arrived in Plymouth on the seventeenth, where the lord mayor feted the Americans before they continued on by rail to

London. The whirlwind began soon after the delegation arrived in the British capital. The Americans were split between the Ritz, where the civilian representatives stayed, and the Mayfair, where Moffett and the rest of the naval and technical staff had their accommodations. On 18 January, the representatives paid a courtesy visit to the prime minister, Ramsay MacDonald, who was head of the British delegation to the conference, followed by a formal dinner at the American embassy later that evening. On the afternoon of the twentieth, King George V received the Americans at Buckingham Palace and that evening hosted a dinner at the Savoy Hotel.[30]

At eleven on the morning of 21 January, the conference opened in the Royal Gallery of the House of Lords. The first plenary session involved little more than a formal introduction to the proceedings of the conference, with a welcoming address by the king and brief speeches by the heads of the various delegations. Moffett wrote to Towers on the twenty-third to tell him that most of the preparatory work had been finished and that he looked forward to getting some "real work" done. During discussions among the American representatives, Moffett and other naval advisers agitated for an increase in the carrier tonnage totals. They found almost no support among the civilians, who were conscious that there was pressure to reduce tonnages at the conference, not to increase them. Everyone was aware, too, that the British wanted to reduce the carrier totals for the two countries to 100,000 tons each. As the Americans hammered out a plan, Moffett (although not giving up hope that it still might be possible to increase carrier tonnages) suggested that each nation be permitted to use a portion of its cruiser tonnage for small aircraft carriers. Admiral Jones was insistent that none of the cruiser tonnage be allocated to small carriers unless there was agreement to increase the tonnage ceilings in the cruiser category, but Pratt was generally favorable to Moffett's idea.[31]

Encouraged, Moffett presented a memorandum to the delegation on 31 January formally proposing that a clause be inserted in the tentative American plan letting the powers use some of their cruiser tonnage for small aircraft carriers. He saw this as a way to satisfy those who wanted big carriers and to meet what he saw as the obvious need for the maximum number of flight decks. Under the plan the United States could conceivably use all of its tonnage in the aircraft carrier category for large ships while reserving part of its cruiser tonnage for smaller vessels. To answer critics like Jones who objected to the reduction of cruisers, Moffett proposed that some of the ships could be built as combination carrier-cruisers. Evidently Moffett's memo was acceptable, because the proposal stimulated a series of feasibility studies of flying-deck cruisers by naval engineers attached to the delegation.[32]

By the second week of February the flying-deck cruiser had become even more attractive, after Moffett realized that an increase in carrier tonnage was unlikely at London. It was also apparent to him that the British would insist on banning all carriers smaller than 10,000 tons because they feared such vessels, depending on their armament, might overlap the cruiser category. Moffett wrote Towers that he had "been doing everything I know to make more aircraft carrier tonnage available, but it looks as if I had lost out. If they do not reduce the 135,000 tons, I will have to be satisfied." Later Moffett told Towers that he had repeatedly brought the question up with Adams and Pratt, who were cool to the idea. Pratt, Moffett said, "was adamant for letting carriers alone; he feels that if we brought it up we might lose," because the British would demand a reduction.[33]

Among the technical advisers Moffett found mostly disinterest in aviation questions. With the exception of Yarnell, they "never mention aircraft. They have no picture in their minds. I have explained all the arguments used against getting an increase, but the fact that the rest of the advisers would not urge any handicapped me greatly. I have constantly endeavored to indoctrinate them all and I think that they know a great deal more about aircraft carriers than they did before and perhaps appreciate them more, but for all practical purposes at this conference, we are through, and all I hope for now is 135,000 tons." Moffett buffered his disappointment by telling Towers that it was unlikely under any circumstances that the United States would build more than five carriers before the expiration of the treaty in 1936.[34] Increasingly, Moffett was drawn to the flying-deck cruiser as the only means of offsetting the British numerical advantage in aircraft carriers.

As the conference wore on and the negotiators waded through the esoterica of offensive versus defensive armaments, gun calibers, and ship specifications, Moffett followed the situation closely. He pored over stenographic copies of meetings of the various technical committees, examining them for information that might be useful in arguing his points about naval aviation and the aircraft carrier. Of particular interest to him were discussions of vessels in the exempt categories and those ships under 10,000 tons that might be capable of operating aircraft. In a letter to Towers on 17 February he gave his impressions of developments so far. He was disappointed by British efforts to reduce total carrier tonnages and the consequent failure of the American delegation to press for increases, but he observed that "it must gall [the British] to be in a position where they have to admit that anybody can claim parity with them and to feel that we are here to make them reduce their navy." Continuing in a reflective mood, Moffett wrote, "I can not help but feel that Great Britain has reached her pinnacle; that they have a glorious history and traditions but are living on traditions too much, in my opinion. They have traditions and what is generally called aristocracy, but while we are comparatively short on both, we have virility and are a young nation, stepping out with vision and confidence, and nothing will stop our being the greatest nation in the world except what we do within ourselves."[35]

When he had the opportunity to break away from the conference proceedings and the seemingly endless rounds of luncheons, dinners, and receptions, Moffett got out of the city to inspect naval and aviation facilities. On 25 February, he visited Calshot and flew around the Isle of Wight as a passenger in a British twin-engine flying boat. Three days later, he traveled to the air station at Hendon and, despite poor weather, made two flights in the vicinity of the base. Before the month was out, he also visited the British airship hangar at Cardington, where the big R-100 was undergoing flight tests. In a letter to Congressman Burton L. French on 5 March, Moffett wrote that he was convinced from his personal observations that "our Naval Aviation is far ahead of theirs, on the whole." The British had a "great advantage" over the United States in aircraft carriers, but they had far fewer aircraft in operation with the fleet. Moreover, "their having a separate Department of Air is a tremendous handicap to the Navy, and they have spent, as one Naval officer told me, about eight years fighting the Air Ministry. They have practically no control over their Air arm and have to take what the Air Ministry will give them."[36] Moffett's assessment was entirely accurate. Not until 1937 did the Royal Navy regain control over the fleet air arm, too late to obtain the specialized aircraft types needed for intensive operations during World War II.

Moffett made several more inspection tours before ending his service in London. On 12 March, he visited Royal Air Force stations at Northolt, Stag Lane, and Heston, and on the fourteenth he flew from Hendon on a three-hour aerial circuit of British air installations in the vicinity of London. Another excursion, on 26 March, was a motor trip to the City of London and Tilbury dock areas. There he saw extensive and modern facilities for handling vast quantities of cargo, but he came away with the impression that the Tilbury docks, controlled by a single gate, were particularly vulnerable to air attack. The last of his side trips was to Paris on 8 April to visit the French military aviation research center at Villacoublay. He returned to London the next day on a scheduled French Air Union flight.[37]

By the middle of February, the Americans and the British had reached a tentative understanding that secured the success of the London Conference. They agreed to a five-year extension of the Washington treaty's holiday from the construction of new capital ships. The United States went along with British demands for two cruiser categories and reduced its demand for twenty-one 8-inch-gun cruisers to eighteen, supplemented by twenty 6-inch-gun ships, ten of which—in the *Omaha* class—had already been completed. For their part, the British agreed to a slightly lower total tonnage ceiling for cruisers, fifteen of the 8-inch-gun ships, and a marginally greater tonnage of 6-inch-gun ships. Resolution of Anglo-American differences on the vexatious cruiser issue forced the Japanese to compromise in their efforts to raise their cruiser ratio across the board from 10:6 to 10:7 and paved the way for understandings on destroyers and submarines.[38]

Despite basic agreement among the three naval powers in all categories of warships, there remained considerable work for the technical advisers at London. Reluctant to go along with any limitations on submarines and unwilling to accede to parity with Italy, France dragged out negotiations for the better part of a month. Near the end of March, Moffett reported that France was unlikely to sign any accord coming out of London and that he saw no chance for a five-power treaty. Some measure of Moffett's frustration is evident in a letter to Comdr. Newton H. White, Jr.: "I am very much bored with the Conference and will be glad when it is over. The Conference might well be called 'much ado about nothing' because they are dealing with obsolete weapons and giving almost no attention to aircraft, or rather, aircraft carriers."[39]

As much as anything, Moffett was relieved when he learned on 31 March that he, Yarnell, and Pringle were to return home. In London he had tenaciously played the advocate role. Almost single-handedly he had fought to preserve the status quo in total aircraft carrier tonnage and through sheer perseverance had persuaded the American delegation to accept the flying-deck cruiser. Admiral Pratt told Moffett at one point that he was "the most persistent man he had ever met." Jones agreed, telling Moffett that "when [he] went to Arlington for the last time, they would find 'aircraft carrier' inscribed on [his] heart."[40] When he left London, it was clear that the British were willing to go along with the Americans on total carrier tonnage and were prepared to accept flight decks on a percentage of ships in the cruiser category. Moffett may not have realized it at the time, but his presence at London had measurably affected the outcome of the conference.

On 11 April, Moffett sailed from Southampton aboard the liner *George Washington,* arriving in New York ten days later. Shortly after leaving the ship, Moffett issued a statement to the press. The London Conference, he said, convinced him that the United States had made real progress in aviation. More still needed to be done in the development of high-performance, fighter-type airplanes and in the lighter-than-air field, but from the perspective he gained abroad, American equipment and operating experience compared favorably with those of any foreign power. To Moffett, a three-power naval treaty "will be a God-send to our country and to the world. If we have the national pride we boast of, we will have parity in fact as well as in name. We have the population and resources to be first and ought to be content with nothing less." Moffett returned to Washington with his aide and several other officers aboard a Navy Ford Trimotor, landing at Anacostia early in the afternoon of 21 April.[41]

Next day, on the other side of the Atlantic, the United States, Britain, and Japan signed the London Naval Treaty. Of the most interest to Moffett were the points in the accord pertaining to aircraft carriers and the flying-deck cruiser. The treaty preserved the 135,000-ton ceiling on total carrier tonnage for the United States and Britain and the 5:5:3 ratio in this type of warship. In a separate article, the London agreement closed the door on small carriers by prohibiting the construction of such vessels displacing less than 10,000 tons and mounting guns larger than six inches. There was also a clause stating that the signatories could add flight decks to capital ships, cruisers, and destroyers without having such vessels "charged against or classified in the category of aircraft carriers." Because the treaty prohibited fitting existing capital ships with flight decks and experiments had demonstrated that destroyers were too small to be so equipped, it was obvious that cruisers were the only vessels suitable for conversion to or construction as aviation ships. But under the terms of the treaty each signatory could equip no more than 25 percent of the ships in the cruiser category with flight decks.[42]

So busy was Moffett with the aviation implications of the London treaty that weeks passed before he was able to resume his full normal work schedule at the bureau. He immersed himself initially in Senate hearings on the treaty. On 22 May, Moffett appeared before the Naval Affairs Committee, where he testified that in London he had successfully opposed a reduction in total aircraft carrier tonnage. He added that he regretted losing the right to build small aircraft carriers and charge them against the cruiser category, but "we could not get everything, and the solution which we have, of putting landing decks on 25 per cent of the cruisers, was a great deal." On the cruiser issue, Moffett agreed with Pratt, Yarnell, and Hepburn that the nation needed a mix of eight-inch-gun and six-inch-gun ships and that eighteen of the larger cruisers was sufficient to meet the Navy's requirements. Had the United States not been willing to accept the smaller cruisers, Moffett doubted that there would have been any treaty at all.

It was almost heresy in light of the preoccupation with the cruiser controversy in London, but Moffett believed "the tonnage of aircraft carriers and the number of aircraft carriers that we can have is of much greater importance than that of any other category or of the question of the 8" vs. 6" gun cruisers." What was important in regard to cruisers, however, was the right to fit a quarter of the ships with flight decks. To Moffett a six-inch-gun cruiser with a flight deck and aircraft was more "than at least equal, and in my opinion, superior to the 8" gun cruiser without landing decks."

Flying-deck cruisers were better than nothing, but they were no substitute for aircraft carriers. The London Conference had helped crystallize in Moffett's mind a vision of future warfare in which the carrier played a vital if not central role. In the event of war in the western Pacific, the scenario was this: The American battle fleet would lead the advance across the Pacific, at least until it got within range of Japanese land-based aircraft. At that point the carriers would take over, launching strikes against enemy shore bases and neutralizing the opposition's air strength. For such a campaign to succeed, it was essential for the United States to maintain in peacetime a clear superiority over Japan in numbers of aircraft carriers.

Approval of the treaty was essential, for Moffett believed that it was unlikely Congress would otherwise authorize or appropriate the money for the numbers of ships needed to keep pace with Britain and to sustain a lead over Japan. To illustrate the problem, he pointed to the failure of Congress to provide for five aircraft carriers to achieve parity with Britain. He said that despite doing "everything I could to get the aircraft carriers built," only *Ranger* had been approved. At least in aircraft carriers the Washington treaty had imposed a total tonnage ceiling. In other warship categories the two nations had engaged in unlimited building, far outstripping the pace of construction in the United States. This was the essence of Moffett's advocacy of the treaty. He wanted ratification "without change and without reservation provided that we build our Navy up to the authorized treaty strength prior to the holding of the next Conference."[43]

But Moffett, Pratt, and other naval officers were a minority in supporting Senate approval of the treaty. On 3 June, Moffett wrote to John H. Gunnell, formerly attached to the bureau and now a captain with the American naval mission in Peru, to complain that those who opposed the treaty were "doing more to sink the Navy than the Japanese have ever done or ever will do. . . . The question of six or eight inch guns is of course of no importance as compared with the right to put landing decks on 80,000 tons of six inch gun cruisers. No one has mentioned Aviation at the hearings except Pratt, Yarnell and myself. They are talking about inches where we are talking about thousands of pounds of bombs."[44]

In a letter the same day to H. Ralph Burton of the National Patriotic League, Moffett expressed many of the same opinions. He believed that approving the treaty was crucial if the United States was to halt its decline relative to the other naval powers. Since the Washington Conference, Congress had consistently failed to initiate a building program aimed at keeping up with Britain and Japan. Without the treaty and the imposition of additional tonnage limitations, there was every reason to believe that the United States would fall even farther behind. "In other words," Moffett wrote, "there are a great many reasons for ratifying the treaty and comparatively few, if any, reasons for not doing so." Somehow Secretary Adams learned of the correspondence and, heeding the administration's policy of restricting public access to information on the treaty until after the Senate took action, forbade Moffett to send the letter to Burton.[45]

With the fate of the treaty still to be determined by the Senate, Moffett launched a campaign in the Navy Department to build the fleet up to the maximum permissible limits in aircraft carriers and flying-deck cruisers. In a memo to Adams on 28 May, Moffett called for the construction of five 13,800-ton carriers and eight 10,000-ton flying-deck cruisers with six-inch guns. The General Board favored immediate authorization of the carriers but was decidedly cool to the flying-deck cruiser. Nevertheless, Moffett secured permission to begin experiments on *Saratoga* to ascertain whether aircraft could operate safely and efficiently from a flight deck of the size contemplated for the cruisers. The success of those tests, coupled with Pratt's active support for the proposed vessel when he became chief of Naval Operations in September, were enough to keep the flying-deck cruiser part of subsequent plans to build the Navy to its treaty limits.[46]

In public appearances following Senate approval of the London treaty on 21 July, Moffett presented the agreement as the best means of increasing the strength of the Navy in general and of naval aviation in particular. On 29 July, at the dedication of the James Clements Airport in Bay City, Michigan, Moffett used the occasion to survey recent progress in naval aviation and to emphasize that the Navy must continue in a position of leadership. He explained why the London treaty was in the best interests of the Navy and the nation. "There were so many reasons for its ratification that I was at a loss to understand the opposition," Moffett said. "Aside from its benefits to peace, international good-will, [and] saving of money, it repairs the most serious defect of the Washington Treaty. We scrapped our battleships, the only Naval power we had, and left the door wide open in all other categories. This blunder has now been retrieved in the London Treaty, by limiting all categories, and for our national pride and self respect we must build to the Treaty limits."[47]

The flying-deck cruiser became the centerpiece in Moffett's efforts to secure additional aircraft platforms for the fleet. In October, the General Board recommended that one of the vessels be included in the construction program for fiscal year 1932. Secretary of the Navy Adams followed up later in the year with a draft naval construction bill setting aside $20,780,000 for an experimental flying-deck cruiser and $27,650,000 for an aircraft carrier. On 18 December, Moffett spoke in support of the measure before the House Naval Affairs Committee. He saw the flying-deck cruiser as a means of partially offsetting the British advantage in aircraft carriers and as the forerunner of a powerful new class of warship. In answer to those critics who charged that the flight deck and aviation facilities on the ship detracted from her ability to carry out her primary mission,

Moffett argued that aircraft actually enhanced the vessel's capabilities in the long-range strategic scouting role and provided an augmented strike capacity that the conventional six-inch-gun cruiser lacked. He broadly asserted that he was "convinced that in single combat one of the 6-inch platform cruisers can even defeat any 8-inch cruiser now afloat."[48]

As Congress considered the fate of the flying-deck cruiser, Aeronautics officers worked with their opposite numbers in the Bureau of Construction and Repair on a series of tentative design schemes for the new warship. They faced a daunting task: incorporating the diverse requirements for speed, an effective main battery, antiaircraft protection, and the maximum aircraft operating capacity without exceeding the 10,000-ton limit. During General Board hearings in December 1930 on the characteristics of the vessel, Admiral Pratt set the tone by insisting that he wanted a cruiser and not a small carrier. Moffett obviously preferred the opposite but knew he needed Pratt's support if the concept were to have any chance of success. He did, however, suggest that the ship's design segregate the aviation and gunnery functions, preferring a preliminary scheme that had all three 6-inch-gun turrets forward. Any design with three turrets and nine guns, he said, was "not open to any criticism of being an aircraft carrier instead of a cruiser."[49]

His predilections aside, Moffett remained sensitive to the prevailing attitude that the ship was to be primarily a cruiser. When the General Board held additional hearings on the ship's characteristics on 23 December, he said he wanted a long, flush deck and hinged funnels to maximize the safety and efficiency of flight operations. He pointed out that the flush deck might actually strengthen the ship's cruiser function by reducing the weight of the superstructure and eliminating top hamper that might be damaged in a gun battle. The General Board thought otherwise, recommending that the vessel have the shortest deck consistent with safety and that it incorporate fixed exhaust stacks in an island set off to the starboard side, although it did concur on locating the guns in three forward turrets.[50]

In the preliminary design that was finally presented to the secretary of the Navy in July 1931, the Bureau of Construction and Repair adhered for the most part to the General Board's mandate. The proposed 10,000-ton ship was to operate twenty-four aircraft. A 65-foot-wide flight deck extending 332 feet and angled slightly to port to clear the island on the starboard side was the principal feature of the design. The ship's main battery consisted of nine 6-inch guns in three turrets mounted forward of the flight deck. Minor alterations to the design resulted from General Board hearings in the summer of 1931, but for all practical purposes the ship's design remained fixed from that point on.[51]

As Moffett should have known from previous experience with ship and aircraft procurement, authorization and plans were not enough to guarantee acquisition. Nevertheless, he expressed dismay when he found out that Congress was not going to take any action on new warship construction before the end of the legislative session in the winter of 1931. To Charles W. Schick, head of the American Legion's National Defense Committee in Chicago, he wrote that the failure of Congress meant that nothing would be done until December at the earliest, ensuring that no new ships would be laid down until after 1 July 1932, the beginning of the new fiscal year. Considering the lead time involved in the construction of major warships, the dilatoriness of the legislators guaranteed that "no ships would be finished before the next Limitation of Armaments Conference in 1935, and that we would again be in the position that we were in at the London Conference, with paper ships instead of real ships."[52]

President Hoover shared the blame with Congress for the failure to secure a naval bill in 1931. Moffett wrote to his friend and classmate Claude Bailey on 30 September 1931 and vented his anger. He felt he had been double-crossed. The Navy, and he personally, had been "absolutely loyal" to the chief executive in all questions relating to the London treaty. "I supported the Treaty, as you know, but I did so with the expectation and belief that the President would build up to it. I don't think he has ever had any intention and I feel sure he has no desire to do so." Moffett was confident that had Hoover demonstrated effective leadership and pushed for the naval construction bill, it would have passed and the Navy would have had its flying-deck cruiser. He told Bailey that he "will be particularly disappointed if not one is even started."[53]

There was a ray of hope that the flying-deck cruiser would be resurrected when Congressman Vinson, the new chairman of the House Naval Affairs Committee, introduced a bill in January 1932 for the construction of one of the ships. But Congress was no more willing to increase naval spending than it had been the previous year, and Vinson, realizing that the measure had no chance of passing, withheld it from consideration by the full House. Born in the expediency of naval arms limitation, Moffett's fly-ing-deck cruiser died in the financial exigency of the nation's worst eco-nomic crisis.[54]

Contemporary critics of the flying-deck cruiser were right; the ship would have been neither a good aircraft carrier nor a good cruiser. Moffett exaggerated the merits of the proposed warship, but there is little doubt he understood that the type was, at best, a compromise that made sense only in the unusual diplomatic and naval climate of the late twenties and early thirties. As much as anyone else at the time, Moffett knew the air-craft carrier met the Navy's aviation requirements far better than did the flying-deck cruiser, and he believed he could justify the hybrid ship only as part of a wider obligation to acquire the maximum number of flight decks. It is also possible Moffett saw the flying-deck cruiser as a precedent, paving the way for the conversion or construction of light carriers similar to those built on the hulls of *Cleveland*-class cruisers during World War II.

Once it appeared likely the Navy would gain at least some additional aviation platforms in the guise of flying-deck cruisers, Moffett initiated a reevaluation of the optimum size of aircraft carriers in the spring of 1931. Following many conferences and probing analyses, the bureau presented data on three ships: 13,800 tons, 18,400 tons, and 20,700 tons. Still hop-ing for the maximum number of flight decks, Moffett remained optimistic that the 13,800-ton ship would be adequate, but that proved not to be the case. The preliminary studies indicated that carriers needed additional protection against dive bombing attacks, something that was impossible to provide in the smallest of the three tonnages. Consequently, Moffett wrote to the secretary of the Navy on 22 May 1931 to urge the construc-tion of three 18,400-ton ships rather than five of *Ranger*'s size. The greater displacement, he argued, allowed higher speed, more compart-mentalization, armor protection for machinery and magazine spaces, and more hangar and flight deck space.[55]

The carrier situation was exceedingly fluid and shifted rapidly during the summer. Admiral Pratt, liking the tactical symmetry of two carriers in each class, indicated that he thought a pair of ships in the 20,000-ton range would be better than three 18,400-tonners, with the remaining treaty tonnage used to build a 15,000-ton near-sister to *Ranger*. Moffett did not believe he was in a position to disagree with the chief, particularly if in the end he got the same number of flight decks. Part of his rationalization, also, was the ever-elusive goal of parity with Britain, which had recently completed the 22,500-ton *Courageous* and *Glorious*.[56]

On 24 July 1931, the General Board held additional hearings on carrier design characteristics. In an attempt to cut through the confusing details of speed, armament, underwater protection, and hangar capacity, Moffett suggested the board first "decide on how we are going to use this tonnage," that is, to determine first how to get the maximum utility out of the total carrier tonnage remaining to the United States. Once that had been done, the board could concentrate on choosing the best specification within the unit tonnage agreed upon. Originally the General Board had concurred with the bureau that the 13,800-ton ship was best, but the terms of the London treaty and subsequent technical developments indicated that a carrier of that size would not necessarily meet the requirements, especially if the board insisted on 32.5-knot speed for the ship. Moffett explained that a small 32.5-knot carrier had little freeboard, was exceptionally "wet" in heavy weather, and was limited to about forty aircraft because the machinery needed to attain such a speed would take up extra weight and space. A 13,800-ton carrier with thirty-knot speed might be adequate, but the bureau doubted that it would have sufficient protection against dive bombing attacks. Therefore, Moffett said, he was "inclined to the solution of a 15,000 and 20,000 ton carrier," provided the ships were in fact carriers and were not loaded down with heavy ordnance or other equipment superfluous to their principal mission. The numbers of flying-deck cruisers were also important and had to be factored into the board's decisions. Because it appeared certain that the choice was to be three new carriers rather than four, the United States needed at least three flying-deck cruisers to match the British potential of nine aviation platforms.[57]

The General Board's recommendation in September that two 20,000-ton ships be included in the fiscal year 1933 building program, followed by the 15,000-ton vessel in 1934, did not end the debate on carriers. Because *Saratoga* and *Lexington* proved to be excellent ships, Secretary Adams asked the board to review carrier characteristics once again, this time considering the possibility of building two 25,000-ton ships with eight-inch guns.

Knowing by then that there was no chance Congress would appropriate money for the flying-deck cruiser, Moffett realized that he might lose another aviation ship if the new carrier proposal were approved. On 13 November 1931, he told the General Board that the 25,000-ton vessel was a mistake. Study after study had indicated that the Navy needed more carriers, not fewer, and that 20,000 tons represented the best compromise as far as speed, protection, and aircraft capacity were concerned. The eight-inch battery of the 25,000-ton ship seriously detracted from the number of aircraft she could operate. Moreover, Moffett foresaw no circumstances under which the carrier would engage in a gunnery duel with enemy surface warships. The sooner everyone realized that the offensive and defensive strength of the carrier lay almost exclusively in her aircraft the better. "We can hardly visualize today the potential power of aircraft, not so much for scouting and spotting, but for bombing and torpedoing. It may readily be the deciding factor in a war." The flurry of interest in the heavily armed carrier passed, however, and plans went ahead to finalize the design for the 20,000-ton ship called for in the board's original recommendation.[58]

Unfortunately, Moffett did not live to see any of these ships laid down, much less completed. Although Congress authorized two 20,000-ton carriers, it failed to appropriate any money for construction in 1932 or early 1933, forcing Aeronautics and the Bureau of Construction and Repair to suspend their collaboration on detailed specifications and plans for the ships. To Moffett this was deeply distressing. On 9 February 1933, he wrote to David S. Ingalls, Warner's successor as assistant secretary of the Navy for Aeronautics (Ingalls had resigned the year before to run unsuccessfully for public office), "Things could not be worse as far as the Navy is concerned. . . . the situation is more outrageous than it has ever been before, and you ought to be thankful you are not here."[59]

Severe budget cuts implied draconian measures, among them placing *Ranger* in reserve as soon as she was completed. For Moffett nothing could have been worse; in withdrawing a carrier from service, the United States would lose ground to Britain and Japan and would, in all likelihood, be stuck in a position of inferiority for years to come. Carriers and flying-deck cruisers were the Navy's salvation, he told Norman Lyon of the American Legion in March 1933. "It is those categories in which we are most deficient, and it is Aviation which can do the most good for the Navy for smallest expenditure of money."[60]

Moffett was disappointed that he had devoted more than three years to the fight for more carriers and had nothing to show for his efforts. It was one of the sad ironies of Moffett's life and career that fate did not grant him only one more year. Then he would have seen *Yorktown* and *Enterprise,* two of the 20,000-ton carriers authorized during his tenure, laid down as part of the Roosevelt administration's public works program. Most important, he would finally have had the satisfaction of knowing that the Navy and the nation were committed to building the number of carriers he thought necessary to fight and win the next war.

10

CONFRONTATION AND COMPROMISE

MOFFETT HAD DONE EVERYTHING IN HIS POWER TO GET THE numbers and kinds of aircraft carriers he thought best for the Navy, only to be disappointed in the end by a combination of economic and political events beyond his control. The carrier issue proved only part of a broader pattern of controversy that had dogged Moffett ever since his confrontation with Billy Mitchell. Wherever he turned in the latter stages of his career, he faced conflict: in the development of the fleet airship and the selection of a base on the West Coast, in the sensitive area of aviation personnel, in procurement policy, and in the looming specter of a united air force. Moffett faced each of these challenges head-on, even welcoming some of them as opportunities to exercise his formidable political muscle and powers of compromise. As with the carrier question, he did not always achieve success, but approaching retirement he could still look back at a record of accomplishment matched by few of his peers.

An important component of the 1926 five-year aircraft program was authorization for the construction of two fleet airships, estimated to cost $4 million each. To Secretary Wilbur in June 1926, Moffett urged that the

Navy get "an early start on the construction of at least one of the large rigid airships," adding that "postponement in starting an airship requiring three years to build is far more serious than delay in starting airplanes requiring about one year to build." Realizing that the Bureau of the Budget and Congress opposed including money for the airship in the fiscal year 1928 appropriation, Moffett suggested issuing a contract authorization, allowing construction to begin but not requiring an immediate outlay of funds. The best Moffett could achieve, however, was the insertion of $200,000 in the 1928 Navy bill—not much, but enough to permit the Bureau of Aeronautics to initiate a design competition and preliminary contract negotiations.[1]

From the beginning of his involvement in rigid airship development Moffett looked to the creation of a self-sustaining domestic airship industry. As he viewed it, part of the Navy's contribution was to stimulate a commercial market for such craft, revolutionizing air transportation and simultaneously ensuring a reliable manufacturing base to meet the demands of the service for large, long-range airships. Above all, Moffett wanted to be certain that the organization selected to build the Navy's first fleet airships was efficient, well-funded, and had the technical expertise and personnel to establish a foundation for the new industrial enterprise. The Goodyear-Zeppelin Corporation of Akron, Ohio, met those qualifications perfectly. Created in 1923 as a partnership between the Goodyear Tire and Rubber Company and Luftschiffbau Zeppelin, the firm combined the know-how and experience of the German manufacturer of rigid airships with Goodyear's capital resources and background in supplying lighter-than-air craft for the Army and Navy.[2]

Because he wanted to minimize delays and he was confident Goodyear-Zeppelin was right for the job, Moffett preferred entering into a negotiated contract with the company. But Congress demanded that the work be opened to everyone on a competitive basis. In the first round of design competition, held between February and June 1927, Goodyear-Zeppelin easily won over thirty-six other entries. The company, however, would not agree to deliver the airship for an estimated fixed price of $4.5 million, and the Navy Department refused to go along with a cost-plus contract. Consequently there was another cycle of design competition in 1928. This time there were only nine submissions, three of which—from Goodyear-Zeppelin, American Brown-Boveri, and Schutte and Company— were sufficiently detailed to warrant further scrutiny. Again, Goodyear won, offering to construct one 6.5-million-cubic-foot airship for $5,375,000 and the second for $2,450,000. In October 1928, the Navy signed a contract to build one of the airships (designated ZRS-4) and secured an option on the second (ZRS-5), which was to be built following the completion and acceptance of the first craft.[3]

After two years of delay, the fleet airship project went ahead with remarkable alacrity. Primary responsibility for the program lay with Dr. Karl Arnstein, Goodyear-Zeppelin's vice president in charge of engineering, while Jerome Hunsaker, who had joined the company in 1928, had general supervisory responsibility for the airship's design and construction. Arnstein and Hunsaker worked hand in hand with Comdr. Garland Fulton, head of the bureau's Lighter-than-Air Design Section, on the detail specifications and design. In the meantime, in May 1929, workers began erecting the first steel arches of the huge airship hangar at Akron's municipal airport.[4]

On 6 November 1929, Moffett and Fulton flew from Anacostia to Akron in a Marine Ford Trimotor to participate in ceremonies marking the laying of the airship's main transverse ring. The next morning, thousands gathered in the still-incomplete hangar to watch as Moffett inserted a small golden rivet into the duralumin girder. In a brief speech, he predicted that the new craft would prove of "great value" as a long-range scout for the fleet. Beyond that, however, the airship was the harbinger of a new age of aerial commerce. "Other nations have airships, and it has been well established that America cannot be without them. We want our country to be the first with this new merchant marine of the air, making seacoasts of inland cities." Equally important, the new airships vindicated the Navy's persistence in the face of adversity. "If the Navy had given up when it received its first blow by the loss of the Shenandoah, this great industry would have been much retarded" and the United States would have fallen behind other nations in this important new technology.[5]

Nearly as meaningful as securing the airships themselves was the choice of a basing site on the Pacific Coast. Moffett initiated the selection process himself in September 1928 during a three-week trip that took him to the National Air Races in Los Angeles and on a tour of naval reserve air facilities at Long Beach, San Diego, San Francisco, and Seattle. While he was in California, he spent a great deal of time aboard Saratoga with Rear Adm. Joseph Mason Reeves (Commander Aircraft Squadrons, Battle Fleet), who told him that he thought tactical and strategic considerations should be weighed most heavily in selecting a location for a major airship base.[6]

Moffett wrote to Reeves on 10 October to thank him for his hospitality during his recent West Coast tour and to run through some of the ideas he had about the planned airship base. Determined to "lose no time" in recommending a site, Moffett thought the most likely choice was Camp Kearny, north of San Diego and now the site of the Naval Air Station, Miramar. The site's closeness to the sea and its propinquity to the Mexican border made it potentially vulnerable to enemy aircraft attack, but even so, Moffett considered it "probably ideal" in nearly all other respects. Farther to the north, Mare Island presented possibilities, but with only about one hundred acres available, it did not appear to have enough room for rigid airship operations. Nor was it certain that the Bureau of Aeronautics would have complete jurisdiction over the Mare Island base once it was completed.[7]

In January 1929, the secretary of the Navy submitted a draft bill to provide for a West Coast airship base at a cost not to exceed $5 million, and six weeks later the General Board held hearings on the subject. Moffett took exception to the recommendation of Rear Adm. Frank Schofield that Mare Island, because it was near the "center of the most important strategic area on the West Coast," was the best location. According to Moffett's estimates, between 640 and 1,000 acres were needed for the base, and that space was simply not available at Mare Island. Camp Kearny, however, had more than enough room, was near the main fleet operating base, had better weather than the San Francisco or Seattle areas, and had sewers, roads, and other facilities already in place.[8]

Moffett headed a board to make a formal recommendation on the site. Convened on 15 May 1929, the board included Reeves, Fulton, Lt. Comdr. Charles E. Rosendahl (a survivor of the *Shenandoah* disaster who was fresh from command of the airship *Los Angeles*), and an engineering officer, Lt. Comdr. Edward L. Marshall. As part of its investigation, the board considered nearly a hundred potential sites and visited many of them during a West Coast tour in July.[9]

Moffett caught up with his family during the West Coast trip. In Seattle, he spent a day with his son George, who had graduated from the Naval Academy the year before and was on temporary duty awaiting orders. Later, Moffett saw George again at San Diego, where the young lieutenant had begun flight training at North Island. On the way back to

Washington by train he stopped in Chicago to see his daughter Janet. Married to Elliot M. Moore for more than three years, Janet delivered a baby boy named William during Moffett's short visit. This was Janet's second child, and he made the Moffetts grandparents for the second time; Janet had given birth to a baby girl (also named Janet) in Washington in July 1927.[10]

In its report, issued on 31 October, the Moffett board narrowed the alternatives for the airship base to Camp Kearny and a site at Sunnyvale, in Santa Clara County south of San Francisco. Of the two locations, a majority of the board thought Sunnyvale was superior, although they concurred that Camp Kearny was a good location for a mast and auxiliary airship facility. Reeves was unconvinced and continued to hold out for establishing the main base at Camp Kearny. To the General Board on 15 November Moffett explained that he had initially favored Camp Kearny and that he still liked it for its proximity to the major fleet operating base at San Diego. But "after the greatest consideration and study of all the information obtained," he believed that Sunnyvale was better. In part, his choice was due to strategic and tactical considerations; in the event of war, the fleet was likely to rendezvous in the San Francisco area before striking out across the Pacific for its fateful encounter with the Japanese. A combination of meteorological factors, more suitable terrain, cost estimates, and the availability of an adequate water supply also helped sway the board to the northern California site.[11]

The board's survey of the various sites did nothing to change Reeves's mind about Camp Kearny, which he believed was superior to Sunnyvale in topography and climate. Reeves downplayed the potential water shortage problem at the site and argued that its further development as an aeronautics facility would help relieve some of the overcrowding at the Naval Air Station, North Island. But the overriding factor in his mind was that Camp Kearny was "next door to the fleet." Locating the base near San Diego would help integrate lighter-than-air with heavier-than-air activities and expedite future joint operations with the Navy's major surface units.[12]

The issue still remained undecided when Moffett learned that he was headed for the London Conference as a technical adviser on the American delegation. Swayed by Reeves's carefully prepared minority report, the General Board recommended Camp Kearny. Caught with a political football on his hands while his boss Adams was in London, assistant secretary of the Navy Ernest Lee Jahncke passed the Moffett report and the General

Board's recommendation on to Congress accompanied by the statement that either site was acceptable. In the meantime, two bills were introduced into the House: H.R. 6808, to build the base at Camp Kearny; and H.R. 6810, to build it at Sunnyvale.[13]

The decision then fell to the House Naval Affairs Committee, chaired by Fred A. Britten, a Republican from Illinois. Moffett appeared before the committee on 26 May and read a prepared statement explaining how his board had chosen Sunnyvale and delineating specific shortcomings of Reeves's minority opinion. In three subsequent days of intense questioning, Moffett explained why he had changed his mind on the location of the base. He admitted that he had been "strong for Camp Kearny," but that "was before I had seen Sunnyvale" and had a chance to evaluate the location thoroughly. Moffett also skillfully fended off suggestions that he might be biased toward Sunnyvale as a result of newspaper opinion and aggressive lobbying by chambers of commerce in the San Francisco area. He maintained that the first time he became aware of the site was on 20 July during hearings in the naval district commandant's office and that he, personally, had not in any way been influenced by external political factors.[14]

No one was more pleased or relieved than Moffett when, after six weeks of hearings, the House Naval Affairs Committee agreed on the Sunnyvale site and sent H.R. 6810 forward with its unanimous consent. But there were more delays, and it was not until 2 February 1931 that the full House took up the measure and approved it by a voice vote. The Senate voted for the bill a week later, and the president signed it on 19 February. Moffett wasted no time getting out to California to inspect the site during a two-week tour of naval air facilities in March. Considering some of the problems that had been experienced at Lakehurst, he paid particular attention to the location of the Sunnyvale hangar in relation to topographical features and the prevailing wind. He was interested, too, in the layout of the runways for heavier-than-air flight operations. The Navy advertised for bids on the hangar in August and on 1 October awarded contracts totaling $2.7 million for its construction.[15]

While concentrating on the problem of a West Coast base, Moffett also worried that the second airship, which had been approved and for which money had been appropriated, might fall victim to economy moves in late 1929 and early 1930. Through Towers, Moffett kept in touch with developments during his stint at the London Conference. Moffett suspected that some "malign influences" in Congress were trying to shoot down the second airship, and he advised Towers to follow the situation closely and to rely on Commander Fulton for help on specific issues. If worse came to worst and Congress canceled the second airship, Moffett thought there would be little immediate savings: most of the money was tied up in the engineering and construction of the first airship and, because of the option clause in the contract, no money would have to go to the second airship until after the first had been placed in commission. Moffett need not have been concerned. In August, Secretary Adams denied that there were plans to cancel the airship, and before the end of the year Congress appropriated $100,000 for preliminary design work and materials acquisition.[16]

As if there were not enough controversy surrounding the Navy's lighter-than-air program, Moffett had to deal with persistent and highly vocal advocates of the metalclad airship, which had been authorized as part of the 1926 building program. The brainchild of Ralph Upson, formerly a Goodyear engineer, the innovative airship's thin duralumin skin, held in shape by the pressure of the helium lifting gas, formed an extremely lightweight monocoque structure. By 1926, Upson's metalclad had received the backing of Carl B. Fritsche, general manager of the Aircraft Development Corporation in Detroit, whose principal supporter was Henry Ford. Fritsche lobbied hard for the metalclad in Congress, touting the superiority of the design compared with the conventional rigid airship.[17]

The metalclad put Moffett in an awkward position as he pressed for the early completion of additional rigid airships. On the one hand, he did not want to discourage innovation or to do anything to alienate Henry Ford, who had put his considerable financial muscle behind aviation and had constructed at his own expense an airship mast at Detroit. On the other hand, Moffett rightly feared that emphasizing the metalclad might divert scarce resources from the conventional airships he wanted so badly. Once Congress committed the Navy to the metalclad, Moffett had no choice but to support the project, but he was hardly surprised when the company ran into problems with the experimental design and encountered delays in completing the first craft. Testifying before Congress in March 1928, Moffett described technical and organizational difficulties that had made it impossible to predict a completion date for the metalclad. Resisting the temptation to say, "I told you so," Moffett explained that "the success, or nonsuccess, of the experiment is problematical, just as it was at the outset. . . . it will be a number of years before metal-clad airships having performance comparable to that of the conventional rigid airships can be built."[18]

Despite his skepticism about the merits of the metalclad, Moffett followed work on the airship with considerable interest. He traveled to Detroit in November 1928 and April 1929 and reported to Congress that the company was making slow but steady progress toward completion of the craft, designated ZMC-2. Fritsche wrote to Moffett on 15 August 1929 to invite him to Detroit for the airship's inaugural flight, noting that "no one knows better than you how many hard problems we have faced, and how much laborious effort has gone into this accomplishment." Moffett declined the invitation but sent a reassuring note to Fritsche on the twentieth congratulating him on the success of the first flight. He hoped that "further tests and flights of the ship will prove her usefulness and durability" and that "the results from the experience with this airship will justify your pioneer efforts in constructing and demonstrating this type of airship."[19]

Service tests of ZMC-2 led to mixed conclusions about the potential development of the metalclad. Fulton told members of the House Appropriations Committee in February 1930 that the airship experienced directional control problems but pilots were "much more favorably impressed than they expected to be" with the craft. Moffett admitted that ZMC-2 had "performed satisfactorily" but that it was too early to judge its merits compared with conventional rigid airships. Largely because Fulton was cool toward a 1930 proposal from Aircraft Development's successor, the Detroit Aircraft Corporation, to design and build a larger metalclad, Moffett decided against putting more money into the program.[20] Usually receptive to such innovations, Moffett had little choice in the political and economic climate of the early thirties but to push for the adoption of the more conservative, "proven" rigid airship. The metalclad unfortunately remained nothing more than an attractive path not taken in lighter-than-air technology.

Whatever disappointment Moffett may have felt about not pursuing a promising new airship concept evaporated by the time ZRS-4, appropriately named *Akron,* approached completion in the summer of 1931. Leaving for Akron on 7 August, Moffett and his wife accompanied the president's wife, Lou Hoover, who was to sponsor the airship. The next day, a throng estimated at more than a quarter million gathered in and around the Goodyear hangar for the christening ceremonies. Following

Goodyear's president, Paul W. Litchfield, to the podium, Moffett spoke of the economic benefits the nascent airship industry would bring to a nation mired in the depths of the Depression. Granted *Akron* was a naval weapon, but she also represented the vanguard of a vast fleet of airships bringing to the United States boundless opportunities for global commerce. Concluding his presentation with a moving quote from a Longfellow poem about the hopes and prayers of a nation resting with the ship of state in troubled times, Moffett stepped aside as Mrs. Hoover formally christened the airship. Four dozen pigeons raced skyward as workmen loosened tethers allowing the great craft to lift off the hangar floor for the first time.[21]

Back in Washington after the launching ceremonies, Moffett reflected on the accomplishment in a letter to his old friend Claude Bailey. "Putting over Lighter-than-air has been the toughest job I ever undertook," he wrote. "The Navy Department, and particularly the General Board were violently opposed to it. It has taken years of constant effort, and I will not breathe easily until the second airship and the Air Base at Sunnyvale, California, are well on their way. These are the marks that I have set for myself, and I will not be content unless they are accomplished."[22]

From his frustrated attempts to build the Navy up to its treaty limits in aircraft carriers, Moffett knew that *Akron's* completion did not assure success for the rigid airship. He was also cognizant that budget constraints and internal bureaucratic dissension could erode support for the program within the Navy's hierarchy. There were those in the service who feared the expansion of naval aviation as a threat to their own positions and authority and who would take whatever steps necessary to impede the development of aeronautics.

One of the reasons for such opposition was Moffett's dogged persistence in the struggle to secure and maintain authority over aviation personnel. Despite the recognition of Aeronautical Engineering Duty Officer status, his success in gaining reappointment, and partial alleviation of the shortage of aviators, personnel questions pursued Moffett through his third term. One of the most vexing of these was flight pay. In 1922, the Joint Board had determined that aviators should receive an increment of 50 percent of their base pay, provided they made a minimum of ten flights or logged at least four hours in the air per month. In the Bureau of Aeronautics, flight pay amounted to more than $700,000 in fiscal year 1926, a considerable sum in those days of tight military budgets. Moffett himself accrued $4,000 in flight pay that year, bringing his total salary to $13,700, more than any other bureau chief and not far from what was paid the chief of Naval Operations. Moffett also had certain perquisites that other bureau chiefs did not enjoy: a car and driver, for instance, ostensibly for transportation from downtown to Anacostia, but the car was parked at Main Navy and liberally employed for other trips in and around the city. In a service where rank and privileges were everything, the exercise of such prerogatives naturally induced jealousy and hostility among Moffett's fellow officers.[23]

Concerned about economy and the possibility for abusing flight pay, Congress began to look critically at the question. In October 1926, Congressman Burton L. French, a Republican from Idaho, asked Moffett in hearings before the House Appropriations Committee about an instance in which a flier had taken a Navy airplane to a dance. Moffett countered with a strong denial that any aircraft had been used for personal reasons, pointing out that cross-country flights had to be authorized by the naval district commandant. He went on to argue that flight pay was one of the most important incentives the Navy had in attracting and retaining aviators and that reducing or eliminating it would exacerbate the already serious shortage of fliers.[24]

In the summer of 1928, the Navy Department created a board headed by Rear Adm. Luke McNamee to study the question of pay in general and flight pay in particular. Moffett wrote to McNamee on 16 August to explain that he understood the board was to make recommendations for increasing pay and to correct some of the shortcomings of the 1922 pay law. A reduction or elimination of flight pay, Moffett argued, would adversely affect morale and almost guarantee the need to detail personnel to aviation. "The efficiency of the organization would naturally be reduced with personnel who are compelled to serve, if indeed they could be made to serve," he wrote. The real question boiled down to paying flying officers and other aviation personnel for hazardous duty. Considering the high death rate among aviators, Moffett asked, "is it unnatural or wrong for [the aviator] to expect extra compensation during his shorter life?" Additional life insurance, as had been suggested by some who wanted to eliminate flight pay, was not a viable alternative, because its purpose was to provide protection for a flier's dependents and not to meet immediate financial needs. It was also extraordinarily expensive, because insurance companies jacked up premiums to cover what they considered the additional risks of flying.[25]

In its report issued on 12 September 1928, the McNamee board agreed with Moffett that flight pay was really hazardous duty pay and that life insurance ought not to be considered as a substitute. But Moffett did not get everything he wanted. Although the board recommended keeping the 50 percent figure, it specified that it be calculated as a percentage of base pay. Moffett had wanted a change to 50 percent of base pay and allowances, particularly because allowances had gone up substantially over the years, while base pay remained relatively static.[26]

Nor did the report lay to rest the flight-pay issue. It arose again in early 1932 when the chief of the Bureau of Navigation, Rear Adm. Frank Brooks Upham, proposed replacing the present system of compensation by grade with one calculated on a flat rate regardless of rank. Moffett was deeply chagrined to get into a dispute over personnel with Upham, one of the officers he had encouraged to enter aviation. Largely at Moffett's urging, Upham had gone to Pensacola as commandant of the naval air station, and there he had demonstrated considerable administrative skills. Following a visit to Pensacola, Moffett wrote to Upham praising him for the "great work you are accomplishing" and expressing the "pleasure" he felt after seeing the many improvements he had made at the base. When Upham left Pensacola for a battleship command in June 1928, Moffett said, "We will all be sorry to see you go and hope that it is only a temporary departure from Aviation." Moffett enthusiastically backed Upham's appointment to replace Admiral Leigh as Navigation chief in 1930, believing that he would be a powerful friend at court.[27]

Imagine Moffett's feeling of betrayal when Upham took the same stand as his predecessor on the flight-pay question. Upham saw no reason to accord aviators special treatment or privileges, making it clear that he thought it was especially unfair for senior officers on aviation duty to receive more compensation than their juniors. In point of fact, he saw no reason for senior officers to fly at all: "In order to exercise the administrative functions of higher grades, the senior officers should not pilot planes any more than should the captain of a ship take the wheel, hence his skill as a pilot is no longer a requisite; and, further, the plane carrying the administrative officer—if, indeed, he be in the air at all—should not expose him to the same hazards as are taken by the younger and active pilots."

Rather than getting more, senior officers should receive less compensation for flying duties.[28]

At the same time, Moffett had to deal with an amendment attached to the naval appropriations bill placing a ceiling of a little over $1 million on extra compensation for flight duties. In a letter to Democratic Congressman W. A. Ayres on 26 April 1932, he asserted that the proposed cap on flight pay was in reality a reduction of more than 20 percent and that it "would upset and disorganize the whole Naval Aeronautic Organization." Hit hardest by the proposed amendment were senior officers, nearly all of whom would have to curtail flying and whose flight duties were "essential to the proper, efficient, and safe handling of Naval Aviation." Moreover, the law stipulated that all officers attached to aviation activities had to fly on a regular basis, which meant that to comply with the pay limitation, the Navy had to reduce the number of aviators.[29]

In December 1932, Moffett prepared a detailed statement on flight pay for presentation to Congress. In it he argued strongly against any moves to reduce or eliminate flight pay or to base it on a flat rate. The issues were simple: aviators had a right to extra pay for extra hazardous duty. He provided detailed information and statistics corroborating the dangers inherent in flying, the stress and medical problems aviators encountered, and the exorbitant insurance premiums they had to pay. In the statement he also made a convincing case for the necessity of flight duty and pay for staff and technical officers. Aerologists, for example, as part of their work had to make observations of weather patterns at higher altitudes; engineering officers had to fly not only to improve their understanding of airplanes but to help inspire confidence in the equipment aviators took up on a daily basis.

As for the question of flight pay on a flat rate, Moffett dismissed the argument that higher-ranking officers were at less risk than their juniors and therefore should receive smaller compensation. Using statistics as evidence, he pointed out that over the last five years the annual death rate of senior officers (lieutenant commander and above) was only marginally lower than that for junior officers. Furthermore, it was ludicrous to suppose that the flying skills of young aviators merited an equal rate of pay with their superiors, whose leadership skills and experience had been garnered over many years in military command. Finally, Moffett compared the pay of naval aviators to that of their counterparts in the Royal Air Force and the civilian airlines in the United States. He found that across the board RAF and airline pilots were paid more—in some cases substantially more—than those in the Navy. To reduce or modify flight pay for the sake of a "comparatively small monetary saving" jeopardized morale and threatened to destroy much that had already been accomplished in naval aviation.[30]

Moffett succeeded in blocking Upham's efforts to fix flight pay on a flat rate, but he was unable to do anything about the lid Congress placed on the total amount of compensation for aviators. The issue remained unsettled in late February 1933, when Moffett sent a confidential memo to Carl Vinson. He predicted that there would continue to be "severe criticism" in Congress of flight pay for senior officers and urged that any drastic changes be made only "after thorough and complete hearings" by all appropriate committees. Moffett said that he "had nothing whatever to do with passing the law" on flight pay and that his earnings were actually less than that of a commandant of a Navy yard or naval station, who received a house and other allowances for which Moffett was not eligible.[31]

On 22 March 1933, less than two weeks before his death, Moffett commented on an article on flight pay that the United States Naval Institute wanted to publish in its *Proceedings*. Suggesting that additional data be included in the piece, Moffett noted that ignorance was widespread in the service concerning what flight pay was and the reasons for it. The failure of his fellow officers to comprehend the deeper implications of the issue had "caused me more trouble than any other subject that I have had to deal with since I have been Chief of Bureau" and had created a morale problem among aviation personnel. He encouraged the institute to publish more articles on aviation topics as a means of educating officers on the importance of aviation to the service as a whole.[32]

Unfortunately, Moffett did not live to see a final resolution of the flight-pay controversy. Shortly after his death, another board met to study the problem. Chaired by Alfred Johnson, now a rear admiral, and including Capt. Arthur B. Cook, assistant bureau chief, the board in its report of 2 May 1933 underscored Moffett's argument that flight pay was fair compensation for hazardous duty and reaffirmed his long-held belief that all officers, senior as well as junior, must be eligible: "Leaders must lead; a leader in aviation duty can not continue to enjoy the respect and confidence of his juniors if he rejects the risks which they must accept." Extra life insurance in lieu of flight pay was not acceptable, if only because it did not mean as much to a bachelor as it did to an officer with dependents.[33]

The Johnson report vindicated Moffett's commitment to flight pay, but his unyielding stand on the issue proved to have been a mistake. Despite his defense of flight pay, the practice was prone to misuse, and too often his statements supporting it sounded like special pleading. To argue that naval aviation and its personnel should be integral with the fleet while simultaneously insisting on extraordinary pay increments was inconsistent at best and counterproductive at worst. Moreover, in continuing to press the issue with Upham rather than seeking a compromise, Moffett missed an opportunity to mend fences with the Bureau of Navigation and establish a more cooperative relationship that in the long run might have worked to the advantage of naval aviation and its personnel.

Another fight with the Bureau of Navigation grew out of remedial measures taken to reduce the high rate of accidents in naval aviation. Fatalities and serious injuries were to be expected in naval flying, particularly during its early years, but that did not make them at all palatable. Moffett was alarmed by a general increase in accidents in 1927, and rumors were circulating that lax discipline at the Naval Air Station, Pearl Harbor, may have contributed to the death of the station's commanding officer, Lt. Comdr. M. Barnett McComb, in a crash in November 1927. To meet the situation head on, Moffett authorized Lt. Charles R. ("Cat") Brown to analyze the aviation accident problem. Brown discovered that modern aircraft with welded-steel fuselages were 75 percent safer than the old stick-and-wire machines of World War I and found that human error caused 80 percent of the accidents.[34]

Aware that the McComb incident and the Brown report demanded immediate action, Moffett sent a letter to all aviation units on 3 January 1928 directing everyone to be more conscious of the "human factor" in preventing accidents. "The subject of aircraft safety and accidents," he noted, "is the most disquieting element to be contended with, and is today of intense interest to the general public as well as those immediately connected with aviation." He went on to emphasize that beyond the loss of life and material, the effect of accidents was "to destroy public confidence in aircraft and in the administration and efficiency of our organization." That twenty fatalities had occurred during low-altitude aerobatics implied loose discipline and ignorance of operational procedures.[35]

At the same time, Moffett hoped to use the Brown report as a means to get more flight time for naval aviators. He told the House Appropriations Committee in March 1928 that the key factor was experience. Pilots with

400 or more hours had 40 percent fewer mishaps than pilots with 100 hours; those with 1,500 hours or more had 75 percent fewer accidents. "The lessons to be learned [from the Brown report] are self evident. The greatest improvement in safety of operation can be brought about through personnel, and the means of improving the flying efficiency of personnel can be brought about by increasing their experience." More flight time for aviators was "economical both of life and material." He assured the lawmakers that the bureau was doing what it could to mitigate the problem by dispatching monthly safety notices and commending those units with the lowest accident statistics.[36]

The safety issue might have passed had not Comdr. Theodore Ellyson and two other officers disappeared in the predawn hours of 27 February on a flight out of Hampton Roads. Forty-three years old, Ellyson was almost legendary as the Navy's first aviator and was executive officer of the carrier *Lexington*. He had learned that his daughter was bedridden with a serious illness in Annapolis, and he wanted to be by her side. His airplane, a Loening amphibian, apparently suffered an engine failure and plunged into Chesapeake Bay near Cape Charles. An intensive search yielded only a few pieces of wreckage; what remained of Ellyson's body was recovered more than a month later.[37]

Admiral Leigh of the Bureau of Navigation used Ellyson's death as an example of administrative shortcomings at the Bureau of Aeronautics and Moffett's failure to exercise adequate administrative control. In a letter to Secretary Wilbur on 19 April, Leigh pointed out that Ellyson had taken off in an airplane that was not properly equipped or checked out for night flying. To Leigh the episode demonstrated negligence on the part of both Ellyson and the commanding officer at Hampton Roads. The accident had not been caused by "faulty judgment" or by a single person's mistake. Rather, "the chief error consists in permitting the employment of imperfectly equipped planes on flights that are not of urgent military necessity." Concluding that "surely there is something wrong with the system of supervision" in naval aviation, Leigh demanded that the entire aeronautic organization be "given close and immediate attention" and that the department take whatever steps necessary to correct the situation.[38]

Two days after receiving Leigh's letter, Wilbur appointed a board headed by Rear Adm. William H. Standley to look into Leigh's charges and to determine whether aviation accidents were the result of disciplinary or organizational problems within the Bureau of Aeronautics. Other appointees to the board were Capt. Donald C. Bingham, Capt. Husband E. Kimmel, Comdr. P. N. L. Bellinger, and Lt. Comdr. Bruce Leighton. Charged with broad responsibility "to inquire into and report upon certain phases of the administration of naval aviation activities," the board met for the first time on 26 April.[39]

Moffett was indignant. Maintaining he "had no knowledge that there was any feeling of dissatisfaction in the Bureau of Navigation" in regard to Aeronautics' accident studies or the circumstances surrounding Ellyson's death, he complained that he had not been given time to comment on Leigh's original letter until after Wilbur had already decided to create the board. In fact, the first he heard of the letter was from a junior officer. To make matters worse, he had not been consulted before the appointment to the board of Bellinger, who at the time was "directly under my command" in the bureau. Leigh's statements to the press criticizing specific bureau personnel were damaging to morale and proof of the "lack of cooperation by the Bureau of Navigation with the Bureau of Aeronautics."[40]

The Standley board and the implications of mismanagement and lack of discipline in naval aviation were the most serious threat Moffett had faced since the loss of *Shenandoah* and the clash with Billy Mitchell. When he received a draft of the board's report about the middle of August, he immediately solicited comments from his staff officers. Fulton, Kraus, Land, and Towers sent back memos highly critical of the board and its findings, which Moffett consolidated in a letter to the secretary of the Navy on 3 October. From the start he wanted Wilbur to know that "aeronautics is a new and complex art. New questions and problems constantly arise. The older established order of things can not always be applied." Moffett had always done his best "to weave aeronautics into the fabric of existing Naval policy, regulations, orders, customs and traditions, resisting all efforts from without and within to separate aeronautics from the Navy." Yet it seemed to him that many high-ranking officers failed to comprehend that salient point.

Moffett found most of the recommendations in the Standley report to be critical without being constructive. The major problem, as Moffett saw it, was that the board did not include any senior aviation officers and had heard from "relatively few" witnesses; the assistant secretary of the Navy for Aeronautics had not even been called to testify. Those who did testify provided absolutely no corroboration of Leigh's charge that it was "common knowledge" in the Navy that aviation personnel were "not held to the same degree of accountability for their acts as the rest of the service." Nothing in the accident analysis indicated any shortcomings in discipline or in the administration of naval aviation, and Moffett reassured Wilbur that naval aviation personnel were treated no differently from other officers and men.

This did not mean that there was no room for improvement as far as aviation accidents and personnel were concerned. Moffett recommended to Wilbur that in the future all crash studies be issued jointly by Aeronautics and Navigation to eliminate friction and to demonstrate cooperation between the two bureaus. He wanted additional staff officers with flight training and experience to administer flight operations, even if it meant detailing them to such duties. In every instance of negligence or wrongdoing on the part of aviation personnel, Moffett told Wilbur, "This Bureau is ready to concur in any measure the disciplinary agencies of the Department see fit to apply." But he was emphatic that the problems in naval aviation did not warrant any major policy changes. Wilbur evidently agreed. The Standley report was never made public, and it did not form the basis for sweeping changes in aviation personnel policy.[41]

The vexing questions centering on aviation personnel never fully resolved themselves before Moffett's death. Neither did the issues surrounding procurement and contracting procedures, which remained nearly as confused after passage of the 1926 Army Air Corps Act as they had before. Moffett remained convinced that his bureau needed more freedom to negotiate contracts with aircraft manufacturing companies. In this he was generally in agreement with the manufacturers, who almost unanimously opposed competitive bidding. But it placed him at odds with Congress, which wanted to use open bidding as a means of preserving and stimulating competition in the industry.

All indications were that Moffett, if anything, drew closer to the manufacturers after the Air Corps Act than he had been before. In January 1929, Moffett wrote Clement Keys, the principal spokesman for the aircraft industry, that he was "looking forward" to seeing him when he was in Washington and that "I have always enjoyed so much our little conferences and have missed not having had any for so long a time."[42] Part of the reason for courting favor with Keys was selfish, in that Moffett in early 1929 was not sure of his reappointment as bureau chief and did not want to rule out a possible job with one of Keys's companies. But he knew, also, that he needed to stay on the good side of Keys and other manufacturers to help ensure the earliest possible completion of the five-year aircraft program.

Under ideal circumstances, Moffett believed, the bureau should advertise for competing designs, let contracts for experimental aircraft from the companies submitting the superior proposals, and then, once tests demonstrated which prototype met the Navy's requirements and specifications, buy more aircraft from the winning company for development purposes. Finally, bidding would be open on a full-scale production contract for as many aircraft as needed or for which Congress had appropriated sufficient funds. But only in rare circumstances was there enough money or time to follow such procedures. In most instances, the bureau had to cut corners by limiting the number of experimental aircraft and by distributing production contracts to firms without competitive bidding. Aeronautics accomplished this by having the Bureau of Supplies and Accounts draw up requisitions including "proprietary certificates" guaranteeing the company's design rights to the aircraft being produced.[43]

Moffett understood that competitive bidding had a tendency to freeze aircraft designs, which he viewed as catastrophic at a time when the technology was in a state of flux and aircraft construction and performance were advancing rapidly. He recognized that the time-consuming process of competitive bidding could lock the Navy into an obsolescent aircraft and that cutthroat competition on prices severely limited the ability or willingness of firms to innovate. By 1929, to get around some of the more restrictive aspects of competitive bidding, the bureau had developed the "gentleman's agreement," whereby the bureau contracted with the manufacturer for a prototype at an estimated price and guaranteed to pay any costs exceeding that estimate. But Moffett had reservations about the gentleman's agreement. The bureau, for example, had not always made up the difference on a cost overrun. In one case, Consolidated Aircraft spent $250,000 more than estimated on an experimental contract, of which the bureau paid only $135,000. A large company like Consolidated could absorb such a loss, but a small firm could not, and Moffett worried that this would limit the number of manufacturers participating in the development of prototypes.[44]

Further complicating the procurement process was a decision handed down by the Navy's judge advocate general in November 1928 that the bureau was legally bound to competitive bidding on all production contracts. Moffett countered that his interpretation of the law was that negotiated contracts were all right as long as entering into them was in the best interests of the government. But he was usually circumspect about avoiding competitive bidding procedures, fearing that Congress might impose even more restrictions than it already had on the bureau's limited flexibility in procuring aircraft.[45]

When the judge advocate general issued a formal ruling on the procurement provisions of the 1926 Army Air Corps Act in January 1931, he narrowly interpreted the law as requiring competitive bidding on all aircraft contracts, even experimental ones. The ruling created a stir in the bureau. In May, Comdr. Sydney M. Kraus, who had been in charge of aircraft procurement in the bureau for more than four years and had recently taken over as manager of the Naval Aircraft Factory, suggested that an informal process could be worked out permitting all manufacturers to submit bids on a contract but making it clear to them that the bureau would accept only the lowest bid for the best airplane. Others argued in favor of negotiated contracts regardless of the potential legal problems they would present.[46]

Meanwhile, the nation's aircraft industry went into a severe slump, caused by the general economic crisis and exacerbated by the termination of the Navy's five-year aircraft program on 30 June 1931. Charles L. Lawrance, president of the Aeronautical Chamber of Commerce of America since January 1931, wrote to Moffett on 4 March 1932. His letter carried a desperate tone, opening with the statement that the "aircraft industry is confronted with an emergency threatening its existence." Moffett concurred with Lawrance "in regard to the situation in the aircraft industry," adding that "you know that I have always regarded the aircraft industry as a part of the national defense and that the failure to appreciate this fact is most unfortunate." He agreed to meet with Lawrance at the earliest possible date to discuss the problem and potential solutions to it.[47]

A month later, Moffett sent a letter to David S. Ingalls, assistant secretary of the Navy for Aeronautics. He confided that he feared the Senate would appoint a special committee to look into authorizations and contracting procedures, subjecting important experimental and development projects to close scrutiny or possibly even cancellation. The gist of the letter was that Moffett thought the bureau would have to finalize a production order with Vought for a large number of new observation planes before Congress delved too deeply into changing existing procurement legislation. He needed all the help he could get from Ingalls to push through the contract with Vought before the Senate took action on the is-sue.[48]

After a long assessment of the procurement situation, Moffett issued a statement on 19 October 1932 in which he tried to articulate the bureau's policy on competitive bidding. He said that because the 1926 law was for the most part satisfactory he saw no reason for congressional investiga-tions or additional procurement legislation. His bureau over the years had established an excellent cooperative arrangement with the aircraft manu-facturing industry and had done its part to foster competition by encour-aging such new companies as the Grumman Aircraft Engineering Corpo-ration to enter the field. The bureau had recognized the manufacturers' proprietary design rights to the extent possible under the law and had tried to see that the firm submitting the best design received a production order sufficiently remunerative to cover its costs and permit a modest profit. Through competitive bidding, the Navy had secured the best price while reserving enough flexibility to ensure that the bidder was responsi-ble and that the article procured met the Navy's requirements.[49] It was an unsatisfactory system, but Moffett had made it work despite the unrealis-tic provisions of the law and the narrow interpretation of what was per-missible under competitive bidding procedures.

Severe budget reductions made Moffett's job of procuring adequate numbers of aircraft even more difficult, especially after the completion of the five-year program. The bureau's preliminary budget for fiscal year 1934, submitted at the end of April 1932, called for an expenditure of ap-proximately $29.8 million, down $3 million from estimates for the previ-ous year. Pared to less than $26.5 million, the estimates received approval from the Navy's budget officer, but the Bureau of the Budget demanded further cuts. In July, Moffett wrote to the Bureau of the Budget to explain that it was impossible for his bureau to tighten its belt more than it al-ready had, considering the need for new aircraft to equip *Ranger,* four new cruisers, and three recently modernized battleships. The Bureau of the Budget responded by slashing the estimates another $5 million, al-though it added $8.1 million in contract authorizations. Moffett managed to squeeze a little more money out of the treasury, but when all was said and done "Aviation, Navy" for 1934 still came in at less than $22 mil-lion.[50]

It proved to be the last budget Moffett saw through to completion, and it was hardly satisfactory. Moffett complained to the House Appropriations Committee that the bureau would be unable to buy the aircraft it needed to sustain the 1,000-airplane inventory and that some badly needed maintenance projects at naval air stations would be held up or canceled. He went on to say that "we have reached the danger zone" in budget cuts and that if Congress or the Bureau of the Budget called for additional economies, they were "likely to seriously impair the efficiency of naval aviation and its usefulness as an arm of our national defense."[51]

Despite Moffett's dire predictions, the 1934 budget reductions, though severe, did not imperil the existence of naval aviation. Renewed efforts in Congress to establish a separate air force did, however, constitute a genuine threat. Like a recurrent nightmare, the independent air force concept emerged again as part of a general effort to reduce government expenditures in the depths of the Depression. Two similar bills, H.R. 4742 and H.R. 7012, came up for consideration in early 1932, both intended to effect economies by creating a department of national defense, encompassing the Army and Navy and spinning off the services' aviation components into a unified air force. Appearing before the House Committee on Expenditures in the Executive Departments on 6 February, Moffett opposed the measures on the grounds that they would seriously reduce the efficiency of the military services. He was also skeptical about the motives behind the bills, because "neither directs nor accomplishes economy, it merely being expected or hoped that, in some way not provided in the legislation, economy will result." In his view, the formation of a department of national defense actually increased government expenditures by adding another layer of bureaucracy.

To subsume naval aviation into an independent air force not only was uneconomical and inefficient but it could have dire consequences for the nation's security. "No one," Moffett said, "is more sincerely devoted to the cause of efficiency and economy in national defense than I am and no one believes more strongly than I do in the real value and importance of aviation in national defense." Nevertheless, it was inconceivable to him that there was "any need or justification" for the creation of a unified air force either as a means of defending the nation or as a way to advance the development of aviation. As he had before the Lampert committee seven years earlier, Moffett elaborated on the special requirements of naval aviation and the need to have naval personnel flying naval aircraft. "It would be easier and more practicable for soldiers to man ships than to have Army aviators man naval aircraft," he maintained. Combined training was nearly impossible because of the disparate demands of army and navy aviation and "would result in second-class aviators in both services." Separation of the Navy's air arm, "or any lack of complete control of its aviation by the Navy," Moffett believed, was certain to "result in disaster at sea, with possible defeat of the country in war."[52]

Normally Moffett counted on the support of David Ingalls in such controversial matters. The Navy's only ace from World War I, Ingalls had replaced Edward Warner as assistant secretary in March 1929. In contrast with his cool and formal association with the cerebral and egocentric Warner, Moffett found Ingalls far more congenial, and the two developed a cordial working relationship. Unfortunately, Moffett learned in the spring of 1932 that Carl Vinson had introduced a bill to eliminate the assistant secretary's position. "I have no idea what made Mr. Vinson do this," Moffett wrote Ingalls on 19 April. When he asked Vinson if he were serious about the measure, Vinson said that "he was not joking, and meant to do it" as an economy move. Ingalls's departure later in the spring to run for the Republican nomination for governor of Ohio deprived Moffett of a vigorous aviation advocate in the Navy Department at a most inopportune time.[53]

Moffett also missed the support of Jack Towers as assistant bureau chief. Towers had left the bureau in June 1931 to become chief of staff to Rear Adm. Harry Yarnell (Commander, Aircraft Squadrons, Battle Fleet). Towers's relief was Capt. Arthur B. Cook. A graduate from the academy in the class of 1905, Cook was a latecomer to aviation, but he proved to be solid and competent in a variety of staff positions before taking over as assistant chief. Cook got along well with Moffett, but he did not have Towers's flair for politics. During the struggle against the unified air force in the spring of 1932, Moffett recalled Towers to temporary duty in Washington, ostensibly to advise the bureau on aircraft characteristics. Instead, Moffett and Towers combined their efforts to convince key members of the House and Senate that the independent air force was not in the best interests of the Navy or the nation, and together they managed to defeat the proposal.[54]

Towers was Moffett's first choice to succeed him as bureau chief at the end of his third term. In early 1932, Moffett broached the idea to Admiral Pratt (now the chief of Naval Operations), only to find that Pratt had doubts about Towers's ranking as a junior captain and preferred someone older, even though Towers at forty-seven was hardly a callow youth. Most important, however, was that Pratt had his own candidate for the post, Capt. George W. Steele, Jr., commanding officer of *Saratoga*. But Steele fell from favor in August when his ship ran aground. Finally, in consultation with Admiral Upham in Navigation, Pratt devised a scheme whereby Moffett would be reappointed for a fourth term in March 1933 and would serve until his mandatory retirement on 1 November of that year. In the intervening eight months, careful consideration could be given to the person most qualified to relieve him. Moffett went along with the plan, although he wanted to make it clear that the fourth term was not his idea and he worried that the extra time would still not be long enough to secure Towers's appointment.[55]

He was concerned, too, that others were casting covetous eyes on the position, and that Ernest King was among them. In an extraordinary letter to Moffett on 27 October 1932, King bluntly informed him that he had "the ambition to succeed you as Chief of Bureau when you retire." After complimenting Moffett on all that he had done for naval aviation, King was deeply apologetic about what had led up to his resignation as assistant chief. "Please let me say, frankly and sincerely, that I regret the manner in which I approached that subject. I wish also to say that I thoroughly appreciate the kindness and consideration which you have continued to show me, and which have led me to hope that you will not count that one lapse against whatever merits I may possess." King went on to assure Moffett that he was "in thorough agreement with your views" on naval aviation and "wholly in sympathy with your aims . . . of making naval aviation even more efficient and of more value to the fleet." He agreed with Moffett that the next bureau chief should be a naval aviator and that because of his seniority he deserved particular attention. On the matter of continuing the development of big rigid airships, King admitted that he was "not an enthusiast about lighter-than-air," but that he had "an open mind" about airships and was not in any way opposed to them. Expecting to learn more about airships and their operations, King had already taken steps to work with the people at Lakehurst and hoped to make a flight soon in *Akron*.[56]

Moffett waited until 18 November before responding to King's letter. Thanking King for his "kind remarks," he said that he understood why he had left the bureau and insisted that he held no grudges against him. He acknowledged King's "very fine, outstanding record in Aviation," but he had "no intention of changing [his] recommendation" of Towers as his relief. Instead, Moffett thought King's next assignment should be as commanding officer at Pensacola.[57] What King thought of the suggestion we can only surmise, but Pensacola was among the least attractive alternatives for a senior captain fresh from command of the carrier *Lexington,* currently enrolled in the advanced course at the Naval War College, and ripe for promotion to flag rank.

King's letter was all the motivation Moffett needed to start another of his by now well-known political campaigns. To Carl Vinson Moffett wrote that he thought "all of Aviation wants to see Towers here," and "I am afraid if something is not done about it that somebody else may get the promise of the position." In January 1933, he told Towers that he had seen Vinson personally and that he had told him that "he was strong" for Towers's appointment. He also urged Towers to do what he could in his own behalf. Obviously thinking about what had worked with his own reappointments, Moffett wanted Towers to write to everyone he could think of in Congress, the Navy, and the aviation industry, "letting them know that you are a candidate for the position."[58]

In the early months of 1933, Upham saw an opportunity to block Moffett's reappointment and gain time to politick for his own candidate for bureau chief, Rear Adm. Henry V. Butler. In a letter to Porter Adams, formerly head of the National Aeronautic Association, on 28 February, Moffett said that Butler had had only limited experience as the battle fleet's commander of Aircraft Squadrons and had been away from aviation for some time. Moffett wanted Towers because he foresaw "a great battle" on flight pay and believed that "it is essential for the Navy's interests, if for no other reason, that the head of this Bureau be an aviator and a real one." Only a few days before the expiration of his term, Moffett told Towers that it appeared as if flight pay had been saved but that "the situation here is very much confused" as to Towers's appointment.[59]

Exactly what occurred in the first few hectic weeks of the new administration of Franklin D. Roosevelt to keep Moffett on as bureau chief is nearly impossible to ascertain. Indications were that Roosevelt, who had known Moffett for years, wanted to see him reappointed, but his secretary of the Navy, Claude A. Swanson, was cool to a fourth term. In any event, the decision seemed to be for Moffett, and Swanson called him over to his office on 14 March to tell him he had the job. The next day, however, Swanson informed him that Roosevelt was having second thoughts about nominating someone for such a brief term in office and that he and the president were trying to work out some way of continuing him without going through a formal nomination process.[60]

When Moffett learned that the White House was trying to work around the nomination, he immediately wrote to Swanson that it was "extremely gratifying" news that the administration wanted him to stay and suggested that there were "numerous precedents" for keeping bureau chiefs on until they reached retirement age. He did not think, however, that he could stay beyond 22 April, the date of his confirmation by the Senate for his third term, without going through the nomination procedure. Swanson checked with the judge advocate general to confirm that Moffett was right on this point. Regardless, Moffett was content that one way or another he would stay as bureau chief until November and that there was, as he wrote Towers on 20 March, "plenty of time" to get everything straightened out.[61] "Plenty of time" turned out to be only fifteen days.

11

The Last Flight

MUCH WAS AT STAKE FOR THE NAVY'S RIGID AIRSHIP PROGRAM in the early thirties. Admiral Moffett and others hoped and expected that exhaustive trials with *Akron* would demonstrate the practicality of the large airship in operations with the fleet and would lead the way to procuring a force of ten such craft. As the dog days of the summer of 1931 dragged by, Moffett anxiously awaited *Akron*'s maiden flight, which could not be scheduled until Goodyear-Zeppelin's technicians completed a battery of hangar tests. By the third week of September everything seemed in order. Moffett, Secretary Adams, and assistant secretary Dave Ingalls came in from Washington for the first flight, scheduled for the twenty-first, only to be disappointed when strong winds caused a two-day postponement. Finally, on the afternoon of 23 September, the ground crew nudged the big airship out of the Goodyear "air dock" hangar, and Moffett and the other dignitaries clambered aboard. A huge crowd cheered as *Akron*'s commanding officer, Lt. Comdr. Charles E. Rosendahl, calmly ordered the airship to be released from her mooring mast and she rose majestically into the sky. For the three hours and forty-seven minutes of the flight, the airship generally performed as anticipated, although at high speeds the elevator and rudder controls were excessively heavy. It turned out that the flight surfaces were overbalanced, a problem that was easily fixed before subsequent flights.[1]

Back on the ground following the flight, Moffett was nearly ecstatic when he met with the press. He extolled *Akron* as "a great ship—the greatest ship of the air." Elaborating, he insisted that the airship's first flight "could not have been better. There was no vibration. The ship was steady—she acted fine in the air." Above all, he was pleased that "the people of this country have the courage to carry on" with the construction of large rigid airships considering the many technical and financial obstacles faced by the program over the years.[2]

Moffett did not attend *Akron*'s commissioning in Lakehurst on Navy Day, 27 October 1931, but he participated in an extraordinary demonstration of radio's new and unique advantages for instantaneous communication. A multiple hookup linked Lakehurst with Goodyear-Zeppelin's president Paul Litchfield, who was in New York; Secretary Adams, aboard the old frigate *Constitution*, which had recently completed repairs in Baltimore; and Moffett, who sat at his desk in Washington. Loudspeakers carried their addresses to the crowd in the Lakehurst hangar. Moffett again praised the American people for their commitment to the rigid airship and restated his belief that *Akron* was the first in what was to be a vast airship fleet flying the flag of the United States. Americans "should be justly proud" of their accomplishments in aeronautics and that their nation was the undisputed leader in lighter-than-air technology.[3]

Akron and her crew were unusually busy in the waning months of 1931. While Admiral Pratt drew up an ambitious operational schedule for her, including a flight to the West Coast and Hawaii in early 1932, Moffett wanted to use *Akron* to showcase the Navy's accomplishments in the air. He arranged a flight on 2 November for himself, a group of journalists, and an NBC radio crew. *Akron* lifted off from Lakehurst shortly after dawn, worked her way down the coast, and then cut across to Washington, circling the city as thousands gaped skyward. During the ten-hour flight, millions of radio listeners around the East Coast tuned in to the NBC broadcast. The next day, back at Lakehurst, *Akron* went up with 207 people, a record number of persons carried in an aircraft. It was nothing more than a stunt, but Moffett used the extensive publicity to demonstrate the potential commercial applications of the airship and its capability for the emergency airlift of troops.[4]

For Moffett *Akron* became both a source of immense personal pride and a glittering symbol of the Navy's aerial might. As much as his packed schedule permitted, he liked to join her on flights from Lakehurst. On 15 December, he was aboard for a planned two-day flight, the longest the airship had made since her predelivery trials at Goodyear-Zeppelin. During the forty-six-hour flight, *Akron* cruised southwest to Mobile, Alabama, then up the Mississippi and Ohio valleys and back to Lakehurst, where she arrived early on the seventeenth. Moffett was aboard again when *Akron* left Lakehurst for Hampton Roads on 16 January 1932. During the flight, the airship circled to the west around a major storm center, yet still ran into low visibility, snow, and sleet in central Virginia and North Carolina before arriving the next day and mooring to the mast on the stern of *Patoka*. Moffett was encouraged. In the face of some of the worst weather any airship had encountered, *Akron* and her equipment performed magnificently and the mooring tests at Hampton Roads came off without a hitch.[5]

From experience, Moffett knew that the publicity game cut both ways. *Akron* had often been the target of negative press coverage, starting with reports while she was still under construction that she was overweight. Although the airship's excess weight fell within the bounds expected in the design and construction of a new aircraft, the revelation did nothing to counter public and congressional forces hostile to the rigid-airship concept. In January 1932, Congressman James McClintic began hearings on *Akron*'s supposed shortcomings as a military airship. Stung by press criticism and McClintic's investigation, Moffett went on the offensive, inviting the congressman and other members of the committee to Lakehurst on 22 January for a flight in *Akron*. Contrary to what Moffett wanted, the overture led to a public relations disaster. As *Akron* emerged from the hangar into a stiff breeze, she broke loose from the heavy beam holding her stern and pivoted around to face the wind, in the process dragging her lower fin across the ground and damaging it severely. The accident caused no major structural damage, but it did little to enhance the airship's public reputation or her image in Congress. Nor did it do much to elevate *Akron*'s esteem within the Navy. While laid up for repairs at Lakehurst, the airship missed the fleet exercises that year.[6]

To Democratic Congressman John J. Delaney of New York Moffett wrote on 24 February that *Akron*'s accident had been caused by an unusual and totally unexpected gust of wind. A preliminary inspection of the airship showed that "the damage was even less than at first thought, and that what damage there is is local. The structural integrity of the ship is in no way hurt, and the damage done can be readily repaired." Moffett took issue with those who said that the accident had revealed major structural weaknesses in the airship and who implied that she was unsafe to fly. "The statement that flying in her will be in the slightest degree unsafe owing to this accident, is entirely unwarranted and not based on any facts or information," Moffett insisted. It bothered him that "a great engineering accomplishment, in which every American should take pride, has had mud thrown at her," and he deplored the "muck raking" that had attended the entire incident.[7]

Repairs to *Akron* consumed nearly two months. While the airship was on the ground at Lakehurst, workmen installed her trapeze. From their inception, *Akron* and her sister ship had been planned as flying aircraft carriers, supporting small scouts and fighters during long-range operations with the fleet. A trapeze fitted to *Los Angeles* in 1929 proved that the idea worked and was instrumental in training the elite group of aviators who later constituted *Akron*'s heavier-than-air unit. Not until the latter part of April was the airship ready to fly again. Wanting to make sure that no one had any doubts about her airworthiness, Moffett invited Secretary Adams to go along with him on the airship's first flight following the repairs. Leaving Lakehurst on the evening of 28 April, *Akron* flew up and down the coast for more than nine hours. The flight was completely uneventful and reassuring to everyone that the repairs had been satisfactorily accomplished.[8]

Akron and her crew logged many hours in the air during the spring and summer of 1932. At Lakehurst there were engineering and test flights, one of which included twelve members of the House Naval Affairs Committee. On other short flights *Akron*'s heavier-than-air unit tried out the trapeze with the new Curtiss XF9C-1 fighter. But the most spectacular flight occurred in May. *Akron* lifted off from Lakehurst on the eighth and set a course to the south and west, her destination southern California and exercises with the scouting fleet. This was only the second time such a flight had been attempted, and it drew considerable public attention. Like *Shenandoah* in 1924, *Akron* and her crew battled headwinds and poor visibility on the stretch through the mountains. Otherwise the flight was comparatively easy, marred only by a freak accident on her arrival at Camp Kearny on 11 May. As *Akron* approached the ground, an inexperienced landing crew grasped mooring lines and prepared to manhandle the airship to the mast. At that moment, an inadvertent discharge of ballast caused *Akron* to lift off, carrying with her three men desperately clinging to the mooring lines. Two slipped away to their death, but a third quickly tied into the line until *Akron*'s crew hauled him aboard. After a month operating from Camp Kearny and the still-incomplete base at Sunnyvale, *Akron* threaded her way east through the mountains and returned to Lakehurst on 15 June.[9]

Under her new commanding officer, Comdr. Alger H. Dresel, who had graduated from the academy with Zachary Lansdowne in the class of 1909, *Akron* stayed close to home for the next few months. Her crew spent much of the time in the air practicing hook-on techniques and generally gaining experience in the operation and handling of her airplane complement. Moffett flew from Anacostia to Lakehurst on 19 July and joined *Akron* later in the day to observe *Akron*'s heavier-than-air unit in action. The flight turned out to be far from routine. Experiments with the trapeze went smoothly, but as dusk fell, *Akron* ran into a vicious summer thunderstorm, punctuated by gusty forty-knot winds and menacing lightning. Following accepted operational procedures, Dresel turned the airship to the west and circled around behind the storm. After more than sixteen hours in the air and unwilling to wait until the evening of the twentieth, Moffett decided to fly back to Lakehurst in the airship's Consolidated N2Y-1, sometimes used to ferry passengers back and forth while *Akron* was airborne.[10]

In microcosm, the flight demonstrated both the airship's flexibility and some of her limitations, especially in the face of bad weather. Moffett knew that at this early stage of airship operations it was best to err on the side of caution, but it was still exasperating to see the big craft in her hangar while airplanes took off and landed under similar weather conditions. Before *Akron*'s delivery to Lakehurst, Moffett wrote to the base commanding officer, Capt. Harry E. Shoemaker, to give him some advice about operations. "I backed airships," Moffett wrote, "only because I was satisfied they could operate under practically all conditions by using masts. I fully realize that there are conditions when the ship can not get out of the hangar, but if this is so,—and it is so,—she should be taken to a mast well ahead of time so that she can be used when she is needed." Given the widespread skepticism of airships, Moffett thought it essential that the craft be shown to "operate under practically . . . any weather conditions" and he urged Shoemaker and others at Lakehurst to do whatever they could to ensure the maximum use of *Akron* and her sister.

Under no circumstances did Moffett want the Navy or the public to perceive airships as expensive fair-weather craft. He told Shoemaker that he had a "feeling, and have had it for a long time, that the ships have not been operated as much as they should have. By this I mean that they have been scheduled to go somewhere and at the last moment have had to say they could not go." The result was an awkward public relations situation, making "it extremely difficult for me to meet criticisms, not only here in the Navy Department but with the newspapers and the press. We are now at the threshold of a great opportunity, and I feel that all Lighter-than-Air personnel must realize this, or be made to realize it, and see that these ships operate to the fullest possible amount." Continuing, Moffett said that if the big airships "can not operate as I have indicated, then they are of little value and we might as well abandon them. It may be advisable to take one of these ships out and keep her out, even looking for bad weather . . . so we can actually find out what these ships can really do and whether or not they are of any value." How Shoemaker and others interpreted Moffett's letter we do not know, but at the time it must have sounded like an ultimatum. It was possible, too, that aggressive officers, fully aware of Moffett's thinking on the subject, might be more willing to place *Akron* in extreme-risk situations than had been the case with either *Shenandoah* or *Los Angeles*.[11]

The Navy's lighter-than-air officers placed a premium on accurate weather forecasting. Situated directly in the path of storms making their way across the East Coast, Lakehurst was far from ideal for airship operations, which were sometimes suspended for days because of bad weather. Once aloft, airships seemed to be no more vulnerable to adverse weather than airplanes, but the accumulation of rain, snow, or ice on their exterior and the heating and cooling of their lifting gases could and did affect their performance. Line squalls or cold fronts and isolated thunderstorms associated with unsettled summer weather presented difficulties for airships, but probably no more so than for the airplanes of the time. On the other hand, airships tended to fly long missions and could not divert to alternative airports if conditions suddenly worsened. Aware of how crucial weather forecasting was for maximizing the efficiency of both lighter-than-air and heavier-than-air operations, Moffett saw to it that the bureau had some of the finest meteorologists in the country. Most of them served at Lakehurst on one occasion or another. Francis Reichelderfer, for instance, was there as base aerologist from 1928 to 1931, flying many times in *Los Angeles* before the bureau dispatched him to Norway for additional meteorological studies.[12]

The more *Akron* flew the easier it was for Moffett to proselytize for the rigid airship within the Navy. On 22 and 23 November, he went up in the airship on a flight to test her redesigned water recovery apparatus, a device used to condense water out of the engines' exhausts, thereby accumulating ballast that partially compensated for the weight lost in the consumption of fuel and that alleviated much of the need to valve expensive helium on long flights. Earlier versions of the water recovery apparatus corroded, leaked, and became clogged with carbon soot and were a constant maintenance headache. But on this flight, Moffett was less interested in water recovery than he was in bringing along Adm. Frank Schofield, long a critic of the rigid airship, to see what *Akron* could do.[13]

Commander Frank C. McCord was in complete agreement with Moffett that the only way to convince the skeptics in the Navy of the worth of the rigid airship was to work *Akron* and her crew as hard as possible. On 3 January 1933, the day McCord relieved Commander Dresel as the airship's skipper, Moffett boarded *Akron* at Lakehurst for a flight to Florida. Twenty-four hours later, on the afternoon of the fourth, *Akron* moored to the new mast at the Naval Aviation Reserve Base at Opa Locka, and Moffett disembarked to attend the big air meet at nearby Miami. *Akron* lifted off from Opa Locka on the seventh and flew to the air race field at Miami, over which her heavier-than-air unit demonstrated hookons with the trapeze. McCord then shaped a course for Guantánamo. *Akron* arrived early the next morning, but she did not land. Instead, Garland Fulton and other officers were ferried to the base in the airship's N2Y-1 to inspect potential sites for a mooring mast. Moffett saw considerable potential in the Opa Locka facility, telling Dave Ingalls after his return to Washington that it might support airship operations in the Caribbean.[14]

As the Navy gained experience with *Akron*, Moffett agitated for the early completion of her sister ship, designated ZRS-5. Under the terms of the 1928 contract, the second airship was to be completed no later than fifteen months after the delivery of *Akron*. Fabrication of subassemblies for ZRS-5 began in the spring of 1931, and shortly after *Akron* cleared the Goodyear-Zeppelin hangar, workmen began putting together the second craft's structure. As the work proceeded in 1932, the question of a name for the airship came up. In a political masterstroke, the Navy Department decided to name the craft after Macon, the biggest city in the Georgia congressional district represented by House Naval Affairs Committee chairman Carl Vinson, a consistently staunch supporter of rigid airship development.[15]

Moffett worried, however, that the completion date for *Macon* might be delayed. He informed Shoemaker in August 1932 that Goodyear-Zeppelin wanted to stretch out the airship's construction in order to maintain a nucleus of key technical people at the company. Two months later, Moffett wrote to Jerome Hunsaker about his fears that "something would happen" to prevent them from having two airships in commission in the spring of 1933. Budget cutbacks threatened postponement of *Macon*'s completion, and there were rumors that *Akron* would be temporarily decommissioned. This meant that unless *Macon* were finished on time, it was possible that no airship would be ready for fleet maneuvers later in the year. The results of delay would be catastrophic: "I am very much afraid that if the MACON is not finished by March it may be good-night to Lighter-than-Air as far as the Navy is concerned." Moffett appreciated the problems Goodyear-Zeppelin faced, but he wanted Hunsaker to be aware of the political situation in Washington and try to do everything he could to expedite *Macon*'s timely completion.[16]

Largely because of Moffett's persistence, work on *Macon* proceeded swiftly through the winter of 1932–33, and she was ready for her christening on 11 March 1933. Chosen as the airship's sponsor was Jeannette Moffett, who had arrived in Akron with the admiral the day before the big event. In contrast to *Akron*'s christening ceremonies, *Macon*'s attracted only about five thousand people, all of whom squeezed into the hangar to escape a biting wind and subfreezing temperatures. Jeannette highlighted the brief ceremony when she announced, "I christen thee *Macon*," and pulled a red, white, and blue cord to open a decorated container, releasing forty-eight pigeons. The craft then gently rose a few feet into the air. Newly inaugurated President Franklin Roosevelt wired Moffett, "It must be a source of gratification to you because of the splendid and continuous record you have made as Chief of the Bureau of Aeronautics since it was created in nineteen twenty one to be able today to complete the Navy's five year aviation program by christening the USS Macon at Akron Ohio. I congratulate you."[17]

After the christening ceremonies, Moffett and his wife were the featured speakers at a banquet hosted by the Akron Women's Chapter of the National Aeronautic Association. Following Jeannette to the podium, Moffett praised the people of Akron for backing the development of the rigid airship and for establishing "a new industry that will mean not only much to you as a city and as individuals, but also to the country." The completion of *Macon* marked the end of the first phase of the Navy's airship program. Coming next would be the rigorous testing of the craft as naval scouts and the demonstration of their suitability as passenger and cargo carriers. He listed the speed and payload advantages of airships and called upon Congress to follow the Navy's lead with legislation to stimulate their construction and operation for commercial purposes. Answering those "doubting Thomases" who criticized airships, Moffett said that the craft "are new, and like all new things are received with suspicion and sometimes ridicule." A bright future beckoned, but to realize it required spirit and imagination. "Let us look forward and upward, and keep America first in this new field where the sky is the limit, and, if we have the courage and vision, keep the leadership we now hold," Moffett told his audience.[18]

Back in Washington, Moffett sent a letter to his son Bill, who was aboard the small bird-class seaplane tender *Gannet* on his way to Seattle to join a team assigned to conduct an aerial survey of the Gulf of Alaska. He reported that the trip to Akron for the christening ceremonies had been "a great success" and that Jeannette had had a "wonderful time." Everyone had been "very kind and cordial to her," and she had done "very well indeed" at the christening and the banquet that followed, both of which had received full coverage over the national radio networks. He hoped that Bill had been able to listen in, because Jeannette had a "wonderful radio voice" and "was as cool and collected as could be." Moffett went on to inform his son that work was "almost finished" at Happy Landings, his retirement home. He had bought the forty-acre site overlooking the Potomac near Leesburg, Virginia, in late July 1931 and had been spending weekends there on and off for the last year or so. It was, he told his friend Claude Bailey, "a very pretty place."[19]

But retirement still lay some time in the future. For the present Moffett tried to get away as often as he could to observe *Akron* and her new commanding officer in action. On 28 March, he flew to Lakehurst from Anacostia and boarded the airship for a long training flight, principally to test the radio homing devices of the airship's Curtiss XF9C-2 scout-fighters. *Akron* left the hangar early in the evening and took off into a stiff wind with gusts nearing thirty miles per hour. During the night and early the next morning, Moffett watched several successful launches and recoveries, which seemed to point the way to round-the-clock operations by *Akron's* heavier-than-air unit.[20]

Moffett's next opportunity to fly in *Akron* came on the fateful evening of 3 April. He boarded the airship an hour or so before she took off into the gloom that had closed in over Lakehurst. Instead of taking *Akron* directly out to sea and north toward Newport, as called for in her flight plans, Commander McCord set a course westward toward Philadelphia and the Delaware River. Upon reaching the city about 2010, *Akron* turned and headed downriver toward Delaware Bay. Then, over Wilmington, she changed direction to the east and worked her way across the pine barrens of southern New Jersey toward Vineland, where she again altered course to the north and east. Throughout the flight, the weather continued to worsen, with gusty winds and lightning streaking the night sky to the south and west. At about 2245, the airship's executive officer, Lt. Comdr. Herbert Wiley, checked the most recent weather map, which had come in over the radio teletype machine, but he found it was about one-third incomplete because of severe radio static. What it did show was alarming: a severe low-pressure center moving swiftly through the Washington, D.C., area and headed their way.[21]

Moffett was in the control car from time to time through the first two hours of the flight. About 2015, he left the control car and walked through the gangway headed aft toward the wardroom. He passed an enlisted man, boatswain's mate Richard E. Deal, who had come on watch fifteen minutes earlier, and wished him good evening. Ten minutes later, Moffett returned, headed back to the control car. Making casual conversation, Deal remarked that Moffett had to like flying in *Akron*. Before continuing on to the forward part of the airship, Moffett replied, "I am very fond of it, much more than the other. It is much better than the *Shenandoah*."[22]

Akron reached the coast over what Wiley thought was Asbury Park. The time was 2145, and heavy rain pelted the airship. McCord, deciding to take *Akron* out to sea, ordered another course change to almost due east. If anything, the storm seemed to get worse, so McCord put *Akron* on a new, slightly southwesterly heading back toward the coast. At about midnight, people in the control car sighted the lights of a town below, which they guessed was Asbury Park. According to the navigator's drift calculations, *Akron* should not have reached the coast so quickly, meaning that the airship had been pushed west and north by a heavy tail wind. McCord, supposedly concerned that the airship might blunder into the skyscrapers of lower Manhattan, then changed course to the southeast, and *Akron* made her way back out to sea. Observers at the Coast Guard station at Barnegat Inlet, about thirty-five miles south of Asbury Park, saw and heard her as she passed overhead. Moffett, who had been taking a catnap in his quarters, came down into the control car shortly after 2400 and talked to Wiley about the violence of the weather, which he compared to a storm the airship had encountered over Alabama in December 1931. Wiley remembered that Moffett left the bridge and entered the small smoking room in the after part of the control car. It was the last time anyone saw the admiral alive.[23]

Akron sped southeastward for the next ten or fifteen minutes at an altitude of about 1,600 feet, skimming over and through dense fog banks. The rain intensified and lightning flashed all around the airship. Wiley later testified that "we have seen very bad storms but never were entirely surrounded." There was mounting tension in the control car but no confusion when *Akron* ran into a sharp downcurrent of air and began a swift descent. McCord, who had been conning the airship through the storm, released ballast, bringing the nose up and initiating a sharp ascent. *Akron* returned to her cruising altitude and stayed there for about three minutes before she encountered another violent downdraft. With the airship rapidly losing altitude, Wiley flashed an emergency "Landing Stations" signal over the internal telephone system, and her crew rushed to their duty stations. Now *Akron* assumed a sharp upward inclination as the elevator man tried to put her into a climb.

At that time, about twenty minutes after midnight, Wiley felt what he thought was a severe gust, which shook the airship and resulted in the loss of rudder control. The angle of inclination sharply increased to about 45 degrees, and, as Wiley grabbed a girder, more gusts seemed to buffet the airship. Wiley did not know it at the time, but *Akron* was doomed. Her tail was in the sea, her lower rudder and fin had been carried away, and, as water rushed into her stern, waves and wind were tearing the airship apart. Just before the forward part of the craft struck the water, Wiley yelled, "Stand by for crash." Only seconds later, the control car struck the sea, rolled over to starboard, and began filling with water. Wiley exited through one of the car's open windows and began swimming, recalling huge waves and heavy rain as he struggled through the freezing-cold water. His first instinct was to swim toward the airship, but the wind and waves carried the wreckage rapidly away from him, so he turned and swam toward the northwest. Luckily he found a small, square board, which he used for flotation. He was semiconscious from shock and hypothermia when a boat put out by the passing German tanker *Phoebus* picked him up about half an hour later.[24]

Three others, Richard Deal, Moody E. Erwin (aviation metalsmith, second class), and Robert W. Copeland (chief radioman), survived the crash to be rescued by *Phoebus*. Deal had been in his bunk only a few minutes when he felt *Akron* plunge on her last, uncontrolled descent. He felt the shock as the stricken airship's lower fin hit the water and observed some of the longitudinal girders come apart as he unsuccessfully tried to make his way forward in the steeply inclined nose section. The radioman's station was in the lower fin, but at the time of the crash Erwin was off duty and resting in his bunk. He recalled feeling the airship roll heavily and hearing the order "All hands forward" before he, like Deal, saw the girders break up as the airship struck the water. His path to the nose of the airship blocked by wreckage, Erwin dived headfirst through a rent in the outer fabric and swam to safety. The boat from *Phoebus* found Deal, Erwin, and Copeland hanging on to an empty fuel tank, all three close to death from exposure and ingestion of gasoline-polluted seawater. Copeland was unconscious and died a short while later aboard the German tanker.[25]

Boats from *Phoebus* diligently searched the crash site about thirty miles east of Little Egg Inlet in the vain hope of finding more survivors. Rescuers heard men in the water, but they could not get to them before the waves swallowed them up. Meanwhile, Wiley had recovered sufficiently to compose a cryptic radiogram informing the Navy Department of the accident and describing the condition of the crew members taken aboard *Phoebus*. Only minutes after *Phoebus* sent out Wiley's message at 0146, news of *Akron*'s crash reached the Naval Communication Service, which quickly alerted ships in the vicinity and passed the word along the Navy's chain of command. Because Moffett's name was on the list of those to be informed in the event of such an occurrence, a phone call went to his

Massachusetts Avenue home, adding confusion and embarrassment to the unfolding *Akron* tragedy.[26]

At 0230, the admiral's youngest child, fourteen-year-old Beverly, got up and answered the phone. She had been disturbed by the storm passing through the city that night and had come downstairs from the fourth floor of the house to sleep in her father's bedroom. She listened as the caller identified himself, explained that *Akron* had gone down, and insisted that he had to speak to the admiral at once. Puzzled, Beverly handed the telephone to her mother, who said that the admiral was not home and that he had left for a flight on *Akron* the previous afternoon. In that one awful moment came the sudden shock of realization on both ends of the wire that Moffett had been lost along with *Akron* and nearly all her crew.

Throughout the day, Jeannette Moffett courageously stood vigil at home, comforted by Beverly and her eighteen-year-old son, Charles. Two other children, Janet and George, were on the West Coast when they learned of the disaster, and they had to make hasty arrangements to fly east to be with their mother. Bill Junior was somewhere at sea off the coast of Alaska, and no one was sure if he had even received word of the disaster. Just after lunch, the president's wife, Eleanor Roosevelt, drove by the Moffett home to offer condolences and support. Mrs. Roosevelt praised Jeannette Moffett: "She is quite wonderful. She has not given up hope and says she won't give up hope."

Then there was the press. Steeped in sensationalism, mesmerized by the adventure of aeronautics, and addicted to tales of disaster, the fourth estate exploited the *Akron* tragedy for every line of type. Few reporters doubted that in the aftermath of the accident they had a compelling human-interest story certain to hold the rapt attention of hundreds of thousands of readers. The admiral would not have been surprised, for he, more than anyone else in the Navy, had understood and manipulated the popular news media. For her part, Jeannette Moffett, too, understood the power of the press, and she had been a Navy wife long enough to know what her duties were. She knew that every time her husband had gone to sea or had taken to the air there was the possibility that he would not return.

Jeannette Moffett met the press at the top of the steps leading to the front entrance to the house. She told the reporters that she had not given up hope that her husband was still alive, adding that the wives and loved ones of other men on the stricken airship should not abandon hope, either. Bravely, she declared, "I have every belief that Admiral Moffett is all right and I shall hear from him. I shall not give up hope until I have definite word from the Navy that he has been proved lost. So many little boats, not equipped with radio, are on those waters that there is every chance that many of the men were saved. The Admiral has a way of coming out of things safely." The wife of Comdr. Harry Cecil was with Jeannette Moffett and said that she, too, believed that there would be more survivors.[27]

More than a personal loss for the families involved, the crash of *Akron* was a disaster of national scope. Seventy-three were dead or missing, making it the worst accident in aviation history up to that point. And it came at one of the most devastating times in American history, as the nation and its people reeled from the effects of the Depression and wondered how the new administration of Franklin D. Roosevelt would cope with the massive economic problems facing the country. The *New York Times* found only "grief and bewilderment" in Washington following the accident and reported that Roosevelt, in office only a month, "talked of little else" after he heard of the tragedy. In his statement to the press on the fourth, Roosevelt said that "ships can be replaced, but the nation can ill afford to lose such men as Rear Admiral William A. Moffett and his shipmates who died with him, upholding to the end the finest traditions of the United States Navy."[28]

There was gloom in Akron, Ohio, too. At the Goodyear-Zeppelin Corporation, Karl Arnstein, the German émigré who had led the team responsible for the airship's design, was stunned, sitting "grim and tight-lipped" at his desk. To initial inquiries from reporters, he replied, "I can say nothing. I must know more." Later in the day, he recovered enough to issue a statement: "News of this disaster comes as a profound shock to me and to the entire organization. . . . it is a staggering loss to the Nation." The *Akron Beacon-Journal* reflected the same feelings. The "destruction of the USS Akron," the paper editorialized, "was a catastrophe that shocks the nation. It was an even greater blow to the city whose creative enterprise had dedicated the airship to the Navy service, and whose long-sustained interest in aeronautics was rewarded by having its first Navy dirigible named in its honor." The newspaper also echoed the common feeling of the time that despite the accident to *Akron* and the heavy loss of life, the Navy and the nation needed to persevere in the development and operation of large rigid airships.[29]

As the days slipped by and the full magnitude of the *Akron* tragedy became known, the Moffett family's confident expectations gave way to resignation that neither the admiral nor any of the others missing from *Akron* would be counted among the survivors. Young Bill Moffett, with *Gannet* in the Gulf of Alaska, learned of the accident over the ship's radio. Before he could make arrangements to get back home, his instinct told him that his father would not be found alive. Meanwhile, at Main Navy there was profound sadness in the realization that the bureau had lost its first and only chief, the beloved "Old Man" whose twelve years of leadership had molded the Navy's air arm. Capt. Dick Richardson said, "The loss to the Service and the nation is irreparable."[30]

Jeannette Moffett's quiet fortitude began to waver as letters of sympathy poured in from around the country. One was a handwritten note from Admiral Pratt, who offered his "deepest sympathy" for her loss. Pratt recalled that he and Moffett had enjoyed remarkably parallel careers. Pratt had graduated from the Naval Academy in 1889, a year before Moffett. As four-stripers, they had both commanded battleships, Pratt in *New York* and Moffett in *Mississippi*. He remembered that they had initiated an informal competition, racing their ships into San Pedro harbor to see who would be first to drop anchor. Both officers had advanced to flag rank within a month of one another in 1921. Pratt expressed incredulity that "it doesn't seem possible that good old Admiral Bill isn't in the department now to drop down and see me as he did almost every day."[31]

While ships continued the grim search for bodies and wreckage and the nation mourned its loss, the Navy launched an inquiry into the *Akron* crash. On 6 April, secretary of the Navy Swanson announced the creation of a board to investigate the accident. Headed by Rear Adm. Henry Butler and including Captain Shoemaker, Comdr. Sydney Kraus, and Lt. Ralph G. Pennoyer, who had graduated with Rosendahl in the class of 1914, the board met at Lakehurst on 10 April. Lieutenant Commander Wiley was the first witness. In two days of testimony, he detailed what he remembered of *Akron*'s last flight. His halting attempts to retrace *Akron*'s track on the night of 3–4 April showed that he thought the airship's position was at least thirty miles farther north than it actually was.

Wiley's uncertain reconstruction of the airship's movements heightened suspicion among some members of the board that Moffett had ordered at least some of *Akron*'s course changes and thus was either directly or indirectly responsible for the airship's loss. When asked, "Who was responsible for the ship on this flight?" Wiley replied that it had been Commander McCord. He added that he was "not absolutely certain of the Regulations, but so far as I know from my own observation, Admiral Moffett had no authority other than that he was the senior officer, but according to Regulations he had nothing to do with the interior control or discipline of the airship." Wiley insisted that McCord alone had been responsible for determining whether *Akron* was to fly that day, and it was he who decided the time of the flight. When asked whether he thought Moffett had either requested or issued orders affecting *Akron*'s last flight, William Moffett, Jr., insisted that his father would never have deliberately jeopardized the airship and was too good an officer to bypass the normal chain of command by telling the captain of an airship what to do or what not to do.[32]

Nevertheless, it is difficult to comprehend what McCord was trying to do that night. In the space of a little more than two hours, he ordered three course changes, taking *Akron* on a zigzag path toward and away from the storm front. He may have been attempting to work his way south and west around the back side of the storm—standard practice, but impossible given the extent of the weather system. Furthermore, he had enough meteorological information to know that this was no ordinary storm but a major disturbance associated with an intense low-pressure area. Another explanation might be that he was trying to penetrate the front. There was at the time debate among airmen about the safest way of doing so, and McCord's course changes may have been part of an attempt to find the optimum heading to pass through the front with the least danger to the airship. We will never know for sure.

On the morning of the tenth, the day the *Akron* court of inquiry convened in Lakehurst, seamen aboard the seventy-five-foot Coast Guard tug *Daphne* recovered Admiral Moffett's body about three miles off Beach Haven, New Jersey. It was only the fifth body found since the airship's crash. *Daphne*'s commanding officer said that the body was immediately recognizable from the khaki overcoat and the engraved cufflinks on the uniform. Apparently some heavy object had struck Moffett on the side of the head, possibly rendering him unconscious at the moment *Akron*'s control car struck the water. A short while later, *Daphne* came into Absecon, New Jersey, with her colors at half mast and Moffett's body covered by a flag. The body was taken to a hospital across the bay in Atlantic City, where Lieutenant Robbins, the admiral's aide, arranged for its transfer to Washington.[33]

The news of the recovery of Moffett's body ended nearly a week of uncertainty for the admiral's family. Jeannette Moffett told newsmen that she was relieved that her husband's body had been found and stoically contained her grief. One newspaper reported that "definite word lifted a load from her mind." The family decided to have a private memorial service at home, leaving the rest of the funeral arrangements to the Navy. Only four of the Moffetts' five children attended; Bill Junior was unable to get back to Washington from Alaska in time.[34]

Thursday, 13 April, dawned bright and unseasonably warm in Washington, in sharp contrast to the storm and gloom the night *Akron* was swallowed by the sea. In the morning, the Moffett clan attended the funeral services for Commander McCord at the Chevy Chase Presbyterian Church. Shortly before one in the afternoon, Admiral Moffett's flag-draped coffin was placed on a caisson and carried through the Fort Myer gate of Arlington National Cemetery. Walking behind was a solemn procession led by secretary of the Navy Swanson and including scores of officers from the United States and foreign navies. Captain Sydney K. Evans, chief of the Navy's chaplain corps, presided over the burial, which took place in a grove of oak trees on a hillside about two hundred yards south of the Tomb of the Unknown Soldier. Pallbearers were Admiral Pratt; Rear Admiral Upham; Rear Admiral Johnson, now assistant chief of the Bureau of Navigation; Rear Adm. Emory Land, who had become chief of the Bureau of Construction and Repair; Captain Cook, assistant chief of the Bureau of Aeronautics; and Capt. Elwood A. Cobey, head of the bureau's Financial Division.

As his friends and shipmates lowered the admiral's coffin into the flower-ringed grave, a volunteer honor guard from the Naval Air Station, Anacostia, came to attention. Sailors fired three volleys into the air, while a bugler sounded the haunting notes of taps. Ten airplanes—five each from Anacostia and the Marine air station at Quantico, Virginia—led by Lt. Comdr. Arthur Gavin, droned over, dropping a wreath on the gravesite. A gap in the flying formation symbolized the aviators' fallen leader. This funeral, like others, evoked both a sad finality and a reassuring sense of continuity in the naval community. While brother officers and their families said good-bye to one of their own, they took comfort in the understanding that their fallen comrade was still part of a seamless fabric of duty and tradition. Deeply saddened by Moffett's death, they remained confident that the Navy's dedicated cadre of aviation people would build on the foundation left behind by a remarkable leader.[35]

On the day of Moffett's funeral, the *Akron* court of inquiry continued its hearings, concentrating on the testimony of aerological officers who were present at Lakehurst on the night of the accident. Lieutenant Frederick A. L. Dartsch, officer in charge of the aerological school at Lakehurst, explained that there had been discrepancies in the forecasts before and during *Akron*'s last flight and confirmed that the airship had been the victim of a particularly severe storm associated with a widespread cold front. After the proceedings moved to the Washington Navy Yard, Comdr. Alger Dresel told the court that his experience in airships had taught him to avoid thunderstorms "whenever possible" and that he had always been wary of low-pressure areas at that time of the year. Commander Rosendahl pointed out that the intense low pressure accompanying the storm might have exacerbated inaccuracies in the airship's barometric altimeter.[36]

If weather, confusion about *Akron*'s movements, and the possibility of erroneous instrument readings raised doubts among the members of the court of inquiry, there was no doubt about the structural integrity of the airship herself or that she had struck the water before breaking up. Appearing before the court on 19 April, Jerome Hunsaker testified that *Akron* was built to a "higher order" of strength than any other airship and that since *Akron*'s loss, Goodyear-Zeppelin had reinvestigated its stress calculations and found them to be correct. He thought the longitudinal girder failures noted by previous witnesses had occurred as a result of excessive loads imposed on the airship's structure as waves tore apart her stern. If an airship at 1,600 feet were caught in a downdraft and needed 1,200 feet to recover, and her altimeter was only slightly off, then "the chances of hitting the water with her tail . . . strike me as very good."[37]

The *Akron* court of inquiry concluded its hearings on 27 April. After a preliminary review of the court's proceedings, Secretary Swanson laid to rest any lingering doubts about Moffett's responsibility for the accident. In a letter of 29 April, he determined that "from the evidence adduced, the Navy Department holds that the death of the late Rear Admiral William Adger Moffett, U.S. Navy, was incurred not as the result of his own misconduct." When the court reconvened on 1 May, it found no single cause for the accident, determining that it was "conjecture" why the airship flew into the sea on the night of the disaster. Nor did it determine individual culpability for the loss of the airship. Lieutenant Pennoyer, who served as judge advocate on the court, lamented, "All of us here have lost close friends, officers and men for whom we had the greatest respect. Naval aviation lost its great chief, the one who has done most for the development of naval aviation and particularly the development of the rigid airship." Some changes in procedures or courses might have prevented the accident, but that was hindsight. If there were any errors in judgment about the movements of the ship, they had been made "without negligence or culpability."[38]

Two days after the *Akron* court of inquiry issued its findings, Ernest J. King succeeded Moffett as chief of the Bureau of Aeronautics. King had actively campaigned for the post, and he had allies in the Navy Department and the Roosevelt administration. Moreover, having been on the list of captains to be considered for elevation to rear admiral since December 1932, he enjoyed an advantage in seniority over Towers, his principal rival for the job. One can only speculate how Moffett, had he lived, would have reacted to King's appointment, but it is safe to say that he would not have been happy. In many ways, King was the antithesis of Moffett; always something of a martinet, he engendered respect more than admiration among his subordinates, and his haughty presence bordered on contemptuousness. Nevertheless, he was intelligent and fair, and he had a firm commitment to the cause of naval aviation.[39]

Not long after taking over as bureau chief, King read and commented on the results of the *Akron* court of inquiry. Generally concurring with the court's findings, he agreed that "the design, construction and maneuverability of the AKRON were adequate to the point of excellence" and that "the material condition of the AKRON was excellent at the time of take-off on 3 April, 1933." Moreover, "the personnel were competent and efficient in their capacity to handle the airship." But King also determined that "there is need to recognize the fact that it is essential, in their present state of design, construction and operation, that airships should avoid bad weather (storm) areas," and he pointed out the accident reinforced the importance of accurate weather forecasting and the need to increase the number of people trained in meteorology.[40]

The naval court of inquiry was not the only probe of the *Akron* disaster that spring. Senator William H. King, a Democrat from Utah, chaired a joint congressional investigation into the accident. The King committee covered much the same ground as the naval court, concentrating on the weather conditions at the time, the circumstances surrounding the decision to fly that day, and the course changes ordered by McCord in the hours before the crash. In its report, issued on 14 June, the committee shed no new light on the loss of *Akron*, but in twelve days of testimony it accumulated a great deal of information on rigid airships and their operation. Perhaps most significant, the committee recommended keeping Lakehurst in operation and going ahead with airship development, including the construction of a new craft to replace *Akron*.[41]

To a certain extent the findings of the Navy's court of inquiry and the congressional investigation into airship disasters amounted to posthumous recognition of Moffett's key role in lighter-than-air development and brought to a close the last chapter in the admiral's controversial tenure as chief of the Bureau of Aeronautics. With Moffett's name already linked to the airship, Moffett's death in the crash of *Akron* fixed his reputation in the public mind as the uncompromising defender of lighter-than-air in the Navy. The association is unfortunate, for Moffett saw the rigid airship as only one component of a complex, powerful naval air force. His advocacy of the rigid airship tended to obscure less spectacular but, in the long run, more important contributions he made in integrating aviation with the fleet. Rather than being thought of only for his enthusiasm for the airship, Moffett should be remembered as the proponent of fleet aviation.

Viewing Moffett's accomplishments in a broader perspective reveals how much he did to bring about the realization of a true air navy during the interwar years. Through persistence and tireless effort, Moffett made the aircraft carrier an indispensable component of the fleet, and he saw to it that there were enough up-to-date airplanes to fly from those carriers. After the 1921 law creating the Bureau of Aeronautics, the 1926 five-year aircraft program was the most important legislation affecting the naval aviation establishment. Not only did it provide for the numbers of aircraft needed by an expanding naval air arm, but it also rescued manufacturers from almost certain doom by guaranteeing orders over an extended period. He did not overcome congressional opposition to more flexible aircraft contracting procedures, but he did establish a rational procurement policy that met the needs of both the industry and the Navy. Moreover,

Moffett's commitment to advancing technological change ensured that American naval aviators flew some of the best airplanes available to any service in the world.

Moffett had an innate sense of what was possible and what was not possible in times of rapid technological change. Though a traditional line officer with little background in engineering, he appreciated the problems of the specialist officer and had some understanding of how aircraft and engines and their ancillary equipment worked. He understood the limits of technology, as well, and strove to ensure that the Navy did not expend large sums on projects that offered only limited potential for success. That was one of the reasons why he, influenced by Henry Mustin, insisted on limiting the bureau's planning to five-year cycles. Beyond that span of time, it was impossible to make reasonable predictions about the technology or to determine accurately the Navy's requirements for new material. To him, the Army's ten-year procurement plans seemed absurd, pie-in-the-sky dreams.

That Moffett accomplished this during an era of restricted budgets and limited enthusiasm for the military was even more remarkable. His political perspicacity was the reason for his success. He quickly learned his way around the civilian and military bureaucracy in Washington and, as he was blooded in the bureaucratic wars, knew how to get what he wanted. The results speak for themselves. In the process, however, he carved out a personal empire and gained considerable celebrity. Fortunately for the Navy and the nation, he never allowed the celebration of the individual to obscure what the individual stood for or to overshadow the importance of institutional goals. Admiral Hyman G. Rickover had a similar influence in the creation of the modern nuclear navy, but Rickover's organization, despite its effectiveness, bore the unmistakable stamp of his tyrannical personality. Moffett, instead, maintained the delicate balance of personal and organizational priorities better than any other military officer of his generation.

One can only speculate about the way things might have been had Moffett lived on into retirement. There seems little doubt that he would have in one way or another continued to influence the course of events through the thirties. Perhaps his continued dedication to the rigid airship would have led to its eventual incorporation into the fleet. Possibly the Navy would have acquired more aircraft carriers than it did before the abrogation of the treaty limits by Germany, Japan, and Italy. Maybe the Navy would have had more and better airplanes and the personnel to operate and maintain them. Aside from such speculation, Moffett at the time of his death had already done more than anyone before or since to secure the place of naval aviation in the military establishment. His tireless efforts laid the foundation for the modern air navy and created the organization and infrastructure on which naval aviation built during World War II. For that alone he deserves acknowledgment and praise for a job well done.

APPENDIX 1
The Moffett Legacy

Within weeks of Moffett's death in April 1933, Ernest King, the new chief of the Bureau of Aeronautics, suggested that a commemorative bust be made of Moffett. The sculpture, by Ralph S. Barnaby, a pioneer Navy glider pilot, was cast in bronze and mounted in Memorial Hall at the Naval Academy in 1934. King also approved the creation of the Rear Admiral William A. Moffett Memorial Trophy, a silver plaque mounted on a wooden base, which was awarded annually to the battleship or cruiser aviation unit with the best safety record.

In January 1934, the keel for the destroyer *Moffett* was laid at Bethlehem Shipbuilding Corporation in Quincy, Massachusetts. The admiral's daughter Beverly sponsored the ship at her launching in 1935, and she went into commission the following year. U.S.S. *Moffett* participated in convoy and antisubmarine warfare duties during World War II before being scrapped in 1947. Beverly Moffett has the ship's bell at her home in North Carolina. The admiral's son William A. Moffett, Jr., and others tried in the eighties to have an aircraft carrier or other ship named for Moffett, but they have not been successful.

The naval air station at Sunnyvale, the location of which had caused considerable controversy, opened only eight days after Moffett's death. In June 1933, the Navy officially changed the name of the base to NAS, Sunnyvale, Moffett Field. Following the loss of the airship *Macon* in early 1935, the Navy turned Moffett Field over to the Army in exchange for additional land at North Island in San Diego. When the Navy began blimp operations on the West Coast in 1942, it reacquired the facility, which became NAS, Moffett Field. In the meantime, in 1940, the National Advisory Committee for Aeronautics (now the National Aeronautics and Space Adminstration) established its Ames Aeronautical Laboratory at Moffett Field. In recent years, Moffett Field has been the principal base for Navy antisubmarine warfare and early warning aircraft on the West Coast, although it is slated for closure before the end of the century. NASA's Ames laboratory will remain as the field's principal tenant.

Sources: Correspondence in 00/Moffett file, box 4149, BuAer, Gen. Corres., 1925–1942, RG 72, NA; *Dictionary of American Naval Fighting Ships*, 4: 406–7; Coletta, ed., *United States Navy and Marine Corps Bases, Domestic*, 318–24.

APPENDIX 2
Naval Aviation Funding

Naval Aviation Estimates and Appropriations, Fiscal Years 1923–1934

Year	Bureau Estimate (millions of dollars)	Navy Budget Allowance (millions of dollars)	Appropriation "Aviation, Navy"	Expenditure
1923	21.5	17.5	$14,683,950	$15,123,704 (Includes carryover from 1922.)
1924	41.5			$27,245,782
1925	22.6	16.0	$15,150,000	$15,135,000
1926	32.07	16.0	$14,790,000	$22,230,000 (Includes $3 million from 1925 deficiency act, $340,000 from 1926 deficiency act, $4.1 million contract authorization.)
1927	33.4	18.9	$19,065,288	$25,403,057 (Includes $9.5 million contract authorization.)
1928	40.1		$25,135,000	$24,211,000
1929	45.6	31.5	$32,189,000	$20,300,000 (Does not include $10 million contract authorization.)
1930	50.1	46.8	$31,430,000	
1931	53.0	35.0	$32,032,211	$28,800,000 (Bureau returned $2 million to Treasury.)
1932	33.5	32.0	$31,145,000	$27,603,897 (Bureau returned $3 million to Treasury.)
1933	32.8	31.5	$25,245,420	$30,960,430 (Includes $5.7 million contract authorization.)
1934	29.8	26.4	$21,957,499	$18,000,000

Navy Appropriations (in millions of dollars)

Year	Direct	Indirect	Total
1921	768.54	250.63	1,019.17
1922	508.16	28.77	536.93
1923	330.61	47.55	378.16
1924	302.86	36.86	339.72
1925	308.81	37.08	345.89
1926	310.60	1.12	311.72
1927	332.08	23.73	355.81
1928	348.34	9.37	357.71
1929	383.15	2.12	385.27
1930	364.70	5.56	370.26
1931	403.25	4.54	407.79
1932	359.20	.45	359.65
1933	333.93	13.23	347.16
1934	313.34	11.43	324.77

Sources (for both tables): Appropriations, "Aviation, Navy," file L1-1 (26–33), BuAer, Gen. Corres., 1925–1942, RG 72, NA; *Hearings Before the President's Aircraft Board* (Washington, D.C.: Government Printing Office, 1925), 1: 203; U.S. Cong., House, *Hearing Before the Subcommittee of House Committee on Appropriations . . . Navy Department Appropriation Bill for 1927,* 69th Cong., 1st sess. (Washington, D.C.: Government Printing Office, 1926); *Aircraft Year Books,* 1922–1933; *Annual Reports of the Navy Department for Fiscal Years 1922–1933;* Lord, "History of Naval Aviation"; Davis, *Navy Second to None.*

APPENDIX 3
Naval Aviation Personnel, 1922–1934

Year	Officer Personnel			Enlisted Personnel		
	Total Navy	Aviation	Percent Aviation	Total Navy	Aviation	Percent Aviation
1922	7,831	595	7.6	88,580	4,631	5.2
1923	7,873	600	7.6	82,355	3,716	4.5
1924	8,126	536	6.6	87,327	3,602	4.1
1925	8,389	554	6.6	84,289	3,308	3.9
1926	8,574	670	7.8	82,161	3,877	4.7
1927	8,904	677	7.6	83,566	4,425	5.3
1928	8,856	737	8.3	84,276	11,421	13.6
1929	8,905	843	9.5	85,284	11,642	13.7
1930	8,985	1,019	11.3	84,872	10,769	12.7
1931	9,260	1,313	14.2	80,863	12,639	15.6
1932	9,423	1,283	13.6	81,093	12,358	15.2
1933	9,449	1,276	13.5	79,206	12,286	15.5
1934	9,582	1,330	13.9	80,312	11,973	14.9

Sources: *Annual Reports of the Department of the Navy for the Fiscal Years 1922–1932; Davis, Navy Second to None.*

NOTES

CHAPTER 1: THE AIR ADMIRAL

1. Richard K. Smith, *The Airships* Akron *and* Macon: *Flying Aircraft Carriers of the United States Navy* (Annapolis: Naval Institute Press, 1965), 73, 77; testimony of Lt. Comdr. H. V. Wiley, 10 Apr. 1933, USS *Akron* Court of Inquiry, file ZRS 4&5/A17, vol. 1, box 5598, Bureau of Aeronautics, General Correspondence, 1925–1942, Record Group 72, National Archives (hereafter cited as BuAer, Gen. Corres., 1925–1942, RG 72, NA); testimony of Lt. Comdr. Jesse L. Kenworthy, 29 May 1933, U.S. Cong., *Hearings Before a Joint Committee to Investigate Dirigible Disasters,* 73d Cong., 1st sess. (Washington, D.C.: Government Printing Office, 1933), 412–13.

2. Testimony of Lt. Comdr. H. V. Wiley, 10 Apr. 1933, USS *Akron* Court of Inquiry, file ZRS 4&5/A17, vol. 1, box 5598, BuAer, Gen. Corres., 1925–1942, RG 72, NA.

3. Ibid.

4. Ibid.; Reminiscences of Eugene E. Wilson, 1962, Naval History Project, Oral History Research Office, Columbia University, 338 (hereafter cited as Wilson Reminiscences, Columbia Univ.); Edward Arpee, *From Frigates to Flat-Tops: The Story of the Life and Achievements of Rear Admiral William Adger Moffett, USN,* "The

Father of Naval Aviation" (Chicago: Lakeside Press, 1953), 238; Smith, *Airships Akron and* Macon, 78.

5. Eugene E. Wilson, *Slipstream: The Autobiography of an Air Craftsman* (New York: McGraw-Hill Book Co., 1950), 45.

6. Memo, Capt. John H. Towers (Asst. Chief, BuAer) to WAM, 30 July 1929, Aer-D-157-FAM, file 00/Moffett, William A., vol. 3, box 4148, BuAer, Gen. Corres., 1925–1942, RG 72, NA; U.S. Patent Office, *Official Gazette* 403 (10 Feb. 1931): 362.

7. Wilson Reminiscences, Columbia Univ., 363–64; Memoirs of Admiral Felix B. Stump, 1963, Oral History Research Office, Columbia University, 77 (hereafter cited as Stump Memoirs, Columbia Univ.).

8. Thomas C. Hone, "Navy Air Leadership: Rear Admiral William A. Moffett as Chief of the Bureau of Aeronautics," in Wayne Thompson, ed., *Air Leadership: Proceedings of a Conference at Bolling Air Force Base, April 13–14, 1984* (Washington, D.C.: Office of Air Force History, 1986), 110.

9. Ibid.; WAM to Lt. Comdr. Claude Bailey, 16 Sept. 1930, roll 1, William A. Moffett Papers, Ms. Coll. 198, Nimitz Library, U.S. Naval Academy (hereafter cited as WAM Papers, USNA).

10. Historian Richard K. Smith suggested Moffett's "three-front war" in "Calvin Coolidge and the 'Airpower' Crisis of 1925–1926" (unpublished seminar paper, University of Chicago, 1964).

11. Clark G. Reynolds, "William A. Moffett: Steward of the Air Revolution," in James C. Bradford, ed., *Admirals of the New Steel Navy: Makers of the American Naval Tradition, 1880–1930* (Annapolis: Naval Institute Press, 1990), 379; Clark G. Reynolds, *Admiral John H. Towers: The Struggle for Naval Air Supremacy* (Annapolis: Naval Institute Press, 1991), 199.

12. In the first half of the twenties, the Naval War College carried out more than a hundred studies of aircraft. See Ronald Spector, *Professors of War: The Naval War College and the Development of the Naval Profession* (Newport, R.I.: Naval War College Press, 1977), 147. The considerable attention given to naval aviation in Stephen Roskill's *Naval Policy Between the Wars: The Period of Anglo-American Antagonism, 1919–1929* (London: Collins, 1968) and *Naval Policy Between the Wars, II: The Period of Reluctant Rearmament, 1930–1939* (Annapolis: Naval Institute Press, 1976) underscores the point.

13. Reminiscences of Jerome C. Hunsaker, 1960, Aviation Project, Oral History Research Office, Columbia University, 95 (hereafter cited as Hunsaker Reminiscences, Columbia Univ.).

14. Hone, "Navy Air Leadership," 93; Reynolds, "William A. Moffett," 379.

15. William F. Trimble, *Wings for the Navy: A History of the Naval Aircraft Factory, 1917–1956* (Annapolis: Naval Institute Press, 1990), 60–80.

16. For an excellent recent study of the aircraft industry and its problems dur-

ing the postwar years, see Jacob Vander Meulen, *The Politics of Aircraft: Building an American Military Industry* (Lawrence: University Press of Kansas, 1991).

17. Archibald D. Turnbull and Clifford L. Lord, *History of United States Naval Aviation* (New Haven: Yale University Press, 1949), 259–61; Vander Meulen, *Politics of Aircraft*, 85–86; Irving Brinton Holley, Jr., *Buying Aircraft: Material Procurement for the Army Air Forces* (Washington, D.C.: Department of the Army, Office of the Chief of Military History, 1964), 48–49; Charles M. Melhorn, *Two-Block Fox: The Rise of the Aircraft Carrier, 1911–1929* (Annapolis: Naval Institute Press, 1974), 98.

18. For a definition of the military-industrial complex, see Benjamin Franklin Cooling, ed., *War, Business, and American Society: Historical Perspectives on the Military-Industrial Complex* (Port Washington, N.Y.: Kennikat Press, 1977), 4–5.

19. Melhorn, *Two-Block Fox*, 106, 110–15.

20. Alex Roland, *Model Research: The National Advisory Committee for Aeronautics, 1915–1958* (Washington, D.C.: National Aeronautics and Space Administration, 1985), 2: 432.

21. Smith, *Airships* Akron *and* Macon, xix–xxii.

22. Douglas H. Robinson and Charles L. Keller, *"Up Ship!": U.S. Navy Rigid Airships, 1919–1935* (Annapolis: Naval Institute Press, 1982), 194–95.

23. Smith, *Airships* Akron *and* Macon, 116.

24. Wilson Reminiscences, Columbia Univ., 203.

25. Ernest Andrade, Jr., "The Ship That Never Was: The Flying-Deck Cruiser," *Military Affairs* 32 (Dec. 1968): 132–40.

26. Melhorn, *Two-Block Fox*, 108–12; Norman Friedman, *U.S. Aircraft Carriers: An Illustrated Design History* (Annapolis: Naval Institute Press, 1983), 57–77. That *Ranger* never operated with the carrier task forces in the Pacific during World War II underscores the limited capabilities of the small carrier.

27. Beverly Moffett Mohan, letter to the author, 29 Apr. 1991; interview with R. Adm. William A. Moffett, Jr. (Ret.), 15 Dec. 1990.

28. Interview with William A. Moffett, Jr., 15 Dec. 1990; George H. Moffett, Jr., letter to William A. Moffett, Jr., 12 Dec. 1990, William A. Moffett, Jr., files, Williamsburg Landing, Va.

29. 30 Oct. 1887 entry, Naval Cadet Diaries, vol. 1, box 1, WAM Papers, Part 2, USNA; Claude Bailey, letter to William A. Moffett, Jr., 24 Mar. 1947, box 6, WAM Papers, Part 2, USNA; interview with William A. Moffett, Jr., 15 Dec. 1990; George H. Moffett, Jr., letter to William A. Moffett, Jr., 12 Dec. 1990, William A. Moffett, Jr., files, Williamsburg Landing, Va.

30. Claude Bailey, letter to William A. Moffett, Jr., 24 Mar. 1947, box 6, WAM Papers, Part 2, USNA.

31. George H. Moffett, Jr., letter to William A. Moffett, Jr., 12 Dec. 1990, William A. Moffett, Jr., files, Williamsburg Landing, Va.; Wilson Reminiscences,

Columbia Univ., 364; Wilson, *Slipstream,* 63; J. J. Clark, with Clark G. Reynolds, *Carrier Admiral* (New York: David McKay Co., 1967), 42–43.

CHAPTER 2: THE FORMATIVE YEARS

1. Walter J. Fraser, Jr., *Charleston! Charleston!: The History of a Southern City* (Columbia: University of South Carolina Press, 1989).

2. *Charleston News and Courier,* 28 June 1875; Historical Record of George Hall Moffett, folder 26, Papers of George H. Moffett, South Carolina Historical Society, Charleston, S.C. (hereafter cited as G. H. Moffett Papers, SCHS).

3. Fraser, *Charleston! Charleston!,* 286–89; *Charleston News and Courier,* 28 June 1875; Moffett genealogy in William A. Moffett, Jr., files, Williamsburg Landing, Va.; Edward Arpee, in *Frigates to Flat-Tops* (pp. 4–5), dates Charles Simonton Moffett's birth as 27 Oct. 1862.

4. *Charleston News and Courier,* 28 June 1875; Arpee, *Frigates to Flat-Tops,* 4–5.

5. *Charleston News and Courier,* 28 June 1875; Historical Record of George Hall Moffett, folder 26, G. H. Moffett Papers, SCHS; Arpee, *Frigates to Flat-Tops,* 5.

6. *Charleston News and Courier,* 14 June 1875, 28 June 1875.

7. Arpee, *Frigates to Flat-Tops,* 5–6; R. Adm. William A. Moffett, Jr., to V. Adm. M. W. Cagle, 26 Sept. 1983, box 6, WAM Papers, Part 2, USNA. The Charleston city directories of 1877–78, 1882, 1884, and 1887 give the Moffett family's addresses. The house on St. Philip Street has been torn down to make room for the expansion of the College of Charleston, and the 131 Coming Street house was demolished for the church's parking lot. Only the 119 Coming Street house is still standing.

8. Fraser, *Charleston! Charleston!,* 306–7; Robert Molloy, *Charleston: A Gracious Heritage* (New York and London: D. Appleton-Century Co., 1947), 158; Arpee, *Frigates to Flat-Tops,* 6; M. F. Sherfesee to Moffett, 23 Oct. 1931, Correspondence S, reel 6, Moffett Correspondence, Eugene E. Wilson Collection, Mic 80, Navy Department Library (hereafter cited as Moffett Corres., Wilson Coll., NDL).

9. 24 Nov. 1887 entry, Naval Cadet Diaries, vol. 1, box 1, WAM Papers, Part 2, USNA.

10. 6 Mar. 1887 entry, Naval Cadet Diaries, vol. 1, box 1, WAM Papers, Part 2, USNA; Arpee, *Frigates to Flat-Tops,* 7–10.

11. 6 Mar. 1887 entry, Naval Cadet Diaries, vol. 1, box 1, WAM Papers, Part 2, USNA; Arpee, *Frigates to Flat-Tops,* 11–12.

12. 6 Mar. 1887 entry, Naval Cadet Diaries, vol. 1, box 1, WAM Papers, Part 2, USNA; Arpee, *Frigates to Flat-Tops,* 12–13, 31; *Register of Alumni, 1845–1956*

(Annapolis: United States Naval Academy Alumni Association, 1956), 159–60.

13. Jack Sweetman, *The U.S. Naval Academy: An Illustrated History* (Annapolis: Naval Institute Press, 1979), 85–87, 135.

14. Ibid., 123–25.

15. For the peculiar social dynamics affecting incoming cadets, see Gerald E. Wheeler, *Admiral William Veazie Pratt, U.S. Navy: A Sailor's Life* (Washington, D.C.: Naval History Division, 1974), 7; *Annual Register of the United States Naval Academy, 1887–88* (Washington, D.C.: GPO, 1887), 28–29; Naval Cadet Diaries, vol. 3, box 1, WAM Papers, Part 2, USNA.

16. 17, 25 July, 10 Aug. 1887 entries, Naval Cadet Diaries, vol. 1, box 1, WAM Papers, Part 2, USNA; Arpee, *Frigates to Flat-Tops*, 15–16, 19. *Constellation* is now a museum ship in Baltimore.

17. *Annual Register of the United States Naval Academy, 1888–89* (Washington, D.C.: GPO, 1889), 38–39; 7, 10 Oct., 6, 26 Nov. 1887 entries, Naval Cadet Diaries, vol. 2, box 1, WAM Papers, Part 2, USNA.

18. 27 July, 1 Aug. 1887 entries, 25 Oct. 1887 entry, 26 Apr. 1888 entry, Naval Cadet Diaries, vols. 1–3, box 1, WAM Papers, Part 2, USNA.

19. William Ravenel, M.D., to Comdr. W. T. Sampson, 1 Oct. 1888, Record of Naval Cadet William Adger Moffett, RG 405, William W. Jeffries Memorial Archives, USNA.

20. WAM to Comdr. W. T. Sampson, 3 Nov. 1888, Record of Naval Cadet William Adger Moffett, RG 405, William W. Jeffries Memorial Archives, USNA; *Annual Register of the United States Naval Academy, 1889–90* (Washington, D.C.: GPO, 1889), 22–23.

21. WAM to Mama (from *Constellation* at Norfolk), 21 June 1889, box 2, WAM Papers, Part 2, USNA; *Constellation* deck logs, 14 June–16 July 1889, RG 24, National Archives (hereafter cited as RG 24, NA).

22. *Annual Register of the United States Naval Academy, 1890–91* (Washington, D.C.: GPO, 1891), 20–21; SecNav to WAM, 31 May 1890, U.S. Navy Orders, 1887–1906, box 1, WAM Papers, Part 2, USNA; Arpee, *Frigates to Flat-Tops*, 31–32.

23. *Pensacola* deck logs, 13 Nov. 1890–23 May 1891, RG 24, NA; R. Adm. W. P. McCann to WAM, 10 June 1891, U.S. Navy Orders, 1887–1906, box 1, WAM Papers, Part 2, USNA.

24. Arpee, *Frigates to Flat-Tops*, 33; *Baltimore* deck logs, 7 Nov. 1891–5 Jan. 1892, RG 24, NA.

25. Wheeler, *Pratt*, 11–12; Arpee, *Frigates to Flat-Tops*, 33; *Baltimore* deck log, 18 Apr. 1892, RG 24, NA; Acting SecNav to WAM, 27 May 1892, U.S. Navy Orders, 1887–1906, box 1, WAM Papers, Part 2, USNA.

26. *Portsmouth* deck logs, 6 July 1892–30 June 1893, RG 24, NA.

27. Acting SecNav to WAM, 2 June 1893, U.S. Navy Orders, 1887–1906, box

1, WAM Papers, Part 2, USNA; Robert Seager II, *Alfred Thayer Mahan: The Man and His Letters* (Annapolis: Naval Institute Press, 1977), 254–57, 278–307.

28. Chief, BuNav to WAM, 2 Jan. 1895, U.S. Navy Orders, 1887–1906, box 1, WAM Papers, Part 2, USNA; Arpee, *Frigates to Flat-Tops*, 33–34.

29. Acting SecNav to WAM, 29 March 1895, Chief, BuNav to WAM, 5 June 1895, 4 Apr. 1896, U.S. Navy Orders, 1887–1906, box 1, WAM Papers, Part 2, USNA; Arpee, *Frigates to Flat-Tops*, 34–35.

30. Acting SecNav to WAM, 30 Apr. 1896, U.S. Navy Orders, 1887–1906, box 1, WAM Papers, Part 2, USNA; Seager, *Mahan,* 160–90; Arpee, *Frigates to Flat-Tops,* 35.

31. Telegram, Navy Dept. to WAM, 13 May 1898, U.S. Navy Orders, 1887–1906, box 1, WAM Papers, Part 2, USNA; *Mohican* deck logs, 19 Mar.–13 May 1898, RG 24, NA; A. Farenholt, "Incidents of the Voyage of the USS 'Charleston' to Manila in 1898," *U.S. Naval Institute Proceedings* 50 (May 1924): 753–55 (hereafter cited as *USNIP*).

32. Farenholt, "Incidents of the Voyage of the USS 'Charleston,'" 756–58; Timothy P. Maga, *Defending Paradise: The United States and Guam, 1898–1950* (New York: Garland Publishing, 1988), 10–11.

33. Arpee, *Frigates to Flat-Tops,* 38.

34. Ibid.; Ronald Spector, *Admiral of the New Empire: The Life and Career of George Dewey* (Baton Rouge: Louisiana State University Press, 1974), 94–97.

35. Dewey to WAM, 1 Dec. 1898, U.S. Navy Orders, 1887–1906, box 1, WAM Papers, Part 2, USNA; Farenholt, "Incidents of the Voyage of the USS 'Charleston,'" 769; Arpee, *Frigates to Flat-Tops,* 38–40.

36. Orders, 17 May, 14 June 1899, U.S. Navy Orders, 1887–1906, box 1, WAM Papers, Part 2, USNA; *Boston* deck logs, 1 July–26 Aug. 1899, RG 24, NA; Arpee, *Frigates to Flat-Tops,* 40.

37. Acting SecNav to WAM, 14 Sept. 1899, U.S. Navy Orders, 1887–1906, box 1, WAM Papers, Part 2, USNA; Arpee, *Frigates to Flat-Tops,* 40.

38. SecNav to WAM, 5 May 1900, U.S. Navy Orders, 1887–1906, box 1, WAM Papers, Part 2, USNA; *Kentucky* deck logs, 15 May–18 Dec. 1900, RG 24, NA.

39. *Kentucky* deck logs, 18 Dec. 1900–9 Apr. 1901, RG 24, NA.

40. Orders, 24 May 1901, U.S. Navy Orders, 1887–1906, box 1, WAM Papers, Part 2, USNA; *Marietta* deck logs, 3 June–17 Sept. 1901, RG 24, NA; Arpee, *Frigates to Flat-Tops,* 41.

41. Arpee, *Frigates to Flat-Tops,* 41.

42. Ibid., 42; *Maine* deck logs, 29 May–14 Dec. 1903, RG 24, NA.

43. *Amphitrite* deck logs, 4 Jan.–10 Feb. 1904, RG 24, NA; Arpee, *Frigates to Flat-Tops,* 42.

44. U.S. Navy Caribbean Sea Frontier, Caribbean Commands, Vol. 2, The

Guantánamo Sector, Caribbean Sea Frontier and the U.S. Naval Operating Base, Guantánamo Bay, Cuba (Historical Section, Guantánamo Sector, 1945), 119–20, 148; WAM to William A. Moffett, Jr., 3 Feb. 1931, William A. Moffett, Jr., files, Williamsburg Landing, Va.

45. Orders, 1 Aug. 1904, and commission for appointment as lieutenant commander, 25 Sept. 1905, U.S. Navy Orders, 1887–1906, box 1, WAM Papers, Part 2, USNA.

46. William A. Moffett Service Record, file 662, National Personnel Records Center, St. Louis (hereafter cited as NPRC); Moffett genealogy in William A. Moffett, Jr., files, Williamsburg Landing, Va.

47. *Maryland* deck logs, 6 Apr. 1908–9 July 1909, RG 24, NA; Arpee, *Frigates to Flat-Tops*, 42–43.

48. Arpee, *Frigates to Flat-Tops*, 43.

49. Ibid.; Moffett genealogy in William A. Moffett, Jr., files, Williamsburg Landing, Va.

50. Arpee, *Frigates to Flat-Tops*, 43–44; Patent nos. 1,077,202 (28 Oct. 1913), 1,087,966 (24 Feb. 1914), Pre-1917, roll 10, WAM Papers, USNA.

51. Lee M. Pearson, "Admiral Moffett and the Bureau of Aeronautics" (unpublished, undated ms.), 5, Historian's Office, Naval Air Systems Command Headquarters, Washington, D.C.

52. Memo, Robert Russell (Judge Advocate General) rel. to examination for promotion of Lt. Comdr. William A. Moffett, 14 Apr. 1911, file 26260–1244, box 1130, General Records of the Navy Department, 1897–1915, RG 80, National Archives (hereafter cited as RG 80, NA); WAM Service Record, file 662, NPRC; Arpee, *Frigates to Flat-Tops*, 44, erroneously dates Moffett's promotion to 4 March 1914.

53. WAM Service Record, file 662, NPRC; Arpee, *Frigates to Flat-Tops*, 44.

54. Reynolds, *Admiral John H. Towers*, 57–62.

CHAPTER 3: COMMAND AT SEA AND ASHORE

1. *Chester* deck logs, 5–13 Nov. 1913, RG 24, NA.

2. Ibid., 14 Nov.–30 Dec. 1913; WAM to Capt. A. P. Fairfield, 25 June 1930, roll 2, WAM Papers, USNA.

3. *Chester* deck logs, 1–2 Jan. 1914, RG 24, NA; Jack Sweetman, *The Landing at Veracruz: 1914* (Annapolis: Naval Institute Press, 1968), 3–25.

4. *Chester* deck logs, 3 Jan.–5 Apr. 1914, RG 24, NA; Sweetman, *Landing at Veracruz*, 27–37.

5. Sweetman, *Landing at Veracruz*, 45–49, 62–65.

6. Ibid., 46–47, 53; *Chester* deck logs, 20–21 Apr. 1914, RG 24, NA; WAM to Comdr. Detached Squadron, U.S. Atlantic Fleet, 23 Apr. 1914, Pre-1917, roll 10, WAM Papers, USNA. *Chester's* deck logs and Moffett's report written after the action vary on the times of certain events. The times cited in the text are from the deck logs.

7. Signals Sent and Received by USS *Chester* Apr. 21 and 22, 1914, Pre-1917, roll 10, WAM Papers, USNA.

8. Sweetman, *Landing at Veracruz,* 96–97; WAM to Comdr. Detached Squadron, U.S. Atlantic Fleet, 23 Apr. 1914, Pre-1917, roll 10, WAM Papers, USNA; Signals Sent and Received by USS *Chester* Apr. 21 and 22, 1914, Pre-1917, roll 10, WAM Papers, USNA.

9. WAM to Comdr. Detached Squadron, U.S. Atlantic Fleet, 23 Apr. 1914, Pre-1917, roll 10, WAM Papers, USNA.

10. Sweetman, *Landing at Veracruz,* 77, 103–7; WAM to Comdr. Detached Squadron, U.S. Atlantic Fleet, 23 Apr. 1914, Pre-1917, roll 10, WAM Papers, USNA; Signals Sent and Received by USS *Chester* Apr. 21 and 22, 1914, Pre-1917, roll 10, WAM Papers, USNA.

11. Sweetman, *Landing at Veracruz,* 107, 113; WAM to Comdr. Detached Squadron, U.S. Atlantic Fleet, 23 Apr. 1914, Pre-1917, roll 10, WAM Papers, USNA.

12. Sweetman, *Landing at Veracruz,* 107, 113; WAM to Comdr. Detached Squadron, U.S. Atlantic Fleet, 23 Apr. 1914, Pre-1917, roll 10, WAM Papers, USNA.

13. WAM to Comdr. Detached Squadron, U.S. Atlantic Fleet, 23 Apr. 1914, Pre-1917, roll 10, WAM Papers, USNA.

14. Sweetman, *Landing at Veracruz,* 123, 151–61.

15. Arpee, *Frigates to Flat-Tops,* 48.

16. Sweetman, *Landing at Veracruz,* 164.

17. Frank L. Owsley, Jr., and Wesley Phillips Newton, "Eyes in the Skies," *USNIP* (Supplement, Apr. 1986): 17–25; Reynolds, *Admiral John H. Towers,* 78–80.

18. *Chester* deck logs, 25 Apr.–25 July 1914, RG 24, NA.

19. *North Carolina* deck logs, 3 July–4 Aug. 1914, RG 24, NA; Reynolds, *Admiral John H. Towers,* 84.

20. *Chester* deck log, 15 Sept. 1914, RG 24, NA; WAM Service Record, file 662, NPRC; Richard W. Turk, "Lake Bluff, Ill., Great Lakes Naval Training Station," in Paolo E. Coletta, ed., *United States Navy and Marine Corps Bases, Domestic* (Westport, Conn.: Greenwood Press, 1985), 273; Hugh W. Fisher, "The Great Lakes Naval Training Station" (ms., 1926), roll 2, WAM Papers, USNA.

21. Turk, "Lake Bluff, Ill., Great Lakes Naval Training Station," 273; Fisher, "Great Lakes Naval Training Station" (ms., 1926), roll 2, WAM Papers, USNA.

22. Arpee, *Frigates to Flat-Tops*, 58; Turk, "Lake Bluff, Ill., Great Lakes Naval Training Station," 273.

23. WAM Service Record, file 662, NPRC.

24. WAM to BuNav, 19 Nov. 1918, roll 2, WAM Papers, USNA.

25. *New York Times*, 8, 9 June 1917; Lt. Comdr. R. S. Robertson to Chief, Bureau of Supplies and Accounts, 12 Feb. 1925, S-3516-11, file 26283-1398:5, box 1759, SecNav, Gen. Corres., 1916–1926, RG 80, NA.

26. Turk, "Lake Bluff, Ill., Great Lakes Naval Training Station," 273–74.

27. Arpee, *Frigates to Flat-Tops*, 56, 59; Turk, "Lake Bluff, Ill., Great Lakes Naval Training Station," 274.

28. Francis Buzzell, *The Great Lakes Naval Training Station: A History* (Boston: Small, Maynard & Co., 1919), 108–25.

29. Comdr. Walter H. Allen, "The Twelfth Regiment (Public Works) at Great Lakes," *USNIP* 47 (Mar. 1921): 367–76.

30. WAM to Frank Carson, 11 Aug. 1931, roll 2, WAM Papers, USNA; Buzzell, *Great Lakes Naval Training Station*, 143–52.

31. Buzzell, *Great Lakes Naval Training Station*, 137–38.

32. *New York Times*, 30 Sept. 1917; Buzzell, *Great Lakes Naval Training Station*, 44–45, 167; Arpee, *Frigates to Flat-Tops*, 69–70.

33. Henry M. Hyde, "A Mother to 25,000 Boys," *Ladies' Home Journal* (June 1918): 25; Buzzell, *Great Lakes Naval Training Station*, 172–73, 201–2.

34. Moffett genealogy in William A. Moffett, Jr., files, Williamsburg Landing, Va. The Sheridan Road house, on the campus of Lake Forest College, has been torn down.

35. Turnbull and Lord, *History of United States Naval Aviation*, 100–101.

36. Eileen F. LeBow, *Cal Rodgers and the Vin Fiz: The First Transcontinental Flight* (Washington, D.C.: Smithsonian Institution Press, 1989), 79; Secretary, Aero Club of Illinois, to William Wrigley, Jr., 23 May 1917, box 14, file 83, Aero Club of Illinois Collection, Chicago Historical Society; WAM to William Wrigley, Jr., 14 Nov. 1924, 17 Dec. 1928, Corres. W, reel 7, Moffett Corres., Wilson Coll., NDL.

37. Paul M. Angle, *Philip K. Wrigley: A Memoir of a Modest Man* (Chicago: Rand McNally & Co., 1975), 12–19.

38. Howard L. Scamehorn, *Balloons to Jets: A Century of Aeronautics in Illinois, 1855–1955* (Chicago: Henry Regnery Co., 1957), 82, 85; "News for August [1917]," file 83, box 14, Aero Club of Illinois Collection, Chicago Historical Society; Arpee, *Frigates to Flat-Tops*, 66.

39. Roosevelt to Bureau of Yards and Docks, 29 Dec. 1917, Op. Air 065-5, file 065-1-25, box 203, BuAer, Gen. Corres. initiated in Office of SecNav, 1917–1925, RG 72, NA; Buzzell, *Great Lakes Naval Training Station*, 125–27.

40. Buzzell, *Great Lakes Naval Training Station*, 24, 127–28.

41. Ibid., 128–30.

42. Ibid., 127–29; Angle, *Philip K. Wrigley*, 19.

43. Memo, Lt. C. S. Baker to DNA, 3 Aug. 1918, Op. Air 065-26, file 065-26-0, box 203, BuAer, Gen. Corres. initiated in BuC&R, 1917–1925, RG 72, NA; Lt. Gordon H. Balch to DNA, 26 Oct. 1918, Op. Air 065-29, file 065-26-50, box 203, BuAer, Gen. Corres. initiated in BuC&R, 1917–1925, RG 72, NA. For Balch and his work during World War I, see Reynolds, *Admiral John H. Towers*, 113–14.

44. *New York Times*, 21 Sept. 1918.

45. Memo, WAM to Judge Advocate General, 8 Aug. 1918, file 26283-1398, box 1759, SecNav, Gen. Corres., 1916–1926, RG 80, NA.

46. WAM to Judge Advocate General, 11 Apr. 1918, Aer-GB, file 26283-1398:5, box 1759, SecNav, Gen. Corres., 1916–1926, RG 80, NA.

47. Weimar D. Nutt to Lt. Comdr. R. S. Robertson, 28 Sept. 1922, Corres. R, reel 7, Moffett Corres., Wilson Coll., NDL; *New York Times*, 3 Mar. 1919.

48. Reynolds, "William A. Moffett," 390.

49. Arpee, *Frigates to Flat-Tops*, 49.

50. *Dictionary of American Naval Fighting Ships* (Washington, D.C.: Navy Department, Office of the Chief of Naval Operations, Naval History Division, 1969), 4: 388–89.

51. Arpee, *Frigates to Flat-Tops*, 51; Hearings Before the General Board of the Navy, 1919, vol. 3 (micro. roll 3), 824; Fred C. Dickey, Jr., "U.S. Navy Ship Plane Units," *Journal of the American Aviation Historical Society* 10 (Summer 1965): 121.

52. Hearings Before the General Board of the Navy, 1919, vol. 3 (micro. roll 3), 826–29; ibid., 1921, vol. 1 (micro. roll 4), 148; Dickey, "U.S. Navy Ship Plane Units," 121.

53. Hearings Before the General Board of the Navy, 1919, vol. 3 (micro. roll 3), 836, 845, 942.

54. Dickey, "U.S. Navy Ship Plane Units," 124; Hearings Before the General Board of the Navy, 1921, vol. 1 (micro. roll 4), 147–48.

55. See 6 Feb., 28, 30 Apr., 5, 7, 16, 27 May, 12 June 1920 entries, Journal (Personal), Capt. H. C. Mustin, USN, box 1, Papers of Henry Crosky Mustin, Library of Congress Manuscript Division (hereafter cited as Mustin Journal, LCMD).

56. 10 June 1920 entry, Mustin Journal, LCMD; Reynolds, "William A. Moffett," 377–78.

57. Arpee, *Frigates to Flat-Tops*, 49–50.

58. Hugh Rodman, *Yarns of a Kentucky Admiral* (Indianapolis: Bobbs-Merrill Co., 1928), 305–7.

59. Arpee, *Frigates to Flat-Tops*, 53; Moffett to Comdr. Paul P. Blackburn, 9 Apr. 1921, box 1, WAM Papers, Part 2, USNA.

CHAPTER 4: CHIEF OF THE BUREAU OF AERONAUTICS

1. WAM Service Record, file 662, NPRC.

2. Ibid.; WAM to Philip K. Wrigley, 27 Jan. 1932, Corres. W, reel 7, Moffett Corres., Wilson Coll., NDL.

3. There is no full scholarly study of American naval aviation in World War I. See Adrian O. Van Wyen, ed., *Naval Aviation in World War I* (Washington, D.C.: Chief of Naval Operations, 1969); Turnbull and Lord, *History of United States Naval Aviation*, 96–149; Trimble, *Wings for the Navy*, esp. 19–39; and Reynolds, *Admiral John H. Towers*, 110–23.

4. Turnbull and Lord, *History of United States Naval Aviation*, 150–56; Richard K. Smith, *First Across!: The U.S. Navy's Transatlantic Flight of 1919* (Annapolis: Naval Institute Press, 1973); Melhorn, *Two-Block Fox*, 28–38.

5. Turnbull and Lord, *History of United States Naval Aviation*, 158–59.

6. Ibid., 36–37, 45.

7. U.S. Cong., House, *Hearings Before the Committee on Naval Affairs . . . On Estimates Submitted by the Secretary of the Navy, 1916*, 64th Cong., 1st sess. (Washington, D.C.: GPO, 1916), 1: 1815–17.

8. Ibid., 1818–19, 1821.

9. Turnbull and Lord, *History of United States Naval Aviation*, 87–89.

10. Ibid., 81, 86–87, 91.

11. William O. Shanahan, "Procurement of Naval Aircraft, 1907–1939," vol. 17, Deputy Chief of Naval Operations (Air), Monographs in the History of Naval Aviation (Washington, D.C.: Naval Aviation History Unit, 1946), 199–201.

12. Lt. G. M. Brush to DNA, 12 Mar. 1919, Serial No. 396678-736-DA, file 602-2, box 308, BuAer, Gen. Corres. initiated in BuC&R, 1917–1925, RG 72, NA.

13. First endorsement, Brush to DNA, 12 Mar. 1919, Bureau of Steam Engineering to DNA, 17 Mar. 1919; third endorsement, Brush to DNA, 12 Mar. 1919, BuC&R to Bureau of Supplies and Accounts, 9 Apr. 1919, file 602-2, box 308, BuAer, Gen. Corres. initiated in BuC&R, 1917–1925, RG 72, NA.

14. "Formation of the Bureau of Aeronautics of the Navy Department: Notes by Commander J. C. Hunsaker," 6, vol. 9, Historical Papers Submitted, folder 25, box 3, Jerome C. Hunsaker Papers, MIT Archives and Special Collections, Massachusetts Institute of Technology, Cambridge, Mass. (hereafter cited as Hunsaker Papers, MIT); Hearings Before the General Board of the Navy, 1919, vol. 1 (micro. roll 2), 485–86, 492–99.

15. Hearings Before the General Board of the Navy, 1919, vol. 3 (micro. roll 3), 883–85.

16. Ibid., 888–90.

17. Ibid., 1004.

18. Memo, Hunsaker to Taylor, 18 July 1919, file 602-2, box 308, BuAer, Gen. Corres. initiated in BuC&R, 1917–1925, RG 72, NA.

19. Frank H. Featherston, "AEDO: A History and a Heritage," *USNIP* 94 (Feb. 1968): 40–41; "Aircraft Division, Bureau of Construction and Repair: Personnel and Organization for Work," 1–6, vol. 10, Historical Papers Submitted, folder 26, box 3, Hunsaker Papers, MIT.

20. Shanahan, "Procurement of Naval Aircraft, 1907–1939," 257; Turnbull and Lord, *History of United States Naval Aviation,* 186–87.

21. Richard Evelyn Byrd, *Skyward* (New York: G. P. Putnam's Sons, 1928), 101–3; Robert E. Coontz, *From the Mississippi to the Sea* (Philadelphia: Dorrance & Co., 1930), 408; Turnbull and Lord, *History of United States Naval Aviation,* 186–87.

22. Turnbull and Lord, *History of United States Naval Aviation,* 181–85; Clifford L. Lord, "The History of Naval Aviation, 1898–1939," Office of the Deputy Chief of Naval Operations (Air) (Washington, D.C.: Naval Aviation History Unit, 1946), 645–46; Melhorn, *Two-Block Fox,* 58–59.

23. Roland, *Model Research,* 52–55.

24. "Formation of the Bureau of Aeronautics of the Navy Department: Notes by Commander J. C. Hunsaker," 6–7, vol. 9, Historical Papers Submitted, folder 25, box 3, Hunsaker Papers, MIT.

25. Hicks to Roosevelt, 16 Apr. 1920, file 3084-A-1, box 161, BuAer, Gen. Corres. initiated in Office of CNO, 1917–1925, RG 72, NA; Roosevelt to Hicks, 26 Apr. 1920, ibid.

26. "Formation of the Bureau of Aeronautics of the Navy Department: Notes by Commander J. C. Hunsaker," 7–8, vol. 9, Historical Papers Submitted, folder 25, box 3, Hunsaker Papers, MIT.

27. Craven to CNO, 8 Sept. 1920, Op-15-GB, file 3084-D-1, box 161, BuAer, Gen. Corres. initiated in Office of CNO, 1917–1925, RG 72, NA.

28. Turnbull and Lord, *History of United States Naval Aviation,* 193; Melhorn, *Two-Block Fox,* 60–61.

29. U.S. Cong., House, *Hearings Before the Committee on Naval Affairs . . . on Sundry Legislation Affecting the Naval Establishment, 1920–1921,* 66th Cong., 3d sess. (Washington, D.C.: GPO, 1921), 116–18.

30. Ibid., 217, 221, 651, 703.

31. Byrd to WAM, 12 Mar. 1921, file 3084-1, box 160, BuAer, Gen. Corres. initiated in Office of CNO, 1917–1925, RG 72, NA.

32. Roland, *Model Research,* 58–60; U.S. National Advisory Committee for Aeronautics, *Seventh Annual Report of the National Advisory Committee for Aeronautics, 1921* (Washington, D.C.: GPO, 1923), 12–14.

33. *Congressional Record,* House, 67th Cong., 1st sess., vol. 51, pt. 1, 92; ibid., Senate, 186; Byrd, *Skyward,* 105–6.

34. U.S. Cong., House, *Hearings Before the Committee on Naval Affairs . . . on Sundry Legislation Affecting the Naval Establishment, 1921,* 67th Cong., 1st sess. (Washington, D.C.: GPO, 1921), 78–80, 83.

35. Ibid., 83.

36. Memo., WAM to CNO, 21 Apr. 1921, Op-15D-2-BB 3084-45, Outgoing Letters File, box 367, BuAer, Gen. Corres. initiated in Office of CNO, 1917–1925, RG 72, NA.

37. U.S. Cong., House, *Hearings Before the Committee on Naval Affairs . . . 1921,* 88–90.

38. Ibid., 104–5.

39. WAM to William Wrigley, Jr., 11 June 1921, Corres. W, reel 7, Moffett Corres., Wilson Coll., NDL.

40. *Congressional Record,* Senate, 67th Cong., 1st sess., vol. 51, pt. 2, 1625, 1665; Byrd, *Skyward,* 108.

41. *Congressional Record,* Senate, 67th Cong., 1st sess., vol. 51, pt. 2, 1731.

42. WAM to William Wrigley, Jr., 11 June 1921, Corres. W, reel 7, Moffett Corres., Wilson Coll., NDL.

43. U.S., *Statutes at Large of the United States of America,* 67th Cong., vol. 42, pt. 1 (Washington, D.C.: GPO, 1923), 140–41.

44. *New York Times,* 19 July 1921; WAM Service Record, file 662, NPRC.

45. Clark and Reynolds, *Carrier Admiral,* 36.

46. Memo, Comdr. W. J. Giles to Lt. Comdr. H. W. Hill, 28 Apr. 1921, Op-15H-AC 4488-709-231, Outgoing Letters File, box 367, BuAer, Gen. Corres. initiated in Office of CNO, RG 72, NA; memo, WAM to CNO, 11 Apr. 1921, Op-29-BGS 4/11 3084 B-2, Outgoing Letters File, box 367, BuAer, Gen. Corres. initiated in Office of CNO, RG 72, NA; *Army and Navy Journal* 58 (6 Aug. 1921): 1293.

47. General Order 65, 10 Aug. 1921, copy in World War II Administrative History, BuAer, vol. 1, Background (Washington, D.C.: Department of the Navy, 1957), 242–45.

48. Memo, Hunsaker to WAM, 3 Aug. 1921, file 602-4, box 308, BuAer, Gen. Corresp initiated in BuC&R, 1917–1925, RG 72, NA.

49. Circular Letter 1, 10 Aug. 1921, in World War II Administrative History, BuAer, vol. 1, Background, 246–51; William A. Moffett, "Organization and Function of Naval Aviation," *Aviation* 13 (28 Aug. 1922): 248–49.

50. Weekly Aviation Conference, 7 Nov. 1921, vol. 1, box 16, BuAer, Confidential Corres., 1917–1941, RG 72, NA; William J. Armstrong, "Henry Mustin: A Clear Voice for Naval Aviation," *Naval Aviation Museum Foundation Journal* 2 (Sept. 1981): 29–33.

51. "Formation of the Bureau of Aeronautics of the Navy Department: Notes by Commander Jerome C. Hunsaker," 8, vol. 9, Historical Papers Submitted, fold-

er 26, box 3, Hunsaker Papers, MIT; Hunsaker to Land, 21 Dec. 1920, folder 21, box 1, Professional Corres., 1920–1921, Hunsaker Papers, MIT.

52. *New York Times,* 28 Nov. 1971; Land to Hunsaker, 3 Mar. 1921, folder 1, box 1, Profes. Corres., 1920–1921, Hunsaker Papers, MIT.

53. Turnbull and Lord, *History of United States Naval Aviation,* 12–13, 18; George van Deurs, *Anchors in the Sky: Spuds Ellyson, the First Naval Aviator* (San Rafael, Calif.: Presidio Press, 1978).

54. Van Deurs, *Anchors in the Sky,* 212.

55. Smith, *First Across!,* 177–78; Patrick Hughes, "Francis W. Reichelderfer, Part I: Aerologists and Airdevils," *Weatherwise* 34 (Apr. 1981): 52–59.

56. *Daily Aviation News Bulletin* 2 (22 Aug. 1921): 1; *Army and Navy Journal* 59 (17 Sept. 1921): 56; Wilson, *Slipstream,* 1, 12.

57. Conference Reports, vols. 1–3, box 16, BuAer, Confid. Corres., 1917–1941, RG 72, NA.

58. "Development of Naval Aircraft, Aircraft Division, Bureau of Construction and Repair: Notes by Commander Jerome C. Hunsaker," 9–10, vol. 10, Historical Papers Submitted, folder 26, box 3, Hunsaker Papers, MIT.

CHAPTER 5: CARRIERS AND CONFERENCES

1. WAM Service Record, file 662, NPRC. An account of the early bombing tests off the Virginia Capes appears in Burke Davis, *The Billy Mitchell Affair* (New York: Random House, 1967), 94–95.

2. WAM Service Record, file 662, NPRC; Davis, *Billy Mitchell Affair,* 97–99.

3. WAM Service Record, file 662, NPRC; Davis, *Billy Mitchell Affair,* 102–11.

4. Turnbull and Lord, *History of United States Naval Aviation,* 200–201.

5. "Interview with Admiral Moffett," Commander News Releases 2 (no date, but most likely Aug. 1921), BuAer, Gen. Corres. initiated in the Office of the CNO, 1917–1925, box 350, RG 72, NA.

6. Ibid.; Turnbull and Lord, *History of United States Naval Aviation,* 199–200.

7. Melhorn, *Two-Block Fox,* 29–37.

8. Ibid., 39–44.

9. U.S. Cong., House, *Hearings Before the Committee on Naval Affairs . . . on Sundry Legislation Affecting the Naval Establishment, 1920–1921,* 736–37.

10. Ibid., 668–69.

11. Thomas H. Buckley, *The United States and the Washington Conference, 1921–1922* (Knoxville: University of Tennessee Press, 1970), 1–34, 49–55.

12. Melhorn, *Two-Block Fox,* 81–82.

13. Ibid., 82; Friedman, *U.S. Aircraft Carriers,* 41–43.

14. U.S., *Conference on the Limitation of Armament, Washington, November 12, 1921–February 6, 1922* (Washington: GPO, 1922), 14–16; Charles E. Hughes to WAM, 3 Nov. 1921, file 00/Moffett, William A., vol. 1, box 4148, BuAer, Gen. Corres., 1925–1942, RG 72, NA.

15. Buckley, *United States and the Washington Conference*, 68–74.

16. Wilson, *Slipstream*, 9–10; U.S., *Conference on the Limitation of Armament*, 414; U.S., *Conference on the Limitation of Armament, Washington, November 12, 1921–February 6, 1922, Subcommittees* (Washington: GPO, 1922), 192, 206.

17. U.S., *Conference on the Limitation of Armament . . . Subcommittees*, 214–16, 224–30.

18. U.S., *Conference on the Limitation of Armament*, 754, 758.

19. Ibid., 758–74.

20. Ibid., 776.

21. Ibid., 778–80, 790.

22. U.S., *Conference on the Limitation of Armament*, 88; Friedman, *U.S. Aircraft Carriers*, 40–41.

23. Buckley, *United States and the Washington Conference*, 119–20.

24. Melhorn, *Two-Block Fox*, 84–85; Friedman, *U.S. Aircraft Carriers*, 43.

25. Buckley, *United States and the Washington Conference*, 172–84; Wheeler, *Pratt*, 186.

26. WAM to William Wrigley, Jr., 11 June 1921, Corres. W., reel 7, Moffett Corres., Wilson Coll., NDL.

27. Entry, 1 Jan. 1922, Personal Financial Ledger, vol. 2, box 2, WAM Papers, Part 2, USNA.

28. Entry, 1 Jan. 1924, Personal Financial Ledger, vol. 3, box 2, WAM Papers, Part 2, USNA; George H. Moffett, Jr., to William A. Moffett, Jr., 12 Dec. 1990, William A. Moffett, Jr., files, Williamsburg Landing, Va.; interview with William A. Moffett, Jr., 15 Dec. 1990. The Ambassador Hotel now stands on the site of the 2019 Massachusetts Avenue house.

29. WAM to R. Adm. W. S. Sims, 28 Feb. 1922, Corres. S, reel 6, Moffett Corres., Wilson Coll., NDL.

30. U.S. Cong., House, *Hearings Before the Committee on Naval Affairs . . . on Sundry Legislation Affecting the Naval Establishment, 1921*, 365–66.

31. Ibid., 365–67.

32. WAM to General Board, 2 Mar. 1922, in Hearings Before the General Board of the Navy, 1922, vol. 1 (micro. roll 4), 58–60.

33. Hearings Before the General Board of the Navy, 1922, vol. 1 (micro. roll 4), 28–54.

34. Ibid., 39.

35. Ibid., 318–23; ibid., vol. 3 (micro. roll 5), 763–64, 795.

36. Ibid., vol. 2 (micro. roll 4), 492–93.

37. Ibid., vol. 3 (micro. roll 5), 786–88; enclosure, WAM to Senior Member of Board to Consider Naval Aeronautic Policy, 28 Apr. 1927, Aer-1-GB, A1-2(1), file A1-2(1), vol. 1, box 10, BuAer, Gen. Corres., 1925–1942, RG 72, NA.

38. WAM to SecNav, Aer-1-HS 601-1 804-1 803-0, 10 Aug. 1922, roll 17, WAM Papers, USNA.

39. Hearings Before the General Board of the Navy, 1922, vol. 3 (micro. roll 5), 766–67.

40. Ibid., vol. 1 (micro. roll 4), 297; Melhorn, *Two-Block Fox*, 153–54.

41. Friedman, *U.S. Aircraft Carriers*, 58–62.

42. Ibid., 62–63; Hearings Before the General Board of the Navy, 1924, vol. 1 (micro. roll 5), 161, 164, 170, 175.

43. *United States Naval Aviation, 1910–1980* (Washington, D.C.: Naval Air Systems Command, 1981), 53; Trimble, *Wings for the Navy*, 181–82.

44. BuNav to Chief, BuAer, 7 Nov. 1922, Nn-312-PG, vol. 1, file 00/Moffett, William A., box 4148, BuAer, Gen. Corres., 1925–1942, RG 72, NA; WAM Service Record, file 662, NPRC; *United States Naval Aviation, 1910–1980*, 53.

45. U.S. Cong., House, *Hearing Before the Subcommittee of the House Committee on Appropriations . . . Navy Department Appropriation Bill for 1924*, 67th Cong., 4th sess. (Washington, D.C.: GPO, 1922), 574–75.

46. *Langley* deck logs, 1–12 June 1923, RG 24, NA; WAM to CNO, 2 May 1923, Aer-P-BB, file 203-2, vol. 3, box 202, BuAer, Gen. Corres. initiated in BuC&R, 1917–1925, RG 72, NA; *New York Times*, 12, 13 June 1923.

47. Capt. S. H. R. Doyle (CO *Langley*) to CNO, 30 June 1923, SHRD-126, file 203-2, vol. 3, box 202, BuAer, Gen. Corres. initiated in BuC&R, 1917–1925, RG 72, NA; *New York Times*, 25, 27, 30 July 1923; WAM Service Record, file 662, NPRC.

48. Melhorn, *Two-Block Fox*, 100–101.

49. V. Adm. N. A. McCully to WAM, 12 Feb. 1924, roll 5, WAM Papers, USNA.

50. "Brief of the Development of Airplane Launching Devices," 8 Feb. 1922, file S83-2, vol. 1, box 4788, BuAer, Gen. Corres., 1925–1942, RG 72, NA; U.S. Cong., House, *Hearing Before the Subcommittee of House Committee on Appropriations . . . Navy Department Appropriation Bill for 1923*, 67th Cong., 2d sess. (Washington, D.C.: GPO, 1922), 944; "Summary of New Catapult Program," 1 June 1925, roll 11, WAM Papers, USNA.

51. Trimble, *Wings for the Navy*, 167–68; "Summary of New Catapult Program," 1 June 1925, roll 11, WAM Papers, USNA.

52. Hearings Before the General Board of the Navy, 1922, vol. 3 (micro. roll 5), 762.

53. Enclosure, WAM to Senior Member of Board to Consider Naval Aeronautic Policy, 28 Apr. 1927, Aer-1-GB, A1-2(1), file A1-2(1), vol. 1, box 10, BuAer, Gen. Corres., 1925–1942, RG 72, NA; H. P. Jones (Senior Member Present) to SecNav, 28 Sept. 1927, G.B. 420-15 (Serial No. 1357), box 109, General Board, General Records of the Department of the Navy, RG 80, NA.

54. "Statement of Department's Policy Together with Steps Taken by Bureau of Aeronautics to Meet Requirement of the Policy," 22 Sept. 1924, roll 11, WAM Papers, USNA; enclosure, WAM to Senior Member of Board to Consider Naval Aeronautic Policy, 28 Apr. 1927, Aer-1-GB, A1-2(1), file A1-2(1), vol. 1, box 10, BuAer, Gen. Corres., 1925–1942, RG 72, NA; "Summary of New Catapult Program," 1 June 1925, roll 11, WAM Papers, USNA.

55. BuNav to Mustin, 30 July 1923, Orders to Duty, box 1, Mustin Papers, LCMD; Reginald Wright Arthur, *Contact!: Naval Aviators Assigned Numbers 1 to 2000* (Washington, D.C.: Naval Aviator Register, 1967), 9.

56. Memo, WAM to CNO, 12 May 1924, Aer-1-HS, 605-2, 601-1, O-57, file 605-2, box 309, BuAer, Gen. Corres. initiated in BuC&R, 1917–1925, RG 72, NA; WAM, "Some Aviation Fundamentals," *USNIP* 51 (Oct. 1925): 1877.

CHAPTER 6: AIRPLANES, AIRSHIPS, AND AIRMEN

1. John B. Rae, *Climb to Greatness: The American Aircraft Industry, 1920–1960* (Cambridge, Mass.: MIT Press, 1968), 1–3; Holley, *Buying Aircraft*, 80–87.

2. Trimble, *Wings for the Navy*, 60–65.

3. Ibid., 66–67.

4. Ibid., 70–71.

5. *Annual Reports of the Navy Department for the Fiscal Year 1922* (Washington, D.C.: GPO, 1923), 382.

6. Vander Meulen, *Politics of Aircraft*, 6–7, 44–45.

7. World War II Administrative History, BuAer, vol. 6, Procurement, Production and Contracts (Washington, D.C.: Department of the Navy, 1957), 7–8; Shanahan, "Procurement of Naval Aircraft, 1907–1939," 301–2.

8. Memo, WAM to All Officers of the Bureau, 22 Mar. 1922, Aer-1-HS, 602-4, 803-7, file 602-4, box 308, BuAer, Gen. Corres. initiated in BuC&R, 1917–1925, RG 72, NA.

9. U.S. Cong., House, *Hearings Before the Committee on Naval Affairs . . . on Sundry Legislation Affecting the Naval Establishment, 1922–1923,* 67th Cong., 2d, 3d, 4th sess. (Washington, D.C.: GPO, 1923), 1747–49.

10. Hearings Before the General Board of the Navy, 1923, vol. 1 (micro. roll 5), 122, 140–50.

11. U.S. Cong., House, *Hearing Before the Subcommittee of the House Committee on Appropriations . . . Navy Department Appropriation Bill for 1926,* 68th Cong., 2d sess. (Washington, D.C.: GPO, 1924), 550–51, 555.

12. Trimble, *Wings for the Navy,* 85–86.

13. Charles J. McCarthy, "Notes on Metal Wing Construction," *U.S. Air Services* 10 (Mar. 1925): 9–11; H. C. Richardson, "Development in Naval Aeronautics," *Society of Automotive Engineers, Transactions* 19, pt. 2 (1924): 662–66.

14. *Aviation* 12 (29 May 1922): 636; Richardson, "Development in Naval Aeronautics," 685; Charles Ward Hall, "Metal Construction of Airplanes," *Aviation* 20 (17 May 1926): 744–48; W. W. Webster, "The Navy PN-12 Seaplane," *Aviation* 24 (14 May 1928): 1366, 1404.

15. WAM, "Naval Aviation," *USNIP* 53 (Oct. 1927): 1081.

16. E. E. Wilson, "Air-Cooled Engines in Naval Aircraft," *Journal of the Society of Automotive Engineers* 19 (Sept. 1926): 224; E. E. Wilson report to the Eberle Board in Hearings Before the General Board of the Navy, 1925, vol. 1, Special Hearings [Eberle Board] (micro. roll 7), 1590.

17. Lt. Comdr. S. M. Kraus, telephone confirmation of J-1 contract, file 736-86, box 123, BuAer, Gen. Corres. initiated in Bureau of Steam Engineering, 1914–1925, RG 72, NA; Robert Schlaifer and S. D. Heron, *Development of Aircraft Engines and Fuels* (Boston: Graduate School of Business Administration, Harvard University, 1950), 167–69.

18. Schlaifer and Heron, *Development of Aircraft Engines and Fuels,* 173–74.

19. Ibid., 173–75.

20. Wilson, *Slipstream,* 53.

21. Ibid., 1–8.

22. Ibid., 12–18; Schlaifer and Heron, *Development of Aircraft Engines and Fuels,* 184–85.

23. Wilson, *Slipstream,* 47–56; Schlaifer and Heron, *Development of Aircraft Engines and Fuels,* 186–90.

24. Transcript of flight log of WAM, roll 10, WAM Papers, USNA; Ladislas d'Orcy, "The Curtiss Marine Flying Trophy Race," *Aviation* 13 (16 Oct. 1922): 490–92.

25. Thomas G. Foxworth, *The Speed Seekers* (New York: Doubleday & Co., 1976), 199–201, 453–55.

26. WAM, "Lessons of the Curtiss Marine Flying Trophy Race," *Aviation* 13 (23 Oct. 1922): 559.

27. *New York Times,* 19 Oct. 1922.

28. *Aviation* 15 (8 Oct. 1923): 436–37.

29. WAM Service Record, file 662, NPRC; BuAer to Comdr. M. A. Mitscher, 4 Oct. 1923, Aer-HS, 800-353, file 00/Moffett, William A., vol. 1, box 4148, BuAer, Gen. Corres., 1925–1942, RG 72, NA; Foxworth, *Speed Seekers,* 36.

30. *New York Times*, 7 Oct. 1923.

31. Ibid., 3, 5, 6 Nov. 1923.

32. Report of Bureau Conference, 15 Jan. 1924, Conference Reports, vol. 2, box 16, BuAer, Confid. Corres., 1917–1941, RG 72, NA; *New York Times*, 5 Aug., 28 Sept. 1924; Foxworth, *Speed Seekers*, 338, 405.

33. *New York Times*, 28 Sept., 26 Oct. 1924; Foxworth, *Speed Seekers*, 257.

34. "Dirigible Defended by Admiral Moffett," *USNIP* 49 (June 1923): 1056; memo, WAM to CNO, 11 Aug. 1921, Op 15C-BB, 8/11, file 3109-57, box 164, BuAer, Gen. Corres. initiated in Office of CNO, 1917–1925, RG 72, NA.

35. Robinson and Keller, *Up Ship!* 11, 57–58, 64; Trimble, *Wings for the Navy*, 57–58.

36. Memo, WAM to CNO, 11 Aug. 1921, Op. 15C-BB, 8/11, file 3109-57, box 164, BuAer, Gen. Corres. initiated in Office of CNO, 1917–1925, RG 72, NA; Robinson and Keller, *Up Ship!* 57–58.

37. Robinson and Keller, *Up Ship!* 45–49; *New York Times*, 24 Aug., 18 Sept. 1921.

38. Robinson and Keller, *Up Ship!* 58–59.

39. Ibid., 66–70; *U.S. Navy Bureau of Aeronautics Weekly News Letter* 3 (6 Sept. 1923): 3; *New York Times*, 5 Sept. 1923.

40. Robinson and Keller, *Up Ship!* 71–74.

41. Ibid., 116–18.

42. Ibid., 118–24.

43. WAM to Comdr. W. P. Beehler, 10 May 1922, roll 1, WAM Papers, USNA.

44. Robinson and Keller, *Up Ship!* 130–38.

45. Capt. William A. Moffett, "Airships and the Scientist," Press Release 089, 28 June 1921, roll 15, WAM Papers, USNA.

46. U.S. Cong., House, *Hearing Before the Subcommittee of the House Committee on Appropriations . . . Navy Department Appropriation Bill for 1925*, 68th Cong., 1st sess. (Washington, D.C.: GPO, 1924), 560–68.

47. Ibid., 560–62; Robinson and Keller, *Up Ship!* 77–82.

48. Report of Bureau Conference, 23 Sept. 1924, Conference Reports, vol. 2, box 16, BuAer, Confid. Corres., 1917–1941, RG 72, NA.

49. Hearings Before the General Board of the Navy, 1925, vol. 1, Special Hearings [Eberle Board], (micro. roll 6), 1063; Robinson and Keller, *Up Ship!* 90–92.

50. Hearings Before the General Board of the Navy, 1925, vol. 1, Special Hearings [Eberle Board], (micro. roll. 6), 1055–57; Arpee, *Frigates to Flat-Tops*, 194–97.

51. Robinson and Keller, *Up Ship!* 92–95; Report of Bureau Conference, 28 Oct. 1924, Conference Reports, vol. 2, box 16, BuAer, Confid. Corres., 1917–1941, RG 72, NA.

52. *Washington Post,* 26 Nov. 1924; transcript of flight log of WAM, roll 10, WAM Papers, USNA.

53. *Annual Reports of the Navy Department for the Fiscal Year 1925* (Washington, D.C.: GPO, 1926), 613–16.

54. Hearings Before the General Board of the Navy, 1924, vol. 1 (micro. roll 5), 66, 235–38.

55. WAM to Chief, BuNav, 19 Nov. 1921, Aer-F-3-HJJ, 803-0, 601-1, file 803-0, vol. 1, box 337, BuAer, Gen. Corres. initiated in BuC&R, 1917–1925, RG 72, NA.

56. WAM to Chief, BuNav, 4 Mar. 1922, Aer-F-HM, 803-0, 804-1, 705-17, file 803-0, vol. 2, and WAM to SecNav, 23 June 1922, file 803-0, vol. 3, box 337, BuAer, Gen. Corres. initiated in BuC&R, 1917–1925, RG 72, NA; *Annual Reports of the Navy Department for the Fiscal Year 1922,* 371.

57. WAM to Chief, BuNav, 28 May 1923, Aer-F-HM, 705-17, 803-0, 601-1, file 803-0, vol. 4, box 338, BuAer, Gen. Corres. initiated in BuC&R, 1917–1925, RG 72, NA; Turnbull and Lord, *History of United States Naval Aviation,* 229.

58. *Annual Reports of the Navy Department for the Fiscal Year 1923* (Washington, D.C.: GPO, 1924), 571; Lt. Comdr. Richard M. Carrigan, "History of Naval Aviation Personnel, 1911–1933," vol. 21, Deputy Chief of Naval Operations (Air), Monographs in the History of Naval Aviation (Washington, D.C.: Naval Aviation History Unit, 1946), 122–25.

59. *Annual Reports of the Navy Department for the Fiscal Year 1925,* 602.

60. WAM to Lemuel P. Padgett, 8 Apr. 1922, Aer-F-HS, 803-0, 99-3, 605-3, file 803-0, vol. 2, box 337, BuAer, Gen. Corres. initiated in BuC&R, 1917–1925, RG 72, NA; *Annual Reports of the Navy Department for the Fiscal Year 1923,* 529.

61. WAM to Chief, BuNav, 27 Mar. 1922, Aer-F-BB, 803-0, 804-1, file 803-0, vol. 2, box 337, BuAer, Gen. Corres. initiated in BuC&R, 1917–1925, RG 72, NA.

62. WAM Service Record, file 662, NPRC; Capt. H. H. Christy (Commandant, Pensacola), 17 June 1922, to Chief, BuNav, 41-3330, vol. 1, file 00/Moffett, William A., box 4148, BuAer, Gen. Corres., 1925–1942, RG 72, NA.

63. Featherston, "AEDO," 40–41.

64. BuNav to Comdr. J. C. Hunsaker, 3 Nov. 1923, folder 21, box 1, Hunsaker Papers, MIT; Hunsaker to SecNav, 30 June 1926, folder 22, box 1, Hunsaker Papers, MIT; Trimble, *Wings for the Navy,* 76; memo, WAM to Edward P. Warner, 21 Sept. 1927, Aer-BB, A1-2(1), OC, file A1-2(1), vol. 1, box 10, BuAer, Gen. Corres., 1925–1942, RG 72, NA.

65. WAM to Lt. Comdr. N. H. White, Jr., 5 Aug. 1924, file 803-0, vol. 5, box 338, BuAer, Gen. Corres. initiated in BuC&R, 1917–1925, RG 72, NA.

66. WAM to Capt. A. W. Johnson, 6 Dec. 1924, Aer-F-AK, 600-376, 803-0,

file 803-0, vol. 4, box 338, BuAer, Gen. Corres. initiated in BuC&R, 1917–1925, RG 72, NA.

67. Carrigan, "History of Naval Aviation Personnel, 1911–1933," 134–44.

68. Chief, BuNav, to CNO, 2 Mar. 1925, MV(1), Nav61-St, file 803-0, vol. 5, box 338, BuAer, Gen. Corres. initiated in BuC&R, 1917–1925, RG 72, NA; Chief, BuNav, to SecNav, 26 June 1925, file A1-2(1), vol. 1, box 10, BuAer, Gen. Corres., 1925–1942, RG 72, NA.

69. Memo, WAM to SecNav, 19 Sept. 1924, Aer-GB, 99-82, 601-1, 605-4, file L1-1(26), vol. 1, box 2807, BuAer, Gen. Corres., 1925–1942, RG 72, NA.

Chapter 7: Moffett, Mitchell, and Morrow

1. Report of a Committee of Officers Appointed by Secretary of War, 17 Mar. 1923, file 707-0, Office Services Division, BuAer, Gen. Corres., 1925–1942, RG 72, NA.

2. Lassiter Board Report, 27 Mar. 1923, file 145.93-101, U.S. Air Force Historical Research Agency, Maxwell Air Force Base, Alabama; U.S. President's Aircraft Board, *Hearings Before the President's Aircraft Board* (Washington, D.C.: GPO, 1925), 1: 249.

3. Richard W. Turk, "Edward Walter Eberle," in Robert William Love, Jr., ed., *The Chiefs of Naval Operations* (Annapolis: Naval Institute Press, 1980), 38–39.

4. Hearings Before the General Board of the Navy, 1925, vol. 1, Special Hearings [Eberle Board], (micro. roll 6), 4–94.

5. Ibid., 150–70.

6. Ibid., 211–12.

7. Ibid., 1314–1337.

8. Turnbull and Lord, *History of United States Naval Aviation,* 244–45.

9. Ibid., 244; Carrigan, "History of Naval Aviation Personnel, 1911–1933," 132–33.

10. Turnbull and Lord, *History of United States Naval Aviation,* 240–41.

11. Trimble, *Wings for the Navy,* 66–70; Report of Bureau Conference, 29 Apr. 1924, Conference Reports, vol. 2, box 16, BuAer, Confid. Corres., 1917–1941, RG 72, NA.

12. *New York Times,* 18 Dec. 1924.

13. *Literary Digest* 83 (13 Dec. 1924): 58–61.

14. WAM to Editor, *New York World,* 19 Dec. 1924, Aer-A-3-MRC, 40-9, 602-0, 300-3248, file 602-0, Office Services Division, BuAer, vol. 1, box 5, BuAer, Gen. Corres., 1925–1942, RG 72, NA.

15. *New York Times,* 23 Dec. 1924.

16. *Washington Post*, 1 Jan. 1925; interview with William A. Moffett, Jr., 15 Dec. 1990.

17. U.S. Cong., House, *Hearings Before the Select Committee of Inquiry into Operations of the United States Air Services*, 68th Cong. (Washington, D.C.: GPO, 1925), pt. 2, 912–37, 1002–3, 1388.

18. Ibid., pt. 2, 1290–91, 1588–1627.

19. Ibid., 1628–29.

20. Ibid., pt. 3, 1633, 1658–59.

21. WAM to Capt. Powers Symington, 16 Feb. 1925, roll 8, WAM Papers, USNA.

22. *New York Times*, 1, 21 Feb. 1925.

23. WAM, "The Sinking of the Washington," no date, Misc. Corres., reel 9, Moffett Corres., Wilson Coll., NDL.

24. *New York Times*, 5 Feb. 1925.

25. WAM to William Wrigley, Jr., 10 Dec. 1924, Corres. W, reel 7, Moffett Corres., Wilson Coll., NDL.

26. WAM to J. Ogden Armour, 11 Feb. 1925, Corres. A, reel 1, Moffett Corres., Wilson Coll., NDL.

27. WAM Service Record, file 662, NPRC; WAM to William Wrigley, Jr., 13 Mar. 1925, Corres. W, reel 7, Moffett Corres., Wilson Coll., NDL.

28. WAM to Capt. Powers Symington, 16 Feb. 1925, roll 8, WAM Papers, USNA; *New York Times*, 4 Feb., 7, 31 Mar. 1925.

29. *New York Times*, 21 Feb. 1925.

30. Ibid., 21, 22, 23 Feb. 1925.

31. Robinson and Keller, *Up Ship!* 142–44; *New York Times*, 16 May 1925.

32. W. B. Tardy to WAM, 30 Apr. 1925, file O-Z-54, box 17, BuAer, Gen. Corres. initiated in BuC&R, 1917–1925, RG 72, NA.

33. *Annual Reports of the Navy Department for the Fiscal Year 1923*, 566; *New York Times*, 30 Mar. 1925.

34. Memo, WAM for SecNav, Nov. 5, 1923, file 26983-1589:13, box 2132, SecNav, Gen. Corres., 1916–1926, RG 80, NA.

35. WAM to SecNav, 8 Nov. 1924, Aer-P-BB, 804-6, file A4-3(7-1), vol. 1, box 141, BuAer, Gen. Corres., 1925–1942, RG 72, NA.

36. Adm. R. E. Coontz (CinC U.S. Fleet) to CNO, 27 Dec. 1924, file A4-3/F(7-6), box 141, BuAer, Gen. Corres., 1925–1942, RG 72, NA.

37. Capt. A. W. Johnson (by direction, Chief, BuAer) to CNO, 14 Apr. 1925, Aer-P-BB, 804-6, 606-10, file A4-3(7-1), box 141, BuAer, Gen. Corres., 1925–1942, RG 72, NA; CNO to Chief, BuAer, 20 Apr. 1925, Op-38-C-MW, 26983:2, file A4-3(7-1), box 141, BuAer, Gen. Corres., 1925–1942, RG 72, NA.

38. Dwight R. Messimer, *No Margin for Error: The U.S. Navy's Transpacific*

Flight of 1925 (Annapolis: Naval Institute Press, 1981), 7–10, 20–28.

39. Hughes, "Francis W. Reichelderfer," 54–55.

40. Messimer, *No Margin for Error,* 12–14, 29.

41. Report of Bureau Conference, 4 Aug. 1925, Conference Reports, vol. 2, box 16, BuAer, Confid. Corres., 1917–1941, RG 72, NA; WAM Personnel "Jacket," 662–2, files of Richard K. Smith; Robinson and Keller, *Up Ship!* 90; *New York Times,* 23 Aug. 1925.

42. WAM Personnel "Jacket," 662-2, files of Richard K. Smith; Messimer, *No Margin for Error,* 29–33, 40–42.

43. Messimer, *No Margin for Error,* 43–48.

44. Ibid., 55–65.

45. Dispatch, BuAer to WAM, 1 Sept. 1925, in WAM Personnel "Jacket," 662-2, files of Richard K. Smith; Naval Message, 79910, BuAer to WAM, 1 Sept. 1925, file 00/Moffett, William A., vol. 2, box 4148, BuAer, Gen. Corres., 1925–1942, RG 72, NA.

46. *New York Times,* 4 Sept. 1925.

47. Robinson and Keller, *Up Ship!* 100–110.

48. *New York Times,* 4 Sept. 1925.

49. Ibid., 6 Sept. 1925.

50. Clark and Reynolds, *Carrier Admiral,* 16–17; *New York Times,* 10 Sept. 1925.

51. Messimer, *No Margin for Error,* 111–32; Wilson Reminiscences, Columbia Univ., 207; Wilson, *Slipstream,* 59–60.

52. *New York Times,* 14 Sept. 1925.

53. Ibid.

54. Wilson Reminiscences, Columbia Univ., 249.

55. U.S. President's Aircraft Board, *Hearings Before the President's Aircraft Board,* 1: 194–210.

56. Ibid., 225–30, 245–46.

57. Wilson, *Slipstream,* 64–65.

58. U.S. President's Aircraft Board, *Hearings Before the President's Aircraft Board,* 1: 495–559.

59. Ibid., 3: 991–95.

60. Ibid., 997–98.

61. U.S. President's Aircraft Board, Report of President's Aircraft Board (Washington, D.C.: GPO, 1925), 11–14, 23–26.

62. Ibid., 26–29.

63. U.S. Cong., House, *Report of the Select Committee of Inquiry into Operations of the United States Air Services,* 68th Cong., 2d sess. (Washington, D.C.: GPO, 1925), 8–9; Davis, *Billy Mitchell Affair,* 239–326; Robinson and Keller, *Up Ship!* 113–14.

CHAPTER 8: A THOUSAND AIRPLANES

1. Nick A. Komons, *Bonfires to Beacons: Federal Civil Aviation Policy Under the Air Commerce Act, 1926–1938* (Washington, D.C.: Department of Transportation, Federal Aviation Administration, 1978), 78–80; Wilson, *Slipstream,* 71.

2. Memo, WAM for Secretary's Council Meeting, 23 Jan. 1922, Aer-A-1-EM, 99-3, 601-1, 600-25, file L1, vol. 2, box 2806, BuAer, Gen. Corres., 1925–1942, RG 72, NA; *Annual Reports of the Navy Department for the Fiscal Year 1923,* 566–67.

3. Annual Report, FY 1924 (ms.), WAM to SecNav, 15 Aug. 1924, Aer-A-HS, 601-6, file 601-6, vol. 3, box 306, BuAer, Gen. Corres. initiated in BuC&R, 1917–1925, RG 72, NA; *Annual Reports of the Navy Department for the Fiscal Year 1925,* 622.

4. Minutes of SecNav Council, 25 Aug. 1924, and memo, WAM to SecNav, 19 Sept. 1924, Aer-GB, 99-82, 601-1, 605-4, file L1-1(26), vol. 1, box 2807, BuAer, Gen. Corres., 1925–1942, RG 72, NA.

5. U.S. Cong., House, *Hearing Before the Subcommittee of House Committee on Appropriations . . . Navy Department Appropriation Bill for 1926,* 550.

6. U.S. President's Aircraft Board, *Hearings Before the President's Aircraft Board,* 1: 207, 3: 994.

7. WAM to R. D. Stephens, 19 Oct. 1925, Aer-HB, L1-1(27), 605-4, file L1-1(27), vol. 1, box 2807, BuAer, Gen. Corres., 1925–1942, RG 72, NA.

8. U.S. Cong., House, *Hearing Before the Subcommittee of House Committee on Appropriations . . . Navy Department Appropriation Bill for 1927,* 69th Cong., 1st sess. (Washington, D.C.: GPO, 1926), 726–27, 771–76.

9. Ibid., 540–53.

10. *New York Times,* 26 Jan. 1926.

11. U.S. Cong., House, *Hearings Before the Committee on Naval Affairs . . . on Sundry Legislation Affecting the Naval Establishment, 1925–1926,* 69th Cong., 1st sess. (Washington, D.C.: GPO, 1926), 700–712.

12. U.S. Cong., House, *Hearings Before the Committee on Military Affairs . . . Department of Defense and Unification of Air Service,* 69th Cong., 1st sess. (Washington, D.C.: GPO, 1926), 686–87, 694–98, 705–6.

13. U.S. Cong., House, *Hearings Before the Committee on Naval Affairs . . . on Sundry Legislation Affecting the Naval Establishment, 1925–1926,* 1243–44, 1246–49.

14. Ibid., 926–39; *New York Times,* 5 Feb. 1926.

15. *New York Times,* 7 Feb. 1926.

16. U.S. Cong., House, *Hearings Before the Committee on Naval Affairs . . . on Sundry Legislation Affecting the Naval Establishment, 1925–1926,* 1640–41; WAM to Capt. E. S. Land, 17 Feb. 1926, Corres. L, reel 4, Moffett Corres., Wilson Coll., NDL.

17. *Congressional Record,* House, 69th Cong., 1st sess., vol. 67, pt. 4, 4462; *New York Times,* 2 Mar. 1926.

18. WAM to Capt. Adolphus Andrews, 24 Feb. 1926, roll 1, WAM Papers, USNA.

19. WAM to Dwight Morrow, 2 Mar. 1926, Corres. M, reel 4, Moffett Corres., Wilson Coll., NDL; *New York Times,* 14 Mar. 1926.

20. WAM to William Wrigley, Jr., 15 Mar. 1926, Corres. W, reel 7, Moffett Corres., Wilson Coll., NDL; *Congressional Record,* House, 69th Cong., 1st sess., vol. 67, pt. 7, 7149–58, 7205–38, 7308–9.

21. WAM to Dwight Morrow, 26 Apr. 1926, Corres. M, reel 4, Moffett Corres., Wilson Coll., NDL; *Congressional Record,* Senate, 69th Cong., 1st sess., vol. 67, pt. 7, 7341.

22. *Congressional Record,* Senate, 69th Cong., 1st sess., vol. 67, pt. 10, 9586, 10585–87, 11447, 11686.

23. U.S., *Statutes at Large of the United States of America,* vol. 44, pt. 2 (Washington, D.C.: GPO, 1927), 764–68.

24. Roger E. Bilstein, "Edward Pearson Warner and the New Air Age," in William M. Leary, ed., *Aviation's Golden Age* (Iowa City: University of Iowa Press, 1989), 114–17.

25. *Annual Reports of the Navy Department for the Fiscal Year 1926* (Washington, D.C.: GPO, 1927), 598; *Annual Reports of the Navy Department for the Fiscal Year 1927* (Washington, D.C.: GPO, 1928), 621.

26. WAM to Jeannette Moffett, Desbarats, Ont., 6 Sept. 1926, William A. Moffett, Jr., files, Williamsburg Landing, Va.; WAM Personnel "Jacket," 662-2, files of Richard K. Smith.

27. Memo, Warner to Chief, BuAer, 4 Dec. 1926, file A1-2(1), vol. 1, box 10, BuAer, Gen. Corres., 1925–1942, RG 72, NA; Memo, WAM to Asst. SecNav for Aero., 18 Dec. 1926, Aer-1-HS, A1-3(27), VT3M1/F1-1, file A1-3(27), box 10, BuAer, Gen. Corres., 1925–1942, RG 72, NA.

28. WAM to All Units of the Naval Aeronautic Organization, 8 Mar. 1927, Aer-A-BB, L1-1(28), file L1-1(28), vol. 2, box 2808, BuAer, Gen. Corres., 1925–1942, RG 72, NA; WAM memo for files, 13 July 1927, Aer-1-BB, A1-3(28), A19(1), L8(1), file A1-3(28), box 10, BuAer, Gen. Corres., 1925–1942, RG 72, NA.

29. WAM to SecNav, 19 Aug. 1927, Aer-A-1-HP, L1-1(29), file L1-1(29), vol. 1, box 2809, BuAer, Gen. Corres., 1925–1942, RG 72, NA.

30. Memo, Warner for Budget Officer, 30 Aug. 1927, BuAer, Gen. Corres., 1925–1942, RG 72, NA; *Annual Reports of the Navy Department for the Fiscal Year 1929* (Washington, D.C.: GPO, 1930), 590.

31. WAM to SecNav, 20 Jan. 1928, Aer-A-1-HD, L1-1(30), file L1-1(30), vol. 1, box 2809, BuAer, Gen. Corres., 1925–1942, RG 72, NA; *Annual Reports of the*

Navy Department for the Fiscal Year 1930 (Washington, D.C.: GPO, 1931), 568–69; U.S. Cong., House, *Hearing Before the Subcommittee of the House Committee on Appropriations . . . Navy Department Appropriation Bill for 1931,* 71st Cong., 2d sess. (Washington, D.C.: GPO, 1930), 495.

32. WAM to SecNav, 18 June 1929, Aer-B-MTM, and WAM to SecNav, 19 Aug. 1929, Aer-GB, file L1-1(31), vol. 1, box 2810, BuAer, Gen. Corres., 1925–1942, RG 72, NA.

33. WAM to SecNav, 18 June 1930, Aer-B-MPM, L1-1(32), file L1-1(32), vol. 1, box 2811, BuAer, Gen. Corres., 1925–1942, RG 72, NA; U.S. Cong., House, *Hearing Before the Subcommittee of the House Committee on Appropriations . . . Navy Department Appropriation Bill for 1933,* 72d Cong., 1st sess. (Washington, D.C.: GPO, 1932), 524; *Annual Reports of the Navy Department for the Fiscal Year 1930,* 568–69.

34. U.S. Cong., House, *Inquiry into Operations of the United States Air Services,* pt. 2, 1628–29; U.S. President's Aircraft Board, *Hearings Before the President's Aircraft Board,* 1: 207.

35. Hearings Before the General Board of the Navy, 1926, vol. 1 (micro. roll 7), 159, 167.

36. U.S., *Statutes at Large of the United States of America,* vol. 44, pt. 2, 784–89.

37. WAM to R. Adm. E. H. Campbell, 10 Nov. 1926, in Shanahan, "Procurement of Naval Aircraft, 1907–1939," 335–36.

38. U.S., *Statutes at Large of the United States of America,* vol. 44, pt. 2, 766–67.

39. R. Adm. W. R. Shoemaker to WAM, 21 Jan. 1925, Nav-312-A, 3031-942, file 803-0, vol. 4, box 338, BuAer, Gen. Corres. initiated in BuC&R, 1917–1925, RG 72, NA.

40. Carrigan, "History of Naval Aviation Personnel, 1911–1933," 148–49.

41. WAM to SecNav, 1 Aug. 1925, Aer-GB, 800-431, 00 File, Land, Emory S., box 4130, BuAer, Gen. Corres., 1925–1942, RG 72, NA; BuNav to Capt. A. W. Johnson, 14 Nov. 1925, no. 6088, 00 File, Johnson, Alfred W., box 4122, BuAer, Gen. Corres., 1925–1942, RG 72, NA.

42. Carrigan, "History of Naval Aviation Personnel, 1911–1933," 150–51.

43. WAM to CNO, 20 Apr. 1925 (3d endorsement), Aer-F-ANZ, 803-0, 804-11, file 803-0, vol. 5, box 338, BuAer, Gen. Corres. initiated in BuC&R, 1917–1925, RG 72, NA; U.S. Cong., House, *Hearings Before the Committee on Naval Affairs . . . on Sundry Legislation Affecting the Naval Establishment, 1925–1926,* 1188.

44. Memo, WAM to SecNav, 17 Apr. 1925, Aer-BB, 804-12, 803-0, file 803-0, vol. 5, box 338, BuAer, Gen. Corres. initiated in BuC&R, 1917–1925, RG 72, NA.

45. R. Adm. W. P. Shoemaker to R. Adm. M. M. Taylor, 28 Sept. 1925, Nav-313, file A1-2(1), vol. 1, box 10, BuAer, Gen. Corres., 1925–1942, RG 72, NA;

WAM to SecNav, 17 Sept. 1925, Aer-GB, 601-1, 803-0, file A1-2(1), vol. 1, box 10, BuAer, Gen. Corres., 1925–1942, RG 72, NA.

46. R. Adm. W. P. Shoemaker to R. Adm. M. M. Taylor, 28 Sept. 1925, Nav-313, file A1-2(1), vol. 1, box 10, BuAer, Gen. Corres., 1925–1942, RG 72, NA.

47. Board of Officers to SecNav, 20 Jan. 1926, reel 9, Moffett Corres., Wilson Coll., NDL.

48. Ibid.

49. Carrigan, "History of Naval Aviation Personnel, 1911–1933," 161.

50. Adm. S. S. Robison to SecNav, 15 Mar. 1926, WAM Papers, Part 2, USNA. Warren Trest of the U.S. Air Force Historical Research Agency provided me with a copy of this document.

51. WAM to Lt. Comdr. Dewitt C. Ramsey, 13 Nov. 1928, Corres. R, reel 5, Moffett Corres., Wilson Coll., NDL. (On the case of Towers, see Reynolds, *Admiral John H. Towers*, 198–207.)

52. WAM to Capt. J. M. Reeves, Comdr. Aircraft Squadrons, Battle Fleet, 22 Mar. 1926, Corres. R, reel 5, Moffett Corres., Wilson Coll., NDL.

53. WAM, memo for files, 18 Jan. 1926, reel 9, Moffett Corres., Wilson Coll., NDL.

54. Memo, WAM to Chief, BuNav, 29 Apr. 1926, Aer-GB, 605-3, 803-0, file 803-0, vol. 5, box 338, BuAer, Gen. Corres. initiated in BuC&R, 1917–1925, RG 72, NA.

55. WAM to SecNav, 13 July 1927, Aer-BB, A1-2(1), OC, file A1-2(1), vol. 1, box 10, BuAer, Gen. Corres., 1925–1942, RG 72, NA.

56. WAM to SecNav, 25 Jan. 1929, Aer-GB, CC, A1-2(1), OC, file A1-2(1), vol. 1, box 10, BuAer, Gen. Corres., 1925–1942, RG 72, NA; Carrigan, "History of Naval Aviation Personnel, 1911–1933," 199–200; Featherston, "AEDO," 43–44.

57. WAM to Julius Rosenwald, 16 May 1928, Corres. R, reel 5, Moffett Corres., Wilson Coll., NDL; WAM to George Tidmarsh, 12 Jan. 1929, Corres. T, reel 6, Moffett Corres., Wilson Coll., NDL.

58. WAM to C. E. McLean, 21 Apr. 1928, Corres. Mc, reel 5, Moffett Corres., Wilson Coll., NDL; Betty to Bill Moffett, Jr., (undated, but during his first year at the academy), William A. Moffett, Jr., files, Williamsburg Landing, Va.

59. Entry, 22 Apr. 1928, Personal Financial Ledger, vol. 4, box 2, WAM Papers, Part 2, USNA; interview with William A. Moffett, Jr., 15 Dec. 1990; interview with Beverly Moffett Mohan, 11 June 1991.

60. WAM to William Wrigley, Jr., 13 Oct. 1928, Corres. W, reel 7, Moffett Corres., Wilson Coll., NDL.

61. WAM to Porter Adams, 6 Jan. 1929, roll 1, WAM Papers, USNA; WAM to W. F. Durand, 14 Jan. 1929, Corres. D, reel 1, Moffett Corres., Wilson Coll., NDL; WAM to William Wrigley, Jr., 18 Feb. 1929, Corres. W, reel 7, Moffett

Corres., Wilson Coll., NDL; William Wrigley, Jr., to WAM, 19 Mar. 1929, Moffett Corres., Wilson Coll., NDL; WAM Personnel "Jacket," 662-2, files of Richard K. Smith.

62. WAM to Wilbur, 21 Jan. 1929, roll 9, WAM Papers, USNA; Paolo E. Coletta, "The Apotheosis of Political Strategy: The Third Appointment of Rear Admiral William A. Moffett as Chief of the U.S. Bureau of Aeronautics, 1929," *American Aviation Historical Society Journal* 36 (Spring 1991): 25.

63. "Admiral Moffett and a Third Term," *Aeronautic Review* (Feb. 1929), clipping in William A. Moffett Printed Matter File, box 93, American Institute of Aeronautics and Astronautics Archives, Library of Congress, Manuscript Division (hereafter cited as AIAA Archives, LCMD).

64. Reynolds and Clark, *Carrier Admiral*, 33; Stump Memoirs, Columbia Univ., 75.

65. WAM to Lt. Comdr. Claude Bailey, USN (Ret.), 3 Apr. 1929, Corres. B, reel 2, Moffett Corres., Wilson Coll., NDL.

66. Hearings Before the General Board of the Navy, 1926, vol. 1, micro. roll 7, 227–28; *Annual Reports of the Navy Department for the Fiscal Year 1926,* 601; Carrigan, "History of Naval Aviation Personnel, 1911–1933," 183–84.

67. *Annual Reports of the Navy Department for the Fiscal Year 1927,* 622–23; memo, Warner to Chief, BuAer, 10 Aug. 1927, file A1-1/P16, vol. 1, box 6, BuAer, Gen. Corres., 1925–1942, RG 72, NA.

68. Memo, Capt. E. S. Land (by direction, Chief, BuAer) to Asst. SecNav for Aeronautics, 28 Sept. 1927, Aer-F-ANX, A1-1/P16, file A1-1/P16, vol. 1, box 6, BuAer, Gen. Corres., 1925–1942, RG 72, NA.

69. R. Adm. R. H. Leigh to CNO, 29 Sept. 1927, A21/P11-1, Nav-10, file A1-1/P16, vol. 1, box 6, BuAer, Gen. Corres., 1925–1942, RG 72, NA; Capt. E. S. Land (by direction, Chief, BuAer) to CNO, 6 Oct. 1927, Aer-1-BB, CC4-1, NC 49, 804-11, file A1-1/P16, vol. 1, box 6, BuAer, Gen. Corres., 1925–1942, RG 72, NA.

70. E. P. Warner to SecNav, 15 Oct. 1927, A21/P11 (271006), file A1-1/P16, vol. 1, box 6, BuAer, Gen. Corres., 1925–1942, RG 72, NA.

71. WAM to Chief, BuNav, 24 Apr. 1928, Aer-F-ANN, A1-1/P16, 804-11, file A1-1/P16, vol. 1, box 6, BuAer, Gen. Corres., 1925–1942, RG 72, NA.

72. R. Adm. R. H. Leigh to CNO, 14 June 1928, A21/P16-1 (6), file A1-1/P16, vol. 1, box 6, BuAer, Gen. Corres., 1925–1942, RG 72, NA.

73. *Annual Reports of the Navy Department for the Fiscal Year 1928* (Washington, D.C.: GPO, 1929), 669–70, 717.

74. *Annual Reports of the Navy Department for the Fiscal Year 1929,* 593–94, 634.

75. *Annual Reports of the Navy Department for the Fiscal Year 1930,* 570, 585; Carrigan, "History of Naval Aviation Personnel, 1911–1933," 207.

CHAPTER 9: "THIS NEW AND POWERFUL WEAPON"

1. Transcript of flight log of WAM, roll 10, WAM Papers, USNA; Clark and Reynolds, *Carrier Admiral,* 26–27, 33; *New York Times,* 7, 8 May 1930.

2. WAM, speech delivered over the National Broadcasting Circuit, 9 May 1930, roll 13, WAM Papers, USNA.

3. Hearings Before the General Board of the Navy, 1925, vol. 2 (micro. roll 7), 418–31.

4. U.S. Cong., House, *Hearing Before Subcommittee of House Committee on Appropriations . . . Navy Department Appropriation Bill for 1926,* 688–91; *New York Times,* 25 Jan. 1925.

5. *New York Times,* 8 Apr. 1925; "Address at the Launching of the 'Lexington,'" 3 Oct. 1925, reel 10, Moffett Corres., Wilson Coll., NDL.

6. Memo, Warner to WAM, 4 Dec. 1926, file A1-2 (1), vol. 1, box 10, BuAer, Gen. Corres., 1925–1942, RG 72, NA; WAM to SecNav, 6 Jan. 1927, Aer-P-1-BB, CV, A1-3(27), file A1-3(27), vol. 1, box 10, BuAer, Gen. Corres., 1925–1942, RG 72, NA; WAM to SecNav, 21 Feb. 1927, Aer-1-HS, A1-2(1), QB/EN 15, file A1-2(1), vol. 1, box 10, BuAer, Gen. Corres., 1925–1942, RG 72, NA.

7. SecNav to R. Adm. Montgomery M. Taylor, 4 Apr. 1927, G.B. 449 (Serial No. 1353), box 191, General Board, General Records of the Department of the Navy, RG 80, NA; Record of Proceedings of a Board Convened at Navy Department . . . to Consider and Recommend upon the Present Naval Aeronautic Policy, 3 May 1927, G.B. 449 (Serial No. 1353), box 191, General Board, General Records of the Department of the Navy, RG 80, NA.

8. Report of Board to Consider and Recommend upon Present Aeronautic Policy, 11 May 1927 (3d endorsement, 11 Nov. 1927), G.B. 449 (Serial No. 1353), box 191, General Board, General Records of the Department of the Navy, RG 80, NA.

9. Ibid.

10. Chief, BuAer, to General Board, 20 June 1927, Aer-1-QB, CV, QB/EN15, roll 11, WAM Papers, USNA.

11. Hearings Before the General Board of the Navy, 1927 (micro. roll 7), 98, 108, 131.

12. Hearings Before the General Board of the Navy, 1928, vol. 1 (micro. roll 7), 34–38.

13. Ibid., 46.

14. Ibid., 261–65.

15. Chief, BuNav, to Land, 13 Aug. 1928, and WAM to Land, 27 Aug. 1928, Aer-0-HD, 3182-27, 00/Land, E. S., 00 File, Land, Emory S., box 4130, BuAer, Gen. Corres., 1925–1942, RG 72, NA; Ernest J. King and Walter Muir Whitehill,

Fleet Admiral King: A Naval Record (New York: W. W. Norton & Co., 1952), 187–88, 207–9; Reynolds, *Admiral John H. Towers,* 220–21.

16. U.S. Cong., House, *Hearings Before Committee on Naval Affairs . . . on Sundry Legislation Affecting the Naval Establishment, 1927–1928,* 70th Cong., 1st sess. (Washington, D.C.: GPO, 1928), 837, 842, 845.

17. WAM to SecNav via CNO, 31 July 1928 (secret), Aer-P-1-KWK, CV, G.B. 449, box 191, General Board, General Records of the Department of the Navy, RG 80, NA.

18. Friedman, *U.S. Aircraft Carriers,* 69–75, 391.

19. Ray Wagner, *American Combat Planes,* 3d ed. (Garden City, N.Y.: Doubleday & Co., 1982), 116–17; Reynolds, *Admiral John H. Towers,* 206, 583; Hearings Before the General Board of the Navy, 1928, vol. 1 (micro. roll 7), 62.

20. CinC Battle Fleet to Battle Fleet, 28 Nov. 1928, and Commander Battle Force to Battle Fleet, 24 June 1931, file A16-3, vol. 1, box 199, BuAer, Confid. Corres., 1922–1944, RG 72, NA. Professor Stephen L. McFarland brought these sources to my attention.

21. Andrade, "Ship That Never Was," 133; R. D. Layman and Stephen McLaughlin, *The Hybrid Warship: The Amalgamation of Big Guns and Aircraft* (Annapolis: Naval Institute Press, 1991), 48–49.

22. WAM to SecNav via CNO, 31 July 1928 (secret), Aer-P-1-KWK, CV, G.B. 449, box 191, General Board, General Records of the Department of the Navy, RG 80, NA.

23. For an overview of the negotiations leading to the London Conference, see Raymond G. O'Connor, *Perilous Equilibrium: The United States and the London Naval Conference of 1930* (Lawrence: University of Kansas Press, 1962).

24. WAM to SecNav, 23 Nov. 1929, Aer-P-1-EMN, CV, A3-1(2-1), VV, (secret), G.B. 438-1 (Serial N. 1464), box 171, General Board, General Records of the Department of the Navy, RG 80, NA.

25. R. Adm. Andrew T. Long to SecNav, 3 Jan. 1930, Aer-P-1-EMN, CV, A3-1(2-1), VV, (secret), G.B. 438-1 (Serial N. 1464), box 171, General Board, General Records of the Department of the Navy, RG 80, NA.

26. Chief, BuNav, to WAM, 4 Dec. 1929, Nav-3-A, file 00/Moffett, William A., vol. 3, box 4148, BuAer, Gen. Corres., 1925–1942, RG 72, NA; ibid., 31 Dec. 1929, Nav-3-M; Wheeler, *Pratt,* 298.

27. Arpee, *Frigates to Flat-Tops,* 147; King and Whitehill, *Fleet Admiral King,* 210–11.

28. Trimble, *Wings for the Navy,* 104; King and Whitehill, *Fleet Admiral King,* 210–11; Reynolds, *Admiral John H. Towers,* 224.

29. Testimony of WAM, London Treaty of 1930, Senate Committee on Naval Affairs, 1–2, item M, roll 17, WAM Papers, USNA; Reynolds, *Admiral John H. Towers,* 225–29.

30. Misc. memos, clippings, and invitations in WAM Scrapbook, 1930 London Conference, William A. Moffett, Jr., files, Williamsburg Landing, Va.

31. Roskill, *Naval Policy Between the Wars, II: The Period of Reluctant Rearmament,* 46; WAM to Towers, 23 Jan. 1930, roll 8, WAM Papers, USNA.

32. Andrade, "Ship That Never Was," 134; Layman and McLaughlin, *Hybrid Warship,* 51.

33. WAM to Towers, 10 Feb. 1930, roll 8, WAM Papers, USNA; WAM to Towers, 17 Feb. 1930, Corres. T, reel 6, Moffett Corres., Wilson Coll., NDL.

34. WAM to Towers, 17 Feb. 1930, Corres. T, reel 6, Moffett Corres., Wilson Coll., NDL.

35. Ibid.

36. Transcript of flight log of WAM, roll 10, WAM Papers, USNA; WAM to Burton L. French, 5 Mar. 1930, Corres. F, reel 3, Moffett Corres., Wilson Coll., NDL.

37. Transcript of flight log of WAM, roll 10, WAM Papers, USNA; WAM notes in WAM Scrapbook, 1930 London Conference, William A. Moffett, Jr., files, Williamsburg Landing, Va.; Arpee, *Frigates to Flat-Tops,* 173.

38. O'Connor, *Perilous Equilibrium,* 71–83.

39. WAM to Towers, 25 Mar. 1930, Corres. T, reel 3, Moffett Corres., Wilson Coll., NDL; WAM to Comdr. Newton H. White, Jr., 29 Mar. 1930, Corres. W. reel 7, Moffett Corres., Wilson Coll., NDL.

40. WAM to David S. Ingalls, 24 Feb. 1930, roll 4, WAM Papers, USNA.

41. *New York Times,* 1 Apr., 22 Apr. 1930. Arpee (*Frigates to Flat-Tops,* 176) erroneously states that Moffett left the conference on 23 Apr.

42. A text of the treaty appears in O'Connor, *Perilous Equilibrium,* 129–44.

43. Testimony of WAM, London Treaty of 1930, Senate Committee on Naval Affairs, 3–4, 6, 9, 14–17, 19–20, 23, item M, roll 17, WAM Papers, USNA.

44. WAM to Capt. John H. Gunnell, 3 June 1930, Corres. G, reel 3, Moffett Corres., Wilson Coll., NDL.

45. WAM to H. Ralph Burton, 3 June 1930, roll 1, WAM Papers, USNA.

46. Layman and McLaughlin, *Hybrid Warship,* 54–56.

47. Press release, Bay City, Mich., 29 July 1930, WAM Papers, reel 13, USNA.

48. U.S. Cong., House, *Hearings Before Committee on Naval Affairs . . . on Sundry Legislation Affecting the Naval Establishment, 1930–1931,* 71st Cong., 3d sess. (Washington, D.C.: GPO, 1931), 3582–85.

49. Hearings Before the General Board of the Navy, 1930, vol. 3 (micro. roll 8), 663–65.

50. Ibid., 714–15; Layman and McLaughlin, *Hybrid Warship,* 66–67.

51. Layman and McLaughlin, *Hybrid Warship,* 68–69.

52. WAM to Charles W. Schick, 9 Feb. 1931, Corres. S, reel 6, Moffett Corres., Wilson Coll., NDL.

53. WAM to Lt. Comdr. Claude Bailey, USN (Ret.), 30 Sept. 1931, Corres. B, reel 2, Moffett Corres., Wilson Coll., NDL.

54. Layman and McLaughlin, *Hybrid Warship*, 71. The flying-deck cruiser reappeared in proposals for the "CF" in 1934 and 1938. See ibid., 88–93, 96–101.

55. Hearings Before the General Board of the Navy, 1931, vol. 1 (micro. roll 9), 270–84, 290–300; Friedman, *U.S. Aircraft Carriers*, 79–80.

56. Wheeler, *Pratt*, 333; Hearings Before the General Board of the Navy, 1931, vol. 2 (micro. roll 9), 555.

57. Hearings Before the General Board of the Navy, 1931, vol. 2 (micro. roll 9), 553–54, 569.

58. Ibid., 713–18.

59. WAM to David S. Ingalls, 9 Feb. 1933, Corres. I, reel 4, Moffett Corres., Wilson Coll., NDL.

60. WAM to Norman Lyon, 24 Mar. 1933, reel 1, Moffett Corres., Wilson Coll., NDL.

CHAPTER 10: CONFRONTATION AND COMPROMISE

1. Memo, WAM to SecNav, 25 June 1926, Aer-M-13-ERG, 601-1-2, file A1-3(27-31), box 10, BuAer, Gen. Corres., 1925–1942, RG 72, NA; *Annual Reports of the Navy Department for the Fiscal Year 1928*, 693.

2. Smith, *Airships* Akron *and* Macon, 7, 15.

3. Ibid., 17–18.

4. USS *Akron* Court of Inquiry, 266–67, file ZRS 4&5/A17, vol. 1, box 5598, BuAer, Gen. Corres., 1925–1942, RG 72, NA; Smith, *Airships* Akron *and* Macon, 33.

5. Transcript of flight log of WAM, roll 10, WAM Papers, USNA; *New York Times*, 8 Nov. 1929; *Washington Post*, 8 Nov. 1929.

6. WAM memo for Chief, BuNav, 23 Aug. 1928, Aer-F-HD, file 00/Moffett, William A., vol. 3, box 4148, BuAer, Gen. Corres., 1925–1942, RG 72, NA; Weekly Aviation Conference, 11 Sept. 1928, vol. 3, box 16, BuAer, Confid. Corres., 1917–1941, RG 72, NA.

7. WAM to R. Adm. Joseph M. Reeves, 10 Oct. 1928, roll 7, WAM Papers, USNA.

8. Hearings Before the General Board of the Navy, 1929, vol. 1 (micro. roll 8), 47–76.

9. R. H. Leigh (Chief, BuNav) to WAM, 15 May 1929, Nav-313-N, file 00/Moffett, William A., vol. 3, box 4148, BuAer, Gen. Corres., 1925–1942, RG 72, NA.

10. WAM Personnel "Jacket," 662-2, files of Richard K. Smith; WAM to

William A. Moffett, Jr., 25 June, 13 Aug. 1929, William A. Moffett, Jr., files, Williamsburg Landing, Va.

11. Hearings Before the General Board of the Navy, 1929, vol. 2 (micro. roll 8), 322.

12. Ibid., 322–28, 339–41.

13. U.S. Cong., House, *Hearings Before Committee on Naval Affairs . . . on Sundry Legislation Affecting the Naval Establishment, 1929–1930,* 71st Cong., 1st and 2d sess. (Washington, D.C.: GPO, 1930), 815–16.

14. Ibid., 2770–80, 2791, 2806.

15. *Congressional Record,* House, 71st Cong., 3d sess., vol. 74, pt. 4, 3790–94; ibid., Senate, 4497; ibid., House, 71st Cong., 3d sess., vol. 74, pt. 5, 4766, 5440; Chief, BuNav, to WAM, 28 Feb. 1931, Nav-311-R, 662-399, file 00/Moffett, William A., vol. 3, box 4148, BuAer, Gen. Corres., 1925–1942, RG 72, NA; *New York Times,* 2 Aug., 2 Oct. 1931.

16. WAM to Towers, 10 Feb. 1930, roll 10, WAM Papers, USNA; WAM to Charles W. Schick, 6 Dec. 1930, Corres. S, reel 6, Moffett Corres., Wilson Coll., NDL; *New York Times,* 5 Aug. 1930.

17. Smith, *Airships* Akron *and* Macon, 15; U.S. Cong., House, *Hearing Before the Subcommittee of the House Committee on Appropriations . . . Navy Department Appropriation Bill for 1927,* 69th Cong., 1st sess. (Washington, D.C.: GPO, 1926), 1053–71.

18. U.S. Cong., House, *Hearing Before the Subcommittee of the House Committee on Appropriations . . . Navy Department Appropriation Bill for 1929,* 70th Cong., 1st sess. (Washington, D.C.: GPO, 1928), 771.

19. WAM Personnel "Jacket," 662-2, files of Richard K. Smith; Carl B. Fritsche to WAM, 15 Aug. 1929, Corres. F, reel 3, Moffett Corres., Wilson Coll., NDL; WAM to Carl B. Fritsche, 20 Aug. 1929, roll 2, WAM Papers, USNA.

20. U.S. Cong., House, *Hearing Before the Subcommittee of the House Committee on Appropriations . . . Navy Department Appropriation Bill for 1931,* 71st Cong., 2d sess. (Washington, D.C.: GPO, 1930), 563–64; U.S. Cong., House, *Hearing Before the Subcommittee of House Committee on Appropriations . . . Navy Department Appropriation Bill for 1932,* 71st Cong., 3d sess. (Washington, D.C.: GPO, 1931), 471; memo, Fulton to WAM, 27 May 1930, roll 13, WAM Papers, USNA.

21. Smith, *Airships* Akron *and* Macon, 39–40.

22. WAM to Lt. Comdr. Claude Bailey, USN (Ret.), 30 Sept. 1931, Corres. B, reel 2, Moffett Corres., Wilson Coll., NDL.

23. U.S. Cong., House, *Hearing Before Subcommittee of House Committee on Appropriations . . . Navy Department Appropriation Bill for 1928,* 69th Cong., 2d sess. (Washington, D.C.: GPO, 1926), 493; Pearson, "Admiral Moffett and the Bureau of Aeronautics," 21–22.

24. U.S. Cong., House, *Hearing Before Subcommittee of House Committee on Ap-*

propriations . . . Navy Department Appropriation Bill for 1928, 494–97.

25. Memo, WAM to Pay [McNamee] Board, 16 Aug. 1928, file L16-4(4), vol. 2, box 3440, BuAer, Gen. Corres., 1925–1942, RG 72, NA.

26. Report of a Board Convened to Consider the Effect upon the Naval Service of the Joint Service Pay Act of June 10, 1922, 12 Sept. 1928, file L16-4(4), vol. 2, box 3440, BuAer, Gen. Corres., 1925–1942, RG 72, NA.

27. WAM to Capt. F. B. Upham, 29 Apr. 1927, roll 9, WAM Papers, USNA; WAM to R. Adm. F. B. Upham, 5 June 1928, Corres. U, reel 6, Moffett Corres., Wilson Coll., NDL; WAM to Porter Adams, 14 Nov. 1929, Corres. A, reel 1, Moffett Corres., Wilson Coll., NDL; Reynolds, *Admiral John H. Towers,* 225.

28. Memo, F. B. Upham for WAM, 16 March 1932, file L16-4(4), vol. 3, box 3440, BuAer, Gen. Corres., 1925–1942, RG 72, NA.

29. WAM to W. A. Ayres, 26 Apr. 1932, roll 1, WAM Papers, USNA.

30. "Aviation Flight Pay," A Statement by WAM, 5 Dec. 1932, roll 14, WAM Papers, USNA.

31. Memo, WAM to Carl Vinson, 21 Feb. 1933, Corres. V, reel 7, Moffett Corres., Wilson Coll., NDL.

32. WAM to Comdr. C. H. McMorris, U.S. Naval Institute, 22 Mar. 1933, Corres. B, reel 2, Moffett Corres., Wilson Coll., NDL.

33. Johnson Board Report, 2 May 1933, file L16-4(4), vol. 4, box 3440, BuAer, Gen. Corres., 1925–1942, RG 72, NA.

34. U.S. Cong., House, *Hearing Before the Subcommittee of the House Committee on Appropriations . . . Navy Department Appropriation Bill for 1929,* 754.

35. WAM to All Aviation Units Ashore and Afloat, 3 Jan. 1928, reel 11, Moffett Corres., Wilson Coll., NDL.

36. U.S. Cong., House, *Hearing Before the Subcommittee of the House Committee on Appropriations . . . Navy Department Appropriation Bill for 1929,* 754–55.

37. *New York Times,* 28 Feb., 4 Mar. 1928.

38. *Army and Navy Journal* 65 (5 May 1928): 705; Chief, BuNav, to SecNav, 19 Apr. 1928, roll 12, WAM Papers, USNA.

39. SecNav to R. Adm. W. H. Standley, 21 Apr. 1928, roll 12, WAM Papers, USNA.

40. WAM comments on Leigh to SecNav, 19 Apr. 1928, reel 9, Moffett Corres., Wilson Coll., NDL.

41. WAM to SecNav, 3 Oct. 1928, roll 12, WAM Papers, USNA.

42. WAM to Clement M. Keys, 7 Jan. 1929, roll 4, WAM Papers, USNA.

43. Shanahan, "Procurement of Naval Aircraft, 1907–1939," 341; World War II Administrative History, BuAer, vol. 6, Procurement, Production and Contracts, 27–28.

44. World War II Administrative History, BuAer, vol. 6, Procurement, Production and Contracts, 32–34.

45. Ibid., 34; Vander Meulen, *Politics of Aircraft,* 86.

46. World War II Administrative History, BuAer, vol. 6, Procurement, Production and Contracts, 34–36.

47. Vander Meulen, *Politics of Aircraft,* 107; Charles L. Lawrance to WAM, 4 Mar. 1932, and WAM to Lawrance, 5 Mar. 1932, Corres. A, reel 1, Moffett Corres., Wilson Coll., NDL.

48. WAM to David S. Ingalls, 6 Apr. 1932, Corres. I, reel 4, Moffett Corres., Wilson Coll., NDL.

49. World War II Administrative History, BuAer, vol. 6, Procurement, Production and Contracts, 36–37.

50. Lord, "History of Naval Aviation," 1301–2.

51. Ibid., 1302.

52. U.S. Cong., House, *Hearings Before the Committee on Expenditures in the Executive Departments . . . Department of National Defense,* 72d Cong., 1st sess. (Washington, D.C.: GPO, 1932), 135–45.

53. WAM to David S. Ingalls, 19 Apr. 1932, Corres. I, reel 4, Moffett Corres., Wilson Coll., NDL.

54. Reynolds, *Admiral John H. Towers,* 233, 240.

55. WAM to Capt. G. W. Steele, Jr., 8 Oct. 1932, Corres. S, reel 6, Moffett Corres., Wilson Coll., NDL; WAM to David S. Ingalls, 7 Sept. 1932, Corres. I, reel 4, Moffett Corres., Wilson Coll., NDL; WAM to Capt. E. J. King, 18 Nov. 1932, roll 4, WAM Papers, USNA.

56. Capt. E. J. King to WAM, 27 Oct. 1932, roll 4, WAM Papers, USNA.

57. WAM to King, 18 Nov. 1932, roll 4, WAM Papers, USNA.

58. WAM to Carl Vinson, 22 Nov. 1932, Corres. V, reel 7, Moffett Corres., Wilson Coll., NDL; WAM to Towers, 13 Jan. 1933, Corres. T, reel 6, Moffett Corres., Wilson Coll., NDL.

59. WAM to Porter Adams, 28 Feb. 1933, Corres. A, reel 1, Moffett Corres., Wilson Coll., NDL; WAM to Towers, 6 Mar. 1933, Corres. T, reel 6, Moffett Corres., Wilson Coll., NDL.

60. WAM to Col. M. H. McIntyre, 17 Mar. 1933, President's Official File 18i, Franklin D. Roosevelt Library, Hyde Park, New York.

61. WAM to Claude A. Swanson, 16 Mar. 1933, President's Official File 18i, Franklin D. Roosevelt Library, Hyde Park, New York; WAM to Towers, 20 Mar. 1933, roll 8, WAM Papers, USNA.

CHAPTER 11: THE LAST FLIGHT

1. Smith, *Airships* Akron *and* Macon, 40–43.

2. *New York Times,* 24 Sept. 1931.

3. Smith, *Airships* Akron *and* Macon, 43–44; *New York Times,* 28 Oct. 1931.

4. Smith, *Airships* Akron *and* Macon, 48–49.

5. Transcript of flight log of WAM, roll 10, WAM Papers, USNA; Arpee, *Frigates to Flat-Tops,* 224.

6. Smith, *Airships* Akron *and* Macon, 37, 51–55.

7. WAM to John J. Delaney, 24 Feb. 1932, roll 2, WAM Papers, USNA.

8. Smith, *Airships* Akron *and* Macon, 27–30, 55.

9. Ibid., 55–62.

10. Transcript of flight log of WAM, roll 10, WAM Papers, USNA; Smith, *Airships* Akron *and* Macon, 65–66.

11. WAM to Capt. H. E. Shoemaker, 17 Oct. 1931, Corres. S, reel 6, Moffett Corres., Wilson Coll., NDL. Portions of this letter are reprinted in Arpee, *Frigates to Flat-Tops,* 236–37.

12. Hughes, "Francis W. Reichelderfer," 55–59.

13. Transcript of flight log of WAM, roll 10, WAM Papers, USNA.

14. Comdr. F. C. McCord to CNO, 31 Jan. 1933, vol. 3, box 5592, file ZRS4/A4-3(1), BuAer, Gen. Corres., 1925–1942, RG 72, NA (notes courtesy of Dr. Richard K. Smith); WAM to David S. Ingalls, 12 Jan. 1933, roll 4, WAM Papers, USNA.

15. Smith, *Airships* Akron *and* Macon, 93–97.

16. WAM to Capt. H. E. Shoemaker, 2 Aug. 1932, Corres. S, reel 6, Moffett Corres., Wilson Coll., NDL; WAM to Jerome Hunsaker, 3 Oct. 1932, roll 3, WAM Papers, USNA.

17. Smith, *Airships* Akron *and* Macon, 97; *New York Times,* 12 Mar. 1933; telegram, Roosevelt to WAM, care of Goodyear-Zeppelin, Akron, 11 Mar. 1933, file 00/Moffett, William A., vol. 4, box 4149, BuAer, Gen. Corres., 1925–1942, RG 72, NA.

18. Address by WAM, USN, before the Women's Chapter of the National Aeronautic Association, Akron, Ohio, 11 Mar. 1933, President's Official File 18i, Franklin D. Roosevelt Library, Hyde Park, N.Y.

19. WAM to William A. Moffett, Jr., 14 Mar. 1933, William A. Moffett, Jr., files, Williamsburg Landing, Va.; WAM to Claude Bailey, 30 Sept. 1931, Corres. B, reel 2, Moffett Corres., Wilson Coll., NDL.

20. Comdr. F. C. McCord to CNO, 31 Mar. 1933, file ZRS4/A4-3(1), vol. 3, box 5592, BuAer, Gen. Corres., 1925–1942, RG 72, NA (notes courtesy of Dr. Richard K. Smith).

21. Testimony of Lt. Comdr. H. V. Wiley, 10 Apr. 1933, USS *Akron* Court of Inquiry, file ZRS 4&5/A17, vol. 1, box 5598, BuAer, Gen. Corres., 1925–1942, RG 72, NA.

22. *New York Times,* 8 Apr. 1933.

23. Smith, *Airships* Akron *and* Macon, 78–79; *New York Times,* 5 Apr. 1933.

24. Testimony of Lt. Comdr. H. V. Wiley, 10, 11 Apr. 1933, USS *Akron* Court of Inquiry, file ZRS 4&5/A17, vol. 1, box 5598, BuAer, Gen. Corres., 1925–1942, RG 72, NA; Smith, *Airships* Akron *and* Macon, 80.

25. Testimony of Deal and Erwin, 11 Apr. 1933, USS *Akron* Court of Inquiry, file ZRS 4&5/A17, vol. 1, box 5598, BuAer, Gen. Corres., 1925–1942, RG 72, NA.

26. Statement by Capt. Karl Dalldorf (CO *Phoebus*), 12 Apr. 1933, in SecState to SecNav, 4 May 1933, file ZRS4&5 L11-1, box 1732, BuAer, Confid. Corres., 1922–1944, RG 72, NA (notes courtesy of Dr. Richard K. Smith); *New York Times*, 5 Apr. 1933.

27. Interview with Beverly Moffett Mohan, 11 June 1991; Beverly Moffett Mohan, letter to the author, 29 Apr. 1991; *New York Times*, 5 Apr. 1933; *Washington Daily News*, 4 Apr. 1933.

28. *New York Times*, 5 Apr. 1933.

29. *Washington Post*, 5 Apr. 1933; *Akron Beacon-Journal*, 4 Apr. 1933 (notes courtesy of Dr. Richard K. Smith).

30. Wilson, *Slipstream*, 181; interview with William A. Moffett, Jr., 15 Dec. 1990; Capt. H. C. Richardson to Mrs. W. A. Moffett, 5 Apr. 1933, box 4, WAM Papers, Part 2, USNA.

31. Adm. W. V. Pratt to Mrs. W. A. Moffett, 7 Apr. 1933, box 4, WAM Papers, Part 2, USNA.

32. Testimony of Lt. Comdr. H. V. Wiley, 10 Apr. 1933, USS *Akron* Court of Inquiry, file ZRS 4&5/A17, vol. 1, box 5598, BuAer, Gen. Corres., 1925–1942, RG 72, NA; interview with William A. Moffett, Jr., 15 Dec. 1990.

33. *New York Times*, 11 Apr. 1933; Arpee, *Frigates to Flat-Tops*, 246–47.

34. Clipping from *Washington Daily News*, 10 Apr. 1933, in "Flights and Aviation Activities of Moffett, William A.," WAM Biographical File, box 93, AIAA Archives, LCMD.

35. *New York Times*, 12, 14 Apr. 1933; *Washington Post*, 14 Apr. 1933; clipping from *Washington Daily News*, 13 Apr. 1933, in "Flights and Aviation Activities of Moffett, William A.," WAM Biographical File, box 93, AIAA Archives, LCMD.

36. Testimony of Lt. F. A. L. Dartsch, Lt. Charles Maguire, 13 Apr. 1933, and Comdr. A. H. Dresel, 26 Apr. 1933, USS *Akron* Court of Inquiry, file ZRS 4&5/A17, vol. 1, box 5598, BuAer, Gen. Corres., 1925–1942, RG 72, NA.

37. Testimony of Jerome Hunsaker, 19 Apr., USS *Akron* Court of Inquiry, file ZRS 4&5/A17, vol. 1, box 5598, BuAer, Gen. Corres., 1925–1942, RG 72, NA.

38. SecNav to Chief of Bureau of Medicine and Surgery, 29 Apr. 1933, and Finding of Facts, 1 May 1933, USS *Akron* Court of Inquiry, file ZRS 4&5/A17, vol. 1, box 5598, BuAer, Gen. Corres., 1925–1942, RG 72, NA; concluding remarks of Lt. R. G. Pennoyer, 1 May 1933, file ZRS 4&5/A17, vol. 1, box 5598, BuAer, Gen. Corres., 1925–1942, RG 72, NA.

39. Reynolds, *Admiral John H. Towers,* 248–49.

40. R. Adm. E. J. King to CNO, via Chief, BuNav, 11 May 1933, Aer-A-6-ERB, ZRS 4&5/A17, file ZRS 4&5/A17, vol. 1, box 5598, BuAer, Gen. Corres., 1925–1942, RG 72, NA.

41. U.S. Cong., *Hearings Before a Joint Committee to Investigate Dirigible Disasters,* 4–7, 203–38; Smith, *Airships* Akron *and* Macon, 89–91.

Bibliography

Manuscript and Archival Material

Aero Club of Illinois. Collection. Chicago Historical Society, Chicago, Ill.
Hearings Before the General Board of the Navy, 1919–1931 (micro. rolls 3–9).
Hunsaker, Jerome C. Papers. MIT Archives and Special Collections, Massachusetts Institute of Technology, Cambridge, Mass.
Moffett, George H. Papers. South Carolina Historical Society, Charleston, S.C.
Moffett, William A.
    Biographical File. American Institute of Aeronautics and Astronautics Archives, Library of Congress Manuscript Division.
    Correspondence. Eugene E. Wilson Collection, Micro. 80, Navy Department Library.
    Papers. Ms. Coll. 198 (microfilm), Nimitz Library, U.S. Naval Academy.
    Papers. Part 2, Ms. Coll. 243, Nimitz Library, U. S. Naval Academy.
    Printed Matter File. American Institute of Aeronautics and Astronautics Archives, Library of Congress Manuscript Division.
    Record of Naval Cadet William Adger Moffett, Record Group 405, William W. Jeffries Memorial Archives, U.S. Naval Academy.
    Service Record. File 662, National Personnel Records Center, St. Louis.

Mustin, Henry Crosky. Papers. Library of Congress Manuscript Division.
National Archives and Records Administration.
   Bureau of Aeronautics, Confidential Correspondence, 1917–1941, Record
      Group 72.
   Bureau of Aeronautics, General Correspondence, 1925–1942, Record Group
      72.
   Bureau of Aeronautics, General Correspondence initiated in Bureau of Con-
      struction and Repair, 1917–1925, Record Group 72.
   Bureau of Aeronautics, General Correspondence initiated in Bureau of Steam
      Engineering, 1914–1925, Record Group 72.
   Bureau of Aeronautics, General Correspondence initiated in Office of the Chief
      of Naval Operations, 1917–1925, Record Group 72.
   Bureau of Aeronautics, General Correspondence initiated in Office of the Sec-
      retary of the Navy, 1917–1925, Record Group 72.
   Deck Logs (*Amphitrite, Baltimore, Boston, Chester, Constellation, Kentucky, Lang-
      ley, Maine, Marietta, Maryland, Mohican, North Carolina, Pensacola,
      Portsmouth*), Record Group 24.
   General Board, General Records of the Department of the Navy, Record
      Group 80.
   General Records of the Department of the Navy, 1897–1915, Record Group 80.
   Secretary of the Navy, General Correspondence, 1916–1926, Record Group 80.
Roosevelt, Franklin D. President's Official File 18i. Franklin D. Roosevelt Library,
   Hyde Park, N.Y.
U.S. Air Force Historical Research Agency, Maxwell Air Force Base, Ala. File
   145.93-101.

PUBLIC DOCUMENTS

Congressional Record.
   House: 67th Cong., 1st sess., vol. 51, pt. 1. 69th Cong., 1st sess., vol. 67, pts.
      4, 7. 71st Cong., 3d sess., vol. 74, pts. 4, 5.
   Senate: 67th Cong., 1st sess., vol. 51, pts. 1, 2. 69th Cong., 1st sess., vol. 67,
      pts. 7, 10. 71st Cong., 3d sess., vol. 74, pt. 5.
United States.
   *Conference on the Limitation of Armament, Washington, November 12, 1921–Feb-
      ruary 6, 1922.* Washington: Government Printing Office, 1922.
   *Conference on the Limitation of Armament, Washington, November 12, 1921–Feb-
      ruary 6, 1922, Subcommittees.* Washington: Government Printing Office,
      1922.
   Statutes at Large of the United States of America, 67th Cong., vol. 42, pt. 1.

Washington, D.C.: Government Printing Office, 1923.

Statutes at Large of the United States of America, 69th Cong., 1st sess., vol. 44, pt. 2. Washington, D.C.: Government Printing Office, 1927.

U.S. Congress, House.

Hearings Before a Joint Committee to Investigate Dirigible Disasters. 73d Cong., 1st sess. Washington, D.C.: Government Printing Office, 1933.

Hearings Before the Committee on Naval Affairs . . . On Estimates Submitted by the Secretary of the Navy, 1916, 3 vols., 64th Cong., 1st sess. Washington, D.C.: Government Printing Office, 1916. vol. 1.

Hearings Before the Committee on Naval Affairs . . . on Sundry Legislation Affecting the Naval Establishment, 1920–1921, 66th Cong., 3d sess. Washington, D.C.: Government Printing Office, 1921.

Hearings Before the Committee on Naval Affairs . . . on Sundry Legislation Affecting the Naval Establishment, 1921, 67th Cong., 1st sess. Washington, D.C.: Government Printing Office, 1921.

Hearing Before the Subcommittee of House Committee on Appropriations . . . Navy Department Appropriation Bill for 1923, 67th Cong., 2d sess. Washington, D.C.: Government Printing Office, 1922.

Hearings Before the Committee on Naval Affairs . . . on Sundry Legislation Affecting the Naval Establishment, 1922–1923, 67th Cong., 2d, 3d, 4th sess. Washington, D.C.: Government Printing Office, 1923.

Hearing Before the Subcommittee of the House Committee on Appropriations . . . Navy Department Appropriation Bill for 1924, 67th Cong., 4th sess. Washington, D.C.: Government Printing Office, 1922.

Hearing Before the Subcommittee of the House Committee on Appropriations . . . Navy Department Appropriation Bill for 1925, 68th Cong., 1st sess. Washington, D.C.: Government Printing Office, 1924.

Hearing Before the Subcommittee of the House Committee on Appropriations . . . Navy Department Appropriation Bill for 1926, 68th Cong., 2d sess. Washington, D.C.: Government Printing Office, 1924.

Hearings Before the Committee on Military Affairs . . . Department of Defense and Unification of Air Service, 69th Cong., 1st sess. Washington, D.C.: Government Printing Office, 1926.

Hearings Before the Committee on Naval Affairs . . . on Sundry Legislation Affecting the Naval Establishment, 1925–1926, 69th Cong., 1st sess. Washington, D.C.: Government Printing Office, 1926.

Hearing Before the Subcommittee of the House Committee on Appropriations . . . Navy Department Appropriation Bill for 1927, 69th Cong., 1st sess. Washington, D.C.: Government Printing Office, 1926.

Hearing Before Subcommittee of House Committee on Appropriations . . . Navy Department Appropriation Bill for 1928, 69th Cong., 2d sess. Washington,

D.C.: Government Printing Office, 1926.

Hearings Before Committee on Naval Affairs . . . on Sundry Legislation Affecting the Naval Establishment, 1927–1928, 70th Cong., 1st sess. Washington, D.C.: Government Printing Office, 1928.

Hearing Before the Subcommittee of the House Committee on Appropriations . . . Navy Department Appropriation Bill for 1929, 70th Cong., 1st sess. Washington, D.C.: Government Printing Office, 1928.

Hearings Before Committee on Naval Affairs . . . on Sundry Legislation Affecting the Naval Establishment, 1929–1930, 71st Cong., 1st and 2d sess. Washington, D.C.: Government Printing Office, 1930.

Hearing Before the Subcommittee of the House Committee on Appropriations . . . Navy Department Appropriation Bill for 1931, 71st Cong., 2d sess. Washington, D.C.: Government Printing Office, 1930.

Hearings Before Committee on Naval Affairs . . . on Sundry Legislation Affecting the Naval Establishment, 1930–1931, 71st Cong., 3d sess. Washington, D.C.: Government Printing Office, 1931.

Hearing Before the Subcommittee of House Committee on Appropriations . . . Navy Department Appropriation Bill for 1932, 71st Cong., 3d sess. Washington, D.C.: Government Printing Office, 1931.

Hearing Before the Subcommittee of the House Committee on Appropriations . . . Navy Department Appropriation Bill for 1933, 72d Cong., 1st sess. Washington, D.C.: Government Printing Office, 1932.

Hearings Before the Committee on Expenditures in the Executive Departments . . . Department of National Defense, 72d Cong., 1st sess. Washington, D.C.: Government Printing Office, 1932.

Hearings Before the Select Committee of Inquiry into Operations of the United States Air Services, 68th Cong. Washington, D.C.: Government Printing Office, 1925. Pts. 2, 3.

Report of the Select Committee of Inquiry into Operations of the United States Air Services, 68th Cong., 2d sess. Washington, D.C.: Government Printing Office, 1925.

U.S. National Advisory Committee for Aeronautics. *Seventh Annual Report of the National Advisory Committee for Aeronautics, 1921.* Washington, D.C.: Government Printing Office, 1923.

U.S. Navy. *Annual Reports of the Department of the Navy for the Fiscal Years 1922–1932.* Washington, D.C.: Government Printing Office, 1923–1933.

U.S. President's Aircraft Board.

Hearings Before the President's Aircraft Board, 4 vols. Washington, D.C.: Government Printing Office, 1925.

Report of President's Aircraft Board. Washington, D.C.: Government Printing Office, 1925.

Administrative Histories

Carrigan, Richard M. "History of Naval Aviation Personnel, 1911–1933," vol. 21, Deputy Chief of Naval Operations (Air), Monographs in the History of Naval Aviation. Washington, D.C.: Naval Aviation History Unit, 1946.

Lord, Clifford L. "The History of Naval Aviation, 1898–1939." Office of the Deputy Chief of Naval Operations (Air). Washington, D.C.: Naval Aviation History Unit, 1946.

Shanahan, William O. "Procurement of Naval Aircraft, 1907–1939," vol. 17, Deputy Chief of Naval Operations (Air), Monographs in the History of Naval Aviation. Washington, D.C.: Naval Aviation History Unit, 1946.

U.S. Navy Caribbean Sea Frontier. Caribbean Commands, Vol. 2, The Guantanamo Sector, Caribbean Sea Frontier and the U.S. Naval Operating Base, Guantanamo Bay, Cuba (Historical Section, Guantanamo Sector, 1945), 119–20, 148. Operational Archives, Naval Historical Center.

World War II Administrative History, Bureau of Aeronautics, vol. 1, Background. Washington, D.C.: Department of the Navy, 1957.

World War II Administrative History, Bureau of Aeronautics, vol. 6, Procurement, Production and Contracts. Washington, D.C.: Department of the Navy, 1957.

Books

Angle, Paul M. *Philip K. Wrigley: A Memoir of a Modest Man.* Chicago: Rand McNally & Co., 1975.

Annual Register of the United States Naval Academy, 1887–88, 1888–89, 1889–90, 1890–91. Washington, D.C.: Government Printing Office, 1887–1891.

Arpee, Edward. *From Frigates to Flat-Tops: The Story of the Life and Achievements of Rear Admiral William Adger Moffett, U.S.N., "The Father of Naval Aviation."* Chicago: Lakeside Press, 1953.

Arthur, Reginald Wright. *Contact!: Naval Aviators Assigned Numbers 1 to 2000.* Washington, D.C.: Naval Aviator Register, 1967.

Bradford, James C., ed. *Admirals of the New Steel Navy: Makers of the American Naval Tradition, 1880–1930.* Annapolis: Naval Institute Press, 1990.

Buckley, Thomas H. *The United States and the Washington Conference, 1921–1922.* Knoxville: University of Tennessee Press, 1970.

Buzzell, Francis. *The Great Lakes Naval Training Station: A History.* Boston: Small, Maynard & Co., 1919.

Byrd, Richard Evelyn. *Skyward.* New York: G. P. Putnam's Sons, 1928.

Clark, J. J., with Clark G. Reynolds. *Carrier Admiral.* New York: David McKay Co., 1967.

Cooling, Benjamin Franklin., ed. *War, Business, and American Society: Historical Perspectives on the Military-Industrial Complex.* Port Washington, N.Y.: Kennikat Press, 1977.

Coontz, Robert E. *From the Mississippi to the Sea.* Philadelphia: Dorrance & Co., 1930.

Davis, Burke. *The Billy Mitchell Affair.* New York: Random House, 1967.

Davis, George T. *A Navy Second to None: The Development of Modern American Naval Policy.* New York: Harcourt Brace Jovanovich, 1940.

Dictionary of American Naval Fighting Ships. Vol. 4. Washington, D.C.: Navy Department, Office of the Chief of Naval Operations, Naval History Division, 1969.

Foxworth, Thomas G. *The Speed Seekers.* New York: Doubleday & Co., 1976.

Fraser, Walter J., Jr. *Charleston! Charleston!: The History of a Southern City.* Columbia: University of South Carolina Press, 1989.

Friedman, Norman. *U.S. Aircraft Carriers: An Illustrated Design History.* Annapolis: Naval Institute Press, 1983.

Holley, Irving Brinton, Jr. *Buying Aircraft: Material Procurement for the Army Air Forces.* Washington, D.C.: Department of the Army, Office of the Chief of Military History, 1964.

King, Ernest J., and Walter Muir Whitehill. *Fleet Admiral King: A Naval Record.* New York: W. W. Norton & Co., 1952.

Komons, Nick A. *Bonfires to Beacons: Federal Civil Aviation Policy Under the Air Commerce Act, 1926–1938.* Washington, D.C.: Department of Transportation, Federal Aviation Administration, 1978.

Layman, R. D., and Stephen McLaughlin. *The Hybrid Warship: The Amalgamation of Big Guns and Aircraft.* Annapolis: Naval Institute Press, 1991.

Leary, William M., ed. *Aviation's Golden Age.* Iowa City: University of Iowa Press, 1989.

Lebow, Eileen F. *Cal Rodgers and the Vin Fiz: The First Transcontinental Flight.* Washington, D.C.: Smithsonian Institution Press, 1989.

Love, Robert William, Jr., ed. *The Chiefs of Naval Operations.* Annapolis: Naval Institute Press, 1980.

Maga, Timothy P. *Defending Paradise: The United States and Guam, 1898–1950.* New York: Garland Publishing, 1988.

Melhorn, Charles M. *Two-Block Fox: The Rise of the Aircraft Carrier, 1911–1929.* Annapolis: Naval Institute Press, 1974.

Messimer, Dwight R. *No Margin for Error: The U.S. Navy's Transpacific Flight of 1925.* Annapolis: Naval Institute Press, 1981.

Molloy, Robert. *Charleston: A Gracious Heritage.* New York and London: D. Appleton-Century Co., 1947.

O'Connor, Raymond G. *Perilous Equilibrium: The United States and the London Naval Conference of 1930*. Lawrence: University of Kansas Press, 1962.

Rae, John B. *Climb to Greatness: The American Aircraft Industry, 1920–1960*. Cambridge, Mass.: MIT Press, 1968.

Register of Alumni, 1845–1956. Annapolis: United States Naval Academy Alumni Association, 1956.

Reynolds, Clark G. *Admiral John H. Towers: The Struggle for Naval Air Supremacy*. Annapolis: Naval Institute Press, 1991.

Robinson, Douglas H., and Charles L. Keller. *"Up Ship!": U.S. Navy Rigid Airships, 1919–1935*. Annapolis: Naval Institute Press, 1982.

Rodman, Hugh. *Yarns of a Kentucky Admiral*. Indianapolis: Bobbs-Merrill Co., 1928.

Roland, Alex. *Model Research: The National Advisory Committee for Aeronautics, 1915–1958*. Washington, D.C.: National Aeronautics and Space Administration, 1985.

Roskill, Stephen. *Naval Policy Between the Wars: The Period of Anglo-American Antagonism, 1919–1929*. London: Collins, 1968.

———. *Naval Policy Between the Wars, II: The Period of Reluctant Rearmament, 1930–1939*. Annapolis: Naval Institute Press, 1976.

Scamehorn, Howard L. *Balloons to Jets: A Century of Aeronautics in Illinois, 1855–1955*. Chicago: Henry Regnery Co., 1957.

Schlaifer, Robert, and S. D. Heron. *Development of Aircraft Engines and Fuels*. Boston: Graduate School of Business Administration, Harvard University, 1950.

Seager, Robert II. *Alfred Thayer Mahan: The Man and His Letters*. Annapolis: Naval Institute Press, 1977.

Smith, Richard K. *The Airships* Akron *and* Macon: *Flying Aircraft Carriers of the United States Navy*. Annapolis: Naval Institute Press, 1965.

———. *First Across!: The U.S. Navy's Transatlantic Flight of 1919*. Annapolis: Naval Institute Press, 1973.

Spector, Ronald. *Admiral of the New Empire: The Life and Career of George Dewey*. Baton Rouge: Louisiana State University Press, 1974.

———. *Professors of War: The Naval War College and the Development of the Naval Profession*. Newport, R.I.: Naval War College Press, 1977.

Sweetman, Jack. *The Landing at Veracruz: 1914*. Annapolis: Naval Institute Press, 1968.

———. *The U.S. Naval Academy: An Illustrated History*. Annapolis: Naval Institute Press, 1979.

Thompson, Wayne, ed. *Air Leadership: Proceedings of a Conference at Bolling Air Force Base, April 13–14, 1984*. Washington, D.C.: Office of Air Force History, 1986.

Trimble, William F. *Wings for the Navy: A History of the Naval Aircraft Factory, 1917–1956.* Annapolis: Naval Institute Press, 1990.

Turnbull, Archibald D., and Clifford L. Lord. *History of United States Naval Aviation.* New Haven: Yale University Press, 1949.

United States Naval Aviation, 1910–1980. Washington, D.C.: Naval Air Systems Command, 1981.

Vander Meulen, Jacob. *The Politics of Aircraft: Building an American Military Industry.* Lawrence: University Press of Kansas, 1991.

Van Deurs, George. *Anchors in the Sky: Spuds Ellyson, the First Naval Aviator.* San Rafael, Calif.: Presidio Press, 1978.

Van Wyen, Adrian O., ed., *Naval Aviation in World War I.* Washington, D.C.: Chief of Naval Operations, 1969.

Wagner, Ray. *American Combat Planes.* 3d ed. Garden City, N.Y.: Doubleday & Co., 1982.

Wheeler, Gerald E. *Admiral William Veazie Pratt, U.S. Navy: A Sailor's Life.* Washington, D.C.: Naval History Division, 1974.

Wilson, Eugene E. *Slipstream: The Autobiography of an Air Craftsman.* New York: McGraw-Hill Book Co., 1950.

ARTICLES

Allen, Comdr. Walter H. "The Twelfth Regiment (Public Works) at Great Lakes." *U.S. Naval Institute Proceedings* 47 (Mar. 1921): 367–76.

Andrade, Ernest, Jr. "The Ship That Never Was: The Flying-Deck Cruiser." *Military Affairs* 32 (Dec. 1968): 132–40.

Armstrong, William J. "Henry Mustin: A Clear Voice for Naval Aviation." *Naval Aviation Museum Foundation Journal* 2 (Sept. 1981): 29–33.

Bilstein, Roger E. "Edward Pearson Warner and the New Air Age," in William M. Leary, ed., *Aviation's Golden Age.* Iowa City: University of Iowa Press, 1989, 113–26.

Coletta, Paolo E. "The Apotheosis of Political Strategy: The Third Appointment of Rear Admiral William A. Moffett as Chief of the U.S. Bureau of Aeronautics, 1929." *American Aviation Historical Society Journal* 36 (Spring 1991): 24–29.

Dickey, Fred C., Jr. "U.S. Navy Ship Plane Units." *Journal of the American Aviation Historical Society* 10 (Summer 1965): 121–26.

"Dirigible Defended by Admiral Moffett." *U.S. Naval Institute Proceedings* 49 (June 1923): 1056.

D'Orcy, Ladislas. "The Curtiss Marine Flying Trophy Race." *Aviation* 13 (16 Oct. 1922): 490–92.

Farenholt, A. "Incidents of the Voyage of the U.S.S. 'Charleston' to Manila in 1898." *U.S. Naval Institute Proceedings* 50 (May 1924): 753–70.

Featherston, Frank H. "AEDO: A History and a Heritage." *U.S. Naval Institute Proceedings* 94 (Feb. 1968): 33–45.

Hall, Charles Ward. "Metal Construction of Airplanes." *Aviation* 20 (17 May 1926): 744–48.

Hone, Thomas C. "Navy Air Leadership: Rear Admiral William A. Moffett as Chief of the Bureau of Aeronautics," in Wayne Thompson, ed., *Air Leadership: Proceedings of a Conference at Bolling Air Force Base, April 13–14, 1984*. Washington, D.C.: Office of Air Force History, 1986, 83–117.

Hughes, Patrick. "Francis W. Reichelderfer, Part I: Aerologists and Airdevils." *Weatherwise* 34 (Apr. 1981): 52–59.

Hyde, Henry M. "A Mother to 25,000 Boys." *Ladies' Home Journal* (June 1918): 25.

McCarthy, Charles J. "Notes on Metal Wing Construction." *U.S. Air Services* 10 (Mar. 1925): 9–16.

Moffett, William A. "Lessons of the Curtiss Marine Flying Trophy Race." *Aviation* 13 (23 Oct. 1922): 559.

———. "Naval Aviation." *U.S. Naval Institute Proceedings* 53 (Oct. 1927): 1081–83.

———. "Organization and Function of Naval Aviation." *Aviation* 13 (28 Aug. 1922): 248–49.

———. "Some Aviation Fundamentals." *U.S. Naval Institute Proceedings* 51 (Oct. 1925): 1871–81.

Owsley, Frank L., Jr., and Wesley Phillips Newton. "Eyes in the Skies." *U.S. Naval Institute Proceedings* (Supplement, Apr. 1986): 17–25.

Reynolds, Clark G. "William A. Moffett: Steward of the Air Revolution," in James C. Bradford, ed., *Admirals of the New Steel Navy: Makers of the American Naval Tradition, 1880–1930*. Annapolis: Naval Institute Press, 1990, 374–92.

Richardson, H. C. "Development in Naval Aeronautics." *Society of Automotive Engineers, Transactions* 19, pt. 2 (1924): 661–92.

Turk, Richard W. "Lake Bluff, Ill., Great Lakes Naval Training Station," in Paolo E. Coletta, ed., *United States Navy and Marine Corps Bases, Domestic*. Westport, Conn.: Greenwood Press, 1985, 273–74.

———. "Edward Walter Eberle," in Robert William Love, Jr., ed., *The Chiefs of Naval Operations*. Annapolis: Naval Institute Press, 1980, 37–46.

Webster, W. W. "The Navy PN-12 Seaplane." *Aviation* 24 (14 May 1928): 1366, 1404.

Wilson, E. E. "Air-Cooled Engines in Naval Aircraft." *Journal of the Society of Automotive Engineers* 19 (Sept. 1926): 221–27.

INTERVIEWS AND ORAL HISTORIES

Memoirs of Admiral Felix B. Stump, 1963. Oral History Research Office, Columbia University.
Rear Adm. William A. Moffett, Jr. (Ret.). Williamsburg Landing, Va., 15 Dec. 1990.
Beverly Moffett Mohan. Deep Gap, N.C., 11 June 1991.
Reminiscences of Jerome C. Hunsaker, 1960. Aviation Project, Oral History Research Office, Columbia University.
Reminiscences of Eugene E. Wilson, 1962. Naval History Project, Oral History Research Office, Columbia University.

UNPUBLISHED PAPERS

Pearson, Lee M. "Admiral Moffett and the Bureau of Aeronautics." Unpublished, undated ms. Historian's Office, Naval Air Systems Command Headquarters, Washington, D.C.
Smith, Richard K. "Calvin Coolidge and the 'Airpower' Crisis of 1925–1926." Unpublished seminar paper, University of Chicago, 1964.

INDEX

Adams, Charles Francis, 180, 211, 214,
217, 222, 223, 227, 234, 236, 255, 256,
258
Adams, Porter, 253
Aero Club of Illinois, 55, 56
Aeronautic Review, 194–95
Aeronautical Chamber of Commerce of
America, Inc., 112, 145, 248
Aeronautical Engineering Duty Officers,
138, 187–88, 238, 190–92
Aircraft: on auxiliary ships, 109; on battleships, 59–60, 61, 101–2, 107–8; on
cruisers, 102, 108; on destroyers, 102,
108–9; engines, 115, 117–20, 121; gunnery spotting by, 60–61; limitation of,
93–95, 212; metal construction of,
116–17; procurement, 10–12, 82,
111–17, 145, 146, 165–66, 167–81,
199, 230, 246–50, 274–75; on submarines, 102, 108–9
Aircraft, types of: Aeromarine 39B, 105;

Consolidated N2Y-1, 259, 261; Cox-
Klemin XS, 108–9; CS torpedo bomber,
147, 148, 181; Curtiss CR-2, 121, 122;
Curtiss CR-3, 122, 123; Curtiss R2C-1,
123; Curtiss R2C-2, 124; Curtiss TR-1,
121; Curtiss TR-3A, 122; Curtiss TS,
117; Curtiss XF9C-1, 2, 258, 264; De
Havilland DH-4B, 209; Ford Trimotor,
232; Hanriot HD-1, 61; Loening
amphibian, 244; Martin MS, 108–9;
Naval Aircraft Factory F-5-L, 87, 105,
115, 116; Naval Aircraft Factory NM-1,
117; Naval Aircraft Factory PT-2, 105;
Naval Aircraft Factory TR-3, 122; Naval
Aircraft Factory TS-1, 118; Navy-Wright
NW-2, 122–23; PB-1, 156, 157, 158;
PN-9, 156–59, 160; Royal Aircraft
Factory SE-5, 60; Sopwith Camel, 60;
Sopwith 1½ Strutter, 60; Vought O2U,
200; Vought VE-7 SF, 105; Wright
F2W-1, 123; Wright F2W-2, 124